ULSTER COUNTY
NEW YORK

The Architectural History & Guide

Published by Black Dome Press Corp.
649 Delaware Ave., Delmar, New York 12054
blackdomepress.com
(518) 439-6512

First Edition Paperback 2011

ISBN-13: 978-1-883789-70-1

ISBN-10: 1-883789-70-2

Library of Congress Cataloging-in-Publication Data

Rhoads, William Bertolet, 1944-

   Ulster County, New York : the architectural history & guide / William B. Rhoads.
      p. cm.
   Includes bibliographical references and index.
   ISBN 978-1-883789-70-1 (trade paper)
   1. Architecture—New York (State)—Ulster County. I. Title.
   NA730.N42U477 2011
   720.9747'34—dc23
                      2011039753

Front cover (top): Abraham LeFever (John A. LeFevre) House, Gardiner, begun c. 1772 and acquired by Ulster County historian Kenneth E. Hasbrouck in 1950 and 1962. (Erma DeWitt photo, 1949; Haviland-Heidgerd Historical Collection)

Front cover (bottom): Historic Mohonk Mountain House, family owned and operated since 1869. Photo by Jim Smith Photography, 2008, courtesy of Mohonk Mountain House, www.mohonk.com. Used with permission.

Building graphic on chapter introductory pages: Wiltwyck Inn, 48 Main St., Kingston, Myron S. Teller architect, 1910–1911. (advertisement in *The Hue and Cry* vol. 2, no. 1, June 21, 1924)

Map: © Ulster County Tourism. Used with permission.

Design: Toelke Associates www.toelkeassociates.com

Printed in the USA

10 9 8 7 6 5 4 3 2 1

ULSTER COUNTY
N E W   Y O R K

The Architectural
History & Guide

William B. Rhoads

BLACK · DOME

www.blackdomepress.com

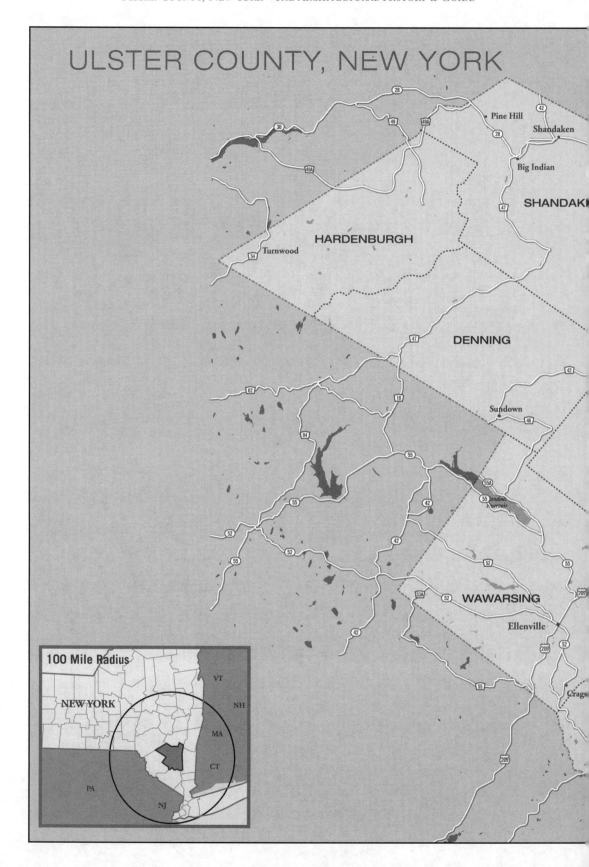

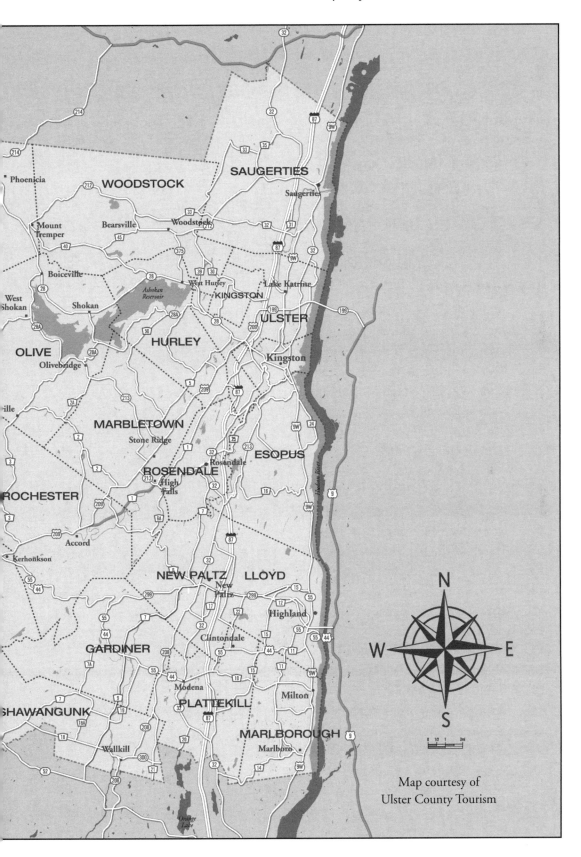

Map courtesy of
Ulster County Tourism

Contents

Foreword

Home is the best place.

William Rhoads has bestowed on us a cornucopia of stories about the buildings we are comfortable with: your house, my house, the neighbor's house, the church, the general store, school and mill, the cemetery and the town hall, the cabin in the woods ...

He tells us about the people who lived in or used these places, when and how they built them, where their ideas about style came from, and what the community was like.

It is important to know these things, not merely to expand what may be our somewhat sketchy learning about architectural history, valuable as that would be. It matters in more profound ways as well.

To increase our understanding of the built environment is to reaffirm our sense that where we happen to have taken root—over generations or only just recently—is a place that is solid, has been created by talented hands, embodies caring, and skill, and determination; in short has distinctive character.

It is to validate our instinctive love for the places we love.

All over the country now, people who live in the nation's immensely various communities are looking afresh at their local, vernacular resources—of habitation, workplace, transportation, cultural life and more—cherishing newly discovered histories that have come to seem significant.

Is this to suggest that scholarly ambition and intellectual depth among the Americans have soared? Perhaps! More likely, it may simply be to suggest that, in a world roiled by constant motion, and dislocation, and hardship, our fond places can provide a longed-for sense of steadiness, and contentment.

Professor Rhoads's careful work affords us this perception. The book in your hand will serve as a most excellent guide, and for the armchair browsing the author recommends, a rich history. It is a meticulous, thoughtful and felicitous account of the structures of Ulster County—of the Empire State's sixty-two counties one of the most historic and bountiful.

Excelsior!

Joan K. Davidson

Joan K. Davidson is a former Commissioner of the New York State Office of Parks, Recreation and Historic Preservation, and is President of Furthermore, the publication program of The J.M. Kaplan Fund.

Introduction

Within Ulster County is a multitude of architectural treasures awaiting discovery by motorists, walkers and now, with this book, armchair travelers as well. Some of Ulster's landmarks, like the early stone houses of Kingston, Hurley, and New Paltz, are relatively well known, but many others—ranging from brick houses in the Federal style to Gothic Revival churches, Arts and Crafts summer colonies, Colonial Revival libraries, and Bauhaus-influenced modern houses—have not received the attention they deserve.

Ulster's architectural treasures do not resemble those of a major city, or even those of Long Island and Westchester where the rich built great mansions. While Ulster does have its grand Payne estate by Carrere & Hastings, architects renowned for their New York Public Library, the rustic buildings of Ralph Radcliffe Whitehead's Byrdcliffe and the relatively modest, Dutch Colonial–inspired Breuchard and Bruyn estates by Myron Teller and Harry Halverson are more characteristic of its country places. For many of us, the simpler structures associated with everyday middle- and working-class life—the inexpensive frame house with a Greek Revival doorway, the pressed-metal storefront, the small-town Romanesque Revival church, the factory-built diner—have an interest and appeal no less great than the architecture of the wealthy.

Ulster County's buildings have long attracted the interest of historians. In 1859 the Ulster Historical Society, as one of its first acts, put out a call for "Descriptions of old churches, houses, and of memorable localities." N. B. Sylvester's invaluable *History of Ulster County* (1880) referred frequently to old landmarks and singled out the "large, two-story gambrel-roofed" Wynkoop house in Stone Ridge, not only for its association with George Washington, who spent a night there in 1783, but also as "a mansion of considerable magnificence at the time of the Revolution." While in 1880 the Wynkoop house was "very much out of repair," it retained "fine specimens of the Dutch tiles in blue and pink that in the old days adorned the dwellings of the wealthier classes." The house was "often visited by strangers" drawn by its connection with Washington and by its historic architecture and design. Barns were discovered later. In 1921 the *Architectural Record*, a leading professional journal, published an article, "The Old Stone Houses of Esopus," with a photo captioned "a well-preserved old Dutch barn." The writer of the article, Helen M. Hastings, found such "huge looking, wide-gabled, low-eaved barns, all more or less real antiquity and worthy of their setting."

It remained, however, for Helen Wilkinson Reynolds, a Poughkeepsie resident and a leader of the Dutchess County Historical Society, to undertake the first meticulous and thorough history of the early architecture of Ulster County as part of her *Dutch Houses in the Hudson Valley before 1776*, published by the Holland Society of New York in 1929 with a foreword by her good friend Franklin D. Roosevelt. Reynolds received advice from Myron S. Teller, Kingston's leading architect in the first half of the twentieth century and an expert restorer and reviver of the old stone houses of the county. Teller condensed his considerable knowledge of these houses in a booklet, *The Early Stone Houses of Ulster County*, published in 1959 by the Ulster County Historical Society. In the 1960s the Junior League of Kingston undertook an ambitious survey of the county's buildings. The survey resulted in a well-illustrated guide, *Early Architecture in Ulster County* (1974) with text by Barry Benepe, that includes buildings from the colonial period through the nineteenth century.

My own aim has been to write an historical guide to Ulster's architecture up to about 1950. When I began concentrated work on the project in 2003, I thought the volume would resemble my *Kingston, New York: The Architectural Guide* (2003), with small photos and relatively brief text in a handy format for use on walking tours. As it turned out, many readers preferred to peruse the Kingston guide in the comfort of their homes, and the present book, while certainly not intended as a definitive history of Ulster's architecture, has grown to a size too great for pockets and glove compartments. Still, after reading and marking pages at home, I hope the book will inspire readers to go on excursions to sites around the county. In doing so, please respect the right to privacy of private property owners and view buildings from the public sidewalk, street, or road.

The structures I have chosen to write about strike me as good examples of the many building functions and architectural styles that catch the eye of the alert county traveler. I have also tried, where possible, to account for the choice of style by the designer and client. Therefore, the focus of this guide is upon the county's buildings and the people who shaped (or preserved) their forms. These people were part of a changing society where farming eventually gave way to industry and tourism, and where transport by horse was supplemented by canal and then railroad before the triumph of the automobile and truck. These changes can be traced architecturally from the eighteenth- and early-nineteenth-century stone farmhouses and frame barns in many parts of the county, to the later-nineteenth-century buildings of the High Falls–Rosendale area when that area grew as a center of the cement industry along the Delaware & Hudson Canal, and then to the summer hotels along the Ulster & Delaware Railroad ascending into the Catskills west of Kingston to Pine Hill. The Hudson River has constantly been an avenue for commerce, and in the nineteenth century the occasional mill, factory, and brickyard rose along its banks. The beauty of the river has long drawn people to build houses and, later, summer colonies and religious institutions on the high ground overlooking it.

My focus is not on historic, political or military events, or on personages whose role in determining building form is doubtful or unknown. As a consequence, missing here are the homes of such notable figures as 1904 Democratic presidential candidate Alton B. Parker and modern artist Marc Chagall. Another volume could be dedicated to such landmarks as Rosemount, Parker's residence on the Hudson in Esopus, and the simple frame bungalow (now altered) near High Falls that Marc Chagall bought in 1946 while "exiled" from Europe.

Freeman House

Buildings associated with abolitionist and women's-rights advocate Sojourner Truth, who grew up a slave in Ulster County, have long attracted interest. In 1886, three years after her death, a local newspaper identified an old stone Hardenbergh house near Rifton as her birthplace about 1797. A house on the Swartekill near its junction with the Wallkill has been pictured in a recent history of Esopus and cited as the birthplace. In Sojourner Truth's widely read *Narrative* of her life, architecture plays hardly any role. Understandably, she did not feel the need to discuss the quarters of her masters. Instead she focused upon the cellar of Charles Hardenbergh's house and inn, where she slept as a young girl with other slaves of both sexes in the same room filled with "noxious vapors." She recalled "this dismal chamber; its only lights consisting of a few panes of glass, through which she thinks the sun never shone but with thrice reflected rays; and the space between the loose boards of the floor, and the uneven earth below, was often filled with mud and water." The building had been recently erected by Charles Hardenbergh. We can only speculate that his own description of the house would have commented proudly on the excellence of its construction and pleasantness of life therein.

How This Book Is Organized

On the following pages, building entries are grouped by town and then by village, hamlet, or proximity within each town. The name of the building is usually the name of its original owner or occupant. A later owner or occupant may be indicated in parentheses. The current address is followed by the date of the building's design and/or construction; if the building no longer exists, its destruction date may be given in parentheses. If the architect or designer is known, that name follows the date. Significant alterations and their designers are also noted. At the end of the heading, the notation "NR" indicates that the building or district is on the National Registers of Historic Places, while "NHL" indicates even higher distinction as a National Historic Landmark (there are eight NHL sites in the county).

Site of Freeman House shortly after its demolition

Buildings that have been destroyed, heavily altered, or are difficult to see from public roads (because of landscape features or owners' objections) are noted with an asterisk (*) after the number. Destruction in the name of progress has long been practiced in the county. In 1907 it was noted that in Lloyd "the construction of the West Shore Railway along the fine river front" meant that "fine country seats were broken up and destroyed by the grading and excavations for the tracks." In 2010, even as *The New York Times* celebrated old Ulster County houses as desirable country places, the historic stone Freeman house in Port Ewen was demolished by the Mid-Hudson Valley Federal Credit Union despite the pleas of local preservationists. On its site the credit union erected an undistinguished but "green" building for its Port Ewen branch. In July 2011 the credit union tore down the former Esopus Library (with a 1939 Colonial Revival façade by Gerard Betz) adjacent to the new branch and its spacious parking lot. In this age of boundless and shameless "spin," the credit union exhibits pictures of the now-vanished Freeman house and library under the banner "celebrating our region."

The endnotes provide a list of sources for each building entry. The captions of illustrations include the source of the illustration and its date, except for photos taken by the author between 2000 and 2011, in which case the source and date are omitted. Photos dating between 1970 and 1999 and not otherwise attributed were also taken by the author. Illustration sources are listed on page 337.

I

Town of Denning

Formed from part of the Town of Shandaken, 1849.
(Note: later boundary changes for each town are not described here.)

Population: 1,044 in 1870; 516 in 2000.

Denning was named in honor of William H. Denning, owner of large tracts of land in the town. The forests of this sparsely populated town of mountains and narrow ravines were cut for lumber and tanning in the mid-nineteenth century; even then there were few farms and settlements. Today, much of the land is again forested. City people have long been attracted to remote Denning. By 1880 "an army of summer tourists" was exploring its mountain scenery. "Neither mountain crag nor lonely glen can elude their eager search." Trout fishing was recommended, for "along the mountain streams are to be found the most romantic, the grandest, the most beautiful and picturesque scenes in nature."

I-1 Lodge of John Quincy Adams Ward

Peekamoose Rd. (County Rte. 42), Peekamoose. c. 1898.

Founded in 1880, the Peekamoose Club (also known as Peekamoose Fishing Club) over the next decade and a half formed a tiny summer colony of well-to-do New Yorkers, including the prominent sculptor John Quincy Adams Ward (1830–1910), at remote Peekamoose, nine miles from the nearest Ulster & Delaware station at West Shokan. The membership, numbering about ten men, enjoyed hunting on some 2,000 acres and fishing the headwaters of the Rondout Creek, but in the 1890s the club was dissolved after its members squabbled violently among themselves—to the delight of local and metropolitan newspaper readers. Ward was a founding member of the club, which in 1880 purchased a tract of land, including Peekamoose Lake at the foot of Peekamoose Mountain, and built a substantial log clubhouse near the lake. The clubhouse, which does not survive, had sleeping accommodations for twenty and a fieldstone hearth with stone lintel inscribed "The Canty [cheerful] Hearth Where Cronies Meet 1880."

(The lintel survives in Ward's later lodge.) The club included financier and author Anthony W. Dimock and John R. Hegeman, president of the Metropolitan Life Insurance Company. In 1884 another member, J. W. Wentworth, and his cosmopolitan artist wife, Cecil de Wentworth, acquired land at Peekamoose and built a Swiss chalet known as the Wigwam with nearby Gothic chapel (see I–2).

The multi-gabled building visible today from Peekamoose Road was Ward's fishing lodge. It grew out of a small stone house, with angular, pointed-topped windows in the Gothic taste, pictured and described by R. Lionel De Lisser as "Old Stone House, J. Q. A. Ward's Fishing Lodge." De Lisser observed that Ward was "converting his keeper's house [the "Old Stone House"] into a picturesque fishing lodge." A fireplace in the extant house is carved with the date 1898, and that is probably the construction date of the expanded house seen in a vintage photo (Albany Institute of History & Art). Before twentieth-century alterations, the lodge displayed a half-timbered upper story (purely wooden, without plaster, in the Stick-style manner), trussed and barge-boarded gables, and fantastic dragon heads at the apexes of the gables. The dragon-headed gables were doubtless inspired

I-1. Ward's Lodge (1984 photo)

by medieval Norwegian precedent, appropriate given the steep slope and cascade directly behind the lodge—a lesser version of the dramatic Norwegian fjords. The designer of the lodge is unknown, although it is tempting to see the hand of the renowned New York architect Richard Morris Hunt, who had designed three earlier houses and/or studios for Ward. Hunt had traveled to Norway in 1867 and occasionally referred to its picturesque wooden buildings in his subsequent work. Hunt died in 1895, however, and no documentation has been found to connect him with the lodge.

I-2* J. W. and Cecil Wentworth Residence, The Wigwam, and Chapel

Peekamoose. c. 1885–1890 (Wigwam torn down by 1983).

The Wentworths' Wigwam, with its broad, gently sloping gable roof, second-story balcony, and rustic woodwork, looked more like a Swiss chalet (appropriate to the mountainous setting of Peekamoose) than an Indian wigwam. Inside, however, adorning the chimney breast above its rustic stone fireplace was a painting of an Indian who appears to be holding the mounted head of an antlered deer. R. Lionel De Lisser's photo in *Picturesque Ulster* also recorded an Indian basket hanging on the wall.

J. W. Wentworth was a wealthy New York businessman who enjoyed hunting and fishing in

I-2. The Wigwam (De Lisser photo, c. 1896)

the wilds of Denning. He had purchased a large tract of land at Peekamoose in 1884 and built this summer home and a nearby chapel, the latter his wife's project. His wife, Cecil de Wentworth (also known as Cecilia E. Wentworth), was a New York–born painter, trained in Paris, who exhibited at the Paris salon annually beginning in 1889. Among her many honors was a medal bestowed by Pope Leo XIII, whose portrait she had painted. As a devout Catholic, she took pride in her title, Papal Marquise. Her accomplishments entitled her to a listing (rare for a woman of her time) in *Who's Who in America* (1906), and the *Pine Hill Sentinel* called her, not quite accurately, "one of the most noted artists in the world." This now-obscure artist was probably responsible for the painted Indian within the Wigwam.

Alf Evers has told the story behind the building of Cecil de Wentworth's picturesque wooden Gothic chapel overlooking Peekamoose Lake. It seems that Mrs. Wentworth discovered a spring whose waters had miraculous curative powers, and so she erected the chapel at the site of the spring and invited Archbishop Michael Corrigan of New York to consecrate it. The well-known sculptor John Quincy Adams Ward, a Protestant and formerly a friend in the Peekamoose Fishing Club, objected strenuously to the chapel, fearing that his nearby tranquil retreat would be overwhelmed with swarms of people seeking "an American Lourdes." This dispute was one of several among Peekamoose's summer residents from the city that entertained newspaper readers for years.

Mrs. Wentworth was also the donor of St. Augustine's Roman Catholic Church in West Shokan. The board-and-batten and shingled building of sophisticated, freely Gothic design was dedicated by the archbishop in 1894, and a few years later it was featured in *Picturesque Ulster*. In 1915, after the church had been condemned for the Ashokan Reservoir, Mrs. Wentworth became embroiled in another public controversy when she sued Cardinal Farley to either build a new church or return the money she had given for construction of the existing building.

I-3 Methodist Episcopal Church
Intersection of County Rtes. 42 and 46, Sundown. 1868.

Standing isolated at a remote crossroads, this church looks perfect in its geometric simplicity. It is a late example of the Greek Revival with gable treated as pediment and with a plain entablature and corner pilasters. Its only oddity is the small scale of the twin front doors in relation to the building as a whole and the side windows in particular. In 1880 this was one of only two congregations in sparsely settled Denning, and the other, the Baptist Church of Sundown, had no identifiable place of worship.

I-3. Sundown Methodist Episcopal Church (c. 1920 photo)

I-4 Julius Forstmann Lodge (Forstmann Castle, Frost Valley YMCA)
2000 Frost Valley Rd. (County Rte. 47). 1915–1916.

Julius Forstmann (1871–1939) was born in Germany to a prosperous family engaged in the woolen industry since the late Middle Ages. In 1904 he arrived in the U.S. and soon established Forstmann & Huffmann Woolen Company in Passaic, New Jersey, which was highly successful despite occasional bitter conflict with its workers. A hunter and fisherman, Forstmann purchased some 2,000 acres near the Sullivan County border in the little-populated Neversink Valley at a place known as Frost Valley. The Neversink had long been a favorite of John Burroughs for trout fish-

ing. Burroughs returned to Frost Valley in old age in 1917 to fish the Neversink and marveled at "the old sweetness and charm of the place ... The soft murmur of the stream fills all the vale."

Burroughs apparently took no notice of Forstmann's new, twenty-three-room hunting and fishing lodge. By 1924 Forstmann presided over a gentleman's dairy farm, manicured gardens, and vast private game preserve cited as a "model for 'sportsmen's paradises.'" The lodge itself, with walls of cobblestone below and shingles above, is composed in the nineteenth-century picturesque manner—corner tower, balconies, and a terrace to take in the views of the Neversink Valley and Slide Mountain. It looms bulkily above the road, and its current owner, the YMCA, calls it "the Forstmann Castle." Its somewhat overbearing quality—in contrast to the more rustic lodges at Peekamoose or Winnisook—can be attributed to Forstmann's wealth and his desire to build in the style of his German origins.

While prospering in America, Forstmann maintained strong ties with Germany. Even during World War I, when Forstmann subscribed liberally to the Liberty bond drive and assisted with uniforms for the American Army, 15 percent of his firm was owned by Germans and consequently held by the U. S. Government's Custodian of Alien Property. Forstmann's luxurious, 3,500-ton yacht, the *Orion*, said to be the largest private yacht in the world when new in 1929, was built "exclusively of German materials" in the Krupp Germania shipyard at Kiel. The *Times* reported that "the furnishings of the dining room recall those of an old German castle."

The interior of the hunting lodge is reputed to be the work of German craftsmen. Its hardware and fine wood paneling have a distinctly Germanic air. Forstmann's dark, oak-paneled office, fitted out with a rustic stone fireplace, was decorated with stuffed birds, deer heads, and watercolors of fish, and illuminated by light bulbs hanging from a circular band of hammered copper, itself suspended from the ceiling by iron chains. Still hanging in the living room is a forest scene with stag painted in 1877 by the German artist Christian Kroner (1838–1911). Also in the living room is

Catskills town. Julius Forstmann began his Germanic hunting lodge in 1915 (see I–4). Earlier, around 1903, Alexander Tison (1857–1938), a Harvard-educated New York attorney, and his wife, Annie H. Stevens Tison (died 1952 at Grey Lodge), built their Japanese-influenced house on a large tract of land along the East Branch of the Neversink southwest of Slide Mountain. Why Japanese? Tison was a professor of English and American law at the Imperial University in Tokyo from 1889 to 1894, and thereafter practiced law in New York while maintaining strong ties with Japan—traveling there on business four times between 1894 and 1907. In 1904 he lent his support to Japan in its war with Russia, and the next year was one of two Americans to speak at a gathering of Japanese citizens celebrating the Russian surrender of Port Arthur. Beginning in 1908, Tison was a director of Japan Society, which fostered American trade, investment, travel, and study in Japan, and he served as its president between 1929 and 1931. The Emperor of Japan decorated him with the Order of the Rising Sun, fourth class, among other honors.

a copy of a portrait of Forstmann in riding attire. The original portrait, painted in 1923 by Nicola Michailow, a Bulgarian painter active in Berlin who also portrayed Kaiser Wilhelm II, has been returned to Forstmann's family.

Forstmann's obituary credits him with designing the interior of the *Orion* himself. Doubtless he was also involved with the design of his hunting lodge, although for his grand, twenty-five-room house (1923) at 22 East 71st Street in Manhattan, he turned to C. P. H. Gilbert, a well-regarded New York architect. Gilbert designed the façade in his usual Renaissance classical manner; it is not Germanic. In 2009 the mansion was offered for sale by Sotheby's for $75 million.

Forstmann's widow Adolfine died in 1953, and the Frost Valley property was sold to the YMCA in 1956. Today the superbly preserved Forstmann hunting lodge is the centerpiece of the vast, 6,000-acre, Frost Valley YMCA camp and conference center in New York State's "forever wild" Catskill Forest Preserve.

I-5 Alexander and Annie Tison Estate, Grey Lodge

Denning Rd. (near the DEC parking area at the northeast end of Denning Rd.) 1903. Benson & Brockway.

Japan and Germany are both represented in the architecture of wealthy New Yorkers in this remote

Much of the design of Grey Lodge is in line with American country houses and hunting lodges of the time: the use of local materials (including cobblestone and chestnut wood); the glassy bay window; the piazzas; the living hall with central fireplace; and the gun room. But historian Clay Lancaster has identified several markedly Japanese characteristics at Grey Lodge: "the hipped roof is modified by gables at the top, thus putting it in the *irimoya* category [of roof construction], and the eaves curve upward at the corners rather severely." He compared the chimney tops to those of the Japanese-influenced Gamble house (1909) in Pasadena,

California, by the renowned Greene Brothers, while concluding that "the double hood over the central bay is a feature unique to the builder."

The Tisons employed a Japanese gardener, Muto, to transform the Neversink Creek near the house into something Japanese "with channels and waterfalls ... a little lake containing islands, and planted ... with flowering trees and shrubbery. ... Lanterns were built up of cobblestones ... A tea house facing the lake was built of rustic timbers, with plastered walls between. A circular window [the "moon window"] in one wall frames the view of the lodge." Ted Hilton's "Introduction to the Tison Japanese Garden" (1985) explains the rich significance of every stone and element of the garden, which appears natural or casually composed but actually follows a precise set of rules. Thus "each pool and island represents real islands and seas of Japan." Mrs. Tison is said to have been frustrated in her attempt to give the house a Japanese name; neighbors called the place Grey Lodge (the exterior chestnut sheathing had weathered to a beautiful grey) to distinguish it from the neighboring Red Lodge, and the Tisons reluctantly adopted the prosaic name.

According to Clay Lancaster, Annie Tison "planned" the house, and it was built by local carpenter Joseph Ertz. Annie Tison belonged to the socially prestigious Cosmopolitan Club in New York, where she was among those who welcomed Japanese Baroness Ishimoto. Mrs. Tison was a guest of Frank Seaman at Yama Farms (see XX–9) in 1930 to celebrate the 70th birthday of author Hamlin Garland, and in 1937 Henry Francis du Pont invited her, along with Stone Ridge's Sarah Lounsbery and Emily Chadbourne, to visit his showplace of American antiques at Winterthur, Delaware. Lancaster reproduced a skillful pencil sketch for a one-story "bungalow" version of the house, but did not identify the draftsman. It is unlikely that Mrs. Tison made the sketch, since plans for the house have come to light that identify the architects as Benson & Brockway of New York. Both John P. Benson and Albert L. Brockway were trained at the École des Beaux-Arts in Paris, and later they were among the few Americans awarded a silver medal for architecture at the Paris Exposition of 1900. Beaux-Arts architects were open to a variety of styles, and the house Benson designed by 1907 for his own family in Plainfield, New Jersey, was American Colonial Revival with cedar shingled walls. Doubtless the architects incorporated Japanese details into the Tison house at the instruction of the owners.

I-5. Grey Lodge

II

Town of Esopus

Formed from part of the Town of Kingston, 1811.

Population: 4,552 in 1870; 9,331 in 2000.

Esopus, a word of Indian origin, takes its name from the seventeenth-century Dutch settlement on the Hudson River and north of Rondout Creek. Today's town lies south of Rondout Creek and the city of Kingston, while the Hudson River forms its eastern border. The Delaware & Hudson Canal (opened in 1828) brought coal from Pennsylvania to its terminus in Rondout (Kingston) and Sleightsburgh. River commerce was also important in the nineteenth century, especially before the arrival of the West Shore Railroad in 1883. Steamboat travelers of the early twentieth century were directed by Wallace Bruce's *The Hudson by Daylight Map* to look out for Esopus landmarks on bluffs overlooking the river (and the more fashionable estates on the eastern, Dutchess County, shore): A. R. Frothingham's house with "Grecian portico"; John Burroughs's "brown stone cottage"; the Monastery of the Holy Cross; Robert Livingston Pell's "Roman villa"; Alton B. Parker's Rosemount; and the "large new building" of the Novitiate of the Redemptorist Fathers. Some riverfront properties, including those of Pell and Burroughs, grew fruit for shipment to New York and beyond.

II-1 Archibald and Helen Russell House, Glen Albyn (Christian Brothers)

Rte. 9W, West Park. c. 1852?

This is one of Ulster's underappreciated architectural and historical landmarks. Although its designer and date remain unknown, it is one of the county's finest and best-preserved examples of the Italian villa from the mid-nineteenth century. Archibald Russell (1811–1871) acquired the property in 1852, and the house was probably built for him.

Glen Albyn's south façade is composed around a dominant three-story tower, the key element in the Italian villa mode. The tower's low, hipped roof projecting well beyond the walls below, the three round-arched windows of the tower's upper story, and the hooded and balconied opening on the middle story—all are characteristic of the Italian villa mode whose sources lie in the vernacular farmhouses of Italy as interpreted in England and then in America by such masters as A. J. Davis, Richard Upjohn, and John Notman. Also characteristic of the mode are the asymmetrical, picturesquely composed low gables to either side of the tower, as well as the bracketed eaves and treatment of the wall as a series of planes, in this case three. Some features could be found in both Gothic Revival and Italian villas—the bay window to the right, and especially the hooded porch with its pendants and broad trefoil below the gable roof.

Archibald Russell was born in Edinburgh, Scotland, graduated from its university

where his father and grandfather had been professors, and went on to study in Bonn, Germany, before coming to America in 1836. Active in the world of business and finance, in 1851 he was a founder and first president of the Ulster County Savings Institution in Kingston, and the next year he acquired this property in West Park. Russell continued as president until 1870 when the bank's new Victorian Gothic building designed by J. A. Wood opened on Wall Street. Russell's interests extended beyond banking, however; he was well known as a philanthropist, serving as a founding trustee and then president for eighteen years of the Five Points House of Industry, which provided meals, lodging, and schooling on Worth Street in one of New York City's most notorious neighborhoods. In the city he was a member of the Church of the Ascension (Episcopal), and in West Park he helped found the Church of the Ascension of the same denomination. He is said to have hired the architect and supervised construction of the West Park church (see II–12), and in 1862 he proposed a columnar monument to the Twentieth Regiment on a height overlooking the home of its late leader, Colonel George W. Pratt (see II–14).

After Archibald Russell's death in 1871, the property was retained by his widow until it was sold in 1885 to Eugene R. and Cynthia Durkee.

II-1. Glen Albyn (c. 1900 photo, formerly Elizabeth Burroughs Kelley collection)

Durkee, the retired proprietor of the country's leading spice business, enhanced Glen Albyn, "adding buildings and enlarging the gardens, with ... landscaping that included a trellised bridge over the ravine." Durkee died in 1903 and his second wife, Harriet, in 1912. The property was then advertised for sale including, in addition to the main house, a dock, boathouse, stable with coachman's rooms, and gardener's cottage. In the twentieth century the property was acquired by the Christian Brothers, who added a large wing on the north of the house.

II-2 Mother Cabrini School (Cabrini Home)
Rte. 9W, West Park. 1935.

In 1890 Mother Cabrini, founder of the Roman Catholic Order of the Missionary Sisters of the Sacred Heart, purchased this site from Jesuits who had conducted a novitiate here for some twenty years. A native of Italy who came to America in 1889 to help impoverished Italian immigrants in New York, Mother Cabrini initiated Sacred Heart Orphanage, a home at West Park for poor and neglected children, one of several schools and institutions she founded on three continents. At her death in 1917, she was buried on these grounds, but in 1933, as part of the canonization process, her body was exhumed, identified, examined for unusual signs of preservation, and reburied in

New York in the chapel of Mother Cabrini High School. The canonization effort was successful, and in 1946 Frances Xavier Cabrini was the first United States citizen to become a saint.

The school resembles many American public schools of the 1920s and '30s in its generally Georgian Revival character—red brick walls with white trim, including keystones over the double-hung sash windows. Roman Catholic churches and schools of the period were often designed in the Georgian style to express the church's strong bonds with the United States and reinforce the notion that, despite its ties to the Vatican, it was not a foreign institution. Both this school and the Van den Berg School of Practice in New Paltz have boldly pedimented door frames that draw attention to the main entrance—here, up a pair of formal staircases.

II-3 Smith House
Rte. 9W, West Park. c. 1889 and 1906 (altered later).

The Smith house is important as a landmark in the history of the education of women industrial workers, but also as a good example of Arts and Crafts architecture. Its symmetrical east front retains the bay windows and diamond-paned casements of the mid-nineteenth-century Gothic Revival, but here merged with the discipline and simplicity of the turn-of-the-century's Arts and Crafts approach. The east front was designed with extensive porches overlooking the river.

According to Elizabeth Burroughs Kelley, this house originated as a farmhouse. It was purchased in 1889 by John Jewell Smith, a wealthy installer of steam heat in New York office buildings, who then remodeled and enlarged it. Smith died in 1901, and the house, called

II-2. Mother Cabrini School (mid-twentieth-century postcard)

Heartsease, was further altered in 1906, presumably for his widow, Mary Helen Smith. (Kelley's suggestion that Stanford White was responsible for the 1906 alterations is undocumented.) Smith's daughter, Hilda Worthington (known as Jane) Smith (1888–1984), graduated from Bryn Mawr College in 1910, pursued graduate studies, and in 1919 became Bryn Mawr's dean. Active in social work in West Park and eventually across the country, Smith helped organize the Bryn Mawr Summer School for Women Workers in Industry, which opened in 1921 at the college with Smith as director. In 1927 Smith published poetry by women workers in a beautifully printed booklet, *The Workers Look at the Stars*, whose title page featured a drawing of the Hudson River as seen though her diamond-paned casements. In the booklet she announced a "new venture in Workers' Education," the Vineyard Shore School for Women Workers, located at her family home. Here, workers from the Bryn Mawr Summer School and other similar schools were to be offered an additional eight months of study. The school apparently operated from 1929 to 1933, when it closed for financial reasons. Beginning in 1933 Smith was employed by New Deal agencies including the Federal Emergency Relief Administration and the WPA. In 1939 the Bryn Mawr Summer School moved to Smith's place in West Park and became the Hudson Shore Labor School, no longer associated with the college. A 1939 press release described the site: "a delightful rural setting on an old estate overlooking the picturesque and historic Hudson River." Here "60 women workers will enjoy healthful outdoor living combined with opportunities for study and discussion of problems of labor and industry."

A postcard of the Smith house from the period when it was occupied by the labor

II-3. Smith House (c. 1940 postcard)

school (it moved to Rutgers University in 1952) suggests that some of the aura of high intellectual aspiration found in Bryn Mawr College's collegiate Gothic campus also hovered about the Gothic casements of the Smith house. The fireplace in the house's main lounge was faced with tiles and flanked by high wooden settles in the Arts and Crafts manner. In the age of steam heat, the open fire still had a sentimental appeal, as it did in the Arts and Crafts interior of the Deanery, the president's house at Bryn Mawr College. Despite the traditional, upper-class tone of Smith's house and despite (or perhaps because of) the friendship and support she received from Eleanor Roosevelt, Smith was accused of communist ties in the 1930s.

II-4 Howell-Frothingham House, Aberdeen (Hudson Valley School of Massage Therapy)
1723 Rte. 9W, West Park. c. 1835.

Aberdeen is Ulster County's most impressive Greek Revival house. From Rte. 9W there is a partial view of the west façade, with its broad gable treated as a classical pediment and the central doorway sheltered by a shallow distyle-in-antis Ionic porch. The more imposing and impressive front, however, faces east, over the river, and was one of the numerous evocations of the white Greek temple pointed out to nineteenth-century steamboat travelers on the Hudson. Its six, tall, fluted Ionic

II-4. Aberdeen

columns supporting an entablature and pediment are comparable to the temple front of six Doric columns overlooking the Hudson at Edgewater (c. 1820) at Barrytown, Dutchess County, although Aberdeen looks more weightily Greek, as it lacks Edgewater's gracefully arched French windows.

Elizabeth Burroughs Kelley has suggested the house was built about 1835 for John Howell, followed by several owners before it was purchased in 1858 by Abraham Frothingham, vice president of the La Mar Fire Insurance Co. of New York. In 1885 the Frothinghams sold the place to Dr. Alexander Gordon's family, who named it Aberdeen. Henry Ford is said to have briefly considered purchasing the house in 1914 when it was shown to him by John Burroughs, whose Riverby is not far away. Perhaps Ford had in mind transporting it to his Michigan museum. During the 1920s Aberdeen was used for the rehabilitation of drug addicts. Hilda Smith purchased it in 1929 and used it, along with her own home (see II–3) for the education of women workers. After her school closed in 1951, the house again became a private residence, but in recent years it has become a school of massage therapy.

II-5 Van Benschoten House, Vinecroft
Rte. 9W, West Park. c. 1884.

A fine example of the Queen Anne style, the west façade of the Van Benschoten house displays a number of its characteristics—a lower story of masonry with an upper story of wood shingles slightly over-

hanging the first, as well as a picturesque composition of oriel window, steeply sloping roofs, and accented chimneys. Like H. H. Richardson's famous and larger Queen Anne house for Watts Sherman (1875) in Newport, Rhode Island, the Van Benschoten house has a cross-mullioned window set into the ground-story stone wall, and a shed roof sheltering the doorway.

According to Elizabeth Burroughs Kelley, William H. Van Benschoten, president of the Knoxville (Tennessee) Iron Company, purchased a frame house on this site in 1883 and rebuilt it as a stone residence. Van Benschoten had studied painting in France and Italy, and incorporated a studio called Bohemia into his residence. He was a companion of his neighbor John Burroughs in climbing Catskill peaks, and entered into friendly competition with Burroughs as a grape grower. Mrs. Van Benschoten had the distinction of naming Burroughs's retreat "Slabsides." Their grandson, William H. Van Benschoten II (1910–1968), an architect trained at Yale in the 1930s, maintained his office at Vinecroft in the 1950s and '60s.

II–6* John Burroughs House, Riverby
Rte. 9W, West Park. 1873. John Burroughs (altered by Julian Burroughs after 1947 fire).

Among Ulster County's most distinguished inhabitants was John Burroughs (1837–1921), the celebrated writer and naturalist, disciple of Emerson, Thoreau, and Whitman. Not so well known is his keen interest in building. Burroughs had grown up on a farm in Delaware County, taught in rural

II-5. Van Benschoten House

schoolhouses in Ulster County and elsewhere in the 1850s, emerged as a writer in 1860, and from 1864 to 1872 worked for the Treasury Department in Washington while enlarging his reputation as an author. In 1867 he built a substantial but plain brick house on V Street at the northern edge of the city, which gave him proximity to the countryside and space for a fruit and vegetable garden, a cow, and chickens.

In 1873 Burroughs sought a home in the country, looking at Long Island and then at the Hudson Valley, where he purchased a nine-acre farm known as the Deyo place on the river two miles from the Esopus post office. There he could have a fruit farm and write, when not traveling to earn an income as a bank examiner. On the property was an old house from the period of the Revolution. Burroughs retained the house for years as a gardener's cottage and sometimes occupied it himself, finding that with "an open wood fire in the old fireplace ... a real feeling of home comes upon me." Burroughs eventually called his farm and the new house he built on it "Riverby," for their location by the Hudson. In England in 1871 he had admired how the middle class and aristocracy named their houses and thereby gave them "added value and importance."

The author proved himself an amateur architect in designing the house for himself and his wife Ursula, whom he left out of the planning process. He wrote to her: "I have made a plan of our house, and have made the house itself in pasteboard. It has taken me three days to build it. It looks very nice. It is half wood and half stone. If we could reduce ourselves to the size of mice, we could go to keeping house in it right off." He ac-

knowledged that the plan was "a modification" of one from a book owned by his Dutchess County friend Myron Benton, who about this time was building his own picturesque Gothic cottage at Troutbeck.

Burroughs's new house would have large rooms and "a glorious old hall, 12 x 16." It would represent the cultural sophistication Burroughs had acquired since leaving the vernacular farmhouses of his youth, and would align him with the taste of his time for the picturesque and Gothic Revival. In Ulster County this taste had found expression in the Rondout studio (1853) of the Hudson River School artist Jervis McEntee, designed by Calvert Vaux, and the Kingston home (c. 1870) of poet Henry Abbey, a friend of Burroughs. Vaux was a disciple of Andrew Jackson Downing and author of *Villas and Cottages* (1869), a popular guide to house design.

Burroughs wrote of his own principles of residential architecture, put into practice in building Riverby, in "House-Building," an essay he published in *Scribner's Monthly* in January 1876. (In 1886 he revised the essay and titled it "Roof-Tree" in his book *Signs and Seasons*.) The practice of architecture was becoming increasingly professionalized in the 1870s, but Burroughs saw no need to defer to the trained architect; just as "the bird is its own architect ... if one can sufficiently master the subject," he thought it well "to dispense with that functionary."

II-6. Riverby (Scribner's Monthly, Jan. 1876)

He did acknowledge that the floor plans of his house "are adapted from Vaux"—probably from his *Villas and Cottages*—and Burroughs allowed that it was prudent to have "a competent architect ... look over and revise the plans" before construction began. Perhaps Vaux performed this service for Burroughs. In any event, Burroughs was pleased when Vaux "commended" his *Scribner's* essay.

The site appealed to Burroughs for its relative proximity to his family in Delaware County, and it provided both a river view and a hillside that allowed him to fit the three-story house snugly into the slope. Moreover, there were heaps of weathered, warm-gray limestone nearby. Beginning to build in August 1873, Burroughs experienced real pleasure in selecting and drawing out stone for masons to lay up in the lower story of his house. The bird when building its nest not only functioned as its own architect, "but the bird is its own builder, too." Burroughs believed that his "positive contribution of genuine manual labor" enhanced the house's "history and ... meaning" for himself. "Every load [of stone] that was sent home carried my heart and happiness with it. The jewels I had uncovered in the debris, or torn from the ledge in the morning, I saw in the jambs, or mounted high on the corners at night." Burroughs discovered that rural "American mechanics" lacked the skill of his Irish-trained stone mason. When his mason was absent from too much drinking, Burroughs took his place, nearly finished the chimney himself, and was pleased to have his work approved by this "most skilled workman!" At first he called his house Rock Ribs, liking its "gritty" sound, before settling on Riverby. He also helped fell trees and took care in choosing the wood for his house, some coming from places familiar to him in the Catskills.

Burroughs's friend Benton called the design "exceedingly picturesque," and it relates to the picturesque and Gothic Revival of Downing and Vaux in its asymmetry, its bay and oriel windows, and the vertical thrusts of the steeply pitched, intersecting roofs. Burroughs argued that the picturesque house with neutral brown or gray walls, "wide projections and deep shadows ... simple strong lines [and] ... ample ... roofs" was admirable in "blend[ing] ...

with the landscape." Earlier, probably sometime between 1863 and 1872, Burroughs proposed that architecture should "adapt ... itself to the surrounding landscape" and "therefore ... perhaps the most perfect architecture ... is the old baronial castle of Feudalism, perched upon a bluff, or crag, or some almost inaccessible peak and appearing more like ... some design of nature than any piece of merely constructive masonry." At Riverby the baronial castle was an impractical model, but the desire to fit in with nature remained.

Burroughs advocated "the picturesqueness of the stone house above all others. Every line is a line of strength and necessity. ... build of stone by all means ... and the rockier the better." He sought out stones suitable in their regularity for the house's seven corners, but also rejoiced in turning up the apparently "ugly customer, a stone with a ragged quartz face, or cavernous, and set with rock crystals like great teeth ... These I needed a sprinkling of for their quaintness, and to make the wall a true compendium of the locality."

The rugged stone base is surmounted by lighter boards reminiscent of Gothic half-timbering in the diagonal patterning. Burroughs favored this patterning of boards as an "architectural device by which the anatomy, the real framework, of the structure ... is allowed to show, or made to serve as ornament." Shakespeare's Stratford-upon-Avon, with its half-timbered buildings, had appealed to Burroughs on a visit in 1871. His acquaintance, the Connecticut author and sometime architect Donald G. Mitchell, published a house design having a first story of stone and the second half-timbered in his *Rural Studies* (1867), and Mitchell's own picturesquely composed residence (1872) at New Haven was half wood and half stone. Burroughs himself cited E. C. Gardner's *Homes and How to Make Them* as recommending wood above stone, and Mitchell's house was lauded by Gardner in his book.

Burroughs's house was finished in 1874, and a little before completion Burroughs professed that "on the whole [I] am ... proud of the design." Significantly, it was not the design's historical pedigree that pleased him, but rather the treatment of the local stone he had gathered.

"The wall has a bold and rocky look which is much heightened by the projections on all the ends or gables." The rough stonework was complemented by the rustic porch with knotty cedar posts. Burroughs would write that "every man's house is in some sort an effigy of himself." This rugged man of the outdoors preferred the rocky and rustic in his house as an expression of his "taste and manners ... humility and simplicity." On the other hand, "false pride or a petty ambition" would be expressed in the houses of those cursed with these character flaws.

Burroughs also carefully considered the choice of wood and details of the interior, but later came to conclude that it lacked sufficient daylight, and that the floor plan was faulty from both his and his wife's points of view. Ursula was an immaculate housekeeper, and the rooms—including carved, hard-to-dust, wooden ornament designed by Burroughs—were distributed inconveniently over three floors. Burroughs had hoped to write in the library, but it had no view of the river; the parlor had this view, but it was too stiff and inhospitable for the author to use. In fact, in his conclusion to "Roof Tree," written in the winter of 1886, he questioned whether all the efforts that went into the design of houses like Riverby resulted in as much "aesthetic pleasure" as came from "the plain unpainted structure that took no thought of appearances." Burroughs's harsh judgment of Riverby was contradicted in 1905 by a visitor, Gustav Stickley, a leading proponent of the Arts and Crafts movement, who ignored the outmoded Gothic exterior while praising the interior with "some features of peculiar attractiveness." Stickley found antecedents of his own "Craftsman ideals" in Burroughs's strict avoidance of paint—"not an ounce of paint on doors, casings or other woodwork." Renowned for

his artistry in oak, Stickley found a congenial spirit in Burroughs, who insisted on "no other finish than a coat or two of oil. The result is that time has given ... [the woodwork] a rich color which makes it exquisite. The natural poetry of the wood is emphasized ... ."

Not until 1881 did Burroughs build a congenial study (NHL), a one-room "plain unpainted structure" about fifty yards from the main house and nearer the river. In an 1882 letter to Walt Whitman, Burroughs called it "my bark-covered shanty." It was a forerunner of his later, larger, and better-known retreat, Slabsides, in having bark-covered exterior walls, here of chestnut bark placed vertically in contrast to Slabsides's horizontal slabs of hemlock. Oriented to the river view, it had two windows facing the river, and Elizabeth Burroughs Kelley remembered that the entrance door, also facing the river, was kept open by her grandfather. Sunlight poured in the bay window on the south. The brick chimney on the north wall did not draw well and was replaced (probably in 1904) by a more rustic cobblestone chimney. The fireplace was the main architectural feature of the interior, as plain bookshelves came to cover virtually every bit of wall.

Writing in 1912, Julian Burroughs described furniture his father had made for the study, "working it by hand from our tough native oak, carving and decorating some of the pieces in simple designs." Gustav Stickley found the room "as cosy and comfortable and untidy as a man of letters

II-6A. Study at Riverby (early-twentieth-century postcard)

and life could wish. The great open fire place, built of boulders ... pleads for fellowship and a quiet chat; the Morris chair and the Craftsman rocker [was this actually a product of Stickley's Syracuse factory?] invite to ease." Burroughs liked to sit on the doorstep, look out upon nature, and muse, but it was in this den that he would do most of his writing, even after building Slabsides. A few feet nearer the river was a rustic, open summerhouse—another site for musing.

The author transferred ownership of the main house at Riverby to his wife before his death, and she willed it to their son Julian. In 1947 it was heavily damaged by fire, and the upper stories were rebuilt in modified form. According to Julian, his father "liked to build yet all his buildings were badly planned ... how many years of my life I've given to correcting the mistakes he made!" Julian designed new, larger windows and a distinctive library with a more spacious and functional hearth.

II–7* Julian Burroughs House, Love Cote

Rte. 9W, West Park. 1902 and later.
Julian Burroughs.

Julian Burroughs, the Harvard-educated son of John Burroughs, lived in his father's shadow but managed to create his own identity as a writer of magazine articles, a photographer, a farmer, an architect, and the keeper of his father's reputation and his father's property. At Harvard Julian had known and admired Charles Eliot Norton, professor emeritus of the history of art. After graduation from Harvard in 1901, Julian bowed to his father's wish that he give up a promising start as a jour-

II-7. Love Cote

nalist and return to Riverby to assist his father by managing the fruit farm. The next year Julian designed and built, under his father's eye and hand, a cottage for himself and his bride Emily about a hundred yards north of the house his father had created in 1873.

Julian had little experience in design or construction and, like his father, had little respect for professional architects. He claimed to have studied "many books and plans (from which I got nothing)" and then went on to make "my own plans in an hour." Julian followed his father's mature taste for the rustic and planned a low, gable-roofed house with walls of bark-covered slabs, placed vertically as in his father's little, bark-surfaced study nearby. The rustic porch with cedar posts resembled Slabsides. Like his father, Julian arranged windows to take advantage of the view of the river. Much more than his father, however, Julian was absorbed by the river, its wildlife and boats. Julian also had hopes of a happier marriage than his parents', and so he and Emily called the house "Love Cote." However, when Clara Barrus resided there (beginning in 1914 when Julian was living on Col. Payne's West Park estate and serving as its superintendent), it was renamed "the Nest." John Burroughs had written, "What is a man's house but his nest ... ?"

Julian's father entered into the construction of the house as if it were his own, again joyfully digging out stones and designing the fireplace, an improvement over the one in Riverby, and assisting his son with bookshelves, wainscoting, and other woodwork. The initials J. B. and date 1902 were formed in pebbles set in cement in the upper stonework of the fireplace; did this represent the pride of the father and/or the son in putting up the house?

Julian did much of the construction himself, joining in the backbreaking labor of digging the cellar. The Harvard graduate's lowly shoveling was featured by local newspapers. Julian also did much of the carpentry after the framing was completed by a master carpenter. The son did manage to include some refinements absent in the bark study and Slabsides—a chimney of more regular blocks of local stone, diamond-paned casement windows in the second story, and wood shingles in the end

II-7A. The Roxy

After his father's and TR's deaths, Julian put up a three-story lookout tower that was approached from the Nest by an arched bridge. The top, open-sided story of the tower was fitted with mission-style settles where Julian could nap or indulge in his favorite pastime of observing river life. Built with stuccoed walls and recycled timbers from a nearby, recently demolished icehouse, the tower blends with its natural surroundings despite its verticality. Its "rustic romanticism" was, as Barry Benepe has written, combined "with a sense of pictorial fantasy ... expressed ... in details of imbedded tiles, cast lobsters, birds and fish, and numerous sculptured details." Julian's family called it "The Roxy" after the glitzy movie palace in New York, not a name and probably not a tower John Burroughs, who avoided architectural eccentricity, would have favored. Julian also designed an eccentrically detailed, rustic stone shop building (1932), with cupola and large arched windows on the second floor, where he repaired and stored shad nets, while making furniture on the ground floor.

gables. The wood trim and furniture were simple and sturdily geometric in the manner of Gustav Stickley's Craftsman designs. Julian, again like his father, made much of the furniture, although Julian purchased a chair from an Adirondack craftsman and others from Montgomery Ward.

The house was a success functionally—more open to the sun and views of the Hudson, less damp and cold than the 1873 stone house, and with a more practical floor plan and fewer stairs. It also succeeded in terms of the Arts and Crafts ideals of simplicity and clear expression of natural materials. Julian's arguments for using slabs and not conventional painted siding were published in Gustav Stickley's *Craftsman* magazine in 1911 along with photos, probably by Julian, of the nine-year-old house and of John Burroughs "inspecting chestnut bark" that was well preserved after twenty-five years on his bark study. When Julian's house was new, President and Mrs. Theodore Roosevelt had come to visit his father, primarily at Slabsides, but the president also lauded Julian's house as "original and American" in contrast to the "Vanderbilt Italian palace" across the Hudson.

II–8* West Shore Station
West Park. 1891 (not extant).

This handsome station built of local rough-hewn stone, including some quartz, replaced a small frame structure designed by Wilson Brothers & Co. According to Elizabeth Burroughs Kelley, the expense of the stone building was borne by five prominent landowners—John Burroughs, John U. Brookman, Eugene R. Durkee, Adam Neidlinger,

II-8. West Park Station (early-twentieth-century photo, formerly Elizabeth Burroughs Kelley collection)

and John Jewell Smith. She identified the architect and builder as Orlando McLain of Esopus, "who for over forty years was known as the foremost builder in the area." John Burroughs is said to have employed McLain when building Riverby, calling him "Old Reliable, true as steel and superior in every way." The stone station burned during or soon after construction and was quickly rebuilt with added space for the post office. The grounds near the station were landscaped with flower beds, lawns, and trees paid for by Brookman and Neidlinger.

II–9 John Burroughs's Slabsides
John Burroughs Sanctuary, Burroughs Drive, off Floyd Ackert Road, West Park. 1895. John Burroughs. NHL

Slabsides, the rustic retreat of writer-naturalist John Burroughs, is among Ulster County's most significant buildings. It stands within the wooded John Burroughs Sanctuary, established in 1921 with nine acres surrounding the cabin, and later increased to some 170 acres with woodland trails. Burroughs chose the wooded site on the edge of a swamp set into a hill more than a mile inland from his home at Riverby (see II–6). In seeking an alternative to Riverby, Burroughs professed weariness with its "extensive water view," perhaps especially with the grandiose Vanderbilt mansion looming across the river. Instead, he preferred Slabsides's more enclosed, "secluded" site. On the hillside, at the foot of a cliff and not far from an appealing spring, he found a refuge from what he called "the vain and noisy world of railroads, steamboats, and yachts." He was also distancing himself from his wife Ursula (the couple had a contentious marriage, and Julian Burroughs, whom they treated as a son, was in fact born to a woman with whom John had an affair) and from visitors who distracted the author at Riverby. At Slabsides he could quietly observe the nest-building of robins, chickadees, chimney swifts, phoebes, and warblers. Yet Burroughs soon chose to welcome an intermittent stream of admirers ranging from President Theodore Roosevelt (in 1903), to naturalist John Muir, and students from New Paltz Normal School and Vassar College. The last visitors before Burroughs's

death were Henry Ford, Thomas Edison, and Harvey Firestone.

In contrast to the more ornamented and more aggressively picturesque Riverby, which Burroughs had designed and built in the 1870s, Slabsides reflected his preference as an older man for a more complete adoption of rustic simplicity in architecture. What could be more fitting for a naturalist famous for writing about the everyday appearance and activities of birds and insects than to build a rustic human nest? In "House-Building," written almost twenty years before he undertook Slabsides, Burroughs had proposed: "What is a man's house but his nest, and why should it not be nestlike both outside and in,—coarse, strong, negative in tone externally, and snug and well-feathered and modeled by the heart within?" As at Riverby, he played an active part in gathering materials and in construction. He helped cut the trees, and in November and December 1895 worked alongside the carpenter and mason in building "my rustic cabin," playing a larger role than he could have in a larger and more complex project. Burroughs took particular pride in the design of his rustic stone hearth and chimney, a design based on his poking his head up a number of old chimneys and discovering that a good draft resulted when "the throat of the chimney [was] long and narrow and the flue above very big." The hard manual labor of laying up wood and stone appealed to the writer who had grown up on a Delaware County farm and who grew celery in the swamp next to Slabsides; "What joy went into the building of this retreat!" he told Clara Barrus, his companion, physician, and eventual biographer.

Slabsides was a name suggested by Burroughs's neighbor, Mrs. William Van Benschoten, and derived from the cabin's exterior cladding of horizontal, bark-covered slabs of hemlock, which gave the appearance of a log cabin. (While much of Slabsides's timber came from the locality, the slabs came by railroad from Hobart in Delaware County.) Some friends argued for a "prettier name," but Burroughs said, "this name just expresses the place, and the place just meets the want that I felt for something simple, homely, secluded—in fact, something with the bark on." Burroughs took

Barrus to Slabsides on their first meeting in September 1901, and she later described its exterior, focusing on its rustic features: "The roomy veranda, with rustic railing and shaggy cedar posts, the sloping roof, the great chimney, the climbing vines, the wide rustic door with latch-string out, and a curiously twisted knurl for a door knob ..."

In "House-Building," Burroughs had advocated simplicity and harmony with the adjoining landscape. Barrus, picking up on this theme, admired Slabsides—"blending with its surroundings, it is coarse, strong, and substantial without." The gray stone of the chimney from nearby ridges and the slabs of the walls from Catskills timber linked the building to the natural landscape. A different linkage, climbing vines, nearly covered the exterior when Gustav Stickley visited in 1905.

The interior of the cabin was also rustic and expressed the companionable spirit of its owner, in contrast to the more formal rooms at Riverby. Like other visitors, Barrus found the cabin "within ... snug and comfortable; its wide door bespeaks hospitality; its low, broad roof, protection and shelter; its capacious hearth [unlike Riverby's constricted fireplace with its cold marble mantle], cheer ..." The door opened directly into the main room with Burroughs's writing table, the hearth where he preferred to cook (although there was also a small kerosene stove in the kitchen area to the rear), and shelves for books and pictures. A bed was partitioned off to one side, and stairs led to a loft with guest bedroom and space for additional cots. Barrus focused on the rustic details: "The seams of the plain boards of the interior are covered with split-birch saplings. Originally the rafters had the bark on, but they have been denuded by woodborers, which have left a delicate tracery instead." The partition designating the downstairs bedroom was of "satiny yellow birch," also used in constructing the bedsteads. "The legs of tables, stands, window-seat, and mantel-trimming, of sumac limbs, have a spiral twist, from the imprint of the climbing bitter-sweet."

Burroughs's seventeen-year-old son Julian was his helper, and later recalled that his father made "much of the interior trim and furniture ... cutting his birch poles, finding natural crooks in the woods, using what was near at hand whenever it was possible." Beyond the pleasure he had in finding and fabricating rustic pieces, Burroughs also saved money doing the work himself.

II-9. Slabsides (1971 photo)

This economy, Julian observed, gave his cranky mother less to criticize.

What was rustic was often simultaneously quaint and old-fashioned: "A smoky iron tea-kettle hangs from the swinging crane in the wide stone fireplace; on the hearth are old-time andirons and tongs." Burroughs felt a strong attachment to memories of his boyhood on the farm outside Roxbury; his simple furnishings at Slabsides included such "treasures" as "patchwork quilts his mother had made; a few of her mulberry-pattern dishes." His slab-sided cabin itself was probably a sentimental tribute to his grandparents, Eden and Rachel Burroughs, who in 1795 had established themselves in a log house with a stone fireplace and chimney near John's birthplace. He recalled that "my grandmother said the happiest day of her life was when she found herself mistress of a little log-house in the woods." John was pleased to think that Eden and Rachel Burroughs built the log house "mainly with their own hands, and doubtless with as much eagerness and solicitude as the birds build their nests."

Burroughs made the connection between Slabsides and his roots in Delaware County explicit when he wrote that one of his mother's uncles "lived in a little house in the woods. His hut was doubtless the original Slabsides." For this author who was well connected to the culture of his time, however, there must have been other "original Slabsides." Burroughs was a devotee of another author and close observer of nature, Henry David Thoreau, who in 1845 had retreated for two years to a shingled hut he built with his own hands in the woods at Walden Pond near Concord, Massachusetts. Burroughs owned an 1881 printing of *Walden* with an engraving of the hut (Vassar College Library), which was smaller and more ephemeral than Slabsides; Burroughs could not find its site when he traveled to Walden Pond in 1883. Then, too, there were log and rustic cabins newly built in the northern Catskills as summer retreats by sophisticated New Yorkers who were part of the international Arts and Crafts movement. Burroughs knew the rustic buildings at Onteora Park, overseen by his good friend Candace Wheeler, and at Twilight Park, which he visited in August 1895 and found "a lovely spot."

Burroughs and Slabsides, in turn, attracted later Arts and Crafts luminaries, notably Elbert Hubbard, who visited Slabsides in 1901, and Gustav Stickley, who came in 1905. However, Hubbard's *Old John Burroughs* (East Aurora: The Roycroft Shop, 1901) focused on Burroughs the naturalist and conservationist rather than on his buildings, and Stickley was more impressed with the artistry in wood within Riverby than with the rustic elements of Slabsides. Ralph Radcliffe Whitehead, founder of the Byrdcliffe colony at Woodstock in 1902 (see XXI–9), was another admirer of Burroughs. In the summers of 1905 and 1906, Burroughs was a welcome guest at Byrdcliffe and compared its "picturesque" architecture favorably to Slabsides.

While Burroughs was building Slabsides in 1895, railroad magnate Frederick W. Vanderbilt and his architects, McKim, Mead & White, were beginning to create across the Hudson the grand, classical Vanderbilt mansion that would so disturb Burroughs. A New Paltz Normal graduate teaching at the academy in Rondout visited Burroughs in 1897 and reported Burroughs's annoyance with the imposing structure's impact on his river view: "Yes, the Vanderbilts like to advertise their millions and this will be a pretty big signboard, I reckon." A decade later Burroughs wrote, "How I do like a hut or cabin! I could not live in a palace, but in a hut I am as well suited as a turtle in his shell. It is reducing life to its simplest terms. One is a part of nature then in a sense he cannot be in a fine house."

Burroughs's books were popular. He was a celebrity, and the reading public came to associate him with Slabsides thanks to the many published photos of the white-bearded, rustic-looking nature writer taken with the rustic architecture of Slabsides in the background. Soon after his death in 1921, the John Burroughs Memorial Association was formed by his admirers—including Julian Burroughs, Kermit Roosevelt, Hamlin Garland, the wives of Henry Ford and Thomas Edison, and the Burroughs estate's attorney, Judge A. T. Clearwater of Kingston—to preserve Slabsides and Woodchuck Lodge in Roxbury. Julian Burroughs and his daughter Elizabeth Burroughs Kelley were dedicated workers for Slabsides's preservation, and today Slabsides remains very much as it was in 1921 thanks to its owner, the John Burroughs Association.

Burroughs encouraged friends to buy land from him and build rustic cottages near Slabsides. Several of these cottages, privately owned and not part of the John Burroughs Sanctuary, can be glimpsed from the preserve and along Burroughs Drive. As early as 1883, Burroughs had proposed a "literary colony" on property near Riverby. In 1894, shortly before undertaking Slabsides, he tried to induce literary friends to build huts and "form a little community" in the Catskills—probably in Greene County where he had enjoyed life at Candace Wheeler's Onteora Park, although he also had good times visiting Ulster County's Woodland Valley. The first friend to build in the vicinity of Slabsides was Ernest Ingersoll (1852–1946), a naturalist and writer who had climbed Wittenberg in the Catskills with Burroughs in 1884. In a letter of September 1, 1895, to Ingersoll's wife, Burroughs offered to sell them a small building site. In the spring of 1896 Burroughs noted in his journal that "Ingersoll is building a house near me, and is stopping with me for a few days." Elizabeth Burroughs Kelley described the house as "on the bluff above the Slabsides spring." Ingersoll was the author of the very popular *Rand, McNally & Co.'s Handy Guide to the Hudson River and Catskill Mountains*, in which he expressed enthusiasm for Burroughs and West Park.

Burroughs hoped his friend and Smith College professor, Ludella Peck, would "want a hut here," promising her "a big rock to build upon." She might be more willing if their mutual friends, Mr. and Mrs. Percival Chubb, would "build a lodge here." Neither Peck nor the Chubbs joined Burroughs. Most of those who did were identified by Kelley as Poughkeepsie businessmen (including William Smith of the Smith Bros. cough drop family) and their wives. George Millard, manager of the Collingwood Opera House in Poughkeepsie, wanted something more than a rustic cottage and built a house with crenellated tower—known as the Castle—visible crowning the cliff a little east of Slabsides.

Anne Winfield was an exception among the cottagers, coming as she did from New York City. The construction of her cabin above Slabsides in 1910 was to have tragic consequences. Clement Demaron, of West Park, was hauling building material to Winfield's site when his team of horses stalled on the hill. To lighten the load, Demaron unloaded some of the material onto land belonging to Louis Victor Seydel, a New York City stock broker who had taken over Ernest Ingersoll's place. Seydel took offense, and the dispute escalated until Seydel shot and killed Demaron. A Kingston jury, after deliberating a minute and a half, acquitted Seydel of murdering Demaron, who was depicted in *The New York Times* as a hot-headed, brutal Italian who threatened the lives of Seydel, his wife, and young children. Julian Burroughs and his father rallied in Demaron's defense, but to no avail. This must have cast a pall upon the colony for Burroughs and others, and may partly explain why it did not grow and why so little has been written about the colony since 1910.

Walkers are welcome to view the exterior of Slabsides throughout the year. An open house is held twice each year—the third Saturday in May, and the first Saturday in October. For information, go to http://research.amnh.org/burroughs/index.html.

II-10* Slabside Inn
Rte. 9W, West Park. c. 1930 (later altered as residence).

This vintage postcard shows the happy union of gas station, roadside eatery ("HOT DOGS" announces a sign in the window), and rustic architecture—the latter in the manner of John Burroughs's nearby Slabsides. For the proprietor of a

II-10. Slabside Inn (c. 1930 postcard)

gas station to trade on the name of the popular naturalist's cabin may seem opportunistic and highly inappropriate, but Burroughs himself was not altogether devoted to the natural world and old-fashioned ways; he took pleasure in driving the auto he received from Henry Ford in 1913. Then, too, Slabside Inn was part of a broad movement around 1930 to eliminate the tawdry gas station/hot dog stand and furnish motorists with tasteful, often quaintly Colonial, alternatives.

Apparently, in the 1930s Slabside Inn became what a stylish matchbook cover of c. 1940 (author's collection) advertised as Lloyd Plass's "HIGH HAT TANK & TUMMIE TAVERN." Would motorists out for a good time be more likely to turn into a place with a funny name than one recalling the late naturalist who had little taste for alcohol? The Tank & Tummie Tavern metamorphosed into Marcel's Restaurant, which in the later twentieth century occupied a more substantial two-story building a few yards from the former Slabside Inn.

II–11 Holy Cross Monastery
Rte. 9W, West Park. 1902–1904; 1915 and later. Henry Vaughan, Ralph Adams Cram, and others. NR

Originally designed by Henry Vaughan, later the architect of the magnificent Gothic-style National Cathedral in Washington, Holy Cross Monastery, like the cathedral, belongs to the Anglican Community/Episcopal Church. The Order of the Holy Cross was founded by Father James Otis Sargent Huntington in New York City in 1884. In 1902 the order constructed Vaughan's design in West Park, said to be "the first monastery built for an Anglican order since the reign of Henry VIII."

Like the owners of river estates, the men planning for monastic life sought seclusion from the bustle of the highway. The building was sited down a slope and about a city block from the road, with a screen of trees between the two, therefore "cut off from any sounds of passers-by." As seen from the west, the red-brick monastery with white cupola looks less like a medieval monastery and more like a college dormitory. Vaughan, who ordinarily preferred the Gothic, is said to have chosen the Dutch or Dutch Colonial here out of respect for the Dutch traditions of the Hudson Valley. The red brick, segmental arches, gables with single step at their bases, and steep roofs with many dormers create a Dutch, if not Dutch Colonial aura; the Hudson Valley Dutch did not build on this large scale, except for their Town House in New Amsterdam, which did not resemble Vaughan's design. His exterior mostly harks back to the late-medieval period in northern Europe. The cupola, with simple classical forms but placed un-classically off the central axis, suggests northern Europe's slow acceptance of the classical in the seventeenth century.

Vaughan's interior reveals the influence of the medieval on the Arts and Crafts movement—good craftsmanship and honest use of materials (e.g., interior walls of exposed, unpainted brick). But sometimes the preference for simple, geometric forms seems almost modern; the fireplace in the ground floor's south room (originally the refectory) is surmounted by a massive brick chimney breast whose bricks project and recede as in a geometric sculpture.

Interior spaces were laid out for monastic use. Four small chapels, ten feet square, each with its own altar "for early celebrations of the Holy Eucharist," were located on the east side of the basement which, because of the sloping site, was fully above ground. Each had an eastern window "prompt to catch the light of the sun as it rises over the hills across the river." The brothers were also to have some conventional comforts of the time; the basement housed a boiler room, gas machine

II-11. Holy Cross Monastery (c. 1925 postcard)

room (for gas lighting), and kitchen with steward's office. Above the basement, a 100-foot-long cloister was recessed into the east side of the ground floor, and its arched openings encouraged meditation in the presence of a beautiful and expansive view up and down the river. The original chapel and refectory were placed at the north and south ends, respectively, of the ground floor. The chapel at first was plain except for brass candlesticks and a large crucifix. The high altar (which about 1910 incorporated an elaborate reredos with Gothic sculpture) was on the north wall, not the east as preferred in Christian tradition. A Women's Gallery rose two feet above the chapel to the south, with an open-work grille to maintain the necessary separation between women and brothers. (At the building's dedication in 1904, a New York reporter found women "visiting every nook and corner, and even peering into the monks' cells, which they never again will be allowed to see.")

Holy Cross's Christian function, not much revealed in Vaughan's exterior except for the cross over the cupola, was clarified when St. Augustine's Chapel, with its bell tower, was begun in 1915 by Ralph Adams Cram, the leading church architect of the time. In 1911 Cram had taken charge of the design of the immense and richly adorned Cathedral of St. John the Divine in New York. Cram, like Richard Upjohn and Vaughan, usually designed Episcopal churches in the Gothic idiom with embellishments in stone and stained glass. Here, though, Cram wrote that he wanted "to express ... something of the quality of the Order of the Holy Cross," and so the monastic function of the chapel (and perhaps the budget) demanded simplicity in the form of the Romanesque style of round, not pointed, arches and broad areas of undecorated wall. Cram acknowledged that his design for the bell tower, or campanile, had "a certain North Italian quality," and the tower's apparently haphazard (but actually carefully studied) blending of locally made brick and locally quarried stone had precedents in early medieval Italy and Spain. Still, he insisted that as a whole the design was so basic that its roots could be found from Syria to Spain and from the Rhineland to Italy over several historical periods.

Today the interior walls of the chapel are stark white, the piers and columns separating the nave from the south aisle are as plain as a medieval character allowed (the columns have rudimentary leafy capitals), and the windows of the clerestory high on the nave walls are small and filled with colorless glass. (There is a low, west window of stained glass depicting St. Chad holding a Gothic church model.) The ceiling is framed with the most basic triangular trusses. The curving east apse (this chapel is correctly oriented) originally had windows; they are now filled in. The austerity of the chapel was almost compromised, however, in 1925 when Kenneth Rexroth, a young bohemian poet-painter, was a guest at Holy Cross and learned that the order was seeking an artist to become a member and complete frescoes or mosaics in the chapel— wall treatment said to have been planned by Cram but never executed. Rexroth did not carry out any murals at Holy Cross; his avant-garde taste for Marcel Duchamp would have made him an unlikely candidate for executing anything the conservative Cram would approve.

Since the time of Vaughan and Cram, additions have been made to the monastery including an octagon (1964–1965, by Hirsch & Cassetti of Elmira) with monks' cells and library connected to Cram's chapel, as well as a glassy octagonal refectory rising from a concrete pedestal and extending assertively toward the Hudson from Vaughan's building.

Today the brothers' primary ministry is to guests on individual and group retreats. They also manufacture incense and operate a gift- and bookshop.

II-12 Church of the Ascension (Episcopal)
1585 Rte. 9W, West Park. 1842.

Built before the Gothic Revival standards of Richard Upjohn came to dominate Episcopal church design, the Church of the Ascension is a simple rectangular block of fieldstone covered by a gently sloping gable roof. The building's proportions are more classical than Gothic. Its designer is said to have been "Mr. Johnston, an architect from New

II-12. Church of the Ascension

York," perhaps the obscure John Johnston who practiced in the city in the 1840s. The entrance at the east and altar at the west reverses the orientation Upjohn and Christian tradition preferred. Pointed-arched windows, buttresses at the corners of the east front, and a tapering spire are significant Gothic details. By 1897 the stone walls were "overgrown with vinery," leading Ernest Ingersoll to compare the little church to "the rural churches of England." A simple and unobtrusive wood-and-glass vestibule of modern design was added in 1967 by William H. Van Benschoten II, who served as consulting architect to the Episcopal Diocese of New York and occupied Vinecroft, the property developed nearby by his grandfather in the 1880s (see II–5).

The interior, one unified space beneath a vaulted ceiling with simple ribs, is enriched with two stained-glass windows, both depicting passively beautiful women and both apparently by Tiffany Studios, although only one is signed. The window on the north wall, representing Faith, is a memorial to Harriet Carleton Durkee (1839–1912) and is signed "Tiffany Studios, New York, 1916." Its counterpart is Hope, on the south wall, a memorial to Sarah Carleton Brookman (1836–1912). The two windows were given by Mrs. A. H. Walker as memorials to her aunts. Mrs. Brookman's husband, John U. Brookman, had been senior warden for forty-one years and gave the church a $30,000 endowment—unless the services became too "ritualistic" or the church became "too much under the influence of the order of the Holy Cross," whose monastery is nearby, in which case the income should pass to local Baptists or Methodists.

Upper-class families living along the Hudson River tended to support construction of Episcopal churches; see examples across the river in Hyde Park (where Esopus Episcopalians worshipped before 1842), Staatsburgh, Barrytown, and Tivoli. The original construction costs at West Park were borne by Mrs. Anna Rutherfurd Watts, who attended the Church of the Ascension in New York; she also donated the silver communion service to the new West Park church. Other early donors included Mrs. Watts's son-in-law Archibald Russell (who has been credited with hiring the architect and supervising construction of the church), Robert Livingston Pell, and John Jacob Astor. In 1878 "the old-fashioned pine seats, pulpit and reading desk, communion table and altar furniture" were "replaced by new and beautiful work in hardwood." The new Gothic Revival pulpit and font are clearly identified as given by General Daniel Butterfield as memorials to his wife Lizzie and their child Edgar, and the similarly Gothic communion table, reading desk, and pews may also have been given by Butterfield. The general was a Civil War hero and summer resident with property near the church. Presidential aspirant Alton B. Parker attended services here for many years before his death in 1926.

The former rectory was built of local stone in 1859 as a picturesque cottage with multiple gables, Gothic arches, drip moldings, and a bay window. In 1929 the Arts and Crafts–influenced parish hall was erected from earlier carriage sheds. In the 1930s President Roosevelt's mother Sara opened several flower shows in this parish hall for her fellow Episcopalians across the river. Later, Eleanor Roosevelt performed similar flower-show duties.

II-13 Colonel Oliver Hazard Payne Estate (Marist Brothers and Marist College)

Rte. 9W (1455 Broadway). Begun c. 1910. Carrere & Hastings; Julian Burroughs; and others. NR

Seekers of Great Estates should travel across the Hudson to Dutchess County or journey to Newport, Rhode Island. Ulster County was not favored by the plutocrats of 1900. Still, Ulster retains one showplace built for a robber baron of the period, Colonel Oliver Hazard Payne (1839–1917), and designed by a leading New York architectural firm, Carrere & Hastings. According to Julian Burroughs, Thomas Hastings was the partner in charge. Colonel Payne, a Civil War veteran and self-described capitalist, made a fortune in iron, oil, and tobacco in Cleveland and New York. He was best known for his association with John D. Rockefeller in Standard Oil, but in 1913, late in his life, he was described as enjoying "the seclusion afforded by a carefully sheltered bachelor life." Perhaps his choice of the relatively unfashionable west bank of the Hudson was part of his effort for privacy away from his New York residence at 852 Fifth Avenue. The colonel resigned as a director of Standard Oil in 1911 to have "more leisure in his advancing years" to spend on his yacht and at his country places in Esopus and Thomasville, Georgia. He formed his vast Esopus estate in 1909 by purchasing and combining two adjoining properties—Waldorf, formerly the Astor and then the Neidlinger estate, and the estate of Anna Pratt.

The gatehouse on Rte. 9W alerts the visitor to the refined good taste of Colonel Payne and his architects. The early Italian Renais-

sance is suggested in the semicircular arches resting on unfluted columns. The red tile roof and classical door and window frames also refer to Italy and its Renaissance of classical antiquity. Passing through the gate, two outbuildings appear that were once joined by a greenhouse, all designed by Carrere & Hastings. (Colonel Payne also had a formal flower garden and rock garden.) The larger of the two buildings was the gardener's cottage, with living quarters on the upper two floors and white-tiled halls for garden and floral work on the ground floor. While the two structures resemble the gatehouse in their smooth, light-toned limestone walls and tile roofs, they are picturesque, not classical, in their steep roofs, asymmetry (notably of the turret and dormers of the gardener's cottage), and lack of classical ornament. The cottage is reminiscent of a miniature French chateau of the late Middle Ages. Just beyond the farther and smaller of these two outbuildings are gates and a drive leading to the entrance façade of Colonel Payne's mansion.

The Payne mansion replaced Waldorf, John Jacob Astor III's somewhat less grand Renaissance-style residence that was razed in 1910. Colonel Payne's façade is a stately and restrained interpretation of sixteenth-century Italian Renaissance palaces. Architectural historian Mark Alan Hewitt relates the Payne mansion to "the most exalted Italian Renaissance masters—Bramante, Vignola, Sansovino, and Palladio." The low tile roof accords with the gatehouse, but the overall massing

II-13. Payne Mansion (early-twentieth-century photo, formerly Elizabeth Burroughs Kelley collection)

is comparable to the firm's greatest work, the New York Public Library on 5th Avenue (1897–1911), although on a smaller scale. While finely detailed and crafted, Colonel Payne's residence lacks the grandeur of the earlier F. W. Vanderbilt mansion with its four giant, two-story porticos across the river in Hyde Park. Payne's richest portico—six, single-story Ionic columns set between rugged arched pavilions—faces east and is fronted by a balustraded terrace overlooking the river. Steamboat travelers were presumably impressed by this terrace and portico. They had no glimpse, however, of the enclosed courtyard at the center of the mansion fitted with a fountain and recessed loggias adorned with frescoes. And few would see the opulent interior, or Payne's collection of fine paintings including works by Rubens, Turner, and Courbet (the colonel's *Venus and Adonis* by Rubens is now at the Metropolitan Museum of Art).

Raymond A. Rich, an industrialist and business leader, purchased the mansion in 1986; in 2009 it was announced that Rich had bequeathed the mansion and sixty acres to Marist College, which will operate it as the Raymond A. Rich Institute, focusing "on developing the communication, interpersonal and social skills necessary to lead complex organizations in a global setting."

A little north of the former gardener's cottage and greenhouse appear other outbuildings grouped around a rectangular court. Colonel Payne's stable, carriage house, and garage were located here, as well as housing for employees. Some of the structures were built to serve the earlier Pratt estate, notably the house at the southeast corner of the court, which was the home of Mrs. Pratt's su-

perintendent. The residence of Anna Pratt, widow of historian and Civil War hero Colonel George W. Pratt, stands just to the east of these outbuildings. The Pratt house—with porte cochère and lower story of stone, and upper story of shingles curving out over the first story—is characteristic of the late-nineteenth-century Queen Anne style. In 1913 it became the residence of Payne's superintendent, John Burroughs's son Julian and his family. Julian had grown up at Riverby and in 1902 had built his own house there, a little south of the colonel's place (see II–7). Julian and his family were accustomed to Spartan quarters at Riverby (daughter Elizabeth recalled its outhouse and hand pump in the kitchen). On moving into the Pratt house, Julian wrote his father that they were "enjoying the advantages of electricity, bath rooms & toilets on every floor, three on the second floor alone, oceans of room & all that."

Julian Burroughs, without professional architectural training, was able to convince his employer to allow him to function as architect and contractor for several building projects including a poultry plant with manager's cottage built of native stone, and an elegant boathouse. Payne was an ardent yachtsman; the staterooms of his steam-powered ocean-going yacht, the *Aphrodite*, were designed by renowned architect Stanford White, and in 1913 Carrere & Hastings designed a boathouse and garden pavilion for the colonel.

It was Julian Burroughs, however, who actually designed and oversaw construction of the stone boathouse (1914–1915) for the *Aphrodite*'s launch. Her master, Captain Charles W. Scott, made a sketch of the proposed dock and boathouse as a basis for Julian's design. Julian wrote his parents excitedly in 1914 about his grand plans for the boathouse: "I think about the boat house a good deal and if they let me build it my way it will be some boat house, I will make a steel and concrete roof covered with imperial red Spanish tile, the doors and windows and cornice will be of bronze, there will be a balcony on south end and east side with a bronze railing which I will design, inside I will have a faience wainscot with motifs of the Hudson done in colors by the Rookwood Pottery Company, the floors will be stone, there

II-13A. Payne Boathouse (1979 photo)

will be an inside balcony with a hand wrought iron railing, etc, etc. The concrete ceiling I will panel in oak. I am not estimating the cost but the picture wainscot of tile will alone cost $2000. My old head buzzes like a bee—I can shut my eyes any time and see patterns for railings, ceilings, designs for doors, etc, etc."

Burroughs became accustomed to spending freely on the colonel's projects, and on most design issues he also had a free hand. Payne's trusted assistant, Emma Larson, wrote Burroughs about the boathouse: "do ... as you think best. We can not help you because we do not know anything about architecture." However, there were limits to the client's tolerance for useless expense, and he did veto balconies on the east side and on the interior.

The boathouse, a rare survivor of its type on the river, is neither Italian Renaissance nor rustic, but somewhere between the two. A four-column classical portico with ornamental frieze graces the south façade, and the red tile roof also ties the building to earlier Carrere & Hastings buildings on the estate. But the textured stone walls and broadly projecting roof supported by brackets connect to the qualities of craftsmanship and solidity associated with the Arts and Crafts movement. Inside, tile wainscoting was interrupted by a fireplace of dubious practical value. Tiles painted with a seascape and historic sailing vessels, perhaps by the renowned Arts and Crafts tile maker, Rookwood Pottery, face the wall over the fireplace. An iron grill with a delicately worked peacock standing on a post functioned as a gate at the boat entrance; the peacock is repeated on a smaller scale in the railing over the south portico. Near the boathouse is an octagonal stone summerhouse with red tile roof, also built under Julian's supervision in 1915.

Colonel Payne's nephew, Harry Payne Bingham, inherited the estate in 1917. During the Depression, in 1933, he gave the deteriorating 484-acre property to the New York Protestant Episcopal City Mission Society for a "convalescent and work-training centre for men and boys." The center, named Wiltwyck, was transformed from "the glorification of past elegance and vast expenditure upon luxury" to "an equally vast service to unemployed men and boys and convalescent boys." The mansion's "great salon" became the institution's chapel. In 1937 the mission formed a school for neglected and delinquent black Protestant boys. In 1942 the school became more inclusive and was incorporated as the Wiltwyck School for Boys; its leaders included Eleanor Roosevelt, and its alumni included boxing champion Floyd Patterson. In 1942 Marist Brothers purchased the part of the estate between Rte. 9W and the Hudson for a preparatory school and later a retreat center. They carried out a number of alterations and additions, some designed by John Allan Ahlers about 1950.

II–14* Twentieth Regiment Monument (unexecuted proposal) Esopus. 1862.

Colonel George W. Pratt (1830–1862), one of the founders of the Ulster Historical Society, died of wounds received at the Second Battle of Bull Run. Colonel Pratt was the son and business associate of Zadock Pratt, a wealthy tanner and founder of Prattsville in Greene County. In 1866 Zadock memorialized his son in a colossal portrait bust carved into the live rock in a park-like setting known as Pratt's Rocks just outside Prattsville. The younger Pratt had traveled and studied in Europe and Egypt, receiving an honorary Doctor of Philosophy degree at age twenty from the First University of Mecklenburg. In 1855 he married Anna Tibbits of Albany, and a few years later purchased a farm along the Hudson in Esopus.

At a meeting of the historical society held soon after Pratt's heroic death, William Lounsbery asked, "Who can replace this fallen column?" The late colonel's Esopus neighbor Archibald Russell proposed to the society that "a simple stone column, massive, substantial and plain," fashioned from "rough mountain stone and made enduring for all ages," be erected on "prominent mountain tops" to each of the regiments from Ulster serving in the war. For Colonel Pratt's Twentieth Regiment, Russell suggested "the top of Shappawnic, as it overlooks the home of the gallant Colonel who has sealed with his blood his devotion to his country's cause." Located about ten miles south

II-15. Payne Barns (c. 1940 photo when Wiltwyck School for Boys)

of Kingston, the peak (more commonly spelled "Shaupeneak") provided distant views in nearly every direction and would also be visible to the many travelers on the Hudson River. At a later meeting of the historical society's Monumental Committee, chaired by Russell and including Abraham Bruyn Hasbrouck, former president of Rutgers College, it was resolved that the proposed monument on Shappawnic be dedicated to all regiments from the district and that $5,000 be raised through subscriptions of $5 each. The monument, however, was never completed, and no drawings for it are known.

II-15* Barns on Colonel Payne's Estate

Rte. 9W. Begun 1914. Julian Burroughs; Walker & Gillette?

The gentleman's country place of the early twentieth century was incomplete without elaborate and picturesquely designed farm buildings. In August 1914, Julian Burroughs proudly wrote his father that Colonel Payne had entrusted to him the design of a new barn. Julian naively believed that the colonel's renowned architect, Thomas Hastings, would be interested in seeing his amateurish drawings for the barn. Hastings's lack of interest did not deter Julian, however. By July 1916 the necessary stone had been cut, and so Julian laid off about a dozen stonecutters. The colonel died in June 1917, and Julian was himself laid off early in 1918 by Captain Harry Payne Bingham, the colonel's nephew, who inherited the Esopus estate. With construction of the barn incomplete, Julian was ordered to take his barn plans to the New York architect who succeeded him. Julian does not identify the New York architect, but it was probably the firm of Walker & Gillette, as Richard Foy cites blueprints by this firm for the project dated October 5, 1917.

Three stone structures compose the barn complex. Two, forming an L, made up the horse barn; the relative simplicity and lack of sophistication of the right segment suggest the hand of Julian Burroughs, while the dominant left segment with its enormous gambrel roof and clock tower crowned with cupola was probably by Walker and Gillette. The third and lowest structure, with silo, was the cow barn. It was no mean shelter, as its entrance is adorned with a French cartouche of the sort usually found on grand public buildings.

Julian Burroughs is buried nearby in the Ascension Church Cemetery, established in the early 1840s and associated with the Episcopal church farther south on 9W. The plaque on his monument was designed by his daughter and biographer, Elizabeth Burroughs Kelley, and is mounted on a rock from Riverby.

II-16 Bridge over Black Creek
Black Creek Road, just off Rte. 9W. 1915. Julian Burroughs.

Driving north on 9W, just beyond Colonel Payne's big stone barns begun by Julian Burroughs, a left turn brings one onto Black Creek Road, which immediately crosses the creek on a bridge designed and supervised by Julian in 1915. Although the road was then a state highway, the bridge was a private project of Colonel Payne. A concrete structure, the arched bridge is faced with local stone and so blends with the landscape—a characteristic of buildings designed by John and Julian Burroughs. One stone on the south wall facing the roadway is carved "1915."

II-17 Cottages on Colonel Payne's Estate (Black Creek Apartments)
Black Creek Road, near Rte. 9W. 1912. Carrere & Hastings.

A few yards north of Julian Burroughs's bridge over Black Creek are "cottages" built for some of Colonel Payne's employees. The six attached houses were designed by Carrere & Hastings around a court open on the west. Their stone walls are sturdy but simple, in contrast to the classical refinements of the colonel's own mansion. The gable roofs, stone walls, and fenestration stem

II-16. Black Creek Bridge

II-17. Payne Cottages (early-twentieth-century postcard)

from Georgian tradition; the arched, recessed entrances show the hand of sophisticated architects of the 1910s, and may, like the grouping around the court, allude to English roots. The ensemble in fact was said to "constitute a reproduction of a typical English country village." The original dormers have been replaced to expand the attics, and other apartment buildings have been added.

II–18* Robert Livingston Pell Mansion House
Esopus. c. 1838 (not extant).

Robert Livingston Pell's place, a "country seat" or gentleman's farm of 1,200 acres, was among the finest along the Hudson. A Yale graduate, Pell (1810–1880) inherited the original section of the estate from his father and settled on the farm soon after his marriage in 1837. He improved it as a fruit farm and was a pioneer in selling American apples to Europe. Pell's mansion was dignified, but low and externally modest. It was described in 1871 as "built of brick, in the Roman style, and painted a beautiful straw color and white. It has columns in front and extensive piazzas, and is about seventy feet square." The grander interior was called "Grecian. On the ceiling of the dining room, which is twenty-eight feet by twenty-four, there are pictures, painted in Rome on canvas, expressly for it, and costing many thousand dollars, representing Guido's Aurora, Raphael's Galatea, Venus drawn by doves, Triumph of Alexander entering Babylon, Morning and Evening by Thorswalden [sic]." The grounds were dedicated to orchards and vineyards, and fish were raised in "ten artificial lakes ... connected by fifteen light and beautiful fancy bridges, constructed on iron rods." Workers were housed in "ornamental cottages."

Another estate owner, Abraham Bruyn Hasbrouck of St. Remy, credited Pell, "a distinguished agriculturist and public spirited citizen," with turning the "long neglected" properties along the Hudson between the Rondout Creek and Orange County into "the chosen resort of wealthy and refined citizens of New York, seeking rural enjoyment and health upon the romantic shores and amid the breezy hills of that pleasant land." Pell's

mansion was razed by the Redemptorist Fathers, who purchased a portion of the estate for their House of Studies (see next entry, II–19).

II–19 Mount St. Alphonsus House of Studies (Mount St. Alphonsus Retreat Center)
Rte. 9W (1001 Broadway), Esopus.
1904–1907. Franz Joseph Untersee.

In 1904, not long after Frederick W. Vanderbilt completed his splendid classical mansion overlooking the Hudson at Hyde Park, Redemptorist Fathers began building a monumental House of Studies on the opposite, Ulster County, side of the river. While the enormous seminary, 444 feet long with some 200 dwelling rooms, was splendidly sited for views up and down the Hudson, its gray stone walls have a severe, even fortress-like quality in contrast to the aura of upper-class luxury that pervades the Vanderbilt estate.

In June 1904, German Catholic Redemptorists, represented by the Rev. Joseph A. Schneider of New York, purchased 235 acres from a larger estate developed in the 1830s by Robert Livingston Pell, a New York aristocrat (see previous entry, II–18). The Redemptorists, with Father Schneider overseeing design and construction of the new House of Studies, razed the Pell mansion whose dining room ceiling was adorned with paintings on pagan themes. Materials for this tremendous construction project—including steel, concrete, Port Deposit granite, Indiana limestone, and North River bluestone—were transported both by river (to Pell's substantial dock) and by rail. A local contractor, H. W. Palen's Sons of Kingston, furnished lumber and woodwork.

Where the Pell mansion had pagan ingredients, the Redemptorists' new building, designed by the Swiss-born, Stuttgart-trained, Boston architect Franz Joseph Untersee (1858–1927), borrowed from the round-arched Romanesque style of medieval German Christianity, the style Untersee favored in designs for the Catholic Church. The Romanesque had been a period of great church architecture in the early twelfth century in Germany and elsewhere in Europe. In the nineteenth century the round-arched Romanesque was again very popular in Germany, where it was known as the *rundbogenstil.*

The very long east front of the House of Studies is Romanesque Revival in its massive walls and round arches, especially in the repeated small round arches of the corbel table that runs across the top of the building. Vertical accents in the way of Gothic pointed arches and tall spires are absent in the Romanesque; thus, in the House of Studies there are pinnacles at the corners of the central tower, flanking cupolas, and side pavilions, but these pinnacles are short and stubby.

The chapel occupies the central of three wings extending west from the long main block of the seminary. Externally, the chapel is marked by a semicylindrical western apse and semicylindrical side chapels projecting below the clerestory windows. Its gray stone walls have the formidable quality of the rest of the complex. Tall chimneys rise to either side of the western apse, odd reminders of the presence of the boiler room below the chapel. Originally the House of Studies was largely separated from the outside world; newspapers were forbidden, to avoid Modernism, and no door for the public opens from the outside directly into the chapel. But today's visitors (male and female) are welcome to enter a door on the southwest wing leading to a gift shop and ultimately to the chapel, a marvel of radiant stained glass (the clerestory windows by Mayer of Munich depicting the life of St. Alphonsus), lustrous polished stone, mosaics, terra cotta, mural painting, and white marble sculpture.

The Redemptorists were originally strongly linked to the German church, and some of their Protestant neighbors were guilty of xenophobia and anti-Catholic feeling. In 1904 the *Kingston Daily Freeman* opined that "the Pell place was in its day the great show place on the west bank of the Hudson." The new seminary would be highly visible, especially to river travelers, but the newspaper, not quite sure what to make of such a large incursion, expressed disappointment that "Father Schneider and those associated with him have not been very communicative in relation to the details of their plans." There were those who imagined the worst about the purposes of the German Redemptorists, especially during World War I when four brothers had to register as "enemy aliens," and Sara Delano Roosevelt reported to her son Franklin the rumor "that the big grey building of the German Brothers across the river from Hyde Park ... is full of ammunition."

During the first half of the twentieth century, the German link gradually weakened as the priests and brothers sought to be known as Americans, "not as members of a 'foreign' order." By the 1970s, beyond preparing more than a thousand students for the priesthood, the Redemptorists had charge of churches in Port Ewen and Esopus, preached

II-19. Mount St. Alphonsus (early-twentieth-century photo, formerly Elizabeth Burroughs Kelley collection)

and encouraged the religious life in other churches in the region, while seminarians sang in Protestant churches and worked with youth clubs, the elderly, and the handicapped in the area. In 1985 the last ordination to the priesthood took place in the chapel. Since 1990, Mount St. Alphonsus has served as a retreat center, but it is scheduled to close January 1, 2012.

II-20 Reformed Protestant Dutch Church (Klyne Esopus Historical Society Museum)
Rte. 9W (764 Broadway), Ulster Park. 1827. NR

The unidentified designer of this church understood that the Gothic pointed arch was suited to a place of Christian worship, given the prevalence of the Gothic in the great cathedrals of medieval Europe. But he had little knowledge of the Gothic style, and so applied Gothic arched doorways, windows, and louvered cupola openings to what was still a classical building in its symmetry and proportions, even in the cornice and rudimentary entablature of the side walls, which end abruptly on the façade, as well as the classical quoins painted on the corners of the brick walls. Moreover, the elliptical-arched fanlight in the front gable is a clear sign of the lingering classical, Federal-style taste of the designer. (Some of the classical details have been obscured by new surfaces.)

Services were last held here in 1965. Today the building functions admirably as the Klyne Esopus Historical Museum. Enclosures in the gallery are said to have marked the spaces allotted to slaves at worship—or to former slaves, as slavery was abolished in New York in 1827.

II-21 Esopus Meadows Lighthouse
Hudson River, visible from Lighthouse Park and Esopus Meadows Preserve off River Road (County Rte. 24). 1871–1872. NR

The vogue for the French mansard roof after the Civil War extended even to lighthouse design. This lighthouse, warning mariners away from the Esopus Meadows mudflats, replaced one built

II-20. Reformed Protestant Dutch Church (1973 photo)

II-21. Esopus Meadows Lighthouse (print by Robert Arnouts, 1998)

A TOURIST CAMP OF
18 ABANDONED TROLLEY CARS CAN
BE SEEN ON THE PROPHETER FARM ON
NATIONAL HIGHWAY 9-W. THESE CARS ONCE
RAN ON THE STREETS OF KINGSTON, N.Y., THREE
MILES TO THE NORTH, NOW FURNISHED AS SUMMER
CABINS, THEY RENT BY THE DAY, WEEK, OR MONTH
—— AN IDEAL VACATION SPOT FOR "JUICE FANS"

II-22. Propheter Park (Railroad Magazine, Sept. 1938)

nearby in 1839 and rises from a sixteen-foot-high granite pier, itself resting on wood pilings and timbers. The wood-frame, clapboarded keeper's house occupied the first and second stories, with the light tower rising from the mansarded second story. The original light was fitted with an optic fifth-order Fresnel lens. In 1965 the lighthouse, then manned by the Coast Guard, was replaced by an automatic light on a twenty-six-foot steel pipe tower. Subsequently, the lighthouse nearly succumbed to weather and vandalism, but in 1990 a volunteer group, Save Esopus Lighthouse Commission, began an extensive restoration of this, the last wooden lighthouse on the Hudson. In 2003 a new light was installed in the old tower as a working navigational aid, and in 2010 tours of the lighthouse by boat from Rondout Landing were begun. For information about tours, see EsopusMeadowsLighthouse.org.

II–22* John D. Propheter Amusement Park and Country Vacation Place
Rte. 9W, Ulster Park. Begun 1930 (not extant).

This site was at the other end of the architectural and social spectrum from the fine estates not far away along the Hudson. When electric trolley service was abandoned in Kingston, John D. Propheter,

owner of Twin Lakes Homestead Farm, purchased the car bodies (not the trucks with wheels and motors) of many of the old trolley cars with the ambitious idea of using them as key elements in an amusement park and country vacation place on his 150-acre farm. Some bodies were to become "double-deckers" raised up on high concrete-block and stone walls—one to serve as a "public waiting station" for those arriving by bus, another as "a watch tower for State Troopers" who would be prepared to nab dangerous "speed maniacs" on the state highway. Most bodies would rest close to the ground. One would be a "Dairy Quick Lunch Car" serving products from Propheter's farm. Some open-sided summer trolley bodies would be placed along the highway as "observation cars for those who on holidays wish to see the world 'roll' by them while they are seated comfortably in a safe place." Others would be placed in wooded nooks for parties desiring "seclusion," or on an elevation for those wishing to take in the view of river, lakes, meadows, and highways. For baseball fans, eight or ten open trolleys would serve as the grandstand, with benches added to their roofs for fans also hoping to sunbathe.

A number of car bodies were envisioned as tourist accommodations, some surrounded by a picket fence and sufficient room to park an automobile, others placed near the lake for the convenience of bathers. While Propheter's plan was hugely impractical, he did manage to have the car bodies trucked to the farm, and at least his vision of trolleys serving as primitive tourist cabins did come to fruition. *Railroad Magazine* in 1938 suggested that the Kingston bodies would be ideal for traveling "juice fans"—electric trolley fans— among its readership. Propheter apparently felt nostalgic over the passing of "the faithful old trolleys" and hated the prospect of seeing them sold for junk. Unfortunately the second life he offered them was short, and no trace of them remains.

II–23 Reformed Church
Main St., St. Remy. c. 1857.

This delightful board-and-batten, Gothic Revival church might be confused with a small Episcopal church by the master of the type, Richard Upjohn. Adding to the church's picturesque charm are the open belfry and, in the front gable, a six-part window framed with overlapping triangle and trefoil. Unlike Upjohn's Episcopal churches, the chancel of this Reformed church is cramped, and what appear on the exterior to be transepts—suited to High Church worship—become internally a Prot-

II-23. St. Remy Reformed Church (DeWitt photo, mid-twentieth century)

estant "lecture room" added in 1884 and closed off from the chancel by sliding doors. In fact, at first the lecture room was to be shared with a secular fraternal lodge that paid for the furnishings.

Abraham Bruyn Hasbrouck (1791–1879) donated land for the St. Remy church (originally a "chapel" or branch of the Reformed Church of Esopus), and Sylvester records that the building "was projected and built mainly by himself and members of his family." Hasbrouck was born in Kingston, educated at the Kingston Academy and Yale College (where he graduated in 1810), trained in the law, became a successful lawyer in Kingston, and served in Congress. In 1840 Hasbrouck was elected the first lay president of Rutgers College, which had strong links with the Dutch Reformed Church, and he served ten years in that post. During this time he developed "a country-seat" at St. Remy for summer use. The core of this country estate was a 1762 stone house to which he made picturesque additions (see II–24). Hasbrouck apparently believed that a gentleman of his stature should provide a village chapel, as did owners of English country seats. Within the chapel is a marble, Gothic-arched monument to his son T. Lawrence Hasbrouck (1827–1865). The inscription indicates the son had some role in the creation of the building: "In this chapel, which his efforts builded, his labours are fragrant memories ... ." An undated document at the church specifies that when $500 has been subscribed, the chapel should be erected "according to a plan now in the hands of T. L. Hasbrouck of St. Remy." Who drew that plan remains a mystery.

Abraham Bruyn Hasbrouck's taste ran towards the Gothic and picturesque, as is indicated not only by the St. Remy chapel and country seat, but also by the Gothic-lettered and decorated membership certificate given Reuben Bernard in 1859 by the Ulster Historical Society, of which Hasbrouck was first president (in the collection of the Ulster County Historical Society). His own monument on the chancel wall of Old Dutch Church in Kingston is in the form of an elegant Ionic temple façade, to be harmonious with the classical interior of that church (1852) designed by Minard Lafever (see VI–3).

*II-24. Abraham Bruyn
Hasbrouck House
(early-twentieth-
century postcard)*

II–24* Abraham Bruyn Hasbrouck House

St. Remy. 1762, mid-nineteenth century, 1912.

Abraham Bruyn Hasbrouck (1791–1879) was a prominent lawyer in Kingston before serving as president of Rutgers College in the 1840s. His portrait by John Vanderlyn is in Kirkpatrick Chapel at Rutgers. Hasbrouck began acquisition of this property in St. Remy in 1840. He must have been attracted by its setting along the Rondout Creek and the presence of a stone house dated 1762 (initials including IVA [for Jan Van Aken], and MVA, and the year 1762 are inscribed on two stones). Hasbrouck's 1879 obituary refers to the building as "an old family place, which he fitted up in a very handsome manner, and which since then has been used as his country residence."

His purchase of the old stone house was a sign of his interest in the history and historic buildings of the area. In 1859 he became the first president of the Ulster Historical Society. Abraham Bruyn Hasbrouck descended from the Hasbroucks of New Paltz, and he acknowledged in his inaugural address as society president that "I cannot but feel for that ancient village the special reverence which ... ever clings to the early homes and sepulchers of our fathers." His grandfather, Colonel Abraham Hasbrouck, was a leading figure in Kingston during the Revolution and believed by his grandson to be "a gentle-

man of considerable antiquarian taste." When he returned to Kingston in the 1850s, Abraham Bruyn Hasbrouck lived in "the old homestead" of his deceased parents, and his own death occurred in this old house in 1879.

Hasbrouck carried out stone additions to the St. Remy house, among them a pyramidal-roofed tower, which made his "country-seat" picturesque—the residential counterpart of the board-and-batten, Gothic Revival, Reformed Church that he put up nearby (see previous entry, II–23). The additions to the house may be attributed to Detlef Lienau (1818–1887), a leading New York City architect who had been trained in Munich and Paris before his arrival in New York in 1848. Lienau designed the Ulster Historical Society's seal in 1859. The pyramidal roof of Hasbrouck's tower, having lower slopes at its base, resembles the tower roof of the carriage house Lienau designed for Edward Bech's estate in Dutchess County, currently the Marist College campus.

Further additions were made in the early twentieth century for Mr. and Mrs. Hermon Kelley. A stone high in one gable is inscribed in the early Dutch manner: H.A.K. + F.K. 1912. Hermon A. Kelley (1859–1925) was a prominent attorney in Cleveland, where he and his wife Florence were supporters of the Cleveland Museum of Art. On their 200-acre St. Remy estate, Mrs. Kelley developed a renowned flower garden. She was a leading figure in the Ulster County Garden Club, a trustee of the Senate House Association, and member of the Ulster County Historical Society.

II–25 Perrine's Bridge
Rte. 213. c. 1844 (restored 1966–1969 by Albert E. Milliken). NR

Now a pedestrian bridge across the Wallkill River and dwarfed by the New York State Thruway bridge a few yards to the west, Perrine's Bridge is a classic example of the nineteenth-century wooden covered bridge that was roofed and sided to protect the structure from the elements. The bridge crosses the Wallkill in a single span of some 138 feet relying on the timber truss design that Theodore Burr (1771–1822) patented in 1817, which combined the structural advantages of a simple timber truss with a relieving arch. Burr lived in Oxford, Chenango County, and built bridges there and elsewhere in the state, as well as across the Delaware River at Trenton and several across the Susquehanna River in Pennsylvania and Maryland. Other bridge builders throughout the Northeast used the Burr truss, but historian Richard Sanders Allen has called Perrine's Bridge "the only sizable example of the Burr arch truss still standing in this state where it was invented."

For the non-engineer, the beauty of Burr's design is the graceful elongated curve of the wooden arch to either side of the roofed roadway.

As early as 1886 Perrine's Bridge was cited by the *Freeman* as an old but substantial landmark. In 1934, when still in use for automobile traffic, it was recorded in measured drawings and photographs by the Historic American Buildings Survey. From information provided by local historian Cornelius I. Lefever, the survey ascribed the building of the bridge to Rosencrans Wood, who lived south of the bridge on a farm owned in 1934 by Oscar Tschirky ("Oscar of the Waldorf"). Closed to auto traffic in 1946, the bridge restoration of the 1960s incorporated steel reinforcement.

II–26* Jeremiah W. Dimick House, Woodcrest
Rifton. 1895 (altered in twentieth century; accessible by appointment).

Falls on the Wallkill River in the Rifton area attracted the construction of mills in the 1820s, including a cotton mill begun in 1827. About 1860 Jeremiah W. Dimick (also spelled Dimmick) began operation of woolen mills that made army blankets during the Civil War. Later, Dimick's

II-25. Perrine's Bridge (1970 photo)

mills made carpeting; in 1891 he employed some 400 workers, including men, boys, and women. Dimick died in 1895, and his son, of the same name, continued to run the mills at Rifton.

The year of his father's death, son Jeremiah built an estate, Woodcrest, with a Colonial Revival main house complete with extensive bay windows, porches, balconies, and a widow's walk, on ground high above the river and mills. A rustic stone pump house with observation tower was constructed over a spring and stands today between Route 213 and the river. Farming—especially breeding Holsteins—was the son's great interest, reflected in several architecturally treated barns that do not survive. Strikes disrupted operation of the mills a few years before Dimick, Jr.'s, death in 1914, and the mills closed in 1915. In 1954 Woodcrest was purchased by the Society of Brothers (Woodcrest Bruderhof), a Christian cooperative community widely known as makers of Community Playthings—sturdy classroom furniture and toys.

II-26. Woodcrest (early-twentieth-century postcard)

III

Town of Gardiner

Formed from parts of the towns of Rochester,
New Paltz, and Shawangunk, 1853.

Population: 1,991 in 1870; 5,238 in 2000.

The town was named in honor of Addison Gardiner, elected lieutenant governor in 1844. The land had been settled in the late seventeenth and eighteenth centuries by the Dutch, French Huguenots, English, and some African slaves, although the first documented settler was a widow, Gertrude Bruyn, of Norwegian origins, who by 1687 was established near what is now Bruynswick. Sylvester describes Tuthill, on the Shawangunk Creek, as "the oldest and most important settlement of the town," but not flourishing in 1880—the Wallkill Valley Railroad, constructed in 1869, had bypassed Tuthill. Now known as Tuthilltown, it retains a gristmill (NR), begun about 1798, which continued to operate by waterpower until the early twenty-first century. The hamlet of Gardiner, now and for many years the main center of activity in the town, was known in the 1870s as Gardiner Station, since the hamlet, which did not exist before construction of the railroad, grew up around the station. The town's western border is formed by the Shawangunk Mountains, which have attracted summer visitors since the mid-nineteenth century.

III–1 Josiah Hasbrouck House, Locust Lawn
400 Rte. 32 South. c. 1814. NR

When community leader Josiah Hasbrouck (1755–1821) built this carefully composed Federal-style house, he embraced classical architectural ideals and rejected his ancestors' functional approach in building their stone houses. From the house he ran a model farm including a sawmill on the Plattekill. The Jean (later Jacob) Hasbrouck house on Huguenot Street (see XI–2) had been Josiah's residence and store until he moved to Gardiner and established what later came to be known as Locust Lawn. While the grand house was under construction, Hasbrouck is said to have lived next door in the old-fashioned, stone Evert Terwilliger house (1738 with later alterations; NR), which subsequently housed tenants who labored on Hasbrouck's farm.

The new house's stylish façade resembles a design published by New England architect Asher Benjamin in his *American Builder's Companion* (first edition, Boston, 1806). A pediment crowns the central segment of three bays and two and a half stories. To either side a single bay of two stories is recessed from the central segment and topped with the corner of a broad pediment overlapped by the central segment. Slender pilasters separate the bays. The Federal style's preference for the oval and elliptical arch is seen in the pattern in the pediment and arch over the doorway. At first glance, a European traveler might assume the façade is of smooth white marble, or at least stucco, but closer inspection would reveal the cheaper American Georgian and Federal-style expedient of wooden boards nailed flush to the frame and painted white. (The side walls of the house are simply white clapboards.) Only the divided (Dutch) front door seems a holdover from the colonial past. This was, as Neil Larson has written, probably "the most elegant" and architecturally up-to-date house in the county in 1814.

Josiah Hasbrouck was a successful merchant and farmer, a lieutenant in the Revolution, later a lieutenant colonel of the Ulster County militia, supervisor of the Town of New Paltz for some twelve years, and a congressman 1803–1805 and 1817–1819. Josiah's son Levi (1791–1861) inherited the property in 1821, and with his wife Hylah furnished the house with family heirlooms and pieces newly acquired in New York and locally. Members of the family, including Levi and Hylah, were the subject of portraits by Ammi Phillips that remain in the house and seem to strive for the elegance of the house while displaying a charming awkwardness. The house itself has some of this awkwardness in, for example, the juxtaposition of flush and overlapping white-painted boards of its front and sides. Slaves who served the family are buried on a hill east of the house, along with members of the Terwilliger family.

The house remained in the family and had been little altered when donated to the Huguenot Historical Society by Miss Annette Innis Young in 1958. At that time, measured drawings of Locust Lawn were made for the Historic American Buildings Survey under the supervision of Dr. James G. Vander Pool of Columbia University. Vander Pool advised on the restoration of Huguenot Street and

III-1. Locust Lawn (1970 photo)

himself owned the shingle-clad Horton house (begun in the eighteenth century) in Esopus that features a handsome Greek Revival doorway.

In 2010 ownership of Locust Lawn and the Evert Terwilliger house was transferred to Locust Grove, the Poughkeepsie historic site whose Italian villa had been the residence of Samuel F. B. Morse and, much later, Annette Young.

III–2 Lambert Jenkins House
44 Jenkinstown Road, Jenkinstown. c. 1850 (façade altered after 1950). NR

The once-busy hamlet of Jenkinstown originated in 1793 when Lambert Jenkins, a transplant from Bergen County, New Jersey, began to build houses as well as grist- and sawmills on the Plattekill, a tributary of the Wallkill River. Ownership of the core of the hamlet has descended in the Jenkins and DuBois family to the present day. Most of the structures indicated in the 1875 Beers atlas have disappeared, but a two-room stone house (c. 1793 with later frame additions) survives, as does the white frame house that appears in a painted portrait of the dwelling that was probably executed in the late nineteenth century. The painting documents the residence of Lambert Jenkins II, grandson of the founder of the hamlet. Lambert Jenkins II (1821–1901) apparently took a frame house, perhaps from the 1790s, and expanded it about 1850 into a one-and-a-half-story house with some of the proportions of a mid-century Greek Revival

house, but with an asymmetrical façade and no Greek pilasters.

Jenkins was a prominent citizen—trustee of the New Paltz Academy and then a local board member of the Normal School—but Neil Larson speculates that Jenkins "resisted creating a full two-story house and inserted only three windows on the façade's second story ... [perhaps] to maintain the proportions of a traditional rural house and avoid the elitist appearance of a two-story, five-bay house." The painting documents the piazza with Gothic tracery that ran across the main façade and an ell to the west (the piazza does not survive). The depiction also demonstrates the mid-nineteenth-century's taste for white walls with green shutters, as well as white picket fences and red farm buildings. The painting's stretcher bears a label of Ward & Logan, 28–34 Front St., Newburgh, which was in business there beginning in 1866. Tradition has it that the artist was a woman.

III–3 Hornbeck-Deyo-Van Orden-Penzato-Aiello House
321 Route 208. c. 1840.

This unusual combination of the gambrel roof—popularly associated with Dutch culture—and Greek Revival porticos was, according to Kenneth E. Hasbrouck, "considered the finest home between Goshen and New Paltz" by nineteenth-century travelers. Ionic columns support a pediment with finely detailed cornice on the east front, while the porch on the north side is graced with smaller Ionic columns.

The house and associated farm remained in the hands of families long associated with the area until the property was sold in 1934 to Joseph Penzato, a

III-2. Jenkins House (late-nineteenth-century painting by unidentified artist)

III-3. Hornbeck House

Sicilian who, although unable to read or write in Italian or English, had achieved some success owning a fruit and vegetable store in New York City. Entirely inexperienced in growing crops, Penzato became a fruit farmer in Gardiner and, always with the help of his wife and children, ran a summer boardinghouse. His daughter Sadie recalled that "some of the villagers were irritated ... [that] this alien looking foreigner, with his wife and five children 'dare' to come in, (and from their point of view) 'take advantage' of the widow [Agnes] Van Orden by buying her lovely estate."

The house, acquired in 1950 by Anthony Aiello (1919–2010) and maintained by him for some sixty years, remains an architectural highlight of Route 208 between New Paltz and Wallkill. The frame house rests on a foundation of massive stone blocks drawn from the Shawangunk ridge. The Penzatos were responsible for the cement floor and stone wall of the porch; a c. 1900 photograph showed taller columns extending down to the wooden porch floor. Across the highway is an early-twentieth-century cow barn with gambrel roof characteristic of barns of that era.

III–4 Kettleborough School (former)
Rte. 208. 1835–1838. NR

The quintessential one-room "little red schoolhouse" has the proportions and doorway with rectangular transom and sidelight that were characteristic of Greek Revival buildings of the 1830s. The thrifty overseers of its construction, however, saw fit to eliminate extraneous details such as corner pilasters, and even cut out the sidelight to the left of the door, resulting in a lopsided entrance comparable to the anatomical irregularities of contemporary folk art. A report for the year 1856 prepared by the school trustees noted that the interior was fitted with "movable desks and benches" and three blackboards. Heat was supplied by a stove. In answer to the question, "How are the rooms supplied with pure air, so important to the progress, comfort, health and life of the children of your district?" the trustees cited eight large windows. They were obliged to admit that they had not "provided separate privies for the sexes."

The school closed in 1932, and its children were sent to school in New Paltz—part of the effort

III-4. Kettleborough School

in that decade to create larger, consolidated schools. Later it was acquired by local historian, preservationist, and schoolteacher Kenneth E. Hasbrouck; his residence, the John A. LeFevre stone house (begun c. 1772; NR), was next door to the north. Carleton Mabee records that Hasbrouck added the diagonally braced hood over the doorway and painted the exterior red, even though it had long been white. Earlier, Henry Ford had been drawn to the mythology of the "little red schoolhouse" and brought an historic example to the village he created near Longfellow's Wayside Inn at Sudbury, Massachusetts. The current owner of the Kettleborough School continues Hasbrouck's preference for red.

III–5 Abram P. LeFevre House
69 Forest Glen Rd. 1851. NR

Finely sited on rising ground just west of the Wallkill Valley Rail Trail, Abram LeFevre's one-and-a-half-story, wood-frame, Greek Revival house can be dated precisely, thanks to a corner foundation stone inscribed with his initials and the year 1851. The other foundation stones are carefully cut rectangular blocks, not the irregular shapes of eighteenth-century stone foundations. While essentially Greek Revival, the house has projecting eaves supported by curving Italianate brackets, a sign of the passing of the more severe Grecian taste and the arrival of the more complex ornament of the mid-nineteenth century. Within

the rear kitchen wing a small, cast-iron oven door alongside a broad hearth is marked "Fishkill Landing Foundry" and furnishes evidence of the trade among Hudson Valley communities.

Abram LeFevre was a farmer and, according to Carleton Mabee, "moderately wealthy, having $15,500 worth of property, mostly in real estate" in 1870. LeFevre provided a strip of land for the building of the nearby railroad, as well as land for the board-and-batten Forest Glen Station (not extant). His house was later occupied by his son and grandson, who were station agents. The house remains within the LeFevre family, which has maintained it so that photos taken today are hard to distinguish from photos taken a century ago.

III–6 Nathaniel LeFevre House (Boys' Industrial Colony)
457 Rte. 208. c. 1820.

A two-story, wood-frame building with a well-ordered, three-bay façade, this LeFevre house has long functioned as a farmhouse, but from 1897 to about 1900 the Industrial Colony Association took it over as a Christian farm school where some twenty-five "slum boys" from New York and Poughkeepsie would "become useful and patriotic citizens." The boys were part of the "influx of foreign population into our great cities" and potentially "a menace to society," but on the Gardiner farm they would learn discipline and the value of labor as part of the Americanization campaign of the 1890s to develop loyal Americans out of wayward foreign children. Well-to-do New Yorkers of old American families who established the Industrial Colony Association sought and received aid from John D. Rockefeller, including two of his former coach horses, renamed Rocky and John D.

III-5. Abram P. LeFevre House

III-6. Nathaniel LeFevre House (c. 1900 photo)

III-7. New York City Water Supply

Protestant clergy and other leading citizens from Gardiner and New Paltz were also enlisted as advisers and supporters.

In New York practitioners of Americanization, like Lillian Wald at the Henry Street Settlement (established 1895), sought to surround their immigrant charges with traditional American architecture that would have its quiet influence on the Americanization process. Publicity for the Industrial Colony in Gardiner pointed to the historic setting. Although the farmhouse was not a century old, it was described as "a typical old Dutch building" with "big chimneys ... enormous fireplaces ... massive rafters ... [and an] old door knocker." Here for a few years in the "beautiful Wallkill Valley," far from the boys' homes in the "most miserable tenements," American values were taught with the aid of the old house and a flag flying from a new flagpole.

III-7 Superstructure, New York City Water Supply
Route 44/55, just east of Route 208. c. 1915. H. Lincoln Rogers?

Close to the highway but off-limits to the public, this small yet imposing building reflects the classical, Beaux-Arts training of architect H. Lincoln Rogers, who was responsible for the larger gate chambers at the Ashokan Reservoir and undoubtedly for this, one of the superstructures over gauging, drainage, siphon, and blow-off chambers

on the aqueduct's route to the city. Industrial-strength quoins outline the doorway over which the cartouche represents windmill sails, beavers, and barrels from the city's official seal, which pays tribute to the city's Dutch origins. Rural Gardiner lacked monumental classical architecture, and so this structure would stand out as an emblem of the stature and power of the city.

III-8 General Store (Majestic's Hardware)
4 Dusinberre Road, Gardiner. c. 1900.

This store, originally built for John Goodgion, was operated for many years by John M. Moran (d. 1956) before becoming Majestic's. It is a rare and little-altered survivor of the turn-of-the-century store, found in many hamlets, which offered a wide variety of merchandise. The doors and display windows are generously glazed (to entice

III-8. General Store

customers to enter), with wood paneling below. The sheltering porch provided a place for exchange of neighborly greetings.

III–9* Wallkill Valley Railroad Station
Gardiner. 1869 (demolished 2002 after fire). Theodore V. W. Swift, contractor.

This was one of the state's oldest surviving stations when it was heavily damaged by fire and then demolished in 2002. Its board-and-batten walls and curving diagonal braces supporting the sheltering roof overhangs belonged to the taste for the picturesque popularized by Andrew Jackson Downing. The station agent seated at the bay window could survey the track to north and south. The northern section of the building was for passengers, the southern for baggage and freight. Passenger service on the line ended in 1937, freight service in 1977.

The station was the root from which the hamlet of Gardiner developed. An 1884 "Historical Sketch" of Gardiner gave construction of the station by contractor Theodore V. W. Swift "a ruling place in the order of events." Swift was the first dealer in lumber at Gardiner's new business center, and he sold building lots near the station.

III-9. Gardiner Station

III–10* Gardiner Hotel
Gardiner. 1869 and later (demolished 1974).

In the era when travel between towns was best accomplished by railroad, hotels sprang up adjacent to stations. The mansard-roofed, Second-Empire-style Gardiner Hotel was built by Wallkill Valley Railroad president Floyd S. McKinstry just across the tracks from the Gardiner station of his railroad. It was a classic example of the inexpensive, small-town, railroad hotel, and its decline accompanied that of the railroad. It was to be sold at auction in 1929 when it was known as Callahan's Hotel. Then it had twenty-two sleeping rooms and a "large ballroom" on the second and third floors, while on the first floor were parlors, dining rooms, kitchen, offices and, during Prohibition, the former barroom.

III-10. Gardiner Hotel (1971 photo)

III–11 Libertyville School (former)
Libertyville Rd. (County Rte. 7). 1838.

Unlike the one-room school in Kettleborough (1835; see III-4), whose doorway is centered on the gable end of the building, this school has two doors on its long side. Probably one door was assigned to boys, the other to girls. The building

III-11. Libertyville School (1977 photo)

resembles the schoolhouse in the well-known painting *Snap the Whip* (1872) by Winslow Homer—who visited Hurley in the early 1870s and may have been inspired to portray a local school—down to the single-panel shutters with vertical boards and cross battens. If the high-spirited boys of Homer's painting had counterparts in Libertyville, the school trustees were doubtless wise to give girls their own entry. The Libertyville School closed in 1929.

III–12* William E. Bruyn Estate, Brykill

Bruynswick Rd. 1927–1929.
Teller & Halverson. NR

William Edmund Bruyn, born in Rosendale in 1878, went to work in New York about 1895 and later joined Littlejohn & Co. on Wall Street, where he became highly successful importing crude rubber for making automobile tires. Along with wealth came prominence in the Republican Party, which chose him as a presidential elector in 1936 and 1940, the year of his death. Bruyn was a member of the Ulster County Historical Society and active in the Holland Society both in Ulster County and New York. In 1926 he had a detailed record of his ancestry compiled by Joseph Brown Turner of Port Deposit, Maryland. Evidently he was proud that in colonial times Bruyns had been wealthy landowners in the southern part of the county, and his estate, Brykill, clearly reflects his wish to connect with those colonial ancestors. But at the same time he was accustomed to the comforts of upper-class life in Manhattan; in 1930 he and his bride, the former Beatrice van der Velde, lived at 485 Park Avenue and were listed in the *Social Register* as belonging to several clubs and the Society of Colonial Wars. At the time of his death, Bruyn was a member of the Metropolitan Club (designed by McKim, Mead & White) and had an apartment in the palatial River House on East 52nd Street. Something larger and more comfortable than primitive colonial quarters therefore would be required for his estate on the Shawangunk Kill, incorporating land in both the towns of Gardiner and Shawangunk.

In 1926 Bruyn purchased from the Hasbroucks an old stone house that was to form the nucleus of his estate. The house was inadequate for Bruyn's needs and was rebuilt and enlarged according to plans by Teller & Halverson between 1927 and 1929. Bruyn took up residence in 1930, and Brykill was featured in a leading professional journal, *Architectural Record*, in November 1930, and in an article by Harriet Sisson Gillespie in *Arts & Decoration* in June 1931.

Gillespie and other writers have misread Brykill's history before Bruyn's purchase in 1926, but Marc B. Fried, with the assistance of Neil Larson, has created an accurate account. Two inscribed stones placed in Brykill's walls by Teller & Halverson, surely at Bruyn's order, have confused visitors to the house. A small stone dated July 1736 has been interpreted to be the datestone for construction of the original house by the Smedes family that was acquired by Bruyn in 1926, but Fried demonstrates that while the house was built in the eighteenth century by the Smedes, the dates of construction are unknown since the stone was actually intended as a gravestone for an infant of the Smedes family. A larger stone is inscribed, "Time is a devourer of all Things • JACOBUS BRUYN 1724 • Virtue is a driver away of all Vices." William Bruyn was a direct descendant of Jacobus Bruyn (1680–1744), yet this stone came not from the site of Brykill but, as William Bruyn acknowledged, from a stone house about a mile away that had burned, probably in the 1880s, and been rebuilt in wood on its old stone foundation. William Bruyn acquired this property in 1927 and presumably then moved the 1724-inscribed stone to Brykill. It is clear that William Bruyn wanted an estate rooted in the land and buildings of his Bruyn ancestors. The land on which Teller & Halverson's Brykill rose had belonged to Smedes, Hasbroucks, and others, but never to a Bruyn before 1926. The 1724-inscribed stone—and perhaps other stones from Jacobus Bruyn's house—were moved and incorporated into the new Brykill to legitimize it as an ancestral manor house of sorts. Near the small stone dated 1736 was laid a stone inscribed "1927/WEB."

Teller & Halverson retained the eighteenth-century kitchen wing to the east, but tore down the main one-and-a-half-story block of the Smedes house to its foundation and constructed a full two-story house with bedrooms above library, center hall, and dining room. A portrait said to be of Jacobus Bruyn hung in the dining room, and the decorator, Mrs. Mary S. Darrow of Saugerties, furnished the house with antiques, including some family heirlooms in maple and mahogany. A new screened porch incorporated the old well and joined the enlarged main block to a new two-story section with lounge below guest rooms. Above the colonial mantle in the lounge was E. L. Henry's popular depiction of the old Shawangunk Reformed Church.

A few yards from the main house, the architects designed a rectangular court formed by new service buildings—garage with chauffeur's quarters, stables with hostler's quarters (Mrs. Bruyn was a horsewoman), and servants' house with laundry. The grouping furthered the idea that here was a colonial manor house, albeit of a kind unknown in colonial Ulster County where Bruyn's servants' house would itself have been a fine residence. The estate also included what a local paper called "perhaps the most ideal dairy plant in New York State."

As was their custom, the architects searched the property and reused old beams and boards, stones from walls, and old hardware, while also calling for new material, including Teller's handwrought hardware, which is found in abundance. In 1984 Harry Halverson took pride in the fact that it was difficult to distinguish new from old construction at Brykill. Halverson also recalled that Bruyn, who enjoyed hunting with "cronies" on his vast estate, was "tickled to death" by the pheasant weathervane the young architect had designed for the stable's cupola. Looking back over his partnership with Teller, Halverson considered the Bruyn estate the firm's "most important" residential work. In their 1933 *Portfolio of Recent Work* they allotted five pages to photos of Brykill, more than given to any other project. (It should be noted that publication of the *Portfolio* by the architects, with advertisements by companies with which they did business, went against the Code of Ethics of the American Institute of Architects. The A.I.A.'s prohibition of advertising by its members may help explain why Teller was not a member and Halverson did not join until 1950, after the ending of their partnership.)

III-12. Bruyn House (Teller & Halverson, Portfolio, 1933)

The architects' site plan identified the property as "Brykill Manor" and the elongated main house as the "manor house." Although remembered by some as a modest man, William Bruyn seems to have thought of himself as a twentieth-century lord of the manor. He contributed to county charities and worked for the betterment of local schools, but he especially gave money and time to assure the preservation of the historic Shawangunk Reformed Church. In its cemetery, where some of his ancestors are buried, there is one mausoleum, William Bruyn's, with his coat of arms in stained glass (see XVIII–1).

III–13* Minnewaska Golf and Country Club (unexecuted proposal)
Gardiner. Late 1920s.

The stone and half-timbered clubhouse proposed for this golf and country club at the foot of the Shawangunks, just below the Lake Minnewaska

resort, was to be of a scale and grandeur more often associated with Westchester than Ulster County. Alfred F. Smiley of Lake Minnewaska Mountain Houses was a director of the corporation, as were leading citizens of Highland, although the president, C. Hunter Carpenter, was a New York businessman and accused bootlegger with a summer home in Gardiner. (In December 1925 Carpenter was among those arrested in the "greatest round-up in the history of prohibition," but he was acquitted in January 1927.) A brochure intended to attract investment in the club featured a photo of golfers and clubhouse along with text announcing that "the well known golf architect and constructor William P. Cleveland has completed the plans for the golf course." The brochure implied the clubhouse had been built, but the ambitious project never came to fruition and apparently was a victim of the Depression. Tillson Lake, a less pretentious, more popular resort with golf and roller skating was developed at the site.

III-13. Minnewaska Golf and Country Club (late-1920s brochure)

IV
Town of
Hardenburgh

Formed from parts of the towns of Denning and Shandaken, 1859.

Population: 629 in 1870; 208 in 2000.

This town in the remote western part of the county was named in honor of Johannis Hardenbergh (the town's name is spelled both Hardenburgh and Hardenbergh), patentee of a large tract in Ulster and adjacent counties. It has always been thinly settled. A century ago it was described as having:

> some of the most rugged and austere natural features to be found in the county. None but the most experienced mountain farmer would be inclined to locate in Hardenburgh. ... And yet the general topographical features are invested with peculiar charm. The towering mountain crags and scattered bits of valley, the wildwood and forests primeval, are dimpled over with beautiful lakes and thickly threaded with purling streams, which abound with trout.

In 1880 water-powered sawmills were scattered along Dry Brook, Beaver Kill, and Cross Mountain Brook. Artists and well-heeled sportsmen were drawn to Hardenburgh in the late nineteenth century, as it was rugged and wild, yet accessible via the Ulster and Delaware Railroad's station in Arkville, Delaware County.

IV-1* Samuel Coykendall Lodge

New York State Balsam Lake Mountain Wild Forest, Alder Lake, near County Rte. 54. 1899–1900 (mostly demolished c. 2009). Downing Vaux. NR

Long unused and uncared for, the ruinous Coykendall Lodge was demolished by New York State after being listed on the National Register of Historic Places. It was one of the county's most significant summer cottages of the kind turn-of-the-century millionaires built in the cool mountains or along the Atlantic coast. Its shingled walls rising above a sturdy stone base (partly preserved for public enjoyment), cross gables with diamond-paned casements, and combination of symmetry with picturesque variety of outline and surface—all suggested a late example of the Shingle Style initiated by major Eastern architects some twenty years earlier.

Samuel D. Coykendall (1837–1913), son-in-law of transportation mogul Thomas Cornell, was himself Kingston's leading businessman of the late 1800s, controlling the Cornell Steamboat Company, Ulster and Delaware Railroad, the Grand Hotel (on the U & D at Highmount), the *Kingston Freeman*, banks, and other enterprises. He enjoyed using his railroad for excursions into the Catskills with friends and associates; in 1886 he led fellow members of the Holland Society on an outing to the Hotel Kaaterskill in Greene County. By 1892 Alder Lake and surrounding land were purchased by the Alder Lake Club, a group of wealthy Kingstonians, including Coykendall, who intended to build a clubhouse and cottages at the lake, which had been enlarged by a dam for trout fishing. The club, several miles from the U & D station at Arkville, apparently was conceived along the lines of Onteora Park, the fashionable summer colony in Greene County. In 1892 Coykendall and his friend and Republican ally Judge A. T. Clearwater visited the lake with a small party of New Yorkers, including Onteora Park founders Francis B. Thurber and his sister Candace Wheeler. Five years later, Ernest Ingersoll described Alder Lake as "a private fish and game preserve, owned by a club of Kingston gentlemen, who sequestrate themselves and their families there in midsummer, and have trout every day."

IV-1. Coykendall Lodge (1989 photo)

However, the Alder Lake Club did not prosper and was dissolved in 1898. The property passed to Coykendall, who had accumulated tens of thousands of acres in the region, selling much of it to the state for the Forest Preserve. The *Times* reported in June 1900 that "during the past Winter, an army of workmen has been on the grounds making roads, building a mansion and barns, and creating fairyland out of wild surroundings. The improvements will cost Mr. Coykendall $70,000. One item is $4,000 for the plumbing of the main house." The main house or lodge rose from a knoll overlooking the lake. Despite the use of local stone and wood, which tied the building to its forest setting, it was still a conspicuous monument to Coykendall's wealth and power; who else in Kingston could command an army of workmen and spend $70,000 on a mansion in the wilds of the Catskills?

Downing Vaux (1856–1926) was identified in *Picturesque Wallkill Valley 1900* as the designer of Coykendall's "country place" at Alder Lake. Son of Calvert Vaux (1824–1895), noted codesigner of Central Park and architect of Coykendall's Rondout mansion (1890), Downing Vaux was trained at Columbia's School of Mines and in his father's office, where he became a partner. Downing Vaux may have been involved with the design of the Rondout mansion, and he definitely designed Coykendall's Kingston Point Park (1893–1897), a pleasure ground where U & D trains for the Catskills met Hudson River steamers.

Samuel Coykendall died in 1913, but the property remained in his family until 1945. In 1980 it was acquired by New York State and added to the forever-wild Forest Preserve, whose policies resulted in the sad neglect and ultimate demolition of the lodge by the state. Stone portions of the lodge have been stabilized as a latter-day romantic ruin. Ironically, Downing Vaux, while working as a "landscape artist" at the new University Heights campus of New York University many years before, had proposed a "picturesque ruin" made up of stones from the university's old building on Washington Square.

IV-2 School-Bus House
Cross Mountain Road (near the Delaware County line). Mid-twentieth century.

Two retired c. 1950s school buses, at least one a GMC product, were converted to serve as inexpensive housing in this remote mountain setting, much as worn-out trolley cars were made over into cottages earlier in the century. Here masonry was filled in where rubber tires once turned. Stove pipes still emerge from one bus body, but the pair is slowly succumbing to the forces of nature. A similar Chevrolet school bus is preserved at The Museum at Bethel Woods to help tell "the story of the '60s & Woodstock," but its psychedelic paint job is in vivid contrast to the drab paint of the pair on Cross Mountain Road.

IV-2. School-Bus House

IV–3 Millbrook Bridge
Millbrook Road at Davis Road. 1902.

Rural Hardenburgh has Ulster County's largest collection of quaint covered bridges, all dating from the early twentieth century. Millbrook Bridge is the town's longest, with a span of nearly sixty-seven feet over Mill Brook. Where Perrine's Bridge in Esopus employed the Burr arch truss (see II–25), Millbrook Bridge uses the Town lattice truss, a less elegant but widely used design patented by architect Ithiel Town in 1820. In 1964 a new bridge adjacent to the old allowed the retirement of the covered bridge to a quieter existence as historic landmark and pedestrian crossing.

IV–4* George Jay Gould Estate, Furlough Lodge
Dry Brook Road. Andrew F. Mason; Henry Neill Wilson; Francis L. V. Hoppin? 1890 and later.

The Gould name is forever associated with financier Jay Gould (1836–1892), widely despised by his contemporaries as a robber baron, but whose modest origins were in rural Delaware County where he was a schoolmate of John Burroughs. In August 1888 Gould took his luxurious private railroad car, the *Atalanta*, into the Catskills on a trout fishing holiday combined with a return to boyhood haunts. He seems to have particularly enjoyed fishing at Furlough Lake, eight miles from the railroad station at Arkville. By January 1890 Gould's son, George Jay Gould (1864–1923), a self-described capitalist and president of several western railroads, bought a large tract of land including Furlough Lake from Thomas Cornell, president of the Ulster & Delaware Railroad, who had contemplated building a clubhouse at the lake. That same year the first section of the rustic log Furlough Lodge was completed to the design of Kingston architect Andrew F. Mason. George Gould's wife, the former actress Edith Kingdon, was assured by Samuel G. Dimmick (a business associate of Thomas Cornell who dealt with the architect on Gould's behalf) that their new lodge would "excell [*sic*] in every particular, any thing in the Catskills"—including, thought Dimmick, the fine log house of Francis Thurber at Onteora Park in Greene County. In 1893 *The New York*

IV-3. Millbrook Bridge

IV-4. Furlough Lodge (early-twentieth-century postcard)

Times reported that Furlough Lodge was to shelter George Gould and male friends on a "shooting trip." After Jay Gould's death, the *Atalanta* continued to serve George, his wife Edith, their children, and guests who could detrain in Arkville and then proceed over the macadam road George had built to the lodge.

Furlough Lodge was well sited on an elevation providing a magnificent view deep into the Catskills from one façade, and a closer view of the lake from the other. The lodge grew over time. When a reporter for a New York paper, the *World*, visited in 1891 it already qualified as "a veritable palace of logs." The large, two-and-a-half-story house had massive, rustic stone chimneys and walls of bark-covered, white-oak logs, while the gable ends were shingled. De Lisser's photo in *Picturesque Ulster* shows the addition of a cross-gabled section with an expanded porch fitted with knobby posts. De Lisser labeled the building "semi-rustic," since the "lower part [was] built on the outside of half logs with the bark still on and shingled above, but finished and very commodious and comfortable inside." By 1914 the lodge had been expanded so that the long façade was closed at both ends by cross-gabled segments of log, shingle, and rustic stone. The *Times* pub-

lished five photos of the "Luxurious Gould Retreat in Heart of the Catskills" depicting the stone boathouse with rustic rooftop belvedere, the main house with its untrimmed porch posts and, inside, the "lounging room" with open-mouthed bearskin rug before the great stone fireplace, as well as the hall with frieze of mounted animal heads and antlers. By contrast, the frilly white Colonial bedroom of Edith Kingdon Gould evidenced nothing rustic, mounted, or shot. (Today the porch posts have smoother, less rustic profiles than appear in early photos; the Colonial white paint of today's exterior was first applied to the logs and shingles about 1929.)

In 1891 Mason was replaced as the lodge's architect by Henry Neill Wilson (1853–1926). Chimneys designed by Mason were flawed, and there were other problems with his work for the Goulds. Wilson was practicing in Pittsfield, Massachusetts, where he designed Berkshire country houses, including the gargantuan Tudor-style estate (1891–1894) of Anson Phelps Stokes, said to have been briefly the biggest house in America. Wilson was also at work on Cincinnati's famous Rookwood Pottery (1891–1904), where he employed appropriate Arts and Crafts motifs. His Red Lion Inn (1897), still a landmark for hospitality in Stockbridge, Massachusetts, resembles the Gould house in its informal design and occasional use of Colonial details.

Among the numerous buildings on the Gould property, the automobile garage with servants' quarters above is in the Georgian style, but with rugged stone walls. It is probably the work of Francis L. V. Hoppin who, on July 14, 1913, wrote a charming letter to "Lady Bountiful" (Edith Gould) in appreciation of a very enjoyable time on the Goulds' yacht along the Connecticut coast. Hoppin, who admitted leaving most of his heart aboard the yacht, illustrated the letter with a portrait of his handsome self at a drafting table with drawing tubes labeled "Garage," "Boat House," and "Ice House." A boathouse (1913) and icehouse, like the garage built of stone, survive today at Furlough Lodge. (In 1915 Hoppin carried out major stone-walled alterations and additions in the Georgian style at Sara and Franklin Roosevelt's Springwood in Hyde Park.)

Like the multimillionaires who occupied log palaces in the Adirondacks—J. Pierpont Morgan, Alfred G. Vanderbilt, Collis P. Huntington—Gould could well afford the cost of large-scale rusticity. After his death in 1923, his assets were valued at over $15,000,000, not including his real estate in Hardenburgh and his Georgian Revival mansion, Georgian Court (1896, by Bruce Price) at Lakewood, New Jersey. His grandson, Kingdon Gould, has long been a good steward of Furlough Lodge and the surrounding Catskills landscape.

V

Town of Hurley

Formed by patent granted 1708.

Population: 2,994 in 1870; 6,564 in 2000.

Hurley, named in honor of the Barons Hurley of Ireland, before 1669 was known as Nieu Dorp, a village established by a patent granted in 1663. Outsiders long noted that Hurley remained little changed as a population and in its architecture, where traditional ways were preferred. In 1824 Spafford's *Gazetteer of the State of New York* observed that Hurley's "inhabitants are principally Dutch, the descendants of the early settlers." Moreover, "the improvements are in the ancient style, and many of the houses are built of lime-stone, which abounds here." In the 1870s Winslow Homer found the old stone architecture and pastoral setting eminently paintable, as in his *Farmyard Scene* (c. 1874; Clark Art Institute, Williamstown, Mass.) Even in the era of the automobile in the 1920s, "Old Hurley," wrote Harold Donaldson Eberlein, "is just as Dutch as Dutch can be—Dutch in its people, Dutch in its houses, Dutch in its looks. ... With characteristically Dutch conservatism, Hurley has slumbered on through its more than two and an half centuries ... little changed in outward appearance ... and tucked away ... in a backwater past which the swirling eddies of feverish American progress have raced." While Helen Wilkinson Reynolds was distressed to find that in fact little of pre-revolutionary Hurley remained, even today many stone buildings survive on relatively quiet Main Street, the core of the Hurley Historic District (NHL).

V-1 Van Deusen House
(Van Deusen House Antiques)
59 Main St., Hurley. Begun c. 1720.

Here at the Van Deusen house the fledgling state government, in the form of the Committee of Safety, briefly found a refuge and meeting place after the October 1777 burning of Kingston by the British. Architecturally it is a rare survivor from pre-1777 Hurley; Helen Wilkinson Reynolds observed that the destruction or alteration of most of the hamlet's early houses "requires the eyes of faith and imagination to visualize pre-Revolutionary Hurley." Her research indicated that the L-shaped stone house was built at one time, despite its irregular placement of front door and flanking windows, because there were no seams in the stonework. Roderic Blackburn proposes that the house was built by Jan Van Deusen soon after he came to Hurley in 1719 to marry. In 1744 it was conveyed by Jan Van Deusen to his son Jan, Jr., whose initials and transfer date ("J V D Jr 1744") are carved in a stone on a rear wall. (Other, later owners and transfer dates are also inscribed in stone.) Reynolds regretted that Dr. George W. Nash (c. 1857–1923), who acquired the house in 1906 and restored some of the hardware, had applied reproduction strap hinges to the outer side of the front door, while she had found such hinges always on the inner side—an opinion that Myron Teller had no doubt confirmed.

Dr. Nash, a Harvard graduate, was a physician specializing in public health, but also a magazine writer whose photographs often accompanied his articles. He wrote on water gardens for Gustav Stickley's *Craftsman* (March

V-1. Van Deusen House (DeWitt photo, 1948)

1913) and on early American hardware and chimney cupboards for the *Architectural Record* (October 1913 and March 1917). His pursuit of a country house was the topic of an article in *Country Life in America* (June 1907). His decision to purchase the Van Deusen house came only after a thorough inspection of houses in Connecticut, Massachusetts, and New Jersey. None could match the Hurley house's combination of "quaint, old stone house ... good roads, lovely drives, fine neighbors," as well as proximity to the Catskills and the train in Kingston. Moreover, he and his wife could afford the asking price of $3,000.

Nash went on to publish in *Country Life* detailed descriptions of his extensive restoration and remodeling of the house. For "delightfully old" effect, he removed the large-paned, late-nineteenth-century window sash and replaced it with small-paned sash with heavy mullions. Bricked-up fireplaces were opened to their earlier dimensions. No purist when it came to the restoration and revival of the colonial past, he added two shed-roofed dormers on the front of the house to light a new "cosy" bedroom. He defended his use of false strap hinges simply as "ornament" on the outer face of the new Dutch door by alluding to the "exceeding plainness of the door itself" in "Catskill country." And he took peculiar pride in a newly built wooden chest thoroughly covered with old

V-1A. Van Deusen House (drawing by Keefe, 1920s)

houses. In the 1920s Keefe captured the picturesque qualities of the Van Deusen house in drawings (author's collection) that he probably intended to turn into prints. His drawing of the wooden lean-to (later altered) at the rear of the Van Deusen house records the old-fashioned charm of its long slope of roof, interrupted by a tall brick chimney, as well as of two inviting benches, one sheltered by a wooden hood, the other by a canopy of vines, both in the romantic tradition descending from A. J. Downing. Keefe also made a colored drawing restoring the front of the house—with 12-over-12 window sash, shutters, Dutch door free of the offensive exterior strap hinges, and none of the existing dormers. In the street is a handsomely turned-out woman seen in profile, suggestive of the gentility and fine manners that the twenties associated with Colonial architecture. As in the case of his drawing of the Spy House (see V–3), Keefe chose to focus on the pretty and refined woman rather than on the stirring masculine drama of Hurley in the Revolution.

V-2 Nieu Dorp (Eugene Morehouse House)

66 Main St., Hurley. Eighteenth century (altered 1938 by Charles S. Keefe).

In the 1930s Myron Teller dominated the restoration and updating of the county's old stone houses, but here Charles S. Keefe was the architect for the improvements undertaken for Eugene Morehouse in 1938. Keefe was a native of Kingston who established a successful practice in New York City in the early 1900s specializing in new Colonial houses, usually of wood or brick, not stone. While practicing in New York, Keefe maintained his residence on Lucas Avenue in Kingston. With the onset of the Depression, he moved his much-reduced office into his Kingston residence. Morehouse was a state Supreme Court stenographer, prominent Mason, and friend of Keefe.

The name of the house, Nieu Dorp, stems from the Dutch name of the village ("New Village") now called Hurley. The house's origins are traditionally dated about 1730, but it acquired nineteenth-century additions that Keefe, like

"Dutch Colonial" wrought-iron hinges and door handles placed for ornamental effect. Nash's treatment of the interior included Arts & Crafts effects; for example, he paneled the lower walls of the living room and applied red burlap to the three feet between the paneling and ceiling beams.

The noted author and sometime Woodstock resident Richard Le Gallienne visited Hurley and was charmed by Nash, "an enthusiastic antiquary." Le Gallienne was invited to ascend to the garret above the kitchen to inspect Nash's "antiquarium," where the guest found "a treasure-cave of old spinning wheels, flint-locks, Indian corn-mills, and such flotsam and jetsam of the past."

Kingston architect Charles S. Keefe was among the many admirers of Hurley and the Van Deusen house. He told the *Freeman* that Hurley (not Kingston or New Paltz) had "the purest types of Holland dwellings" in the county. Keefe's opinion was no doubt influenced by the fact that he had two Hurley clients, Eugene Morehouse and George Kent, who owned old Dutch Colonial

V-2. Nieu Dorp (1984 photo)

*V-3. Du Mond or Spy House
(drawing by Keefe, 1920s)*

Teller, felt obliged to modify or remove as un-Colonial and unattractive. In 1945 *House & Garden* published Keefe's alterations that were meant "to unify the design in the spirit of the old Hudson Valley Dutch original." These alterations included the substitution of Colonial shed-roofed dormers for a broad front gable that had been added to make the second story habitable, as well as the substitution of a veneer of stone for the frame side walls of the nineteenth-century lean-to at the rear. Keefe also designed a new Colonial stoop and replaced window sash having 2-over-2 panes with 12-over-12 sash. The magazine, no doubt caught up in the spirit inspired by the restoration of Colonial Williamsburg in Virginia, called Keefe's changes a "scholarly restoration," which it was not. Keefe was not prepared to take on the research necessary for a restoration of the kind being attempted at Williamsburg.

V-3 Du Mond or Spy House (George C. Kent House)

37 Main St., Hurley. Eighteenth century (1942 addition by Charles S. Keefe).

Architecturally this early stone house is distinctive because of the steep pitch of its gable roof (with a scalloped verge board from the nineteenth century), but its reputation rests upon the tradition that here the British spy, Lieutenant Daniel Taylor, was held prior to his hanging in October 1777. The Colonial Revival architect Charles S. Keefe drew two views (author's collection) of the house, probably

in the 1920s, one with a woman in old-fashioned dress approaching the quaint house, while in the other the house is bedecked with signs indicating its modern use as a store and gas station. Keefe drew the quaint view in reverse, perhaps because he intended to use it in making an etching. In both drawings he eliminated the verge boards, undoubtedly thinking them Victorian and ugly. In 1942, for his friend George C. Kent, Keefe designed a stone-veneered addition to the north that functioned as a store and later as a post office. Kingston architects Myron Teller and Augustus Schrowang recorded the Du Mond house for the New Deal's Historic American Buildings Survey in 1934. Teller, called the "squad leader," wrote a detailed description of the house, identifying early features and alterations, and drew full-size details of the hand-forged hardware, while Schrowang was responsible for most of the measured drawings.

V-4 Matthew or Matys Ten Eyck House (Henry Paul Farm)

Hurley Mountain Rd. 1750 and later.

Beautifully sited on a bend of Hurley Mountain Road and above the fields of the Henry Paul Farm, the Matthew Ten Eyck house has long been a scenic attraction. In 1899 the promotional booklet *Summer Homes and Tours on the Line of the Picturesque West Shore Railroad* featured R. Lionel De Lisser's photo of the Ten Eyck house (then known as the DeWitt Homestead) on a page of "Old & Rustic" buildings. Helen Reynolds identified the original owner as Matthew Ten Eyck (1728–1809), and dated first construction in 1750 thanks to his initials and date cut into a stone on the south wall and large iron figures on the same wall. She theorized that the original two-room house was soon expanded to the north, and a shed-roofed dormer and granary door cut into the eastward slope of the roof. The sequence of construction remains a puzzle, some suggesting that the house was begun as early as 1722. Reynolds saw in the parlor a masterful but unsigned portrait of Matthew Ten Eyck dated 1733 and attributed to Peter Vanderlyn. Ten Eyck poses attired as a very young gentleman with an idealized architectural and landscape background. In 1782 Ten Eyck was president of the board of trustees of the Town of Hurley and read an address welcoming George Washington as he passed through the village.

The Maverick

Along Maverick and Muse Roads, about two and a half miles from the village of Woodstock, are significant remnants of the Maverick, an important music, art, and literary colony established in 1905 by Hervey White (1866–1944). Poet, novelist, dramatist, printer, but also amateur architect, builder, and "dreamer of marvelous dreams," White had had a role in the creation of Byrdcliffe and was influenced by Ralph Radcliffe White-

head's plain, wooden, Arts & Crafts buildings. White's structures, however, were more rustic, makeshift, and unpretentious than Whitehead's. Where the wealthy Whitehead lived well in a Catskills version of a manor house, White, never rich, lived inexpensively, close to nature, with few modern conveniences. He rejected the artifice and pretensions of sophisticated people and their architecture, and he attracted musicians, writers, artists, and other creative thinkers who were like-minded or whose poverty made them grateful for the cottages, huts, and tents White rented cheaply to them. He provided not only inexpensive housing, but also essential encouragement. In the 1920s and '30s the Maverick was, in part, a successful art colony—Eugenie Gershoy, Harry Gottlieb, Arnold and Lucile Blanch, Carl Walters, Austin Mecklem, Wendell and Jane Jones, and Eugene Ludins were among the artists who occupied houses on the Maverick. In the 1940s the aging White withdrew from participation in Maverick activities and built himself a primitive, one-room-and-porch hut called Six by Eight, where he lived simply until his death in 1944.

V–5 Maverick Concert Hall
Maverick Rd. 1915–1916. Hervey White. NR

White believed that "music is almost akin to religion, the highest, the most divine of all the arts," and the concert hall was White's most ambitious architectural project. Still, as in his other buildings at the Maverick, White spurned the employment of a professional architect or skilled craftsmen. He served as designer (taking special pride in using his knowledge of physics to attain fine acoustics) and

V-4. Ten Eyck House (early-twentieth-century postcard)

V-5. Maverick Concert Hall

supervised the construction by unskilled local men and their horses, with minimal machinery. He remained committed to the rustic and hand-made; it was to be "a rustic music chapel among tall trees." White had studied Gothic cathedrals when a student at Harvard, and the concert hall he designed resembles the Gothic in its broad areas of glass. However, no Gothic cathedral makes use of stock window sash tilted to give the effect of diamond panes and pointed arches, and none used tree trunks as flying buttresses. (These rustic buttresses were later removed and internal tie rods substituted.)

White employed rustic effects to integrate the building with its natural setting: trees from the vicinity went into its framing and buttressing; a tree was allowed to rise through the porch roof, rather than be cut down; and walls were initially rough, unpainted, knotty pine boards that weathered to a dark tan, blending with the surrounding trees. Oddly tilted windows lighting the performers' platform were actually intended as "two tree-like arrangements." Those among the audience who were "lovers of nature" and were willing to forego the comfort of the rough pine benches inside were welcome to sit outside beyond the great open doors. The concert hall is little changed from White's original design and continues to offer excellent chamber music to summer audiences. The symbol of the colony, the wooden *Maverick Horse*

carved with an axe by John B. Flannagan in 1924, has been moved from the roadside to the concert hall interior, however.

V–6 Bearcamp
Maverick Road. c. 1908. Hervey White.

White designed and helped construct this, his cabin home and the printing shop of his Maverick Press. Using unskilled local labor, White erected a barn-like frame of young chestnut tree trunks on a concrete floor—practical for a printing press. Bearcamp resembled Byrdcliffe's cottages in being a story-and-a-half, gable-roofed block constructed of local timber and fitted with horizontal window bands. The horizontal, flush board siding of the gable ends also resembles Byrdcliffe construction, although the rustic stone hearth and chimney dif-

V-6. Bearcamp

fered from Byrdcliffe, where stucco and brick were favored. Bearcamp's lower walls may have been originally slab-sided under the influence of John Burroughs, although later these walls were brick covered with plaster.

In 1916 *The New York Times* suggested White "lives a contemplative bachelor existence in a cabin of his own building," and so was "akin" to Henry David Thoreau. White, however, unlike Thoreau, lived in the midst of a colony of men and women whose creative life he nurtured. Among the young artists White befriended was Raoul Hague, who occupied and later owned Bearcamp. Hague and Philip Guston, whose house and studio were near Bearcamp, stood out as the most renowned Maverick artists in the period after White's death.

V-7* Raymond and Mildred Pitcairn Estate, Glen Tonche
Pitcairn Road, Shokan. 1928–1930.
Mellor & Meigs.

Pennsylvania in the Catskills. Raymond Pitcairn (1885–1966), wealthy philanthropist and builder of Bryn Athyn Cathedral outside Philadelphia, employed the prestigious Philadelphia architects Mellor & Meigs to design Glen Tonche, mountaintop aerie, a mansion overlooking the Ashokan Reservoir. A local man, Jay W. Rifenbary of Kingston, was the builder.

Raymond Pitcairn's father, John Pitcairn, was a follower of the eighteenth-century Swedish scientist, mystic, and religious philosopher Emanuel Swedenborg, and the elder Pitcairn was a cofounder in 1883 of the Pittsburgh Plate Glass Company, which became the world's largest manufacturer of plate glass. Raymond married Mildred Glenn in 1910; both had been raised in the Swedenborgian community of Bryn Athyn north of Philadelphia, where they continued to reside. Raymond Pitcairn came to the Catskills seeking a site for his family's summer home on high ground with vistas, and found it on Big Tonche north of the Ashokan Reservoir. Pitcairn loved to design and build. By 1914 he had given up his law practice in Philadelphia and devoted himself to the design and construction of a great Gothic cathedral at Bryn Athyn. The cathedral was originally designed by the renowned Gothic Revivalist, Ralph Adams Cram, but Cram's services ended in 1917 as Pitcairn assumed full control. Major construction was completed in 1928, although work on wood and stone carvings and metalwork continued into the 1980s. Some of the stone for building the cathedral (and for Glencairn, the Pitcairns' imposing Romanesque residence completed in 1939 in Bryn Athyn) was transported by the O & W Railway from Accord, where it had been quarried by men of the Lawrence family, while craftsmen responsible for the hinges and door locks of the cathedral also made hinges and locks for Glen Tonche.

Pitcairn, who was elected to membership in the American Institute of Architects despite his lack of formal training, apparently took an active part in the design of Glen Tonche, using three-dimensional models to work out his ideas as he did in completing the

V-7. Glen Tonche (1995 photo)

design of the cathedral. In 1995, a few years before the Pitcairn family sold the house at Glen Tonche, visitors were shown a model of one of the living rooms assembled before construction of the room and later used by the Pitcairn children (there were nine) as a playhouse. Architects Mellor & Meigs did, however, produce some sixty-six drawings for Glen Tonche. The compound's several blocks have steep gable roofs and prominent chimneys, which demonstrate the ongoing taste for the picturesque in mountaintop locations, although the architects produced similarly picturesque houses for less dramatic sites in and around Philadelphia. Mellor & Meigs were drawn to English Tudor compositions, but wall surfaces (here white-painted clapboards on stone foundations) are flat, stripped of ornament under the influence of the Arts & Crafts movement and of modernism. Not surprisingly, window glass occupies much of the wall surface. The glass walls of the porch off the living room were installed at Raymond Pitcairn's insistence over the objections of his architects.

Within, a wooden Gothic hall also has severely simple lines, but is a magnificent space with its high, timber-trussed ceiling and lofty stone chimney breast above the arched fireplace. A color photo of Raymond Pitcairn with the Curtis String Quartet from Philadelphia, all dressed informally in the hall, appeared in the March 1962 *National Geographic*. Furniture is pushed back against the walls, but Pitcairn's connoisseurship is still in evidence—an antique tapestry representing David anointed by Samuel hangs on the white-painted chimney breast. The Pitcairn family sold Glen Tonche in 1998; a 2005 Associated Press photo shows another stone hearth in a room dominated by the recording equipment of Allaire Studios, which offered outstanding facilities and mountain vistas to musicians such as David Bowie.

The Pitcairn boathouse on Kenozia Lake is visible from a distance on Route 28. It was designed by the Kingston firm, Augustus R. Schrowang Associates, in the 1960s.

V–8* Methodist Episcopal Church
West Hurley. 1853 and 1867–1868 (not extant).

Destroyed by the creation of the Ashokan Reservoir, the façade of this church was an unscholarly but pleasing combination of the Gothic (crenelations atop the bell tower, corner turret, and roof gable) with the Italianate (quoins and round-arched windows and doorway). The turret was not quite tall enough to hide the (later?) brick chimney rising behind it.

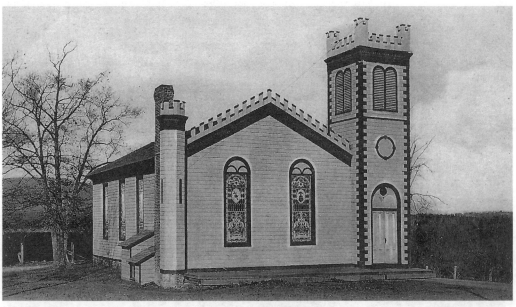

V-8. West Hurley Methodist Episcopal Church (c. 1905 postcard)

VI
City of Kingston

Formed in 1872 by merger of the villages of Kingston and Rondout.

Population: 21,914 (Town of Kingston) in 1870;
23,456 (City of Kingston) in 2000.

Kingston is the county seat and only city in Ulster County. The city traces its origins back to the Dutch settlement of Wiltwyck (now uptown Kingston), named in 1658 by Petrus Stuyvesant, Director General of New Netherland. Stuyvesant ordered construction of a stockade for protection of the settlement from attack by Native Americans. While the stockade is long gone, early stone houses whose walls withstood the burning of the village by the British in 1777 remain well preserved in remarkable numbers within the Uptown Stockade Historic District. Rondout, located on the Hudson River at the mouth of the Rondout Creek, had been the site of a fort/trading post under the Dutch, while in the nineteenth century it flourished as a center of commerce and industry after the opening of the Delaware & Hudson Canal in 1828. The canal ran from the coal regions of northeastern Pennsylvania to the Hudson River at Rondout. For more information about Kingston's architecture and the city's architects, see William B. Rhoads, *Kingston, New York: The Architectural Guide* (2003).

VI-1 Matthewis Persen House
74 John St. at Crown St. c. 1661 and later. NR

While resembling a number of other early stone houses altered in the nineteenth century, the Matthewis Persen House has been the subject of intense architectural and archaeological scrutiny, which has revealed its importance as a building whose origins go back to the earliest period of European settlement. Archaeologist Joseph Diamond uncovered at the site evidence of a fire set in 1663 during the Second Esopus War, waged by the Esopus tribe of the Delaware Nation, and of the stockade that protected Wiltwyck in the 1660s. Architect Kenneth Hewes Barricklo, who has made a detailed analysis of the existing fabric and surviving records, believes that the building grew in several stages from a one-and-a-half-story structure with stone basement, one room on the main floor, and garret above. This small house, at the northwest corner of the present house, may have been built of wood, not stone, above the basement, and nothing of it may survive above ground. Before 1776 additions were made, of stone, to the south and east. The wing on John Street with doorway and two windows on either side functioned both as house and public house (tavern) before the Revolution. When burned by the British in 1777, the property was owned by Matthewis Persen.

In the mid-nineteenth century, stone gables were added over the Crown and John Street façades, as well as Gothic Revival bracketed hoods over the doorways on the two streets. Charles W. Romeyn, the accomplished New York architect who was a native of Kingston and designer of several Kingston buildings, owned the house with his wife Estelle before selling it to Ulster County in 1914, but none of its design can be attributed to him. (Romeyn was the only son of Hiram Radcliffe Romeyn, who at his death in 1904 owned much real estate in the Kingston area.) In recent years the exterior has been restored, including the robust bracketed door hoods that had been replaced in the twentieth century.

VI-2 John Sudam House (Friends of Historic Kingston, Fred J. Johnston Museum)
63 Main St. at Wall St. c. 1812. NR

The immaculately preserved, Federal-style Sudam house, along with the Old Dutch Church across Wall Street, provides a welcome note of classical dignity to a key Kingston intersection. Its classical details are modest, but the wood-frame house

VI-1. Matthewis Persen House

is substantial and the details are unified into a perfectly harmonious whole. Despite this, in 1938 the site (then known as the Van Leuven House, after longtime owners) was ripe for development as a gas station. Happily, demolition was avoided and that same year Fred J. Johnston (1911–1993), a rising young antiques dealer, purchased the house, which would serve as his shop and residence until his death. (In 1960 Johnston erected, behind the house on Wall Street, a new, Federal-style building, designed by Albert Edward Milliken exclusively for shop purposes.) Johnston had dropped out of school in the 10th grade to help support his family, working in factories and briefly for architects Teller & Halverson while training himself to become a leading dealer in American antiques. He rapidly achieved his goal, selling antiques to important American museums and private collectors. In later years he determined that, after his death, the Friends of Historic Kingston should maintain the Sudam house as an historic house museum, complete with his antique furnishings and decorative touches. The Friends have carefully carried out his wishes.

The interior is furnished primarily with American pieces from the eighteenth century and Federal period that might have been in the house when new and owned by lawyer (and later state senator) John Sudam, whose friends included Washington Irving and Martin Van Buren. Johnston called the basement room illustrated here the "Seventeenth Century Room." (It is believed that Sudam built his house on the foundations of a Dutch house burned by the British in 1777.) When this photo was taken in the 1970s, the room was dominated by a kas or kast, a two-door cupboard of the kind widely associated with eighteenth-century households in the Hudson Valley. Johnston believed that it was locally made, attributing it to the Elting-Beekman furniture makers in Kingston. While the objects shown in the photo were mostly later sold by Johnston, the kas remains in the house, but is now given a place of honor on the first floor.

When Johnston purchased the Sudam house, Henry Francis du Pont, creator of the great Winterthur Museum of American decorative arts, was already his client, mentor, and friend (see VI-19,

VI-2. "17th-Century Room," Sudam House (1970s photo)

XIX-2, XX-1, and XX-24). Johnston visited du Pont at Winterthur, near Wilmington, Delaware, for three days in the summer of 1937, when Winterthur was still du Pont's private collection of period rooms and not yet a public museum. Johnston thanked his host effusively for "the most interesting days of my life. I am so very grateful for this honored opportunity to study first hand, and unhurried the finest collection of American furniture in existence. ... I would much rather roam through Winterthur than go to heaven." Later Johnston would refer to his home as a smaller version of Winterthur, or "Winterthur-on-Hudson." Yet Winterthur was clearly an institution created by a very wealthy collector, while Johnston's museum, as Roderick H. Blackburn points out, was to be "devoted to the role of the antiques trade in American life." Visitors today are encouraged to understand that "antiques are not works of art to be admired from a distance, but are meant to be lived with."

VI-3 First Reformed Protestant Dutch Church ("Old Dutch Church")
272 Wall St. at Main St. 1850–1852. Minard Lafever. NHL

Fine as the exterior of Old Dutch Church surely is, with its bell tower and spire still emblematic of the historic culture and traditions of the city, it is the meticulously preserved interior that reminds even the secular-minded visitor how some indefinable perfection in space, surface, and mass can result in a place suited for reflection if not worship. Architect Minard Lafever looked back to the English churches of Christopher Wren and James Gibbs and American Georgian churches such as St. Paul's Chapel on Broadway to arrive at the vaulted nave with Corinthian columns rising to support the galleries to either side and, indirectly, the vaulted ceiling. The columns directly support round arches, creating an arcade on either side of the nave. Above the nave arcades are clerestory windows ("mock," since they do not open to the outside, but Lafever designed the roof above them with skylights to furnish a dim light) separated by arches that span the nave and divide the vaulting into bays.

In the Reformed tradition, the pulpit is raised at the end of the central aisle, the communion table subordinate at the base of the pulpit. The pulpit's design was wholly integrated with the rest of the interior, as was recognized in the 1880s by another prominent architect, Calvert Vaux who, when offered the opportunity of redesigning the pulpit, declined saying, "I cannot change a thing without impairing the exquisite unity." Although the church did not originally have stained-glass windows representing biblical figures (perhaps because of a desire to avoid the practices of Roman Catholicism), the Tiffany window depicting The Presentation in the Temple (1891–1892) seems now a fitting backdrop for the preacher and conclusion for the architectural composition. On the west side of the chancel is an Ionic pedimented memorial to Abraham Bruyn Hasbrouck (1791–1879), president of Rutgers College and owner of a country estate at St. Remy, near Kingston (see II-24).

The architect Minard Lafever, who had a successful practice in New York, was adept at designing in a variety of historic styles. In the 1840s, for Holy Trinity, an Episcopal church in Brooklyn, Lafever had employed the Gothic Revival. There is reason to believe that the Kingston congregation of 1850 wanted to avoid the Gothic as the style of High Church Episcopalians, but also of the rival Fair Street Reformed Church (1850) a few blocks away, preferring instead the round arch and classi-

VI-3. "Old Dutch Church" (Al Nowak photo)

cal details labeled "Roman" in a detailed description of the building (*Ulster Republican*, September 28, 1852) undoubtedly written by the architect.

In 2008 Old Dutch Church received the rare distinction of being named a National Historic Landmark.

VI-4* Kingston Academy
Academy Green. 1830–1831, 1850s, 1883 (demolished 1916). Henry Rector (1830); Charles W. Romeyn (1883).

Kingston Academy, a private institution whose alumni included the important Neoclassic painter John Vanderlyn, was founded in 1774 and occupied a two-story stone building still standing at the southwest corner of John and Crown streets. In 1831 the academy's new four-room, two-story building was completed on spacious grounds still known as Academy Green. Thus the old utilitarian stone academy was replaced by stylish quarters designed by Albany architect Henry Rector, an early example of Kingston securing the services of a professional architect from a larger town. Rector is best known for his classical design of State Hall (1832–1842; later altered and now the New York State Court of Appeals). For the façade of the brick academy building, Rector planned a flattened version of a classical temple, with pilasters rather than columns supporting the pediment, and similar pilasters articulating the side walls. Roman-derived arches appear in the window within the pedi-

VI-4. Kingston Academy (drawing by T. D. Lewis, c. 1880)

ment and openings in the belfry, while a faceted dome topped the belfry, which resembled the one added to the Shawangunk Reformed Church in 1833 (see XVIII–1). After completing the academy, Rector designed another classically inspired building in Kingston for the Reformed Protestant Dutch Church (1832–1833) on Main at Wall Street (since 1869 St. Joseph's Roman Catholic Church, with extensive alterations).

Rector's original building was expanded several times, including an expansion in 1852–1853 required by the addition of a boarding department. The private academy became public in 1864, serving as Kingston's high school while retaining its original name. Sometime between 1853 and 1883, T. D. Lewis (listed as a photographer in the 1899 Kingston *Directory*) made a pencil drawing (UCHS) of the academy with boys playing baseball while a man wearing a stovepipe hat with walking stick stands to the rear.

In 1883 Charles W. Romeyn, a native of Kingston who trained in Calvert Vaux's office and had a successful architectural career in New York, designed alterations and additions, including a tower on one side of the building and a third story overall, with freely adapted Romanesque and classical forms in a version of the Queen Anne style. The next year Romeyn would design another towered Queen Anne building, for the New Paltz Academy, and in 1886 he was responsible for ad-

ditions to Ulster Academy in Rondout. The new Kingston High School was completed on Broadway in 1915, and a year later the Rector-Romeyn Kingston Academy was torn down, although its trustees continue to oversee Academy Green.

VI-5 Burgevin Building
Fair and Main Sts. 1904–1905.
Myron S. Teller. NR

For this commercial building constructed early in his career, Myron Teller adopted red brick with white classical trim to create a Georgian Revival design within the broad Colonial Revival. He used the same style in designing the De Witt Roosa House (c. 1905; see VI-7) at 212 Fair Street; note the triglyphs that appear in the frieze over the Fair Street entrances of both buildings.

VI-5. Burgevin Building

However, in designing a larger, three-story commercial building, Teller took liberties with the Georgian beyond those he employed at the Roosa house—the wide, first-floor shop windows (of plate glass) with arched tops like fanlights, and the corner entrance cleverly recessed behind a single, fluted Doric column of wood that conceals a load-bearing iron column. Did Teller intend this Doric shaft to echo the twin Doric columns of the 1839 Kingston National Bank on the diagonally opposite corner? In 1905 he designed alterations and additions to this bank.

Remarkably, a flower shop has occupied part of the ground floor at this key intersection for more than a century. In the nineteenth century, Valentine Burgevin operated a large nursery with greenhouses at the head of Pearl Street. After his death in 1899, his sons George and David commissioned Teller to design this building with their flower shop at the corner marked by the single Doric shaft.

Elsewhere on the ground floor Miss Mary Kenney, who was active in the woman's suffrage movement, operated the Wiltwyck Inn, with a "tea parlor" facing Fair Street and a dining room facing Main Street. On the third floor she opened a hall for a variety of social events. In 1910–1911 she was able to put up her own building, the Wiltwyck Inn, at 48 Main Street, only a short distance from the Burgevin Building. In planning the new Wiltwyck Inn, Myron Teller turned away from the Anglo-American Georgian and adopted Dutch Revival stepped gables, appropriate for an inn named for the seventeenth-century Dutch settlement that ultimately became the city of Kingston. Teller and Kenney may have been spurred on by the enthusiasm for all things Dutch encouraged by the 1909 Hudson-Fulton celebration of Henry Hudson's 1609 voyage up the river later

named for him. As part of the celebration Governor Charles Evans Hughes was served luncheon at the earlier Wiltwyck Inn, which was decorated with Hudson-Fulton and American flags.

VI-6 The Kirkland
Clinton Ave. and Main St. 1899 (restored 2006–2007). NR

The English Tudor style, signaled here in the decorative half-timbering of dark painted boards against light stucco in the upper stories, set this boardinghouse (later hotel) apart from its rivals. Passersby would be attracted by The Kirkland's tower at the corner, capped with a polygonal bell-shaped roof. The fourth story of the tower was originally an open belvedere, and the low, shallow porch that wrapped around both street fronts suggested the pleasures of rocking chairs in a rural setting, just as the several picturesque gables suggested the wood-framed, rural or mountain-top hotel rather than one in a city, even a small city like Kingston. The half-timbered patterns of the gables called up images of quaint and merry olde England: City Historian William C. DeWitt wrote in the 1940s that "the architecture of The Kirkland is of the Elizabethan Era," and neighboring buildings—Stuyvesant Motors and LaSalle Cleaners (demolished)—had followed the same English style "so as to make strangers think for a moment they are near Shakespear's home."

While the architect of The Kirkland has yet to come to light, the client was Mrs. Margaret S.

VI-6. The Kirkland
(c. 1905 postcard)

VI-7. De Witt Roosa House

and detailed cornice at the eaves and in the side gables, treated as pediments.

Another red-brick Georgian house designed by Teller with abundant classical ornament was the Parsonage of the Reformed Church of the Holy Comforter (1905), which survives at 51 Wynkoop Place. The foundation bears a stone inscribed "Nisi Dominus Frustra 1893" (loosely translated as "Unless the Lord is with us, our labor is in vain"); construction halted after completion of the foundation, to be resumed later according to a new design by Teller. Across the steep, cobblestone street, in the church's cemetery, is the impressive monument of the Wynkoop/Reynolds family, donors of the parsonage.

Also among Teller's early houses is the gambrel-roofed house he designed above Marius Street for the pastor of Old Dutch Church, the Rev. Dr. J. G. Van Slyke (1903). It is well sited for views on a hillside. Described in the *Freeman* as "of the Colonial style of architecture," it combines Georgian symmetry and fanlights with the more informal Shingle Style in its dark shingled walls and paired brackets.

Conklin, described by De Witt as "a very exceptional lady with a host of friends" who, until 1917, presided over a boardinghouse distinguished for its "refinements and homelike atmosphere." In 1922 new owners designated The Kirkland a "hotel." Thirty years later Max and Ruth Brugmann opened the Dutch Rathskeller in the basement, which became a favorite of local politicians. Renovations in 1972 removed the porch and tower roof while enclosing the belvedere. Later the building stood vacant and endangered before its restoration was undertaken in 2002 by Rural Ulster Preservation Company.

VI-7 De Witt Roosa House (Myron S. Teller House)
212 Fair St. c. 1905. Myron S. Teller.

An early work by Myron Teller, this house was built for a prominent attorney, De Witt Roosa, but was later purchased and, from about 1928 to 1949, occupied by the architect and his second wife, Ruth. It is curious that Teller, with a national reputation in the 1920s and '30s as a restorer and reviver of the old stone architecture of Ulster County, would choose to live in a generic, red-brick Georgian-style house. The white-columned porch and white doorway with sidelights and elliptical-arched fanlight were standard elements of the Georgian Revival across the U.S. in the early twentieth century. Here Teller enriched the classical aura with Doric triglyphs in the porch frieze, columns in the second-story three-part window,

VI-8 Conrad Elmendorf House (Elmendorf Tavern)
88 Maiden Lane at Fair St. c. 1725 and later.

City Historian Edwin M. Ford confirms that during the Revolution "this house was the meeting place for the Council of Safety ... appointed by the New York Convention in February 1777 to provide for the safety of public property and records." A stone on the west side bore the now-obscure inscription, "1725 KED BED"—apparently

VI-8. Conrad Elmendorf House

commemorating the house's construction in 1725 for Coenradt Elmendorph (variously spelled) and his (second) wife, Blandina. In 1777 Conrad Elmendorf, Jr., was proprietor of a tavern here when the Council of Safety met and when the building was burned by the British, along with most of Kingston. Unusual for a Kingston building before 1776, the stone walls rose a full two stories, and organization of the main door and flanking windows approached symmetry.

In the nineteenth century the building was the residence of some of the city's leading citizens including John Van Buren, member of Congress 1841–1843, and Dr. Charles W. Deyo, county clerk and banker, and his wife Cornelia. While the building's importance as a landmark of the Revolution was acknowledged during their time, it was still subjected to Victorian alterations—brackets supporting the hood over the Maiden Lane doorway, two cast-iron anchors above this doorway joining the stone wall to the interior frame, and the finely cut bluestone window lintels and sills. Bracketed door hoods were fashionable additions to old stone houses in Kingston around 1870. Other examples can be seen on Crown Street at the Persen House (VI–1) and Frantz Rogen House, as well as at the Colonel Abraham Hasbrouck House, 135 Green Street.

VI–9 Frank A. Palen House
76 St. James St. 1892. NR

In 1892 Frank A. Palen was a twenty-six-year-old building materials merchant whose father, Henry W. Palen, had been a carpenter before opening a sash and blind factory in 1877. The business was reorganized in 1892 as H. W. Palen's Sons. Frank Palen's own house served as a visually striking advertisement of the quality of the woodwork from the newly renamed firm.

Like many architects of the early 1890s, the unknown designer of the Palen house combined a Queen Anne composition with classical details of a semi-Colonial sort. The picturesque asymmetry of the second-story rounded bay, multiple gables, and variously shaped windows is characteristic of the Queen Anne, as is the combination

of masonry wall (here rough-surfaced bluestone) for the first story and wood shingles for the upper stories. Still, the Palladian window, gables treated as pediments, Adamesque foliate relief decoration, and porch columns that apparently were originally fitted with small Ionic scrolls were probably sufficient in 1892 to label the design of the house "Colonial." This would have been so despite the Queen Anne ingredients, as well as the Gothic diamond panes in the bay window and un-Colonial stained glass in several other windows. In the 1910s and '20s, architects like Myron Teller and Charles Keefe would reject the architecture of the Victorian era and turn away from that period's vertical, picturesque compositions filled with bold details from a wide range of historical sources, and instead adopt a more restrained and accurately Colonial approach.

VI–10 John Pettit House
97–101 Clinton Ave. c. 1872 (later altered).

John Pettit was a powder keg manufacturer when his Gothic Revival house was pictured in the 1875 county atlas, but before 1860 he had been a carpenter and in the sash and blind business. Pettit's

VI-9. Palen House (1980 photo)

VI-10. Pettit House (Beers, **Atlas,** *1875)*

house bristled with three steeply pitched gables fitted with decorative wooden barge boards and spikey pinnacles, and the second-story windows were pointed-arched. In the Town of Marbletown, the façades of the Hardenbergh-Davenport and Oliver houses also sported three Gothic gables in the 1870s (see IX–9 and IX–13).

By 1980 the Pettit house had been enlarged and altered—stripped of many of its Gothic details, including the finials and bargeboards, although there was a second-story Gothic oriel window that was not evident in 1875. In the present century the long-vacant and endangered house was purchased by the city and Rural Ulster Preservation Company and transformed into four condominiums.

VI–11 John H. Trumbull House
80 Marius St. 1876. Arthur Crooks.

Hidden away on a quiet street and in disrepair, the Trumbull house came to light when historian Annon Adams discovered its publication in the *American Builder* (December 1876) as "a very pretty frame house" by Arthur Crooks, the New York architect who designed two of the county's most prominent buildings, Kingston's City Hall and St. Peter's Roman Catholic Church in Rosendale. For the Trumbull house Crooks adopted a variety of Gothic Revival called "Stick Style" by Yale historian Vincent Scully. The upper walls are formed of narrow vertical boards

with pointed lower ends. The horizontal boards of the lower walls are overlaid with vertical boards that divide the walls into vertical segments. Additionally, boards are placed in X patterns in panels between the first- and second-story windows. A 1907 photo indicates that these X patterns were painted a dark color and resembled Gothic half-timbering in contrast to the light-colored horizontal boards that substituted for the light-colored plaster of true half-timbering. The steep slopes of the polychrome slate roof belong to the post–Civil War Gothic Revival.

Little is known about John H. Trumbull. In 1877 he was one of a large group of Kingstonians planning to observe the centennial of the founding of state government. He was deceased when his property was advertised for sale in *The New York Times* in 1881. The grounds were described as "under fine cultivation" with an "abundance of choice fruit and shade trees." From the "beautiful suburban location on Golden Hill," there was said to be a "magnificent view of the famed Esopus Valley, the Catskills, and Shandaken Mountains." Today this view is hard to imagine from Marius Street. Trumbull's widow Sarah M. continued to reside in the house for a number of years after 1881.

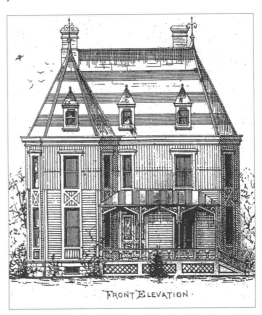

VI-11. Trumbull House (Crooks drawing, **American Builder,** *Dec. 1876)*

VI-12 Augustus Schrowang House

249 Pearl Street. c. 1940. Augustus Schrowang.

Fred J. Scharp House

245 Pearl St. c. 1940. Augustus Schrowang.

For these two Colonial Revival houses, Kingston architect Augustus R. Schrowang (b. 1893) adopted the style of seventeenth-century New England—seen most clearly in the Scharp house's second-story overhang with wooden pendants at the corners—rather than the local Dutch brand of Colonial favored by Myron Teller. Schrowang had been educated in Kingston schools, studied architecture at the Drexel Institute in Philadelphia where he graduated in 1912, worked as a draftsman in the offices of Myron Teller and Gerard Betz in Kingston, and served in France during World War I. He set up his own practice in Kingston in 1926.

No. 245 Pearl was built for Fred Scharp, a plumber. Next door Schrowang occupied 249 Pearl with his wife Mary and two sons, Edward and Augustus, Jr.—the latter joined his father's architectural office in 1960 after graduating from Pratt Institute. The interior of 249 Pearl is distinguished by a curious tightly winding semicircular Colonial staircase to the second floor and by handwrought Colonial hardware by Myron Teller.

Although the Teller hardware is not visible from the street, its presence indicates friendly relations between Schrowang and his former employer.

Schrowang had previously designed two other Colonial Revival houses for himself and his wife Mary. The small but charming house (c. 1925) at 62 Marius Street was the first building completed to his design—a clapboard, gable-to-the-street house whose original appearance is known from his watercolor rendering (given by Augustus Schrowang, Jr., to the Friends of Historic Kingston), one of the few Schrowang drawings to survive. By 1932 he and his family resided at 19 Mountain View Avenue, a mildly eccentric house in having a front door but no windows on the first floor front—there was a screened porch to the rear. Mrs. Schrowang had an antiques business, a factor in their brief residence (c. 1939–1940) in an old stone house at 28 Green Street, which Myron Teller had restored for Mrs. Mae K. Gordon in 1920. For the Schrowangs, the house functioned as residence, architectural office, and antiques shop. Next came 249 Pearl Street, followed by another, larger Colonial Revival house (c. 1956) at 45 Burgevin Street, also designed by Schrowang.

In the neighborhood of the Pearl Street houses are other Colonial Revival efforts by Schrowang, including a diminutive, beautifully detailed cottage for Ottilia M. Riccobono (c. 1949) at 35

VI-12. Schrowang and Scharp Houses

VI-13. Schmidt House (1980 photo)

Mountain View Avenue. Miss Riccobono was a dance teacher and clerk; her brother's wife was the architect's secretary.

VI-13 F. G. Schmidt House
Off North Manor Ave. 1909.
Albro & Lindeberg.

A country home within the city, this residence was designed by Lewis Colt Albro and Harrie T. Lindeberg, both of whom had apprenticed in the celebrated office of McKim, Mead & White. Between 1905 and 1914 the firm of Albro & Lindeberg—with Lindeberg the principal designer—became outstanding purveyors of sophisticated country houses for the elite of Long Island and Westchester County, but also designed Tracy Dows's great estate (1907) in Rhinebeck and other country places as far away as Minneapolis and Houston.

For Fritz G. Schmidt, an optician at 11 East 42nd Street in New York, the architects planned a smaller estate in Kingston. Despite its relatively modest size, the house was considered among the architects' best works and was widely published. Its picturesque composition, stucco walls with bits of half-timbering, small-paned casement windows, and roof apparently of thatch (but actually of wood shingles steamed and bent into curved shapes for ridges and eaves)—all indicated English cottage sources or, as the *Architectural Record* said, "Elizabethan models." But the architect brought the roof down unusually close to the ground—and the first floor was only six inches above the ground—so the house had "much more repose, and is much better fastened to the ground than any purely Elizabethan house." Even when the house was new, the *Record* found it "already has the dignity and respectability of age. It settles down naturally into its surroundings." Low wings—one for a billiard room, the other for the kitchen and servants' rooms—had the appearance of being later additions to the central block. The house also seemed long settled because it was surrounded by old elm trees whose preservation required shifts in the floor plan, according to Phil M. Riley's "A House That 'Fits'" in *Country Life in America* (1910).

Admirers of the new Schmidt house failed to point out that to build the rooted English cottage it was necessary to tear down a genuinely old stone house, which William De Witt believed was the mysterious manor house of Kingston's founder, Thomas Chambers. In 1908 Kingston architect Thomas P. Rice and William S. Neice had been commissioned by Schmidt to plan "colonial" alterations and additions to the existing stone house, but Albro and Lindeberg replaced Rice, and English triumphed over Colonial.

In 1922, after the dissolution of the Albro & Lindeberg partnership, the English country house (NR) of Metropolitan Opera singer Mme. Amelita Galli-Curci was built on the Ulster-Delaware County border at Highmount to the design of Harrie Lindeberg. It, too, is firmly rooted to its site, but in this case on a high elevation with magnificent views. The estate's shingled barn and caretaker's house (close to Galli Curci Road, County Route 49A) have American Colonial sources.

VI-14. Paynter House

VI-14 Justus S. Paynter House
371 Albany Ave. 1911. William S. Neice.

Described when under construction as a "bungalow ... of hollow tile block, covered with stucco, and a red tile roof," this big bungalow is comparable to the Samuel J. Moore bungalow (1910) in Poughkeepsie designed by Gustav Stickley and built with hollow tile walls covered with cement. Characteristic of the bungalow, the Paynter porch is recessed under the broadly sweeping gable roof, and there is a hint of modernity in the severe geometry and nontraditional materials of the walls. But there are also surviving bits of traditional design in the bracketed eaves, truss patterns in the gables, and simple classical forms of the porch piers.

William S. Neice is an obscure figure among Kingston architects. Apparently from a family of carpenters and contractors, he was employed as a draftsman by architect Thomas P. Rice in 1907. Rice and Neice were engaged in 1908 to design alterations and additions to the stone house acquired by F. G. Schmidt on Manor Avenue, but in the end the existing house was replaced by a new one by the prestigious New York firm of Albro &

Lindeberg (see preceding entry, VI–13). In 1912 Neice drew plans, "Colonial in style," for the Lake Katrine Grange Hall.

VI-15 James Millard & Son Building (former)
Broadway and Prince St. 1915–1925. Myron S. Teller?

The subtly detailed white façade of the Millard Building provided an attractive showcase for the sale of Ford cars and other Ford products by John R. Millard (1863–1945), whose father James had operated a foundry on this site in the late nineteenth century. In 1915–1916 Myron Teller made preliminary drawings for new Ford showrooms and their Broadway façade, but construction was delayed until 1925. Originally to include rich ornament in terra-cotta, the simpler façade finally built was composed of a crowning parapet and cornice above slender piers, segmental arches, and large show windows. (Teller's plans for the 1925 construction have not been located, but he probably remained Millard's architect.) The façade's free, spare classicism must have fitted in nicely with the earlier and more accurately classical Post Office (by James Knox Taylor, 1904) that dominated this key intersection until the Post Office's much-lamented demolition in 1969.

The Millard Building was characteristic of auto sales buildings of the time, whose fronts

VI-15. Millard Building

resembled fine office buildings and provided a sense of refined good taste to encourage customers to buy from this dealer and not one in lesser quarters. In New York City, even Model T Fords were sold in 1917 from a salesroom or salon that, writes Chester Liebs, "boasted high-coffered ceilings, plush armchairs, oriental rugs, chandeliers, potted palms, walnut paneling, and a grand staircase." Similarly, the Millard showrooms were described as "large, modern ... light, airy," and dominated by "a mammoth open grate. This fireplace [not now visible] is built of cobble stones and is surmounted by a mantelpiece upon which rest crossed sabers carried by John Millard's uncle during the War of the Rebellion. The fireplace gives a most comfortable appearance to the big show room and is the pride of John Millard." A second-floor showroom was curtained off as a motion picture theatre where Millard showed films of the making and use of Ford products. Like other buildings for auto dealers, the more utilitarian, factory-like spaces were to the rear.

Millard, who died in 1945 at age eighty-two, was hailed in his *Times* obituary as a "pioneer automobile dealer" who had been honored by Henry Ford during the New York World's Fair (1939–1940) "as one of the five oldest Ford automobile dealers in the world."

VI-16 Holy Cross Episcopal Church
30 Pine Grove Ave. 1891–1892.
William J. Beardsley.

This Gothic Revival church was sited in an area of factories and working-class houses, yet it is no simple affair, especially within. Exterior walls are of roughly cut Ulster County bluestone up to the windowsills, then brick, with stone trim over the Gothic-arched façade windows. The belfry is an unpretentious wooden design. The church's young architect, William J. Beardsley, maintained offices in both Poughkeepsie and Kingston in the 1890s, but was primarily active in Poughkeepsie where he developed a large practice, eventually designing courthouses across the state.

Holy Cross was founded as a mission chapel by the Rev. Lewis T. Wattson (1863–1940), rector of St. John's Episcopal Church, whose stone, medieval-looking façade (1861) signaled wealth and influence in the midst of Kingston's commercial Wall Street. (In the 1920s the façade was taken down and reassembled on Albany Avenue, where it stands among fine late-nineteenth and early-twentieth-century houses.) Wattson was an advocate of high church ritual (his use of incense caused a number of parishioners to leave St. John's) and of bringing the church to working-class families living in the vicinity of the West Shore Railroad. A c. 1896 photo of Holy Cross's interior shows a spacious chancel, as wide as the nave, and a large altar suited to Wattson's style of worship. Departing from the rectorship of St. John's, Wattson became a Franciscan friar, still within the Episcopal Church, and in 1899 founded a Franciscan community at Graymoor, near Garrison-on-Hudson. In 1909 Wattson and the Graymoor friars were received into the Roman Catholic Church. At Graymoor, Wattson—then known as Father Paul—established a home for homeless men known as St. Christopher's Inn.

VI-16. Holy Cross Episcopal Church

Holy Cross was subsequently enlarged to the east, and elaborate altars designed within an otherwise plain Gothic interior. In 1925 an impressive High Altar was dedicated that rises twenty-three feet at the east end of the church. The altar was designed by Angelo Lualdi of Cambridge, Massachusetts, with the advice of the Reverend Father F. C. Powell. Lualdi was a noted woodcarver whose work is found in the National Cathedral, Washington, and in All Saints' Church, Ashmont, Massachusetts, the latter designed by the great Gothic Revival architect, Ralph Adams Cram. Holy Cross's High Altar can be closed with doors on massive hand-wrought-iron hinges. Opening the doors reveals the central figure of Christ reigning from the cross, flanked by Mary and John, all carved in low relief by Angelo. There are also intriguing smaller polychrome figures including Samuel Seabury, first bishop of the Episcopal Church, Reverend Mother Harriet, the American founder of the Community of Saint Mary, and Edith Ellison Van Wagenen (1874–1923), in whose memory the altar was given.

Holy Cross's finest stained-glass window, by Mayer & Co. of Munich and New York, represents St. James and St. Paul and was given by John E. Kraft, a Democratic mayor of Kingston, editor of the *Kingston Leader*, and senior warden of Holy Cross. Kraft was the "right hand" of Ulster's most famous Democrat, Judge Alton Brooks Parker, a vestryman at Holy Cross and the father-in-law of the Rev. Charles Mercer Hall, Rector of Holy Cross when Parker was Democratic candidate for president of the United States in 1904.

VI-17 Charles Bray House
262 Broadway. c. 1868 (altered in twentieth century). George E. Woodward. NR

Charles Bray publicized himself as the cashier of the First National Bank of Rondout by having his fashionably picturesque house portrayed in the 1875 county atlas. Bray had served as cashier since 1863 under bank president Thomas Cornell, Rondout's most powerful businessman, and Bray later became a bank president and mayor. Although the original Gothic bargeboards and porch

VI-17. Bray House (Beers, Atlas, *1875)*

have been lost, the polychrome slate roof, quaint dormer, and (not evident in the 1875 print) cast-iron fence on rusticated stone blocks are evidence of the property's original character.

Bray's architect, George Evertson Woodward (1829–1905), practiced in New York City and was well known for a series of popular illustrated books on house design. In his *Country Homes* (1865), Woodward professed to "revere the memory of Downing" and advocated that "clerks and subordinate officers in ... banking ... institutions" enjoy the pleasures of life outside New York in its suburbs,

much as Bray would enjoy on his admittedly small landscaped grounds above the commercial blocks of Rondout. The stone posts with low pyramidal tops that support the cast-iron fence resemble designs in Woodward's chapter on gates.

VI-18 Edgar B. Newkirk House
10 East Chestnut St. at Broadway. c. 1870 and later. NR

The residence of Edgar B. Newkirk, cashier of the National Bank of Rondout, was pictured in the 1875 county atlas, as was the neighboring place on Union Avenue (now Broadway) of Charles Bray, cashier of the First National Bank of Rondout (see preceding entry, VI–17). Newkirk's towered Italian villa on extensive grounds, and the lithograph depicting them, outshone the more modest Bray residence. Was this a case of conspicuous consumption, one cashier outdoing a rival? (At the time, the role of cashier was close to that of a twentieth-century bank president.)

The distinguishing feature of the Italian villa style—the tower with balconies, arched windows, and low but projecting hipped roof—was prominent at the front of Newkirk's house. Also common in buildings of the style are the quoins accenting the corners of the house, as well as its

VI-18. Newkirk House (Beers, Atlas, *1875)*

several low-pitched gable roofs. The extended piazza, along with the tower and its balconies, served as elevated points for viewing Newkirk's landscaped grounds and more distant blocks of Rondout descending to the waterfront. In the lithograph, the grounds are dotted with willow trees, and a latticed, two-level summerhouse (similar to one illustrated in *Country Homes*, 1865, by George E. Woodward, Bray's architect) rises near a picturesquely gabled birdhouse. Outside the low fence, on Union Avenue, two horses pull a streetcar at a good clip, emblematic of the energetic spirit of commerce in Kingston at the time. In the 1890s Dr. David Kennedy, who grew rich from concocting patent medicines with his picture on the bottle, lived here, and the house as photographed in De Lisser (1896) differs from its 1870s appearance. Today the top of the tower, still in place in 1896, is gone.

VI–19* Hone St. Storefront
9 Hone St. c. 1830 (1945 removed to Winterthur Museum).

One of Rondout's architectural treasures was lost not to fire, neglect, greed, or urban renewal, but to the high-minded efforts of Kingston antiques dealer Fred J. Johnston, who procured the elegant storefront at 9 Hone Street for inclusion in Shop Lane within Henry Francis du Pont's renowned Winterthur Museum in Delaware. Johnston wrote du Pont, May 26, 1945:

> Dear Harry:
> Are you still interested in a store front? I have located an early nineteenth Century one with very beautiful detail which is in the old part of Kingston commonly known as Rondout. It is beautifully designed in the Federal period. ... It has never been remodeled and has two show windows on both sides of a recessed door. These show windows have fan light details with some interesting carving, as well as fluted columns. The front ... has a charming feeling of early Kingston. ... I think [it] will fit into the bowling alley without much change."

VI-19. Hone Street Storefront (c. 1945 photo before removal to Winterthur)

Du Pont did purchase the storefront, which Johnston believed had been erected for Dr. Jacob (or Jacobus) Mellon in or before 1827 (just before the opening of the D&H Canal). The disassembled storefront was modified to fit within the former bowling alley in du Pont's mansion.

VI–20 101 Broadway (Reher Bakery Building)
c. 1870. Cast-iron storefront by Rondout Iron Works. NR

This is a notable survivor of the urban renewal of the 1960s that decimated Rondout's commercial buildings. It preserves, flanking the storefront, cast-iron piers produced locally by the Rondout Iron Works; see the name of the foundry cast into the base of the piers. In 1871 the proprietors of the ironworks were John McEntee and John Dillon. As was often the case in Rondout, the second- and third-story front is of brick with segmental-arched window lintels of cast iron, while bluestone was employed for window sills and a belt course between the upper stories. A modestly scaled cornice runs atop the first-story shop front, and a prominent bracketed cornice crowns the whole façade. The corner piers, segmental arches, and cornices all reflect the influence of the Italian Renaissance and belong to the Italianate style.

Edward Cloonan and Andrew Eubank purchased the site of 101 Broadway in 1868 from

VI-20. 101 Broadway

Rondout's richest entrepreneur, Thomas Cornell. Eubank and various Cloonans ran grocery, provision, and soda water businesses in this or nearby buildings by 1871. From about 1883 to 1900, James Van Buren had a "leather and findings" business here—note Van Buren's weathered,

ghostly sign painted on the bricks of the side wall facing the Rondout Creek. Through most of the twentieth century, a bakery owned by the Rehers, a Jewish immigrant family who lived in the upper two floors, occupied 99 and 101 Broadway. Currently efforts are underway by the Jewish Federation of Ulster County to open the building, with its exceptionally unchanged interior, as a museum of mercantile, immigrant, and Jewish life in Rondout and Ulster County.

VI-21 Moses Yeomans House
254 Delaware Ave. Before 1777 (altered mid-nineteenth century). NR

Benson Lossing, author and illustrator of the *Pictorial Field-Book of the Revolution* (1851–1852), identified and sketched this stone house on a knoll close by today's Delaware Avenue as a noble landmark surviving from the war. In 1777 British troops on their way to burning the village of Kingston tried to burn the house, but thanks to the efforts of a "negro woman," the house was saved. Charred timbers remain within the house, which is apparently the only stone house from the colonial era to survive in the Rondout-Ponckhockie sections of the city. While commonly known as the Moses Yeomans house, research by Kevin McEvoy has revealed that Yeomans purchased the house in 1779 from Moses Cantine III.

As recorded by Lossing and still obvious today, the Yeomans façade is pleasantly asymmetrical. The wide Dutch door with old hardware is off center, with two windows to the right and one to the left. Structural evidence suggests that the stone portion of the house was built all at one time.

VI-21. Yeomans House

Picturesque additions made in the mid-nineteenth century include a bay window on the west end, and dormer window and large cross gable in the roof of the south front. Lossing's sketch shows, above the doorway, an apparently unsupported pentice (roof of single slope)—an early Dutch feature, later replaced by a conventional nineteenth-century porch. In 1853 the house was owned by the dominant local industry—the Newark Lime & Cement Manufacturing Company—and its bookkeeper, David Brainerd Abbey, resided here. At that time an unobtrusive concrete addition was put up at the rear.

VII
Town of Kingston

Chartered as Wild-wyck, 1661; incorporated by patent as Kingston, 1667; reorganized as town, 1702.

Population: 21,914 in 1870 (including villages of Kingston and Rondout); 908 in 2000.

The eighteenth-century Town of Kingston was later much diminished when the villages of Kingston and Rondout were removed from its jurisdiction to form the City of Kingston, and by the formation of the towns of Saugerties and Esopus in 1811, and the Town of Ulster in 1879. The creation of the latter was particularly contentious as it was carried out to form a non-Irish town, one free of the sometimes boisterous Irish immigrants who lived just west of the city of Kingston and who were mostly employed at bluestone quarries. These immigrants had dominated Town of Kingston politics in the 1870s. According to Kathleen Burton Maxwell, "the Irish leaders ... used strong-arm tactics to support corrupt officials of the Democratic Party." New York State, therefore, took action to relegate the Irish to the surviving fragment of the Town of Kingston, while the larger and more populous part of the town became the Town of Ulster. The primary landmark in the present Town of Kingston is the historic church of these Irish workers.

Some idea of the living conditions of the impoverished Irish quarry workers can be gathered from the tales told by the bemused and condescending author Ernest Jarrold in his *Mickey Finn Idylls* (1899). Mickey, the son of a quarry worker, lives with his parents in "a plain, unpainted, one-story structure, vulgarly known as a shanty," which, with the adjoining pig sty, make up the "Finn estate ... in the Irish style of architecture." The Finns' three-room shanty—in or near Ponckhockie in the city of Kingston—would have resembled workers' housing outside the city.

VII-1 St. Ann's Roman Catholic Church

Sawkill Rd. near Halihans Rd. 1913.

St. Ann's Church (founded 1860s) stands at the heart of the Town of Kingston. It is a simple, vernacular example of the Gothic Revival church in wood, not stone, despite the presence of nearby bluestone quarries that employed its parishioners. The plain wooden church, built on the site of an earlier wooden Gothic church destroyed by fire in 1913, is expressive of the limited means of the local Irish Catholic population for whom quarrying re-mained a key source of income. Monuments in the adjacent cemetery document the Irish origins of parishioners—for example, Mary Callahan Hannon born in County Cork and died at age 52 in 1882, and her husband John Hannon, born in County Limerick and died at age 56 in 1888. The flight of stone steps leading up to the church reaches, just below the church, an outdoor altar and shrine (1938, 1944) built, presumably, of local stone. At least one miraculous cure is said to have occurred at the shrine. The church was closed in 1971, but fortunately it has been maintained by local residents.

VII-1. St. Ann's Roman Catholic Church

VIII
Town of Lloyd

Formed from part of the Town of New Paltz, 1845.

Population: 4,224 in 1870; 9,941 in 2000.

Eltings, Hasbroucks, and Deyos—families that were among the founders of New Paltz—were early large landowners in what became the Town of Lloyd in 1845. Highland, an unincorporated village and Lloyd's most populous center, developed about 1820 on high ground above New Paltz Landing, the town's earlier business center that furnished the inland settlement of New Paltz with river access. Since Highland lies just across the Hudson from the city of Poughkeepsie, Highland citizens have often been drawn to Dutchess County's chief city, rather than its Ulster County rival, Kingston. Thus the 1939 Highland High School (now a middle school) was designed by Poughkeepsie architects Edward C. Smith and Donald Emley, and not Kingston architects Teller & Halverson or Gerard Betz.

In 1870 Lloyd's bluffs overlooking the Hudson were dotted with fine country seats, few of which survive today. Krum Elbow, a large river estate with a Queen Anne–style house (not extant), observation tower, boathouse, and some twenty-five other buildings, achieved notoriety in 1938 when its owner, Howland Spencer, sold it to followers of Father Divine. Spencer had come to detest Franklin Roosevelt's New Deal and disputed FDR's adoption of the name Krum Elbow for his own Hyde Park estate. In selling to the controversial black leader, Spencer enjoyed the prospect of discomfiting Roosevelt, although Spencer also came to admire Father Divine's principles.

VIII-1 Poughkeepsie Bridge (Walkway over the Hudson State Historic Park)
1871–1873, 1876–1878, 1886–1888.
Thomas Curtis Clarke, Charles Macdonald, and others. NR

In his definitive history of this bridge, Carleton Mabee writes: "The Poughkeepsie Railroad Bridge was the first bridge to be built over the Hudson River from the ocean all the way up to Albany. It was a technological wonder. Opened in 1889 soon after the Brooklyn Bridge opened, it is not only higher above the water than the Brooklyn Bridge, and founded deeper in the water, but also longer. When it opened, its promoters claimed it was the longest bridge in the world." Why then is the Poughkeepsie Bridge relatively little known? Perhaps because, unlike the Brooklyn Bridge, it was not intended to be a civic landmark with mighty stone piers, Gothic arches, and a roadway beautifully suspended from cables—although an 1871 design for Poughkeepsie did propose a suspension bridge. Instead it was to be a functional, economical means of bridging the Hudson for rail traffic. The bridge's chief engineer from 1886 to its completion, Thomas Curtis Clarke of the Union Bridge Company, was aware of the distinction. He remarked that in America "where so many [bridges] have to be built in a short time, aesthetic considerations are little regarded. Utility alone governs their design. So long as they are

strong enough, few care how they look." Clarke readily conceded that his Poughkeepsie Bridge was "'not a thing of beauty,'" yet he boasted it was "a considerable piece of engineering ... one of the great bridges of the world." The American bridge historian David Plowden agrees, calling it one of "the great engineering achievements of the nineteenth century."

The Poughkeepsie Bridge Company was chartered by the state in 1871 to create a rail link between New England and the country south and west of the Hudson. As things stood then, trains had to cross the river at Albany. A number of factors caused completion of the bridge to take seventeen years: the steamboat lobby in Albany resisted the building of piers, which would be obstacles in the river; the mid-1870s saw the country in hard economic times; and the design and construction of a bridge over such a wide and deep river challenged a series of engineers. The ultimate solution worked out by Clarke and his associates involved constructing cantilever spans of steel with four narrow piers in the river that would minimally interfere with shipping. Their narrowness, however, dictated that cantilever spans should alternate with truss spans, which would help stabilize the cantilever spans. The truss spans were erected on falsework or scaffolding, but the cantilever spans were (daringly) erected without expensive and time-consuming falsework. From an engineering standpoint, however, the most difficult

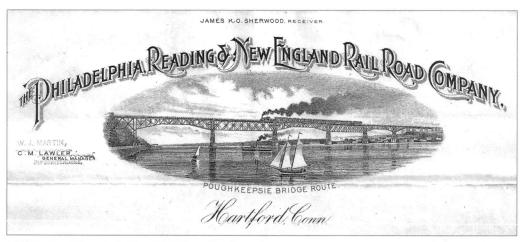

VIII-1. Poughkeepsie Bridge (1896 letterhead)

task was establishing the piers on hard bottom, going down sixty feet of water (at low tide), then seventy feet of mud and clay. Concrete formed the base of the piers, while bluestone (some from Ulster County quarries) was used to face the piers up to thirty feet above the river. From there the piers were composed of well-braced steel columns that rose to support the cantilever and truss spans. The bridge, completed the last day of 1888, had a river span of 3,094 feet and rose 212 feet above the Hudson. Including approach viaducts, the bridge extended well over a mile (6,768 feet).

Trains were originally operated by the Central New England and Western; later they were operated by the New York, New Haven & Hartford, and finally by Penn Central. As locomotives and freight trains became heavier, the bridge was strengthened in 1906–1907 and again in 1917–1918—at least the latter strengthening under the direction of Ralph Modjeski, who in the 1920s would play a key role in the design of the nearby (and handsomer) Mid-Hudson Bridge. A fire on the bridge in 1974 resulted in the termination of rail traffic over the bridge. After decades of discussion about alternate uses, in 2008 the commitment was made to transform the railroad bridge into a pedestrian bridge; it was said that it would be the longest pedestrian bridge in the world. In October 2009 it was opened for walking, running, biking, and skating, and to those who would gaze over the railing and take in the magnificent views of the river and shores of Ulster and Dutchess counties. Any who have enjoyed the adventure of walking across the Brooklyn Bridge are now able to experience the higher and longer trek across the Hudson between Highland and Poughkeepsie (www.walkway.org).

A relic of the abandoned rail line to the bridge is the St. Elmo station (1888). Now used for storage, it has been moved a short distance from its original site and can be glimpsed from County Route 21 in the Town of Shawangunk near the Orange County border.

VIII–2 Mid-Hudson Bridge (Franklin D. Roosevelt Mid-Hudson Bridge)

Rtes. 44/55 over the Hudson River to Poughkeepsie. 1924–1930. Ralph Modjeski and Daniel E. Moran, consulting engineers.

Motorists negotiating the narrow lanes of the Mid-Hudson Bridge during rush hours should not contemplate the visual spectacle of this suspension bridge or reflect on its historic importance, but their passengers might take time to admire the patterns of its piers and cables and recall the roles of the designers, engineers Ralph Modjeski and Daniel E. Moran, and the governors, Alfred E. Smith and Franklin D. Roosevelt, in bringing about this link between Ulster and Dutchess counties, replacing the slow ferry between Highland and Poughkeepsie. Modjeski and Moran were both renowned engineers. Modjeski (1861–1940) was born in Poland, the son of the great actress Helena Modjeska (one of the variants from the original Polish spelling), and trained in Paris where he graduated at the head of his class at the École des Ponts in 1885. His career as bridge designer, however, was purely American. From offices in Chicago and New York, he designed bridges in states across the country. At his death, he was hailed as "the world's leading bridge builder." Moran (1864–1937) was an 1884 graduate of Columbia University's School of Mines and became an expert on bridge foundation work. He was involved with the design of the George Washington Bridge (completed 1931) farther down the Hudson.

The George Washington Bridge is longer than the Mid-Hudson (the span between the GW piers being 3,500 feet vs. 1,500 feet for the Mid-Hudson) and more celebrated, thanks in part to its visibility from New York City. Still, the Mid-Hudson was singled out by the noted industrial designer Norman Bel Geddes in 1932 as illustrating "the proper relation between use and appearance" through a design of "utmost simplicity." The suspension bridge's "main supporting elements, the cables, hang between their supports [the twin pier towers] as naturally and as gracefully as loose rope. The roadway is suspended from the cables by regularly spaced hangers. The location and direction of the cables and hangers conform to the natural lines of the action and stresses within them, permitting the most economical use of material in their structural design. There are no superfluous or inefficient members. Inevitably, when all the elements of which the bridge is composed are organically assembled, the structure assumes a pleasing form." Bel Geddes did not comment upon the form of the twin pier towers, perhaps because the Gothic-arched form of the void over the roadway was inspired by history, not use and efficiency. The pier towers of the Brooklyn Bridge (John Augustus Roebling, 1867–1883) had earlier been designed to serve as Gothic monuments to the importance of Brooklyn and Manhattan, and the piers of the Mid-Hudson Bridge also serve as monumental portals to the two counties. Noted photographer and bridge historian David Plowden calls the Mid-Hudson Bridge—and particularly its towers—"superbly beautiful."

Completion of the bridge was delayed by difficulties in placing the 19,000-ton caisson for the east pier; for months it lay tilted at a 43-degree angle, its tip rising above the river, before it was righted and put in place. The ceremonial opening of the bridge August 26, 1930, attracted some 25,000 people and was broadcast on radio station WGY. Mrs. Smith first cut the ribbon on the Poughkeepsie end, then Mrs. Roosevelt on the Highland end, with Modjeski and Moran at her side. The ladies' husbands both spoke, first in Poughkeepsie, then repeating their speeches across the river. Governor Roosevelt generously told the crowd that he was merely the bridge's "godfather," his predecessor Al Smith was its "official father"— Smith had laid the cornerstone in Poughkeepsie in 1925 with FDR in attendance. Roosevelt was proud of his role in assuring that the bridge would be successfully completed. In 1939 he approved a sketch by Charles Rosen for a mural in the Poughkeepsie Post Office depicting the city from Highland with the Mid-Hudson Bridge looming large on the right. FDR expected that this mural would remind future generations of the great public works the governor and president from Hyde Park had brought into being for the people of the Hudson Valley and beyond.

VIII–3* Patrick's Diner
Rte. 9W, Highland. 1945–1946 (entirely altered later). Kullman Dining Car Company.

The 1945 Patrick's Diner, arguably Ulster County's handsomest streamlined modern diner, no longer lures motorists on Route 9W. Like other diners of its decade, Patrick's exterior glistened with stainless steel, bright enameled panels, and broad windows. But this Kullman Dining Car also sported glass blocks by the entrance and at the rounded corners, which lent an extra air of sophisticated modernity to this eatery for everyman, despite the somewhat-dated raised monitor roof, reminiscent of an early-twentieth-century railroad

VIII-2. Mid-Hudson Bridge (1937 Curt Teich postcard)

VIII-3. Patrick's Diner (1948 Curt Teich postcard)

passenger car or trolley. The Kullman company, founded in 1927, was, like most diner manufacturers, located in New Jersey, first in Newark and later in Harrison.

Patrick's can be said to live on through the postcard reproduced here, the product of the distinguished Curt Teich firm of Chicago. The card promoted Patrick's as: "The Most Modern Diner in Ulster County. Opened Jan. 3, 1946. Featuring home cooked meals, complete fountain service, an all modern kitchen with the latest in refrigeration, spacious parking area. Cleanliness and sanitation are stressed throughout. Tony Patrick & Sons, Prop."

The Gateway Diner, the current incarnation of Patrick's, was renovated by Paramount of Oakland, New Jersey, and reflects today's nostalgia for c. 1950 stainless-steel diners, although the stainless strips seem pumped up on steroids.

VIII–4 First Methodist Episcopal Church of Highland (First United Methodist Church of Highland)
57 Vineyard Ave., Highland. 1868–1869. J. A. Wood.

The formidable brick façade and tower of the Methodist Church dominate the traditional center of Highland, indicative of the prominence of Protestants in the late-nineteenth-century community. The church's cornerstone was laid October 28, 1868; the design was by the mid-Hudson region's leading architect, J. A. Wood, whose office was just across the river on Market Street in Poughkeepsie.

Wood adopted the round-arched Romanesque Revival style, commonly chosen for Protestant congregations seeking a plainer alternative to the Gothic of Roman Catholic and Episcopal churches. Not only are doors, windows, and the drip moldings above them round-arched, but so too are the small arches of the corbel tables that indicate the stages of the tower and run just below the broad, sloping gable of the façade. Gothic pinnacles once ornamented the top of the tower and the corners of the façade. Inside, the main worship space was planned for seeing and hearing the preacher; brightly lit by tall windows, it is a unified space without separate side aisles or chancel. J. A. Wood also designed the Presbyterian Church in Marlboro about the same time and in the same style (see X–4). In 1871 a local writer was of the opinion that the Highland church was the "one building here, public or private, that can claim much architectural excellence." Only nitpickers "have spoken of it in slight terms, because they could not discover absolute perfection in every arch, corner and curve."

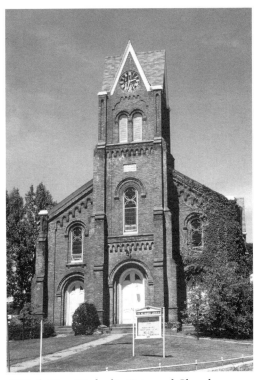

VIII-4. First Methodist Episcopal Church (1976 photo)

VIII–5 First National Bank of Highland (Sawyer Savings Bank)
71 Vineyard Ave., Highland. 1922–1923.
Gerard W. Betz.

The siting of this small but stately classical bank at the intersection of Vineyard Ave. and Main St., "at the village square, adds greatly to the appearance and prestige of the community," stated the *Highland Post* at the bank's opening in 1923. Kingston architect Gerard Betz created a compact, Roman classical building in Indiana limestone with the interior finished in marble and mahogany. The main doorway is accented by a pair of brackets supporting a cornice with a Roman thermal window above (thermal indicating that the form stemmed from ancient Roman baths). Two lampposts resembling classical columns with globes atop also grandly define the entrance. The limestone façade itself lacks expensive rounded columns; instead there are two pairs of simple pilasters supporting a frieze originally with the name of the bank for all to see. Above the frieze, a low parapet and balustrade hide the roof.

For more than a century, American banks had turned to the Greek or Roman temple or treasury as a form proclaiming the dignity and stability of the banking institution. The Kingston National Bank (1839) on Main St. at Fair St. resembled an ancient Greek treasury, and the Highland bank, while not so explicit in its references, also belongs to the Greco-Roman, temple-treasury tradition. Harcourt J. Pratt (1866–1934) was a Highland businessman and a director of the local bank since 1900. In 1921 he also became a director of

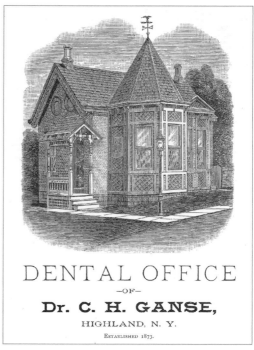

DENTAL OFFICE
—OF—
Dr. C. H. GANSE,
HIGHLAND, N. Y.
ESTABLISHED 1873.

VIII-6. Dr. Ganse's Dental Office (engraving, New Paltz Normal School, Auld Lang Syne)

the Kingston Trust Company that occupied the Kingston National Bank building. Perhaps because of Betz's success with the Highland bank, he was hired to carry out extensive alterations to the Kingston bank in 1927.

VIII–6* Dr. C. H. Ganse's Dental Office
Highland. c. 1890 (not extant).

Dr. Ganse advertised in the New Paltz Normal School yearbook (1892) and other regional publications using this engraving of his picturesque Gothic and Queen Anne office, possibly designed by Poughkeepsie architect Arnout Cannon. Was the dental chair in the low turret? Were patients' anxieties calmed by the charming, small-scale domesticity of the building? A later Ganse ad showed friendly Brownies in the style of illustrator Palmer Cox swarming over the exterior of the building to indicate "The Effect of Dr. Ganse's Low Prices and Free Extracting." The office stood across the street from Dr. Ganse's residence, altered by Cannon in

VIII-5. First National Bank (1975 photo)

1893 and, since 1930, the Highland Free Library at 30 Church Street.

VIII–7 Ezekiel S. Elting House
Rte. 9W and Tillson Ave., Highland. 1858.

Here, surrounded by the disorder of commerce along Route 9W, is an oasis of grass, trees, and dignified architecture—the house having a classical, five-bay façade with bracketed eaves. (The house has lost its original porch, and there have been other exterior changes.) Ezekiel S. Elting (1821–1909) was a merchant, farmer, and Republican leader in the town. His son Clarence J. Elting (1860–1942) continued to live in the house and was a student of local history, genealogy, and architecture. Clarence provided information and photos to Helen Reynolds in 1925 when she was researching her book on early Dutch architecture. He did his best to furnish only accurate information, quoting Josh Billings on the matter: "it iz better not to kno so mutch than to kno so menny things that ain't so." Judge A. T. Clearwater, on the other hand, was guilty according to Elting of slipshod research: "When the Judge wants an historical date, he draws on his well stocked imagination."

In 1934 Elting opposed the campaign by some members of the Ulster County Historical Society to acquire and preserve the derelict Johannes Hardenbergh house in Wawarsing (see XX–1), predicting it would become "the whitest kind of a white elephant." He argued that the soci-

ety should instead acquire a house in Stone Ridge or Napanoch. In fact, the society took over a Bevier house in Marbletown. After Clarence's death, his widow Lottie donated Victorian parlor furniture and portraits that continue to be exhibited in the Bevier house as a memorial to Clarence Elting.

VIII–8* Aaron Rhodes House
White St. (later Route 9W) and Milton Ave., Highland. 1896 (demolished 2002).
William J. Beardsley; George F. Barber.

Poughkeepsie architect William Beardsley appears to have pulled out all the stops in designing the spindles and railings for the porches and porte cochère of this Queen Anne–style house. However, research by Chris DiMattei reveals that Beardsley in fact simplified an even more elaborately ornamented design published by Knoxville, Tennessee, architect George F. Barber in one of his pattern books.

Beardsley's client was Aaron Rhodes, a Civil War veteran wounded at Antietam, and later a successful fruit farmer. How proud Rhodes must have been to stand on his porch enframed in its great horseshoe arch with radiating spindles. About 1905 he gave land in front of his house for a monument (erected 1908) to the 156th Regiment, New York State Volunteer Infantry and its service, 1862–1865. By 1976 the house had been stripped of much of its ornament. In 2002, despite the strenuous efforts of the Town of Lloyd Historical Preservation Society, it was demolished by the

VIII-7. Ezekiel S. Elting House (Pennington photo, 1931)

VIII-8. Rhodes House (early-twentieth-century postcard)

New York State Department of Transportation for the widening of Route 9W.

VIII–9 Oliver J. Tillson House
Vineyard Ave., Highland. 1874.

The splendid mansard roof of the Tillson house is remarkable for its polychrome slates, paired dormer windows, iron crest, and tall central section that derives from the monumental mansards crowning the pavilions of great public buildings of the era such as Philadelphia's City Hall (1869). Closer to home, the roof resembles J. A. Wood's carriage house for Thomas Cornell in Rondout (1872), although less richly ornamented. Both the Cornell carriage house and Tillson house are low, one-story buildings dominated by their mansards.

In 1852 Oliver J. Tillson, a native of Rosendale and twenty-year-old surveyor, collaborated with P. Henry Brink of Saugerties and Jay Gould, then of Delaware County and later the notorious robber baron, in preparing and publishing a detailed map of Ulster County. In 1858 he moved to New Paltz Landing and, by 1871, was a "fruit raiser and farmer" with 150 acres. An early-twentieth-century postcard of the Tillson house shows park-like grounds, including a series of man-made

ponds, in front of the house. In 1991 Ethan P. Jackman purchased and restored the house.

VIII–10 Lloyd Rural Cemetery (Highland Cemetery)
Vineyard Ave., Highland. Organized 1856.

This hillside cemetery is crowned by a Civil War memorial obelisk (1869) "erected by the Ladies Monument Association of Highland" and made by Bissell Brothers of Poughkeepsie, whose Volunteer Fire Department Memorial (1871–1873) is one of the master works in the Poughkeepsie Rural Cemetery. Near the Highland Civil War memorial is a poignant monument with circular text identifying "The Pastor's Son / James Ostrom Liebenau," who died at age twenty in August 1863 in the hospital at Port Hudson, Louisiana, after declaring, "I am every inch a soldier."

Captain Abraham Elting (1785–1859) and members of his family lie beneath an imposing monument with Gothic tracery framing their names. The monument maker was again a Poughkeepsie firm, although its name, carved at the base, is no longer legible. Captain Elting had a highly successful freighting business. His sloop sailed Saturdays for New York with both passengers and

VIII-9. Tillson House (1977 photo)

A small shaft a few yards to the south of the Civil War memorial marks the grave of Lilly Martin Spencer (1822–1902), a leading American genre painter who lived in Highland from about 1879 to 1892 at Rock Nest, a board-and-batten house on property overlooking the river. Her husband, Benjamin R. Spencer, appears as the bumbling spouse in several of her amusing paintings of family life. Benjamin is also memorialized on the shaft.

Perhaps the most unusual, but also appropriate, monument in the cemetery is the circular stone, similar to a millstone, mounted vertically to memorialize Archibald Palen (1823–1902). He is listed in the 1871 Ulster County *Business Directory* as A. Palen, Jr., a millwright and farmer in Stone Ridge.

VIII–11 Electa and John Thompson House (Loyd and Cynthia Lee House)
27 Maple Ave., Highland. c. 1855.

VIII-10. Highland Cemetery

the products of local farmers. Elting's residence, conveniently near the Hudson, was a brick, Greek Revival building that in the nineteenth century also served as a hotel. A balustraded porch graced each of the two major stories, and a Grecian cupola was fitted with acroteria (ornamental forms placed at the corners of a pediment). Altered, the building survives today as an apartment building.

This is one of the county's best examples of the Italian villa as promoted by A. J. Downing's publications. The low corner tower with groupings of three windows in the upper story, the gently pitched roofs, and the blocky, asymmetrical massing are all characteristic of the era's picturesque Italian villas (a capacious porch was added about 1904). In the early 1850s, Samuel F. B. Morse, with the aid of Alexander Jackson Davis, had created an Italian villa for his family across the river, south of Poughkeepsie.

This house was built for John Thompson (1802–1891) and his wife Electa Ferris Thompson (c. 1807–1902). John was a Massachusetts native who became a wealthy Wall Street banker, founder of the First

VIII-11. Thompson House (1976 photo)

VIII-12. Church of the Holy Trinity (1971 photo)

National Bank in 1863, and an organizer of the Chase National Bank in 1877. Electa was a native of Highland and a primary donor for construction of the Episcopal Church of the Holy Trinity (see VIII–12). In the 1871 Ulster County *Business Directory*, Mrs. John Thompson is listed—not her husband—as a summer resident on the property's eight acres. However, John Thompson's obituary notes that "about forty years ago the fine brick residence on Maple Avenue was erected on a portion of the Ferris homestead farm, and here Mr. and Mrs. Thompson have spent their summers ever since."

VIII–12 Church of the Holy Trinity (Episcopal)

Grand St. at Wilcox Ave., Highland. 1870–1873 (rectory, later parish house, 1900).

This small Gothic Revival church resembles the work of Richard Upjohn, but it does not appear in the published list of his commissions. The façade's narrow, pointed-arched windows (or lancets) above the entrance vestibule, the corner buttress-

es, and the steep, gable roof are standard elements of Upjohn's small Gothic parish churches. Also characteristic is the dominant nave with lower chancel to the east and small robing room to the north. The walls are of gray stone of various sizes, shapes, and textures, while sills and other trim are of brownstone. The cost of these stone walls would have been higher than the board-and-batten construction of many of Upjohn's small churches (see the Upjohn-influenced design of All Saints, Milton, X–10). Oliver J. Tillson and others gave stone, but the expense of laying up the walls would have remained. The site was donated by John J. Ferris who, like Tillson, was a fruit raiser and farmer. The principal donor of construction funds was Electa Ferris Thompson, a native of Highland who, with husband John Thompson, a New York banker and founding trustee of the church, returned to Highland each summer to occupy their nearby Italian villa (see preceding entry, VIII–11). Electa Thompson's obituary observed that she had built Holy Trinity and that it was "one of the monuments that will perpetuate her memory."

The neighboring village of New Paltz had no comparable church, and the New Paltz *Independent* in 1870 welcomed the prospect of "a picturesque church—such as we usually see built by this denomination." When the church was opened for worship in 1873, the same paper judged "the interior ... to be tasteful and attractive" despite opinions to the contrary. "The designs may be somewhat antique, but who wants the monotonous architecture that usually characterizes country villages?" That "monotonous architecture" presumably was represented by the Greek Revival of New Paltz's Reformed Church and of many other village churches in the county. The same writer was pleased to see that "a gilded cross [no longer present] adorns the front gable and small ones the interior." One of his acquaintances was on record as opposing crosses: "They look too much like Roman Catholicism." Our enlightened observer, however, believed "what better emblem of Christianity is there than the cross?" He also admired, above the altar, a stained-glass window of Christ the Redeemer, which some would have condemned as too Catholic.

In 1875 an effort to raise funds to build a bell tower failed despite an offer from Mrs. Thompson to provide a bell when the tower was completed. The financial picture did not improve at the turn of the century when the parish trustees refused to build a rectory for their new minister, the Rev. George A. Nicholas, who then took matters into his own hands and found the funds to build, a few feet from the church, the board-and-batten rectory whose picturesque lines were in harmony with the church.

VIII-13 Union Cemetery of Lloyd (Lloyd Cemetery)
841 New Paltz Rd. Organized 1861.

After parking inside the ornamental iron cemetery gates, the visitor may wish to walk back to them and contemplate the cast-iron relief of a semi-nude Father Time with scythe and hourglass and the companion relief of a robed and winged angel kneeling at a classical tomb. The core of the cemetery is defined by orderly rows of evergreens sheltering a

variety of Victorian monuments. Among the most imposing and first to be seen is the brownstone obelisk (c. 1872) of the Deyo family. The stone obelisk was a popular form for monuments to the dead in the nineteenth century, most famously to commemorate George Washington in the District of Columbia. The obelisk's verticality was eye-catching, and its association with ancient Egypt seemed to assure the preservation of the dead, either as a corpse or, at least, as a memory. The pagan associations of ancient Egypt might trouble Christian families, but these associations could be neutralized by wrapping the base of the obelisk in the Gothic forms of Christian architecture, here pointed arches and quatrefoils. The monument is identified (in a carved inscription) as the work of Miller & Van Wyck of Poughkeepsie. An advertisement in the 1873 Poughkeepsie directory describes them as operating a "marble and granite works" on Main Street where they sold "marble mantels." There were also "monuments, tomb and grave stones of every variety on hand" and "granite monuments cut to order from original designs to suit customers' views."

VIII-13. Lloyd Cemetery (1974 photo)

The Christian Gothic also is evident in the diamond panes of glass and decorative barge-boards of the small wooden building near the gate, currently the cemetery office. While its walls have been resurfaced, it retains an attached two-door outhouse.

VIII-14* Raymond Riordon School
Chodikee Lake. 1913–1914 and later (not extant).

Raymond Riordon (1877–1940), an educator who believed conventional private schools and universities produced dissipated "parasites," ran schools in the Midwest and then near Highland that trained boys to be good citizens through learning by doing. The American pioneer who constructed his own log cabin, built his own furniture, and worked his own fields was Riordon's ideal. Riordon had connections with two leading figures in the American Arts and Crafts movement, Elbert Hubbard and Gustav Stickley. In 1911 Riordon was briefly superintendent of the Roycroft School of Life for Boys at Hubbard's Roycroft campus near Buffalo. At the Interlaken School in Indiana, Riordon lived in a modified Stickley Craftsman bungalow. He also wrote articles on education for Stickley's magazine, *The Craftsman*, in 1912 and planned a school for Stickley's New Jersey estate, Craftsman Farms. The school was scheduled to open in June 1913, but never did. Soon thereafter, in 1913–1914, Riordon set about establishing on Chodikee Lake in Lloyd, with "Gustav Stickley's friendly offer of cooperation," a boys' school known as the Raymond Riordon School, which he maintained until his death in 1940.

The property acquired by Riordon included the Chodikee Lake Hotel, a wood-frame building with extensive porches and a cluster of bungalows, as well as several hundred acres of farm, orchard, and wooded land. Riordon's choice of the site was clearly influenced by the proximity of John Burroughs in West Park; Riordon admired Burroughs as a "naturalist and worker," and both men had a taste for rustic architecture. After Burroughs's death, the Riordon School had New York State designate land near Big Indian as the John Burroughs Forest under the school's care. The school placed a tablet designed by its sculptor, Seamus O'Brien, at the forest's entrance.

Stickley published Riordon's self-promotional article, "An Outdoor School for Boys, Where Development Is Gained from Work as Well as Books," in the April 1914 *Craftsman*. Illustrations

VIII-14. Riordon School, interior of the main building (c. 1920 postcard)

VIII-14A. Riordon School, students outside the main building (c. 1916–1920 photo)

included a photo of a rustic "garden house at the edge of Chodikee Lake," as well as elaborate architectural renderings of a four-story horizontal log and shingle schoolhouse and a workshop also to be built of logs by the boys. Neither the schoolhouse nor workshop was built as designed. The school opened in 1914 with eight bungalows and the former Chodikee Lake Hotel, a "large modern hotel with accommodations for one hundred." Riordon regretted that when the school opened "the boys must endure the luxury of a steam-heated hotel ... and be surrounded with all the man-killing comforts of the present-day home." Within two years, however, he expected that the boys would build their own quarters, each small building housing three boys.

In December 1915 the hotel Riordon so disliked burned down—early reports were that the fire was caused by an oil-stove explosion in a Japanese servant's room. A newly completed gymnasium was spared. The rebuilding of the school's main building was undertaken primarily by the boys, guided by Harry Lynn Dabler, an engineer from Raquette Lake. Photos published in 1920 of the dining and living rooms show interior walls of vertical logs, more massive log posts supporting ceiling beams, as well as rustic furniture and rustic light fixtures. The schoolrooms were described as having "log walls ... that throwback to the days of the pioneer school house." Vertical logs also

composed the exterior walls of the bulky main building, while basement and exterior staircase walls were of rough stone, as was a great chimney. Upper window sashes were fitted with diamond panes. Riordon credited Stickley's Craftsman enterprise with assistance in designing buildings at the school, but the interiors should be credited primarily to Riordon, who described himself not only as an educator but also as a "builder and designer of log camps" and "interior decorator." (He designed and built log camps at Raquette Lake and Horseshoe Lake near the Canadian border.) Soon after Riordon's death, it was said that his preference for "the rustic motif" stemmed from his belief that his boys would later "live within walls of brick and steel," but "in their youth, he would have them experience the pioneer's own emotions by building dwellings out of the surrounding forest." The main building, however, had "all the modern conveniences," including steam heat, electric lights, and hot and cold water in each sleeping room.

Riordon maintained contact with Elbert Hubbard's Roycrofters, who printed an early promotional booklet for the school in handsome Arts and Crafts style that listed, on the Honorary Advisory Board, "Gustav Stickley, Designer, Master Craftsman, New York City." Even after Hubbard's death in the 1915 sinking of the *Lusitania*, the Roycrofters continued to design and print school booklets, and Hubbard's son and heir to the Roycroft enterprise, Elbert Hubbard II, wrote an essay promoting the school and titled "The Boy and Opportunity." Moreover, copper plaques commemorating anniversaries of the school's founding resemble Roycroft products.

At the time of Riordon's death in 1940, the school included the main building with classrooms, rustic dining room, and dormitory rooms, as well as a dozen "bungalow dormitories," several of which were built about 1929 with rough stucco walls and rubble-stone foundations and chimneys. Others were "bungalows built by boys where every rafter and each timber, hewn log and nail, and peg, represents the working creative idea of some boy who has gone before ... bungalows not unlike those substantial hand-hewn homes which the forefathers of these boys lived in when Thirteen States made the Nation."

The Riordon School outlived its founder by only a few months. Enrollments had fallen from over one hundred boys to about twenty. In 1942 Marist Brothers expressed interest in purchasing the property, but instead acquired the former Payne estate. Later the property was purchased by New York State and became the Highland Training School. Apparently none of Riordon's buildings survives.

❧ IX ❧
Town of Marbletown

Formed by patent 1703; town organized 1788.

Population: 4,224 in 1870; 5,854 in 2000.

The town was named for its abundant limestone, and its principal hamlet, Stone Ridge, was built along the old King's Highway, which at this point follows a narrow crest of stone. Marbletown is fittingly the site of many eighteenth- and early-nineteenth-century houses built of the local stone. In the vicinity of Rest Plaus Road and within the Rest Plaus Historic District are several eighteenth-century stone houses and, out of sight, a mid-eighteenth-century gristmill. The Rest Plaus Mill, whose timber frame resembles a barn's, was restored to waterpowered operation by the Hansen family in the 1960s. The hamlet of High Falls is named for the considerable falls of the Rondout Creek, below which the Delaware & Hudson Canal crossed the creek on an aqueduct designed by J. A. Roebling. Early taverns built of stone were Sally Tock's in Stone Ridge and Simeon Depuy's in High Falls. Both survive, and until recently Depuy's was still providing food and drink to travelers. Taverns were abundant in Ulster in times past; a list of Marbletown taverns in 1806 includes some twenty names (however, Marbletown then incorporated more territory than at present).

IX–1 Wynkoop-Lounsbery House
3721 Main St. (Rte. 209), Stone Ridge.
c. 1719 and c. 1767–1772. NR

President Franklin Roosevelt recognized the singular importance of this pre-Revolutionary stone house, completed by 1772 for Cornelius E. Wynkoop (1746–1795), and used his presidential power to help assure its preservation. Roosevelt was surely moved by the high regard his friend Helen Reynolds had for the house. Miss Reynolds, not given to overstatement, wrote confidently that "in size and dignity, in elegance of finish and in a certain sophistication the Wynkoop-Lounsbery house is conspicuous in Ulster County."

The house rises a full two stories with a great gambrel roof enclosing a vast, two-level space for storage and perhaps for slave quarters. Its long façade broke with Ulster County precedent in being organized in the English Georgian way with a central doorway (the door itself divided in the Dutch manner) and symmetrically placed windows. Remarkably, the original 12-over-12 sash and the paneled shutters remain in place. The windows are separated by broad areas of stone wall—the weighty stone walls dominate the openings—a holdover from regional, pre-Georgian practice. The stones of this façade, facing the old King's Highway (now Route 209), are cut in rectangular shapes, unlike the irregular stones of the other walls, and the façade is crowned with a simple, classical, Georgian cornice. The gambrel, while often considered a Dutch feature, was more common in early New England than in the Dutch Hudson Valley. According to Gary Tinterow, it is "one of only two large, gambrel-roofed stone houses extant in New York State that was expressly designed in its current configuration"—the other being the c. 1760 Coeymans-Bronck House in Coeymans. A smaller wing to the rear, built with cruder masonry, was probably erected about 1719 as a two-room house with jambless fireplace and gable end to the road. The front porch of the main block was added about 1870 and resembles the porch of the Gothic-gabled Oliver house to the north on Route 209 (see IX–13).

Long-standing tradition holds that George Washington spent the night of November 15, 1782, in the home of Major Cornelius Wynkoop as the Revolution drew to a close. Washington, who designed his own Georgian house at Mount Vernon, no doubt appreciated the Georgian wood paneling within Wynkoop's house, although it was more modest than Washington's own. Reynolds was impressed (as are scholars today) by the paneling, especially since "original paint of unusual shades of blue and of mulberry ... [are] still visible." Several English-style fireplaces on the first and second floors are framed with Delft tiles of the kind made in the 1760s. The spacious central hall incorporates a formal staircase whose balusters, Gregory Long notes, appear "chunky," because of lingering Dutch influence. Historians since at least 1880 have proposed that Washington would have been assigned the best bedroom up those stairs, one with a paneled chimney breast painted blue and with blue Delft tiles around the fireplace.

In 1818 the house was sold to the Lounsbery family, who continued to own it until the death of Miss Sarah Lounsbery in 1988. In the 1910s Sarah ran the Sally Tock tea room across the highway (see IX–2). During the Great Depression she and her father William were hard-pressed financially, and she sought the assistance of powerful men to obtain the postmastership of Stone Ridge, a position that would allow her to maintain the family home. The wealthy antiques collector Henry Francis du Pont visited the house in August 1933, inspired by a reading of Reynolds's *Dutch Houses*, and was especially interested in its interior woodwork. Returning to Winterthur, his Delaware estate, du Pont wrote President Roosevelt as author of the "admirable preface" to Reynolds's book. He reminded the president that the Lounsberys' house was "the finest example of architecture extant in Ulster County," and described Miss Lounsbery as "an exceptionally intelligent lady who takes the keenest interest in her house and is trying to preserve it in its original condition." He found the house "is in rather bad repair," however, and father and daughter "are not very well to do." She told du Pont that to be appointed postmaster (as some of her ancestors had been) would allow her

IX-1. Wynkoop-Lounsbery House

to "look after the house properly," and he urged FDR to make this appointment. As a Delawarean, du Pont was reluctant to interfere with a New York appointment, but "I feel very strongly ... that if anything can be done to help Miss Lounsbery it will also be helping to preserve one of the best and most interesting houses in New York State."

The president replied quickly to du Pont: "I know the Wynkoop house well, and I will take up the post office matter with the Postmaster General," and he indeed asked Postmaster General Farley to appoint Miss Lounsbery so as "to keep up the repair of an historic, old house." In 1935, when the incumbent postmaster's appointment expired, Miss Lounsbery replaced him and served until her retirement about 1961. She was able to preserve her house without further assistance from du Pont. In the 1950s he was still so taken with the blue of some of its interior woodwork that he sought to reproduce the color in a small space he called the Wynkoop Room, whose sole relation to the Stone Ridge house was its color. When the famous collector wrote Miss Lounsbery that he was using her blue, she failed to reply. Du Pont supposed she might be dead, but she survived until 1988.

While Miss Lounsbery was able to maintain the house, the Dutch barn that stood just north of the house (visible in the photo of the house published by Reynolds) collapsed about 1970. Between 1999 and 2001, Gary Tinterow and James Joseph replaced it with a Dutch barn (c. 1830) that had stood near Cooperstown in Otsego County before being taken down and reassembled in Stone Ridge under the supervision of Harry Hansen.

IX–2 Sally Tock's Inn
Main St. (Rte. 209), Stone Ridge. Eighteenth century (1919 addition by Myron S. Teller). NR

This two-story stone house, with entrance on the left side of the façade, was built close to the old King's Highway and is said to have been operated as a tavern by Johannes Tack (pronounced and sometimes spelled "Tock") during the time of the Revolution, and then from 1790 by his wife Sally. Washington spent the night of November 15, 1782, at the Wynkoop house, directly across the highway, and tradition has it that his officers were entertained at Tack's inn. While the inn's stonework resembles the Wynkoop house, the

*IX-2. Sally Tock's Inn
(c. 1915 postcard)*

façade is less orderly in its arrangement of door and windows. In 1798 the building had only one and a half stories. The addition of a full second story several years later may explain the irregular arrangement. The Federal-style front porch or stoop with seats built into its sides is of unknown date.

In 1914 Miss Sarah C. Lounsbery, whose family had long owned the Wynkoop house, opened a tea room, called Sally Tock's Inn, in what had been the colonial tavern. On a card printed with a silhouette of a lovely Sally Tock and the date 1772, when the inn was said to have opened, Miss Lounsbery advertised "Tea ... Light Luncheons. Card and Dancing Parties Accommodated. Automobile Picnic Luncheons Prepared if Notified in Advance." The silhouette and date also appeared on an "old time swing sign at the doorway," updated as a large roadside sign illuminated by electric light bulbs to attract motorists. Miss Lounsbery's brochure, however, focused on the colonial origins of the inn and the likelihood that Major Wynkoop and General Washington had entered the inn and "tossed off a bumper or two of cider, or perhaps a refreshing drink of tea!" Therefore, "today the motorist would scarcely wish to whizz by and miss a visit to the quaint old tavern, likewise a cup of tea brewed by a direct descendant of Sally Tock"— presumably Sarah Lounsbery.

No rowdy tavern or working-class diner, Miss Lounsbery's colonial inn catered to refined patrons, including these full- or part-time residents of the county: Mrs. Gerard W. Betz, wife of the Kingston architect; Jules Breuchaud, a client of Myron Teller; W. A. Carl, another Teller client; Florence E. Cordts, of the brick-making family; Julia Dillon, artist; Mr. and Mrs. Watson M. Freer, clients of Wilson Eyre; Mrs. George Hutton, of another brick-making family; Mrs. George Inness, Jr., wife of the artist; H. Lincoln Rogers, architect at the Ashokan Reservoir; Olive B. Sarre, of Yama Farms; Andrew J. Snyder, of Rosendale; and Myron and Jane Teller, the architect and his first wife. On July 28, 1916, Myron and Jane Teller signed separately, he giving his address as Kingston, she as West Shokan (her Watson Hollow Inn would soon supersede Sally Tock's). Others sought out the inn from a greater distance—Mrs. John E. Adriance came from Poughkeepsie, Mrs. J. Gardner Cassatt from Philadelphia, Miss Edith Elliott from Boston, Mr. and Mrs. Gilbert H. Grosvenor from Washington, Mr. and Mrs. William Barclay Parsons from New York, Mr. and Mrs. Homer Ramsdell from Newburgh, and Mrs. Edmund P. Rogers from Hyde Park. These names appear in a beautifully bound guest register with entries from May 23, 1914, through August 21, 1916, kept on a table with quill pen and candlestick near the front door.

The upper-class enclave of Stone Ridge added another member, probably in 1917, when Emily Crane Chadbourne (1871–1964), a wealthy and cosmopolitan heir of the Crane plumbing fortune, took ownership of the inn as her summer home. Chadbourne, a notable collector of art and antiques, shared the home with her companion, Ellen Newbold LaMotte, a member of the Huguenot Society of America, a Johns-Hopkins-trained nurse on World War I battlefields, and later an author who attacked the opium trade. In June 1919 Myron Teller acquired photos of the old building before drafting plans for its alteration and enlargement in July. Teller added a substantial stone wing to the rear of the inn that included a large third-floor bedroom and ground-floor kitchen. The plans called for fireplaces on three levels, "hewn rafters," and "old oak beams." However, the house expanded for a Crane was anything but primitive in its up-to-date heating, plumbing, and electric service.

Chadbourne and LaMotte lived in Paris in the 1910s, where they were part of the artistic-literary and lesbian world of Gertrude Stein and Alice Toklas. Chadbourne's portrait (now in the Art Institute of Chicago), painted in Paris in 1922 by the fashionable Japanese artist Tsugouharu Foujita, is a contrived image of icy preciousness, idleness, and sophistication—occupying a world apart from early America and from nearly all her Ulster County neighbors. (Her sometime neighbor, Besse Leggett, was a friend; see IX–6.) Chadbourne collected a wide range of art from around the globe, including American decorative arts, and Helen Reynolds credited her in the 1920s with making the inn "a noteworthy repository for Americana." In 1937 Henry Francis du Pont visited the inn when he came to admire the Wynkoop house, and du Pont subsequently hosted Chadbourne for lunch and a tour of his collections at Winterthur. It is an open question whether the building expanded for Chadbourne can—as Kevin Murphy has argued in the case of Colonial expansions and revivals for gay and lesbian New Englanders—be identified as characteristic of the kind of space preferred by gays and lesbians, thanks to its relative isolation in the rural

hamlet of Stone Ridge and the complexity and seclusion of the spaces Teller added at the rear.

Chadbourne willed Sally Tock's to William Walton (c. 1910–1994), her niece's former husband, who continued to maintain it as a summer residence. Walton was a journalist, painter, and close friend of President John F. Kennedy. He served as chairman of the U. S. Commission of Fine Arts, overseeing federal monuments and construction in Washington from 1963 to 1971.

IX–3 John Lounsbery House (Stone Ridge Library)
3700 Main St. (Rte. 209), Stone Ridge. 1798. NR

The façade of this building appears as a more ordered, more Georgian version of the two-story, three-bay, side-entrance façade of Sally Tock's Inn, built earlier a few doors south on Main Street. (The construction date of 1798 is firmly established; according to Stone Ridge historian Charles Cullen, the 1798 Federal Direct Tax list indicates that the two-story stone house of John Lounsbery, a blacksmith, was new and not yet finished.) The sidelights flanking the door here, another feature in the Georgian period, are absent at the inn. However, the stones of the inn's façade are more regular and rectangular than the rubble or fieldstone of John Lounsbery's house.

The building was owned by members of the Lounsbery and Hasbrouck families until 1909, when Julia Hasbrouck Dwight, who had resided here as a child, presented it to the community for

IX-3. John Lounsbery House (DeWitt photo, 1941)

use as a library, which was established that year. In 1946 Louise Hasbrouck Zimm wrote appreciatively of the library: "The old stone house with its two-section Dutch door, its square entry hall, banistered staircase and fireplaces has a homelike, hospitable quality, enhanced by its rare old furniture, portraits and other gifts." Although the library has been expanded and its facilities modernized, much of the charm of the historic library remains. Its important local history collection includes photos gathered by Myron Teller of early buildings in the county, and Teller apparently was responsible for Colonial Revival renovations to the library in the 1910s.

IX–4 Dr. Jacob Louis Hasbrouck House (Maple Lawn)
3705 Main St. (Rte. 209), Stone Ridge.
1843. NR

An alternative to the pedimented, temple-fronted Greek Revival house, this façade is dominated by a broad, low, six-column Ionic porch. Above is a compressed second story with windows cut into the entablature, while below, the basement rises high enough to merit shuttered windows. Small Ionic columns define the main doorway. Two tall windows, extending to the floor, open into the front parlor.

The house's composition is not a common Greek Revival type, yet it does closely resemble the Powers House (today known as Beattie-Powers Place), built in the 1830s in the village of Catskill, Greene County. And it is a worthy neighbor of the magnificent Wynkoop-Lounsbery house next door.

IX-4. Maple Lawn

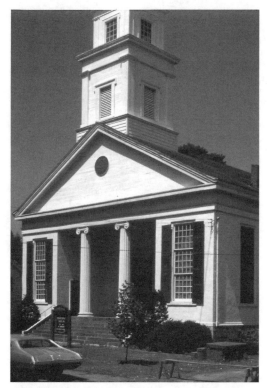

IX-5. Marbletown Reformed Protestant Dutch Church (1971 photo)

IX–5 Reformed Protestant Dutch Church (Marbletown Reformed Church)
Main St. (Rte. 209), Stone Ridge. 1851. NR

The cornerstone of this Reformed church was laid June 17, 1851, and the building was dedicated in 1852. Among the inscribed foundation stones is one marked "JOHN BRODHEAD / Anno Domini 1792"—the year a previous Marbletown church had been erected. The present church's Greek Revival façade is unusual for Ulster County in being distyle in antis—two columns (here of the Ionic order) placed between projecting walls (here the plain antae lack their characteristic pilaster-like moldings). This format allowed for a sheltered porch and the dignity of two columns without the expense of four. It also permitted an un-Greek opening up of the façade with a large window on each side of the recessed porch. The columns and antae support an entablature and substantial pediment. An early-twentieth-century photo shows a three-stage cupola, the lowest with louvered openings characteristic of a belfry, and the highest with an open railing topped by acroteria and pinnacles. Since c. 1969 the lower two stages have supported a pointed spire unknown to the Greeks.

Devotees of the Greek Revival will also want to see the Doric monument to Elizabeth W. O'Neil (died October 12, 1847), daughter of Edward and Delia O'Neil, in the cemetery of the North Marbletown Reformed Church on Route 209.

IX-6 Francis H. Leggett Estate, Ridgely Manor (Vivekananda Retreat, Ridgely)
101 Leggett Rd., Stone Ridge. 1892.

As seen from Leggett Road, Francis Leggett's manor house resembles one of the lesser mansions put up in Newport, Rhode Island, in the 1880s, such as the H. A. C. Taylor house by the renowned architects, McKim, Mead & White. Francis Leggett's architect was possibly Charles C. Haight, a notable New York architect said to have been chosen by Leggett to design a portico and belfry for St. Peter's Episcopal Church, now the Marbletown Community Center. The manor house carried over from McKim's Taylor house the clapboard walls, hipped roof, prominent chimneys, semicircular porch (on the south façade), and details from Georgian and later Classical Revival architecture in America. An open loggia on the southwestern corner mingles stately Ionic columns and the promise of the pleasures of country life. The opposite, north, façade has a grander, six-column Ionic portico evocative of the Old South. It also is graced with an arched window (lighting the staircase) and other windows whose asymmetrical placement in a generally classical composition was a foible of McKim's seen in his Edgar house (1884–1886) in Newport. While certainly designed under McKim's influence, the manor house was, according to Francis Leggett's daughter Frances, intended to be reminiscent of an old house in Delaware admired by her father and owned by the Misses Ridgely, who were distant relatives. The cornerstone of the manor house is inscribed "Ridgely 1892."

Francis (Frank) H. Leggett (1840–1909) was a wealthy wholesale grocer in New York. His estate included the c. 1750 stone house of Isaac Hasbrouck as well as a c. 1842 inn, and he put up other buildings in addition to the manor house, among them a stable and carriage house, casino with bowling alley, and a large house known as the Big Cottage or Clematis. By spring 1894 Leggett's estate caught the attention of *The New York Times*: "Stone Ridge ... has changed from a sleepy country village to a smart place since Francis H. Leggett of New-York erected his palatial Summer residence, Ridgely Manor, there. The house is large and handsome and cost $30,000. Last year Mr. Leggett spent about $100,000 on the place, building a carriage house and stables and laying out roads. He has built several cottages near his home, which during the Summer are occupied by guests." In fact, Leggett advertised three "mountain cottages to rent": The Shawangunk (also known as The Inn) had sixteen rooms with an

IX-6. Ridgely Manor (1998 photo)

eight-room annex; The Clematis had nineteen rooms; while Valley View had fourteen. The grounds were handsomely landscaped as a pastoral, upper-class English park. The plantings took into account the views of the Catskills to the north and the Shawangunks to the south, which had attracted Leggett to the property.

Ridgely Manor was, among other things, a visible display of wealth, as the figures quoted in the *Times* were to confirm. The Leggetts—in 1895 Francis married Besse Sturges (1852–1931), a widow—were socially ambitious. The 1909 *New York Social Register* identifies him as a member of the Union League and Metropolitan Club. The latter club had been organized by J. P. Morgan "primarily for his friends who were not accepted in others" and occupied an opulent Renaissance Revival palace (1893) designed by McKim's firm. The estate allowed the Leggetts to enjoy a social life that made its way into the society news of the *Times*. Christmas 1899 house parties at Seward Webb's estate at Shelburne Farms, Vermont, George Vanderbilt's at Biltmore, North Carolina, and Frederick Vanderbilt's at Hyde Park-on-the-Hudson all were noteworthy, but the Leggetts' party at Ridgely Manor was written up as "one of the largest." Ridgely Manor was a visible sign of wealth and social prestige. Moreover its name and colonial appearance signified Francis Leggett's ancestral connection to a leading family of colonial Delaware; Ridgelys still maintained an eighteenth-century house next to the State House in Dover. Leggett and his wife were not to be confused with one of the new millionaires from the uncouth immigrant class.

According to upper-class notions of the Gilded Age, a manor like Ridgely was unsuited for year-round occupation. Moreover, Besse had social aspirations higher than her husband and New York offered, and she found that her taste in architecture differed from Francis's. For her, the Stone Ridge house was too "plain-quiet-colonial." Her taste ran toward English and Continental upper-class people and design. In August 1901 the *Times* reported that Mrs. Leggett had arrived from England, would spend the late summer and autumn at Ridgely Manor, then return to occupy

a house in London for the season. In 1905 her daughter Alberta married a man who expected to become the ninth Earl of Sandwich. He did, Alberta became the Countess of Sandwich, and their son was known as Viscount Hinchingbrooke. The Leggetts—especially Besse and her unmarried sister Josephine—were also attracted to a Hindu monk from India, Swami Vivekananda, who visited the estate in 1895 and 1899. In 1997 his followers undertook the purchase and careful preservation of Ridgely Manor, now the Vivekananda Retreat.

IX-7 Sanger and Harriet Carleton House
Cottekill Rd., Stone Ridge. c. 1800, 1860, 1932.

Myron Teller's hardware is abundant throughout this handsome house that Teller apparently altered about 1932 for Dr. Sanger S. Carleton (1882–1947), a Manhattan dentist, and his wife Harriet Hasbrouck Carleton (1904–1981). In 1941 *The New York Times* reported that Mrs. Sanger Carleton was assisting Frances Leggett with a country dance at Ridgely Manor (see preceding entry, IX–6) to benefit the British-American Ambulance Corps. The Carletons' barn was fitted with a dance floor and minstrel gallery, while the attached shed housed a long bar, and behind the barn was a stone terrace and fireplace—all, it seems, to meet the partying needs of the Callabar Club, a group of Stone Ridge friends.

IX-7. Carleton House

IX-8. Hardenbergh House (c. 1920 photo from Myron Teller collection)

IX-8 Hardenbergh House and Barn
Mill Dam Road. c. 1762 and later.

Near the stone-ended but frame-fronted house built by Leonard Hardenbergh about 1762 stands a deteriorating Dutch barn (undoubtedly of later date) whose structural members are increasingly visible as the wooden siding disappears. The barn

IX-8A. Hardenbergh Barn

is characteristic of barns erected in the Dutch-settled regions of New York and New Jersey in the eighteenth and nineteenth centuries in its wooden construction (here with a substantial stone foundation), gable roof, and wide entrance (the doors now missing) centered under the triangular gable end. Wagons pulled into the central area of the barn, used as a threshing floor and work area, while animal stalls were typically located to the sides. Hay, corn, and other field products would be stored in the vast loft defined by the triangular gables.

An early waterpowered gristmill stood near the house in 1935 when the property was cited as having remained in the Hardenbergh family for over 200 years, but now only bits of its stone foundation are visible. Nearby, on Bogarts Lane, is the well-preserved Bogart barn, a c. 1790 Dutch barn joined to two early-nineteenth-century barns, and, a few yards away, an early stone house.

IX–9 Hardenbergh-Davenport House
Rte. 209 at Mill Dam Rd., Stone Ridge.
c. 1815 and 1870.

A prime and highly visible example of the Gothic Revival in the county, this house represents the updating of an earlier and plainer house. Only after mid-century, when the taste of Andrew Jackson Downing for the Gothic was ascendant, would an unidentified designer have added the triple front gables with bargeboards and finials, as well as the bay window to the side of the porch. The tall windows, reaching down to the floor of the two main rooms, suggest the summertime pleasure of opening up the interior to the porch; a c. 1900 photo shows a gentleman in a rocking chair on the porch with an open window behind him.

IX–10 Bloom House (Parsonage of the Dutch Reformed Church; Katharine Hasbrouck's Shop in the Garden)
3385 Rte. 209, Stone Ridge. c. 1751 (1926 altered, probably by Myron S. Teller).

This appealing eighteenth-century stone house with an asymmetrically placed front door was remodeled in 1926 as a residence for Miss Katharine Hasbrouck. In 1929 she opened it as a tea and gift shop, which she ran with her companion Anna Budenbach. Louise Hasbrouck Zimm described the enterprise in 1946: "The Shop in the Garden, whose proprietor is Katharine Hasbrouck, of the old Stone Ridge family, is a gift shop of unusual charm in an old stone house once the parsonage of the ... Dutch Reformed Church. Tea, with toast, jam and cakes served either next to the shop or in her beautiful garden, is another attraction of the place, which is visited by shoppers from a wide area." Delicately colored postcards printed by the Albertype Co. portrayed the lovely combination of old stone house and garden "bowered in bloom" where, as newspaper publicity suggested, "one may happily reminisce back to the good old days of the walloon." Cards written by women to women recorded delightful times spent in the charming garden or, in winter, by the quaint living-room fireplace.

Miss Hasbrouck followed after another woman of old Stone Ridge family, Sarah Lounsbery, whose quaint Colonial tea room at Sally Tock's had catered to a similar clientele before World War I (see IX–2). One postcard of Miss Hasbrouck's house shows the road frontage defined by a white picket fence with lovely morning glories, and the gate fitted with prominent hardware, probably by Myron Teller. The 1926 alterations were undoubtedly by Teller, since the shed-roofed dormers, front porch, and rear, glassy lean-to resemble others that Teller added to stone houses. Moreover, Teller put photos of

IX-9. Hardenbergh-Davenport House (1976 photo)

IX-10. Bloom House (Shop in the Garden)
(c. 1930 Albertype Co. postcard)

IX-10A. Shop in the Garden (c. 1930 Albertype
Co. postcard)

the Shop in the Garden in his Stone Ridge scrapbook (preserved at the Stone Ridge Library). In the garden a small structure with porch and terrace was reminiscent of the setting for outdoor tea at Jane Teller's Watson Hollow Inn (see XII–5). Teller's inn attracted automobile parties touring the Ashokan Reservoir, as did Miss Hasbrouck's shop—a postcard map that she distributed pictured the shop with roads to the reservoir.

The similar stone house (but with three shed-roofed dormers and symmetrical façade) just to the north at 3355 Route 209 has been identified as the John Broadhead house, built in 1791. It was altered and enlarged by Myron Teller in 1920 for Katharine Hasbrouck's brother, Dr. John Roswell Hasbrouck of New York City.

Still another old stone house north on Route 209, just beyond its intersection with Old Tongore Road, was restored in the 1930s for *Saturday Evening Post* illustrator Samuel Nelson Abbott (1874–1953). In 1941 Abbott made a sketch suggesting the appearance of the Reformed Dutch Church of Marbletown (1744–1746), a gable-roofed stone building with cupola. The restoration of Abbott's house was credited to "craftsman" William Turner, a carpenter who certainly repaired the woodwork and made new shutters and an oak chest. However, the shed-roofed dormers and the porch with elliptical arch and side benches resemble Teller's work, and Teller's Stone Ridge scrapbook includes photos before and after the restoration. Turner also built a one-room studio for Abbott near the barn behind the house.

IX–11 P. A. Cook House (President's Residence, SUNY Ulster)

3312 Rte. 209, Stone Ridge. c. 1929.
Verna Cook Salomonsky.

This dignified white Colonial Revival house was designed by one of the few prominent women architects of the time, Verna Cook Salomonsky (1890–1978), who was trained at Columbia University's School of Architecture and at the École Speciale d'Architecture in Paris. She worked in the office of noted architect Dwight James Baum before establishing an office in Manhattan in 1920 with her husband Edgar Salomonsky. In 1937 she became a member of the American Institute of Architects, and *The New York Times* described her as "the only woman architect admitted to membership in the Architectural League," a prestigious professional society in New York. She had by 1937 designed hundreds of houses, many in Westchester County. Tragically her husband committed suicide in their Scarsdale home on Christmas Day 1929, the first Christmas of the Great Depression. In 1923 the Salomonskys had published *An Exemplar of Antique Furniture Design: A Collection of Measured Drawings of Furniture in the Metropolitan Museum of Art*, and in 1931 the widow published a similar portfolio, *Masterpieces of Furniture Design*.

Although the front door of the Cook house is divided in the Dutch manner, and benches flanking the door recall a Dutch stoop, the design

IX-11. Cook House (1976 photo)

cept "standardized designs" or consider houses to be like "automobiles, prefabricated and bought ... off the shelf." The house she designed for the "Town of Tomorrow" at the 1939 New York World's Fair was Colonial, but with walls of hollow tile and stucco.

In 1968 the Cook house was purchased to serve as President's Residence of SUNY Ulster.

IX-12 Bevier House (Ulster County Historical Society)
2682 Rte. 209. Begun c. 1690. NR

of the house belongs not so much to the Hudson Valley Dutch Colonial Revival but rather to the New England–inspired Colonial Revival widely adopted across America in the twenties. There is little ornament, but careful attention is paid to proportion and composition. The massive chimney, the broad surfaces of roof and walls, and the dormer windows rising from the upper wall into the roof are found in other houses by the architect. In January 1935 the Cook house was published in the *American Architect*, a leading professional journal. Later it was featured in an ad for Cabot's "double-white" paint, which had been applied to the shingled and stucco walls, while the roof had been treated with Cabot's "creosote shingle stain." Not only did Verna Cook Salomonsky's work appear in professional journals, but she was a frequent contributor of articles and designs to popular magazines, including *American Home*, *House Beautiful*, and *House and Garden*. In 1938 the *Times* reported that she joined other Westchester architects in advocating the continued use of Colonial forms. She was open to the influence of modernism, but doubted homeowners would soon ac-

This underappreciated landmark preserves a wonderful collection of old-fashioned furnishings, artifacts, and curiosities within its walls of limestone blocks quarried on or near the site. The architectural history of the house, the complex evolution of its form over time, has yet to be unraveled, despite a number of serious studies. It was recorded in measured drawings by the Historic American Buildings Survey in 1940–1941, and studies by architects Myron S. Teller in 1953 and Kenneth Hewes Barricklo in 2002 indicate that the oldest section of the house included the west-facing window and door of today's kitchen. This one-room house (with cellar and garret loft) was constructed for Andries Pieterse Van-Leuven, a soldier and farmer born in the Netherlands. (However, architectural historian Neil Larson points out that VanLeuven's house may have been elsewhere, and the oldest part of the Bevier house may date after 1700.) Additions were made in the eighteenth century, first by the

IX-12. Bevier House prior to 1800 (reconstruction drawing by Teller)

IX-12A. Bevier House (1971 photo)

VanLeuvens, and after 1715 by the Beviers. Louis Bevier (1684–1753) purchased the property in 1715, and his descendants owned the house until it was given to the Ulster County Historical Society in 1938. By 1800, according to Myron Teller's 1953 reconstruction drawing, the original house had become an appendage to a larger, story-and-a-half house whose façade consisted of a doorway with three windows to the left and two windows to the right, the basis for the present façade facing Route 209.

One of the sections of the present house was built in 1751 for Louis Bevier, Jr. (1717–1772), whose account book provides a wealth of information about the construction of one room and its hearth by some eighteen skilled and unskilled men working under Johannis Bevier, head mason, and Levi Pawling, head carpenter. Louis Bevier, Jr., owned several slaves, but their labor is not recorded in the account book. Neil Larson, with the assistance of Eric Roth, discovered this document in the archives of the Huguenot Historical Society. It is an extremely rare record of stone-house construction (unique for Ulster County), and Larson has used it to elucidate how such buildings were erected, as well as the roles and status of the men who did the building.

Tradition says that the house burned in 1800 and was rebuilt using much of the earlier fabric of the house while expanding it to two and a half stories with a hipped roof. By 1870 this expansion included the raising of the stone walls of the earliest, c. 1690, segment so that the house took on its present boxy shape. Louis Bevier (1822–1911)

made extensive changes to the interior, including the removal of wood-burning fireplaces in favor of cast-iron stoves and the substitution of 2-over-2 window sash for the old 12-over-12 sash. He also added an observation room atop the roof and a front porch, both later removed. Among the many mysteries concerning the chronology of the house is the date of the stone with finely carved sundial markings at the southwest corner of the house.

The historical society has altered the appearance of the property since 1938 when the house and about an acre of land were given to the society by Louis Bevier of New York City and his sister, Mrs. Ralph G. Wright of New Brunswick, New Jersey. The carriage house was demolished in 1945, apparently at the instigation of Emily Crane Chadbourne of Stone Ridge who, with Judge G. D. B. Hasbrouck and Edward Coykendall, had supported the acquisition of the Bevier House by the society. Myron Teller's detailed 1953 survey of the house included a six-page report, plans, and photos and notes on five early doors and their hardware, his special interest. He was responsible for the restoration of the hardware of the c. 1690 doorway, using two pairs of old strap hinges removed from cellar doors as well as new hand-forged pieces. Teller also opened a fireplace in the onetime kitchen, where he found an early crane, and loaned hardware from his collection to complete the picture of an old hearth. After Teller's death the historical society in the 1960s secured a larger meeting space in the central first-story room by removing the stairway added by Louis Bevier about 1870. In the same period the society transformed the old rear lean-to, once used as a scullery or summer kitchen, into a room to display early tools. This room was the project of John Paul Remensnyder of Saugerties, a retired chemical industry executive, president of the society from 1963 to 1974, and a notable collector of antique stoneware and metal crafts whose stoneware collection was exhibited at the Smithsonian Institution in 1978. In 2007 the room was named in honor of Peter Sinclair to recognize his advocacy for the study of early American crafts and trades.

IX-13. Oliver House
(1977 photo)

IX–13 Oliver House
2455 Rte. 209. c. 1840 and 1876?

Here the early stone house building tradition was refined with regularly cut stonework, and it encountered the Gothic Revival. Three Gothic gables face the highway, each with a finial and decorative bargeboards, while both sides of the house are fitted with a pair of similarly treated gables. The Oliver gables resemble the three at the front of the Hardenbergh-Davenport house, south on Route 209, even to the T-shaped cutouts in the bargeboards (see IX–9). Below each Gothic gable of the Oliver façade are Italianate features—a circular window with keystone-accented frame and a two-part, round-arched window. Beneath the central circular window is a stone that appears to be marked: ReB 1876/CCO. The "CCO" may refer to Cornelius Oliver, listed in the 1871 Ulster County *Business Directory* as a Marbletown farmer of 120 acres.

Barry Benepe suggests that this is an example of the "gothic vernacular"—no architect is known to have been involved with the design—and that the rear wing of the house is earlier, about 1840, from the period of the Greek Revival. The John Pettit house on Clinton Avenue in Kingston, illustrated in Beers's 1875 *Atlas* (see VI–10), also belongs to the "gothic vernacular" and had three Gothic gables distinguishing the façade (with another on the side elevation).

IX–14 Schoonmaker House
(Van Aken Farm)
Rte. 209 at County Rte. 2. c. 1785.

This house, identified with the Schoonmaker family, attracts the attention of motorists keen about colonial antiquities, standing as it does on a rise above Route 209. Since Erma DeWitt photographed the house in 1947, it has acquired additional dormer windows, and Route 209 (the Old Mine Road) has been shifted away from the house. Still, it is evidently very much a fieldstone farmhouse of the old, non-gentrified sort—a weathered barn stands close to the house, and in 2007 *Kingston Daily Freeman* photographer Tania Barricklo recorded Elsa Wilber, daughter of Arthur L. Van Aken who bought the farm in 1909, selling eggs from her side doorway. Helen Reynolds admired such places worn by time and used by

IX-14. Schoonmaker House (DeWitt photo, 1947)

Dutch-descended generations, but she did not include it in her book, presumably because it dated after her 1776 cut-off point.

Five of the seven bays facing Route 209 are organized around a central doorway as English-influenced stone houses tended to be after the Revolution. The two-bay section to the right may be earlier; the gable end of this section includes a projecting Dutch beehive oven and a doorway facing County Route 2.

IX–15 Kripplebush School (Kripplebush Schoolhouse Museum)
County Rte. 2, Kripplebush. 1857 (closed 1951). NR

From Route 209, County Route 2 curves through the picturesque hamlet of Kripplebush, passing around the Greek Revival–style Methodist Church (1857) and shortly arriving at this nice example of the one-room school, typical of its kind but for the little window pushed to the far right of the front wall. The deed for the schoolhouse land, dated September 14, 1857, is preserved within the museum, open summer Sunday afternoons. Next door is the c. 1910 Lodge Hall with material relating to the history of the area.

The 1857 Kripplebush school must have been better constructed than many of its predecessors. A schoolhouse erected about 1763 in Marbletown was described in a letter written that year by Charles Dewitt from Hurley as being "built ... after the old fashion ... a large heap of white oak,

black oak and perhaps other sorts of timber piled up to convenient height and two or three holes cut in for the children and light to pass." This was apparently a log schoolhouse.

In *Small Wonder: The Little Red Schoolhouse in History and Memory*, Jonathan Zimmerman points out that by the late 1990s some 450 one-room American schoolhouses had been restored and opened to the public as "sentimental icons." Americans of many political stripes idealized the "rural school as a quaintly beautiful institution that encouraged individual initiative and self-reliance, drew local citizens together, and protected students from the confusion, corruption, and commercialism of the big city."

IX–16 Reformed Church (former)
Lower Bone Hollow Rd. off County Rte. 2, Lyonsville. 1857–1859 (closed 2001).

The white-painted, green-shuttered Lyonsville church was a perfect example of the Greek Revival adapted to the needs of a small congregation—a gable-roofed rectangular box, with one-story cupola sheltering a bell, was made to resemble (however modestly) a Greek temple through corner pilasters supporting an entablature and front gable treated as a pediment. The doorway and cupola were fitted out with pilasters and crowning cornice. Sadly, this was among the last functioning survivors of a type of diminutive rural church meant to serve families in the vicinity in the pre-automobile age.

IX-15. Kripplebush School

IX-16. Lyonsville Reformed Church (c. 1980 photo)

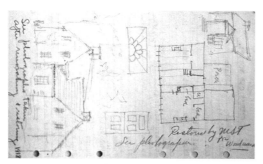

*IX-17. Van Demark House
(sketches by Teller, c. 1918)*

IX-17 Van Demark or Van Dermarke House (Van Lear Woodward House)

115 Buck Rd. Before 1797, 1810 (altered by Myron S. Teller 1917–1918 and before 1925 for Eda Perry Woodward and Van Lear Woodward).

Finely sited on a slope with views to the south, this early stone house received the improving touch of Myron Teller. A stone at the corner of the façade is inscribed "Jacob S. Vandemark/ 1810," but the 1797 assessment for Marbletown indicates that Vandemark was already the owner of a 21-by-26-foot stone house, apparently then enlarged in 1810. In 1917 Teller undertook the restoration and remodeling of the house, which he referred to as the "Van Dermarke Homestead," as a summer home for Eda Perry Woodward and her husband Van Lear Woodward (c. 1890–1951). A few years later Teller designed other improvements (including modern lighting, heating, and plumbing), allowing the house to become the Woodwards' permanent residence. Eda Perry Woodward claimed old New York ancestry, including "the celebrated Lefferts of Brooklyn," as well as a link to Oliver Cromwell. Van Lear Woodward was a New York businessman proud of his Dutch ancestry—although his seventeenth-century forebears settled in Maryland rather than the Hudson Valley. His blue blood permitted his inclusion in the *Social Register* and rise to the rank of major in the "silk stocking" Seventh Regiment, New York National Guard.

The architect added dormers, joined the hall and parlor to make a large living room, transformed "the old farm kitchen" into a dining room, created a new Colonial staircase, and repaired and installed old wrought-iron latches and hinges. Teller included a photo of the restored house with his article, "Early Colonial Hand Forged Iron Work," in the *Architectural Record* (May 1925). Sometime after 1933 the front porch was removed and a screened porch with stone piers built on the west end of the house.

IX-18* Benjamin I. and Rachel Hasbrouck House
2468 Lucas Turnpike (County Rte. 1). 1752 and 1806.

Although very close to the highway, this landmark has been effectively screened from roadside observation. Still, thanks to earlier photos by Erma DeWitt and others, as well as studies by Helen Wilkinson Reynolds in the 1920s and the Metropolitan Museum of Art in recent years, the history of this early house can be determined with an unusual degree of certainty. Reynolds identified two inscribed stones on the exterior, one with the initials I B V, F K, E L, and the date 1752, and the other with the initials B I HB, R HB, and the date 1806. The 1752 builders/owners of the house are not yet known, but Reynolds identified Benjamin I. and Rachel Hasbrouck as the married couple responsible for the 1806 expansion.

The 1752 house probably consisted of two rooms, both facing south. The west wall of the

*IX-18. Benjamin and Rachel Hasbrouck House
(DeWitt photo, mid-twentieth century)*

to the doorway, suggesting that the façade was lengthened at least once. Sally Tock's Inn nearby in Stone Ridge is also a two-story stone inn, but its façade of doorway and two windows to the right was never lengthened.

Opened as a restaurant by John Novi in 1969, the inn was restored (including 2-over-2 sash replaced with 12-over-12 sash) and became a celebrated culinary destination.

IX-20 Delaware & Hudson Canal (ruins and museum)
High Falls. 1828 and 1847–1850. NHL

Visitors should begin with a stop at the D & H Canal Historical Society and Museum (23 Mohonk Road, just off Route 213), which has exhibits relating to the canal that operated between the anthracite coal regions of Pennsylvania and the Hudson River at Rondout between 1829 and 1898. Especially interesting is a working model of a lock. The museum is housed in the former and much-altered St. John's Episcopal Church (1883–1885), originally a building blending the Gothic Revival and Shingle Style, and in the church's former parish hall (1902–1903).

With a map obtained at the museum, explore the hamlet's historic sites and take the "Five Locks Walk" on the towpath along a stretch of the canal that was rerouted when the canal was enlarged in the 1840s to accommodate 140-ton boats. The walk begins near the famous Depuy Canal House (see IX–19) at Lock 16. The lock's well-preserved stone walls are things of beauty fashioned of precisely cut stones laid without mortar. It is also possible to walk to the surviving masonry abutments of the High Falls Aqueduct, the canal's

western room had an English-style fireplace and gumwood paneling with cupboard doors and fluted pilasters. In 1806 the house was extended to the south, with a new south façade, and some of the paneling in the west room was removed. The remainder of the west wall paneling was acquired by the Metropolitan Museum in 1933—no doubt after a careful reading of Reynolds's book—and the next year was reconfigured and permanently installed in the museum's American Wing. The 1806 façade bears signs of the Federal or Neoclassic period in the classical treatment of the doorway with arched fanlight and the pair of semicircular windows under the eaves. Similar openings in the gables are false windows. The front dormer was added at a later date.

IX-19 Depuy House (Depuy Canal House Inn)
1315 Rte. 213, High Falls. 1797 and later. NR

The inscription "S. & A. DEPUY A.D. 1797" on a stone above a second-story window on the east façade identifies the original owners of this roadside tavern; in 1806 Simeon Depuy paid a license fee for a public house here. The inn profited from the opening of the Delaware and Hudson Canal in 1828. At first the canal ran a little to the west of the inn, but a rerouting in 1847 brought the canal and new lock 16 to within a few steps of the east front. While the first- and second-story windows are aligned vertically, they are not balanced in relation

suspension aqueduct over the Rondout Creek. The aqueduct was designed by engineer John Augustus Roebling, later to gain fame as the designer of the Brooklyn Bridge (begun 1867). The abutment on the south side of the creek is more easily accessible; the northern abutment is difficult to reach, but retains a stone block inscribed "J. A. ROE-BLING, {SUPERSTRUCTURE/ G. WATSON, {MASON/ Built A.D. 1849." This aqueduct replaced one built with masonry arches and was a great wooden trunk suspended from wire cables anchored into the rock on either side of the Rondout Creek. A fire about 1917 destroyed the trunk, and the cables and iron suspender rods were later removed.

The canal's telegraph office, although in disrepair and not easily seen, is directly on the abandoned towpath at the site of Lock 15 (the Collector's Lock). The simple wooden building retains many original details—doors, 6-over-6 window sash, shutters, and roof projecting toward the towpath—so that its weathered surfaces seem to embody the spirit of the long-past canal era. Nearby is a transportation relic of the next century, a c. 1950 streamlined trailer that by the 1990s was primitive housing embedded in nature.

IX-20. Delaware & Hudson Canal Lock 16

IX–21* Mohonk Mountain House

Lake Mohonk (a small portion of the Mountain House is in the Town of Rochester). 1879 to 1902, with later alterations and additions. Wilson Brothers & Co., Napoleon LeBrun & Sons, James E. Ware & Sons, and others. NHL

The Mountain House at Lake Mohonk is among the county's greatest architectural treasures, placed in a landscape setting of mountaintop lake and cliffs, with glorious vistas. The site has attracted painters since the time of the Hudson River School. The artist Daniel Huntington discovered Mohonk as a landscape subject in 1837 and many years later was a regular guest at the Mountain House, which published his endorsement of its surroundings: "Bold and savage features are combined with the gentle and picturesque in inexhaustible variety. Those huge masses of rock tumbled in wild confusion, contrasted with rich forest, distant views of mountain ranges and smiling valleys, with the clear lake reflecting at your feet, form together a scene most impressive and delightful, of which the artist and lover of nature can never weary." Countless overnight guests have enjoyed the architectural and landscape spectacle that is Mohonk, but the hotel itself is on private property and not open to casual inspection by the public. However, by reserving overnight accommodations, or simply a treatment in the spa or a meal in the dining room, the curious visitor can experience the wonderfully well-preserved interior and exterior of the hotel.

The origins of the Mountain House lie in a plain, utilitarian inn with bar operated by John Stokes in the 1860s on the site of the present Parlor Wing. In the summer of 1869, the Poughkeepsie *Eagle* observed that while Stokes's new guest rooms were "comfortable," rooms in the "old part are very small and very old fashioned, in fact might be called 'Dutchy' in the extreme"— "Dutchy" presumably suggesting cramped and primitive. That fall, Quaker schoolmaster Albert K. Smiley (1828–1912) acquired Stokes's inn at the recommendation of his twin brother, Alfred, and built additions over the next several years, employing carpenters from New Paltz and

Kingston. Alfred, who served as Albert's manager at Mohonk through the 1870s, reported to his brother in 1869 that he had "spent one whole day with Elting C. [*sic*: T.] Deyo, an intelligent & responsible carpenter from Paltz, in making plans & estimates." These early additions were probably designed by Alfred and his carpenters with little or no professional architectural assistance. (Deyo, however, was sometimes described as an architect; see Deyo's own house, XI–22.)

Alfred had greater confidence in his abilities than did brother Albert. When Albert wrote suggesting an architect be called in to plan a new kitchen in 1872, Alfred found the idea "*extremely absurd*." He was about ready to start construction, "and with one of the plainest & simplest kind of buildings what in the world is there for an architect to do?" Even construction of the more public parts of the hotel, Alfred believed, could proceed without the intervention of an architect, or, to satisfy Albert, an architect could be consulted merely to check Alfred's plans. Any architect consulted, Alfred warned his brother, "will be pretty sure to make all sorts of additions that will cost a great deal of money." In the late 1870s Alfred gradually withdrew from Mohonk to establish his own resort at Minnewaska, which he apparently designed himself (see XIV–

13). By 1882 the relationship between Mohonk and Minnewaska was described as "friendly rivalry."

Albert's and Alfred's architectural taste was clearly for the picturesque and influenced by the writings of Andrew Jackson Downing; still at Mohonk (in the Daniel Smiley Research Center of the Mohonk Preserve) is Downing's *Rural Essays* (1854) bearing Albert's signature. Mohonk's guests were also devotees of the picturesque; among them was Mrs. J. T. Headley whose "cottage in the Rhine style," built on a "picturesque" site near Newburgh, was illustrated and described in Downing's *Cottage Residences*. By 1876 the Mountain House's variety of peaked roofs and expansive balconies for taking in the glories of water, rock, plant, and sky inspired appreciative comments in the *New York Evening Press*: "The House ... is itself a veritable Swiss chalet on a large scale, and blends picturesquely with lake and mountain." The highly ornamented Office Wing of 1881 was more obviously Swiss than were the earlier additions. The somewhat haphazard effect of the whole was what struck a writer for the *Times* in 1882:

> Instead of the great hotel building that one expects ... there is what appears to be a veritable young village. One house

IX-21. Mohonk Mountain House, Parlor Wing (c. 1980 photo)

is perched high on a rocky hill; others are built on the slope; another stands boldly out over the water at the base of the hill, and yet others nestle among the trees in the background. Some are tall, others are flat like Swiss cottages; one is painted brown, others white ... With its varied architecture, its gabled roofs and windows, its verandas to every room front and back, the rocks and water at its base, and trees towering above it in the background, it is needless to say that the Lake Mohonk Mountain House is picturesque.

Enhancing the landscape were rustic summerhouses placed to offer shelter to seekers of picturesque views, while themselves being picturesque forms within the landscape. Alfred wrote his brother in September 1874: "I have built a small summer house on the rock E of [the] new parlor down the ravine just by the water—with a cover like one of those new fashioned hats that ladies wore here so much. It looks odd and quite picturesque." He was trying to complete several summerhouses before having publicity photos taken—they "help the pictures so much." Two weeks later he sought Albert's opinion in switching from straw roofing for the summerhouses to roofs of small green chestnut tree trunks split in two because, "in my judgment they look more rustic and more in keeping with wild scenery."

The oldest section of the present Mountain House is the multi-gabled Rock Building, built of wood but upon rock, designed in 1878 and completed in 1879. Here architects of high standing, Wilson Brothers of Philadelphia and New York, were employed and produced fine drawings still preserved (along with many later architectural drawings) at the Mohonk Mountain House Archives. The lake front elevation called for intricately detailed porches and balconies, as well as a crowning lookout tower.

The earlier, pre-1879 portions of the Mountain House were taken down in the late nineteenth century for a series of improvements and enlargements designed by prominent architects and supervised by Albert and his much younger half-brother, Daniel Smiley (1855–1930). In 1899 Albert told the assembly at the dedication of the New Parlor that he had bought for Daniel "all the books I could on architecture and he is fully competent." Daniel's very extensive architectural library, also preserved at Mohonk (in the Mountain House and at the Mohonk Preserve's Daniel Smiley Research Center), included volumes by Downing on landscape gardening and rural architecture, as well as *Villas and Cottages* by his disciple Calvert Vaux.

After 1879, as before, little attempt was made to unify the several segments, with walls of various materials—wood, stone, and brick—and in various styles. Nevertheless, the overall silhouette was always varied and broken, picturesque, and so appropriate to the mountaintop terrain. Rooftop observatories provided guests with shelter for group admiration of lake and valley views, while the guest room in the tower rising from the Parlor Wing furnished a more private observatory. One observatory-like projection, however, turns out to be a bulkhead for elevator machinery.

New York architect Michel LeBrun (1856–1913) of Napoleon LeBrun & Sons, best known for the Metropolitan Life Insurance tower (1909) on Madison Square, designed the Central Building (1887–1888) and then the Grove Building and present Dining Room and Kitchen Building (all 1891–1892). LeBrun confirmed that it was the client's intention to "treat the whole structure as a series of independent buildings." LeBrun's buildings represent the arrival of the Shingle Style at Mohonk; a letter from Michel Lebrun to Albert Smiley includes a delightful little sketch of a rooftop dormer for the Central Building with smoothly rounded hood. The very handsome central staircase, set off by ranks of spindles, lies within the Central Building. The enormous dining room with wooden walls and lofty ceiling—LeBrun referred to this high but secular space as the "nave"—was designed for air circulation before air-conditioning. An extension to the dining room in the form of a curving wall filled with windows looking out upon the Catskills to the northwest was added in 1910.

LeBrun's firm was succeeded by James E. Ware & Son, also New York architects, who were responsible for the Stone Building (1899–1902) and the Parlor Wing (1899). The Mountain House is sometimes called a castle, and the two cylindrical towers, one with crenellated battlements, on the west side of the Stone Building appear to justify the term, despite the conventional hotel windows and balconies distributed over their six or seven stories. The east side of the Stone Building is not so castle-like as suggestive of Mediterranean or California influence because of the curving gables and tile roofs; Albert and Daniel Smiley wintered in Redlands, California, and the A. K. Smiley Public Library there (dedicated 1898) has a tile roof and curved and stepped gables drawn from Spanish colonial tradition.

Perhaps the finest section of the Mountain House is the Parlor Wing (originally with the office below the parlor, and thus called the New Office and Parlor Building) and adjacent east porte cochère (1899; the similar west porte cochère is also from 1899). This wing's rough boulder arches are even more primitively powerful than those earlier designed by the influential Boston architect Henry Hobson Richardson. The wing and porte cochère were designed by James E. Ware & Son. Albert Smiley credited his half-brother Daniel with devising the wing's "general plan ... with some assistance by me." Contemporaries referred to the Parlor Wing as the "Swiss Chalet"—its broad, gently sloping roof, "piazzas" sheltered by this roof, and sturdy, unpainted wood frame and walls explicitly evoke

the traditional mountain architecture of Switzerland. However, this American chalet of 1900, as seen from the lake, rests upon a prominent steel truss devised by modern engineers.

The Ware firm also was responsible for the Power House (1900–1901), whose up-to-date steam-powered electric generators were cloaked in brick walls with stone trim in the old Dutch or Flemish manner. Segmental arched windows are cross-mullioned, and a wrought-iron weathervane rises from the parapet gable. The quaint style of the early colonists' motherland must have softened the impact of modern technology on this place whose owner so valued old-fashioned quiet that he served no alcohol, allowed neither dancing nor gambling, and limited Sabbath activity.

During the decades following Albert K. Smiley's death in 1912, four generations of Smileys have taken care to retain the Victorian character of Mohonk while modernizing the facilities. Thus a new ice-skating pavilion and a spa with fitness center were designed by Saratoga Associates in such a way that these new architectural elements coexist happily with the old.

IX–22 Clove Chapel
Clove Rd. 1876.

This board-and-batten, Gothic Revival chapel shared picturesque qualities with contemporary construction at the Mohonk Mountain House atop the nearby ridge. The effect of Gothic, pointed-arched windows was achieved at the chapel very simply with straight boards. Also Gothic is the wooden bracing of the gable roof over the entrance and of the smaller gable roof sheltering the bell (now missing) resting on the ridge of the entrance

IX-22. Clove Chapel

IX-23. Yaple House
(1980 photo)

roof. However, the historian Vincent Scully's term, "Stick Style," would also apply to the complex play of "sticks," or boards, here. The high, almost pyramidal hipped roof is fitted with small, triangular dormers; the steep pitch of the roof enhances the picturesque and Gothic character of the design. The foundation is of Shawangunk grit. Although there is no conventional cornerstone, a large stone on the grounds near the entrance is carved "Erected A.D. 1876."

Guests at Mohonk contributed funds for construction costs and later expenses. In 1880 the chapel was described as "a union house [served by several Protestant preachers, including the Methodist and Reformed pastors of High Falls and Alligerville], and in the season of summer tourists has a congregation of considerable numbers."

John F. Stokes (1802–1873), proprietor of the inn that preceded Albert Smiley's Mohonk Mountain House, is buried in the small cemetery across Clove Road from the chapel.

IX-23* Adam Yaple House (Owned by Smiley Brothers, Inc.)
Mossy Brook Rd. 1798 (repaired 1931).

A rare survivor of the log houses that were built in the area after 1760 for the less wealthy families who worked difficult mountain land, this was the farmhouse of Adam Yaple, son of German

immigrants, and his Dutch wife, Arrientje Hendrickson. The Yaple house, today surrounded by forest, was built into a sloping hillside, with basement kitchen entered by a door on the downhill gable end. As Thomas Ryan has pointed out, this form of "bank house" is associated with German and Swiss settlers in the Mid-Atlantic region. It resembles contemporary stone houses in its single story, gable roof, end chimneys, and overlapping boards covering the triangular end gables. As in some stone counterparts, there are two doors at the front of the house (one door for each of the two rooms within), but here there are fewer windows—only two in 1798.

The 1798 Federal Direct Tax list for Marbletown assessed the house at $151.50, while Marbletown's finest and highest-assessed house, the three-story, thirteen-room, stone-walled Wynkoop house in Stone Ridge, was assessed at $2,100. Despite the Yaple house's inexpensive construction, as Barry Benepe observed, "there is great beauty in the use of irregular trimmed logs chinked with mortar and stone slivers."

X

Town of Marlborough

Formed as a precinct 1772 and as a town 1788.

Population: 2,974 in 1870; 8,263 in 2000.

At the southeast corner of the county, Marlborough, named for the Duke of Marlborough, became a town in 1788 after earlier, in 1772, being established as a precinct out of Newburgh precinct. Its ties to Newburgh and Orange County have remained strong. Marlborough seemed distinct from the rest of Ulster County in 1841 since, as one writer then observed, its "inhabitants are more generally of English origin than any other town in the county." It is probably not by chance that the county's sole English-inspired church by the master architect Richard Upjohn is in Marlborough.

In 1880 the unincorporated village of Marlborough (also spelled Marlboro) had several mills and factories and was a shipping center, two steamboat lines making regular stops there. Milton was also a river port. Grapes, berries, and apples were important agricultural products in 1880, and fruit is still widely cultivated in the town.

The famed landscape painter George Inness appears on the 1880 Marlborough census list. He summered in Milton, staying at the attractive boardinghouse of Sarah Hull Hallock and her sister Dorcas Hull while using a nearby old barn in an apple orchard as his studio. (These sites are described in "Historic Trail of the Hamlet of Milton" presented by Friends of the Milton-on-Hudson Train Station.) Other artists who worked in Milton in the 1870s and '80s include the painter Will Low, with a studio in an old tool house, and Mary Hallock Foote, a native of Milton and well-known magazine writer and illustrator who in later life recalled that she "had no studio—the whole house was my studio." Another generation of artists was drawn to Milton with the founding of the Elverhoj Art Colony in 1912.

X-1 Gomez Mill House and Dard Hunter Mill

11 Mill House Rd., Marlboro (on the Orange County line). House c. 1717 and c. 1772; Mill 1912–1913. NR

The Gomez Mill House is celebrated as "the oldest standing Jewish dwelling in North America." In the 1910s it became the residence of Dard Hunter, an important figure in the Arts and Crafts movement who built a small half-timbered paper mill on Jew's Creek, which is very near the house but just across the county line in Orange County.

In 1714, Luis Moses Gomez, a successful trader and businessman in New York, purchased some 6,900 acres including the site of the Mill House. Probably soon thereafter, he built a one-story blockhouse or trading post with thick stone walls that form the first story of the present building. Gomez, whose primary residence was in New York, was the first *parnas*, or president, of Shearith Israel, America's oldest Jewish congregation.

In 1772 the building erected by Gomez was purchased by Wolfert Acker, who is remembered as a Revolutionary patriot whose business interests included packet sloops and a grist- and sawmill. Acker added a second story of finely crafted brick said to have been made on the site by his slaves. Front, second-story windows are topped with brick segmental arches, and the east wall has a Dutch-inspired heart-in-diamond pattern in blackened brick. However, a Palladian window centered on the second-story front gave the symmetrical, five-bay façade a distinctly English Georgian quality; this window lost its side elements in a nineteenth-century alteration.

Edward Armstrong acquired the house and 350 acres in 1835. He did not occupy the relatively modest place, preferring a grand Greek Revival residence (1834) nearby on the river at Danskammer, in Orange County. (This was demolished in the early 1930s; the Ionic columns from its portico now stand on the grounds of the Storm King Art Center and overlook the Thruway.) Edward's son William Henry Armstrong, a gentleman farmer and author, occupied the old Gomez-Acker house from about 1862 to 1904, and added the kitchen wing.

John A. Staples, a furniture merchant and friend of Arts and Crafts entrepreneur Gustav Stickley, owned the house in October 1909 when Natalie Curtis published an article about the house in Stickley's magazine, *The Craftsman*. Curtis credited Staples, "a native of Newburgh who values the old traditions of the Hudson River," with undoing "modern innovations" imposed upon the house in the past fifty years and restoring it "to its old Colonial dignity." The tastes and aims of the Colonial Revival and Arts and Crafts movement overlapped. The simplicity and handmade character of the old house would appeal to both, as did its two large, open hearths in rooms with low ceilings. In one of the rooms built by Gomez, Curtis admired the removal of later fireplaces to reveal Gomez's "huge stone fireplace, whose opening is at least eight feet wide and between five and six feet deep." She imagined, in good romantic fashion, that "the Indians warmed themselves when they came in winter

X-1. Gomez Mill House (1991 photo)

X-1A. Dard Hunter Mill (1981 photo)

to barter furs. What a picture it makes for the fancy—the pioneer Jew and the Indians in the broad, low-ceiled room, lit by the roaring fire of mammoth logs."

In 1912 Dard Hunter (1883–1966) purchased the property then known as Wolfert's Roost, but renamed the Mill House by Hunter. A native of Ohio, Hunter began his career in 1904 as an Arts and Crafts designer for Elbert Hubbard's Roycroft shops in East Aurora, near Buffalo. He had also studied Secession graphic design in Vienna and traveled to England where he absorbed the picturesque rural architecture that had earlier influenced William Morris and other English masters of the Arts and Crafts movement. The Mill House—old, solid, relatively simple, and set in a lovely landscape with flowing stream—was Hunter's version of Morris's home at Kelmscott. Hunter apparently retained Craftsman furnishings by Gustav Stickley placed in the house by Staples. Hunter did add an iron doorknocker in the form of a seahorse that was designed by W. W. Denslow and made by Roycrofters. (Stained-glass windows that Hunter designed for the house are no

longer there.) The house functioned as the home of Hunter and his wife Edith, but also as his printing shop and type-foundry.

In England Hunter had been fascinated by the possibility of making fine paper by hand. He purchased the Marlboro property with construction of a paper mill in mind; Jew's Creek offered a supply of pure water and a dam from a flour mill that no longer stood. In 1912 he began work on his paper mill, whose design, he later wrote, resembled an old Devonshire cottage. Like quaint English cottages, the windows had diamond-shaped panes set in lead, and the walls were half-timbered with brick infill. Hunter used old oak beams from the former gristmill and discarded handmade bricks from Acker's time. The roof was thatched with straw harvested from Hunter's land, while the eight-foot wooden waterwheel was fabricated by a local millwright, Joseph Kniffen, although the gearing, shafts, and bearing boxes were apparently products of modern industry. From the outset, the building looked old and part of its site. The foundation and fireplace were made with fieldstone, and the porch was built around a mature tree. The paper Hunter made here was used in remarkable books he created almost entirely himself; he made the type and paper, then carried out the printing on an old Washington hand press. He did not, however, bind the books. Two small books, *The Etching of Figures* (1915) by William Aspenwall Bradley and *The Etching of Contemporary Life* (1916) by Frank Weitenkampf were made for the Chicago Society of Etchers. Although Hunter had great difficulty in printing the books and considered the experiment in one-man, hand-made, book creation disappointing, it has been recognized as a landmark in the history of the Arts and Crafts movement.

Hunter discovered that the creek's volume was insufficient for his needs, and the house was too cold and small for his growing family. He put the house up for sale in 1917 and moved to an apartment in Newburgh while maintaining his press in Marlboro until selling the property in 1918 to Martha Gruening. A Smith College graduate and social activist for the NAACP and woman's suffrage, Gruening briefly ran a libertarian school at the Mill House.

In 1922 Dard Hunter's reputation encouraged noted type-designer and printer Frederic W. Goudy (1865–1947), then seeking a place to live and work amid picturesque surroundings, to consider the purchase of the Mill House property. Goudy wrote Hunter that he and his printer-wife Bertha Sprinks Goudy (?–1935) found the property "delightful," but the mill was too small and the house too hard to heat. Happily, they found, further down Jew's Creek, an old wooden house with an early mill (Goudy thought it dated c. 1790) large enough for his Village Press. The Goudys purchased this property in 1923 and named it Deepdene. It became a shrine for devotees of fine printing, but the mill-workshop was destroyed by fire in 1939, and their house was demolished in 1978.

After World War II, the Mill House property was preserved by the Starin family. In 1984 ownership passed to the Gomez Foundation for Mill House, which opens it to the public. The much-decayed paper mill was rebuilt in 1991.

X–2 Christ Church (Episcopal)
426 Old Post Rd. near Rte. 9W, Marlboro.
1858. Richard Upjohn and Co.

Picturesquely sited on a gentle rise, Christ Church was the creation of the leading firm of church architects of the time, headed by Richard Upjohn and including his son Richard M. Upjohn and his son-in-law Charles Babcock. Their office was in New York on Broadway, next to Upjohn's Gothic Revival masterpiece, Trinity Church (1839–1846). Drawings for Christ Church, dated March 30, 1858, and signed "Richard Upjohn and Co.," are preserved in the Avery Library of Columbia University. Construction was completed October 20, 1858.

Richard Upjohn chose the Early English Gothic as the historical style best expressive of the English roots of his beloved American Episcopal church and of his wish to return to the Christian faith and practice of the Middle Ages, before the Protestant Reformation. Gothic are the narrow, lancet-shaped, pointed-arched windows separated by buttresses along the north and south walls, as well as the dominant west window with its quatrefoil above two lancets. The polygonal walls to the east indicate the spacious chancel. Upjohn's preference in his mature works for asymmetry accounts for the placement of the tower (with entrance in its base) at the southwest corner. Had the point-

X-2. Christ Church (early-twentieth-century postcard)

ed spire been completed to its planned height of eighty feet, the Gothic sense of verticality would have been enhanced. The architect's drawings depict crosses surmounting the roofs; non-Catholics often frowned upon such crosses as signs of papal intrusion into America. What today looks to be a small decorative finial atop the west gable is clearly shown by the drawings to be a chimney; Upjohn's office was not eager to reveal such an un-Gothic element as a chimney for a hot-air furnace.

Richard Upjohn followed the English architect Augustus Welby Northmore Pugin in his devotion to the Gothic as *the* Christian style, but his firm was also influenced by English critic John Ruskin, who praised the Italian Gothic for its permanent polychrome—seen in Christ Church's colorfully patterned slate roof and walls of red brick with brownstone trim.

The church's interior is distinguished from Reformed, Methodist, and Presbyterian churches of the time by its spacious, semi-octagonal chancel with central altar (until 1967 placed against the east wall) and subordinate, off-to-the-side pulpit to accommodate the medieval ritual favored by Upjohn. Worship would be conducted in semidarkness with no view of the outside world, but with Christian images and spiritualized, colored light provided by the enameled and stained-glass windows, common in the Gothic tradition. The earliest windows are probably those with simple geometric and decorative patterns, although by 1880 the central chancel window was a rendition of Joshua Reynolds's figure of Faith. This key space is now filled by a 1926 window of Christ militant.

The very fine pictorial memorial windows are mostly the creations of Helen Maitland Armstrong (1869–1948), who designed hundreds of windows for buildings from New York to Florida to California. The earliest (and perhaps best) of these at Christ Church appears to be one dated 1891 on the south wall of the nave. Composed of richly colored pieces of glass of various thicknesses, almost like a relief sculpture, this representation of the Virgin and Child was made by Armstrong in collaboration with her father, David Maitland Armstrong (1836–1918), in memory of a child, Bayard Stuyvesant Armstrong (1887–1890), one of Da-

vid's sons. David was a prominent artist (he was responsible for the sixteen windows in the dome of St. Paul's Chapel at Columbia University) and served as a vestryman of the parish. He is memorialized on the north wall by a tablet painted in the manner of a Gothic manuscript—a figure in medieval armor with halo and wings kneels prayerfully within the letter T. Unsigned, this tablet may be by Helen or her sister Margaret N. Armstrong (1867–1944), a well-known designer of book covers. Helen's later windows, such as the militant Christ dated 1926 and again suited in medieval armor, located at the center of the chancel wall, differ from the 1891 window in being less colorful, flatter, and more linear. This window is a memorial to Samuel Hawksley (1814–1855), a tutor of David Maitland Armstrong and later rector of Christ Church and missionary to other towns in the county.

Outside, near the northeast corner of the church, is a brownstone memorial to Hawksley with round-arched Romanesque corbelling, possibly the work of the Upjohn firm. The Hawksley memorial (now shorn of its cross at the top) marks the beginning of the church cemetery on ground sloping steeply down toward the Hudson. Here are found the modest tombstones of Helen and David Maitland Armstrong, as well as other members of their family connected to Danskammer, the Hudson River estate (just over the border in Orange County) of Edward Armstrong, David's father and in 1837 a founder of the mission church that preceded Christ Church. This first church, a wooden structure, was destroyed by fire two days after Christmas 1857.

X–3 St. Mary's Church (Roman Catholic)
Main St. (Rte. 9W), Marlboro. 1922. John P. Draney (with partner William J. Beardsley).

Poughkeepsie architect John Draney designed St. Mary's in the Gothic Revival style, still the prevailing mode for Christian churches between the world wars. However, the Gothic Revival of the early twentieth century, led by Ralph Adams Cram and Bertram Goodhue, differed from that of the Victorian period. Polychrome effects are

X-3. St. Mary's Church

more subdued, and there are broad, unadorned surfaces, which contrast with areas of elaborate decoration based on historic prototypes—here the rose window, enframement of the main doorway, and gargoyles at the corner of the tower.

X-4 First Presbyterian Church of Marlboro

98 West St. at Dubois St., Marlboro.
1868–1869. J. A. Wood.

Close observers of Ulster County churches have long been struck by the strong similarity between Marlboro's Presbyterian Church and Highland's

X-4. First Presbyterian Church (early-twentieth-century postcard)

Methodist Church (1868–1869), both designed in the Romanesque style by Poughkeepsie architect J. A. Wood (see VIII-4). The choice of the round-arched Romanesque style (Wood called the style "Norman") by the Presbyterians helped differentiate them from Episcopalians whose nearby Christ Church (1858) had been designed by the Upjohns in the Gothic Revival style. Presbyterian worship focused on the preacher in the pulpit, which retains its central position within the Marlboro church. Presbyterians formed the oldest religious body in Marlboro, and from the outset they set themselves apart from the beliefs and forms of Anglicans and Catholics; documents dating 1763 and 1765 relating to the building of their first place of worship refer to it not as a "church," but as a "meeting-house" or simply "house."

X-5* Marlborough Central High School and Grade School (Marlboro Middle School)

1375 Rte. 9W, Marlboro. 1936–1937
(altered later). Gerard Betz.

The façade of this insensitively altered school was originally a simple version of the Art Deco designed by Kingston architect Gerard Betz and constructed during the Depression as a project of the Federal Public Works Administration. (Another PWA project was the Highland High School of 1937–1939.) Three of the doorways are still topped with sculptural reliefs, probably of cast stone. Two are identical and represent the reading of a scroll in ancient times. The third portrays a woman of the 1930s

X-5. Marlborough Central School sculpture

reading aloud to a boy in knickers while a girl works at an abacus, all under the influence of an owl radiating wisdom. The sculptor took pains to represent contemporary details down to the shoelaces. Although the sculptor's identity is unknown, the reliefs were probably commissioned by the WPA. The WPA/Federal Art Project produced thousands of sculptures using media like cast stone that allowed inexpensive yet inspirational art to be widely distributed to schools and institutions.

X–6* West Shore Railroad Stations
Marlboro. c. 1883 and c. 1910 (neither extant).

The earlier Marlborough station was designed by Wilson Brothers of Philadelphia with a picturesque three-story tower complete with balcony for surveying the tracks. Another of the firm's towered

X-6. Marlboro Station (c. 1905 postcard)

West Shore stations survives in barely recognizable form as apartments in Highland. At Lake Mohonk, Wilson Brothers designed a portion of the Mountain House (1878–1879) with a tower allowing guests to take in the splendid mountaintop view.

The later Marlborough depot, a simpler example of the Shingle Style adapted to railway needs, resembled the Wallkill Valley Railroad station in New Paltz (opened 1908; much altered for restaurant use) and the West Shore Railroad Depot in Malden (see XVI–19). Lacking towers, these stations merely had ground-story bay windows for the agent to observe train activity.

X–7* Lewis Du Bois House
Rte. 9W, Marlboro. 1757 or 1763 and later.

Sited on high ground not far from the river and barely visible from the highway, the house built for Lewis Du Bois (1728–1802) is said to be among the oldest frame houses in Ulster County. Helen Reynolds mistakenly thought frame houses were uncommon before 1800, and accepted only this house and one built for Louis J. Du Bois (a first cousin of Lewis) on the Wallkill River three miles south of New Paltz as surviving examples. Reynolds and others valued the house for its associations with the Revolution; Lewis was a colonel of the Fifth Regiment, Continental Line and, in October 1777, a British ship on its way to destroy Kingston fired toward the house of this known rebel. Ralph Le Fevre reported in 1909 that over the years cannonballs had been found in an earth bank a little west of the house. Some were preserved at Washington's Headquarters in Newburgh, while Reynolds credited John Rust (actually, John Rusk), an attorney who purchased the house about

X-6A. Later Marlboro Station (c. 1910 postcard)

X-7. Lewis Du Bois House

early feature, similar to the roof of the Hasbrouck house (Washington's Headquarters) in Newburgh. Whatever the merits of his architectural observations, Eberlein's understanding of social history was flawed. He held that the many slaves who cultivated Colonel Du Bois's land "found life, in the main, comfortable and happy, certainly far more protected and care-free than they did after they had been emancipated."

X–8 C. M. Woolsey Building
59–63 Main St., Milton. 1896.

1905, with preserving the Du Bois house (as his residence) and a cannonball. Two balls are displayed in the house by the current owner, George Rusk, Jr., great-grandson of John Rusk.

Reynolds described the clapboarded walls as brick-filled, with the house otherwise originally similar to eighteenth-century stone houses—one-and-a-half stories, gable roof, and one file of rooms on the first story. However, the fine Georgian paneling of the southwest parlor and the arched panels on the outer west wall set the house apart from most of its stone contemporaries. Reynolds regretted minor changes made in the nineteenth century—porch, window frames, shutters, and dormers. (The dormers are unusual in having a second glazed window, lighting the attic, behind the outer window, lighting the second floor.) Worse was the rebuilding of the gable roof into one "of peculiar and individual design" probably, she thought, carried out for Lewis's son after his father's death. Writing a few years before Reynolds, Harold Donaldson Eberlein had accepted the jerkin-head roof as an

This large and stylish commercial building, bearing stones inscribed "C. M. Woolsey" and "1896," comes as something of a surprise to visitors to the hamlet of Milton. It seems to have strayed from the streets of Newburgh or Poughkeepsie, and can be compared to the latter city's Dutchess County Court House by William J. Beardsley. The classical cornice (now unfortunately removed), round-arched windows, and blocky brick quoins at the corners of the end pavilions are common enough in small-city Renaissance Revival buildings around 1900. However, the scrollwork embellishing the circular windows at the center of the façade, the elegantly detailed iron fire escape, and steel beams exposed above the first-story windows infer a client seeking a bold presence in an up-and-coming community.

X-8. Woolsey Building (1979 photo)

Cyprian Meech Woolsey (1841–1924) was a graduate of New Paltz Academy, a Civil War cavalry officer, a lawyer, a Republican politician, and author of *History of the Town of Marlborough* (1908). He maintained his law office in this building. The Sarah Hull Hallock Library, since 1924 located across the street, was an original occupant, and the Milton Post Office has long been anchored here at the center of the hamlet.

X–9* Friends Meeting House and Friends Cemetery
Maple Ave., Milton. 1829–1830 (meetinghouse demolished 2009).

First a Friends (Quaker) meetinghouse, later a storage shed, this house-like place of worship, even in its longtime ruinous state, demonstrated the Quaker insistence on simplicity and avoidance of worldly or churchly ornament. The gentle slope of its gable roof and symmetrical organization of its door and flanking windows did, however, suggest the period of classical influence.

In 1828 the Quakers of the area split between Hicksite and Orthodox branches. The Hicksites retained the meetinghouse, obliging the Orthodox to erect this building. In 1887 the Orthodox moved to a new meetinghouse of a more worldly character. Remaining across Maple Avenue is the well-maintained Friends Cemetery (established c. 1830) with plain monuments to various members of the locally prominent Hallock family.

X-9. Friends Meeting House

X–10* All Saints Episcopal Church (former)
Sands Ave., Milton. 1854–1856 (by 1996 altered as residence).

This small board-and-batten Gothic Revival church closely resembled designs Richard Upjohn published in his *Rural Architecture* (1852). The verticality sought in picturesque Gothic designs was here seen in the narrow lancet windows, battens running up the walls, and steep gable roof. Upjohn and High Church Episcopal preference for roomy chancels was apparent here in the eastern section of the building whose roof was slightly lower than the nave's. In the twentieth century the building became a grange hall before being heavily altered for residential use.

X-10. All Saints Episcopal Church (1971 photo)

X–11 West Shore Railroad Station, Milton
41 Dock Rd., Milton. 1883 and c. 1890. Wilson Brothers & Co.

Although this served as both a passenger and freight station, its most distinctive feature, decorative lettering cut into boards in the north gable, proclaims: "Freight / NY WS & B R Co." The New York, West Shore & Buffalo Railway was a predecessor of the New York Central Railroad. A similar station survives in Saugerties (see XVI–12). After its closing as the Milton station, the building was long used for wine tasting, but the Town of Marlborough and Friends of the Milton-on-Hudson Train Station

X-11. Milton Station

are undertaking its restoration for use as a community center.

The architects, Wilson Brothers & Co. of Philadelphia, designed many stations for the Pennsylvania Railroad, but also a number for the New York, West Shore & Buffalo including, by 1885, those in Ulster County at Marlboro (see X–6), Milton, Highland, West Park, Mount Marion, and West Camp.

X–12* Elverhoj Art Colony (former)
Old Indian Rd., Milton-on-Hudson. c. 1840, 1912 and later.

Visible from the Hudson River and standing directly above the West Shore Railroad tracks is a long, low, stuccoed building with two bands of windows looking out upon the river—once the main building of the Elverhoj colony. Long out of operation and its buildings closed to the public, Elverhoj was established as a colony of artists and craftsmen with summer classes on this site in 1912–1913. The founders were two Danish-American silversmiths, Anders H. Andersen (or Anderson) and Johannes Morton, who had originated the colony in 1906 in Racine, Wisconsin. Their plans for a "model art colony" in Milton were ambitious; while modeled after Byrdcliffe in Woodstock, it was intended to be on an even larger scale.

At first, Elverhoj (Danish for "hill of the fairies") was primarily known for jewelry and silverware entirely designed and made by individual art-

ists, including Andersen, Morton, Joseph Popelka, and James Scott. (Scott later became a well-known landscape painter in the region.) Andersen, the colony's director, had been trained at the Art Institute of Chicago and had studied for two years in Prague and Dresden. In June 1915, C. R. Ashbee, prominent in the English Arts and Crafts movement, visited Elverhoj and found some members of the colony "were building their houses; little timber chalets in the woods overlooking the Hudson." Ashbee admired Elverhoj's way of life and work, while judging its craft objects and paintings second-rate. Still, Elverhoj was awarded a gold medal at the 1915 Panama-Pacific Exposition in San Francisco. Ashbee had been invited to Elverhoj by an early member of the colony, Ralph M. Pearson, a printmaker also trained at the Art Institute of Chicago. Pearson was a friend of Arts and Crafts designer and paper maker Dard Hunter, who in 1912 acquired the historic Gomez house not far away in Marlborough (see X–1) and later collaborated with Pearson in designing Elverhoj's distinctive letterhead.

Elverhoj's main building was a house built about 1840 with a classical portico and Greek

X-12. Sears House, Elverhoj (c. 1915 poster)

X-12A. Studio at Elverhoj (c. 1915 postcard)

Revival doorway overlooking the Hudson. It had been the home of Sherburne Sears, a whaling captain. Just as Hunter valued the Colonial architecture of the Gomez house, the Sears house at Elverhoj was admired as "an old colonial mansion" whose "old-fashioned rooms give a grateful sense of space and quiet"—so wrote Hanna Astrup Larsen in Gustav Stickley's *Craftsman* (September 1916). The old mansion served as the colony's "tea room," about the time tea was being offered by Sarah Lounsbery in Stone Ridge's Sally Tock's Inn; both took advantage of the vogue for tea drinking in old-fashioned Colonial settings.

Elverhoj's artists were housed in several small wooden cabins. The most elaborate of the picturesque studio-houses, featured in a colony postcard and an etching by Pearson, had a broad rubble-stone chimney alongside a doorway sheltered by a rustic wooden porch. The studio-house was not Colonial, but it was clearly handmade and related easily to the landscape and to the colony's motto, "live close to nature for inspiration." A few decades earlier, landscape painter George Inness had occupied a small frame house nearby (just

up the long slope from the river) when, according to Hanna Larsen, he had created "an American school of painting." Now, she wrote, Elverhoj's "earnest workers are striving to develop an American school of decorative art" with "designs founded on American flora."

In the 1920s theatrical productions became an important aspect of the colony, although crafts were still made. The theatre (built c. 1920, collapsed 1980s) was a frame building above the West Shore tracks (patrons were warned that the performance would stop for the cacophony of passing trains); locust tree trunks functioned as rustic interior posts. Yet theatergoers were offered an exotic alternative to the rustic in "the Moorish Terrace, Your Dining Mecca." This was created as a Moorish/Mediterranean-style building by radically altering and enlarging the old Sears house so that its river front was obscured by the dining terrace. The Moorish Terrace's west, or entrance, façade was graced with a three-arched loggia with polychrome capitals and, above, sculptured relief panels and iron grillwork. A Moorish pointed arch topped the main door, which sported elaborate but false iron hinges. Within, the eclectic decoration included Viking ships in stained-glass panels and a painted wall relief sculpture, as well as a trident motif in wood strips atop wainscoting. The public could choose between an upper terrace, open to the sky or, directly below, an enclosed terrace with band of casement windows overlooking the Hudson. (West Shore trains could be heard, but not seen because of the steep drop down to the tracks.)

The theatre continued to function at least through 1936, but Elverhoj never approached the scale or had the impact of Byrdcliffe, and Andersen lost the property in 1934 when a bank foreclosed on the mortgage. Followers of Father Divine, the charismatic and controversial black leader, purchased it in 1938, although Andersen continued to live in a cottage on the property and is said to have become an "enthusiastic adherent" of Father Divine's movement.

Elverhoj became one of Father Divine's most popular missions, easily reached by boat from New York to Elverhoj's own dock. According to an account in the *Times*, the artists' colony was now, for Divine's followers, "a paradise—shaded groves of oak and elm, winding woodland paths and trellised arbors of honeysuckle ... a tumbling mountain stream crossed by rustic bridges." The Moorish Terrace, called a "Spanish style clubhouse," provided views of the Hudson and nearby hills, and its kitchens and dining rooms were expanded to serve 500 diners; the upper, river-facing terrace was roofed and more casement windows installed. On the broad lawn, white-painted stones spelled out "Father-God-Divine." Carleton Mabee has found that "Divine's followers continued to call the site an art colony" and consulted with Andersen in the transformation of the Moorish Terrace into a hotel with vast dining areas. Embedded in an exterior wall is a glazed polychrome circular relief, with dark-skinned men, women, and children portrayed in front of a more decorative version of the Moorish Terrace. Was it added during Father Divine's time? How does it relate to a relief on a lower wall at Elverhoj showing bathers with white skins? Divine's followers sold the property in 1947, and it is now in private hands.

X-12B. Main building at Elverhoj as expanded by Father Divine (c. 1940 photo)

XI

Town of New Paltz

Patent granted 1677; town incorporated 1785; village incorporated 1887.

Population: 2,040 in 1870; 12,830 in 2000.

Three factors have been key in the creation of today's New Paltz, a village within a town, both with an outsized reputation: its founding in the 1670s by Huguenots (French-speaking Protestants) whose eighteenth-century stone houses near the Wallkill River have been the object of preservation sentiment since the nineteenth century; the establishment of the New Paltz Academy in 1833, which has grown into the State University of New York at New Paltz (in 2008 the "Hottest Small State School in America"); and the Shawangunk Mountains, whose beauty and drama have long drawn lovers of nature from metropolitan centers to Lake Mohonk and its mountaintop hotel, just over the town line in Marbletown and Rochester.

Huguenot Street (NHL Historic District)

New Paltz was established along the east bank of the Wallkill River in 1678 by Huguenots or Walloons, French-speaking Protestants from northern France and the Spanish Netherlands, or Flanders, who left their homeland to find religious freedom and a livelihood. They settled for a period in the German Rhineland, but ultimately in the Hudson Valley. The name of the community indicates the Huguenots' regard for the shelter offered by the German Protestants of *Die Pfalz*, or the Palatinate. Their first houses in New Paltz, built with wooden walls, do not survive, although archaeological probing is beginning to reveal their forms. The existing stone houses concentrated on Huguenot Street, begun in the 1690s and early eighteenth century, were built on or near the sites of their predecessors and convenient to land cleared for farming.

As early as 1841 New Paltz was known for its old stone houses. John W. Barber and Henry Howe described the village as having "about 30 dwellings, principally of stone, in the ancient Dutch style." By 1898 the distinction between Dutch and Huguenot settlers was apparent, and visitors to New Paltz were advised that they would find "an entire Huguenot village just as it stood two centuries ago. The houses occupy both sides of a broad avenue, shaded by immense elms of great antiquity, and are still owned by the direct descendants of the original settlers." On every side "Huguenot Street" was surrounded by "the modern town of New Paltz" whose growth depended on the State Normal School. Yet, "only one of the old houses has been modernized, the others being carefully preserved with all their original features." There had, in fact, been more changes than the writer acknowledged—church buildings removed and new ones built, houses altered or demolished. The romantic vision of unspoiled Huguenot Street has had a long life; popular historian Harold Donaldson Eberlein found Hurley still remarkably Dutch in 1924, and "in many ways New Paltz resembles Old Hurley," he wrote, "only ... it is more perfect in its seventeenth century aspect, although surrounded by modernism on all sides. ... New Paltz ... has grown, but the growth has gone on ... outside of the old Huguenot settlement and left it almost untouched, so that the one original village street presents today much the same appearance that it did more than two hundred years ago." In some quarters this vision of an eternally preserved street remains in force today.

XI–1 DuBois Fort
c. 1705 and 1830s.

Pedestrians on Huguenot Street have long accepted the loopholes opening out onto the sidewalk as confirmation that this hospitable-looking stone building—today the visitor center of Historic Huguenot Street—was once a fort. Further, the iron numerals higher on the same wall would seem to indicate that the building was completed in 1705. Recent studies of the building have not disproved that the building was a fort as well as a house of the DuBois family in the eighteenth century. (New Paltz has yet to be attacked, so the loopholes have never been used.) The numerals, however, were not placed in their present positions in 1705. The original building was probably a one-and-a-half-story stone house with gable end facing the street, much like the Bevier-Elting House across the street.

In the 1830s major additions were made, including a full second story and the delightful, south-facing, two-level porch. This was the time when Washington Irving and others were discovering the history and lore of early Hudson Valley settlements—Irving rebuilt his residence, Sunnyside, with old-fashioned Dutch gables in 1835. The Fort's iron numerals, reminiscent of the dates worked into the beam anchors of Dutch buildings in New Amsterdam, may well be eighteenth century. However, when the numerals were repositioned in the 1830s remodeling, they lost their earlier structural function (anchoring the internal wood beams to the exterior stone wall) to become ornamental reminders of the antiquity of the original building.

A century later, enthusiasm for buildings and furnishings from the colonial past was still greater, in part thanks to the opening of the American Wing at the Metropolitan Museum of Art in 1924 and the beginning of the restoration of Colonial Williamsburg in 1926. Robert Deyo ran an antiques shop in the Fort for a period in the 1930s before moving his shop to the smaller frame building next door at 85 Huguenot Street. Apparently the Fort housed a tea room in the late 1920s and early 1930s. Then, in 1937 the Fort's owner, Louise duBois Berry Dingman, began alterations to accommodate a restaurant. In 1938 "The Old Fort" offered a full Christmas dinner including turkey with chestnut dressing and bisque tortoni for $1.50. "Large, comfortable rooms" for two, with meals, were available for $25.00 a week. Afternoon tea with cinnamon toast was 35¢. The Old Fort was operated as a restaurant by Elsie Hanna Oates and Alice Crans for over fifty years until, to the regret of its many devotees, Miss Crans retired as cook and proprietor in 1990.

Like many restaurants and tea rooms in old or new Colonial settings, this was run by women for those seeking a "quiet, refined atmosphere." By contrast, the New Paltz Diner in 1940 was managed by "Jack and Harvey," whose dinners were only 50¢ and where quiet and refinement probably didn't reign. In 1968 the DuBois Fort was purchased by the Huguenot Historical Society with funds from the DuBois Family Association. In its current role as visitor center, its displays have included a recreation of a corner of the historic restaurant.

XI-1. DuBois Fort

XI-2 Jean or Jacob Hasbrouck House
c. 1712 and 1721. NHL

This grand old stone house differs from other eighteenth-century stone houses in the county in its tall, steep gable roof that provided vast storage space in the loft or attic. In the early nineteenth century, grain was stored in barrels here. The space is shaped, in fact, a good deal like that of a Dutch barn. Similar roofs appear in Pieter Brueghel's paintings of village life in sixteenth-century Flanders. Hasbrouck ancestors would have been part of this north European culture before seeking refuge in the Palatinate and then the Hudson Valley.

The façade is a simple composition of central doorway with shed-roofed porch and a single window lighting the front room on either side of the central doorway, which opens into the central hallway. Neil Larson proposes that the house's large size and its orderly façade and central hallway—uncommon in the area in the early 1700s—are indications of Jacob Hasbrouck's wealth and status in the community. Four wrought-iron beam or wall anchors can be seen on the façade; they help join the interior wooden beams to the exterior stone wall. To the left of the doorway is a stone marked "I.H."—the "I" for either Jean or his son Jacob (born 1688). An 1894 history of the house published in the *New Paltz Independent* also identified the date 1712 worked into the mortar near a front window. Although the house is generally known as the Jean Hasbrouck house, the 1894 writer suggested that son Jacob may have been the builder. Twenty-first-century dendrochronology indicates that most of the house was built in 1721, although part of an earlier house from Jean's time may have been incorporated.

XI-2. Jean or Jacob Hasbrouck House (c. 1893 photo)

The front, northeast, room was long used as a store and bar—the bar railing has been preserved. The kitchen, in the southwest room, has what is apparently the only original Dutch jambless fireplace to survive anywhere in New York and New Jersey. In the high loft, the chimney for this fireplace appears as a great tapering mass of thin, handmade bricks. These were long assumed to have been made in Holland, but in fact were locally produced.

By the 1890s the house had been occupied for decades by tenants, and the extensive Queen Anne–style additions to the 1692 Deyo house across the street aroused fear that the Hasbrouck house would suffer a similar or worse fate. As early as 1869 *New Paltz Independent* editor Ralph LeFevre expressed the hope that "the old mansion may survive the storms of time for another century ... for it is one of the few links that connect our place with the past." The Huguenot Patriotic Monumental & Historical Society (HPM&HS) rallied preservation sentiment and in 1894 recommended that the house be purchased "as a store house of ancient relics." The building itself was valued for its association with the ancient Hasbrouck family, down to Josiah Hasbrouck, who ran a store and lived in the house before building his elegant Federal-style mansion now known as Locust Lawn. Josiah's daughter Elizabeth and her husband Josiah DuBois likewise deserted the ancestral home for a new brick house in 1822. In 1894 the old stone house was also admired as a piece of

hand-craftsmanship by the "home carpenter" and "home blacksmith," and for such historic architectural features as the wide, jambless fireplace in the kitchen. The craftsmanship seemed superior to that of the 1890s—"there was evidently no 'slighting' of the work by mechanics in those days." The early builders "meant their houses should be for their descendants as well as themselves." Although wealthy, the eighteenth-century Hasbroucks had been content with "a very plain edifice," while the nineteenth-century Hasbroucks, like others of their time, had "learned to be discontented with the plain, old stone houses of their ancestors"— hence the need for a society to preserve the house.

In 1899 the HPM&HS succeeded in purchasing the house as a memorial to the Huguenot founders of New Paltz. More than a century later it remains the outstanding house in the collection of its successor, the Huguenot Historical Society (Historic Huguenot Street). Oddly enough, given tensions in the later twentieth century between the state college and the historical society, there was a proposal in the 1890s that the society should turn over the property to the state as a museum, a part of the Normal School whose campus adjoined it to the south. With the Normal School's move in 1909 to the heights above the ancient houses, interest in merging school and historic house apparently faded, although in 1919 Ralph LeFevre expressed the hope that the state (not specifically the Normal School) would buy "all the stone houses on Huguenot Street" and open them "as object lessons where people might learn how hand weaving, basket making, lace making, etc., were carried on in the old days." By the 1950s the growth of the state college and the community was viewed by some in the historical society as a threat to the preservation of Huguenot Street.

In 2007–2008 the failing north wall was taken down and rebuilt with the stones in their original configuration. In taking down the wall, parts of two early window frames were discovered, sufficient to justify the insertion of new casement windows in the rebuilt wall. Daniel M. C. Hoppin, in his 1940 measured drawings of the house for the Historic American Buildings Survey, noted that the earlier windows had been casements.

XI–3 French Church (Huguenot House of Prayer; Crispell Memorial) and Burying Ground

c. 1717–1720 (1972 reconstruction by Bernard E. Guenther).

On August 30, 1972, a helicopter delivered a metal cupola, made locally by Fall Fittings, to the roof of the newly reconstructed French Church, or Huguenot House of Prayer. The original building had stood a few yards away until demolished in 1772. Its stones were eventually used in constructing the village school in 1812, a building that survives in altered form at 15 North Front Street (see XI–8). The reconstruction was spearheaded by Kenneth E. Hasbrouck (1916–1996), who presided over the Huguenot Historical Society and was for decades the key figure in the preservation of Huguenot Street. The rebuilding was sponsored by the Crispell Family Association (descendants of patentee Antoine Crispell), and the contractor was Stanley E. Hasbrouck, Jr. The architect was Bernard E. Guenther, a New York architect with a second home in New Paltz, who generously offered his services. In the city Guenther had planned large-scale, modern housing projects, as

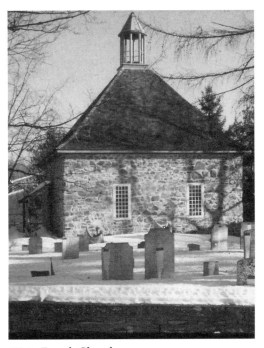

XI-3. French Church

well as the True Light Lutheran Church (1948) in a design appropriate to its site in Chinatown. Columbia University historians Everard M. Upjohn and James Van Derpool provided advice on the design of the reconstruction.

The church has some handcrafted details—e.g., hardware copied by local blacksmith G. B. Palkowics from examples in early New Paltz houses—as well as modern materials and methods. Stones for the walls were drawn from old walls surrounding the fields of Kenneth Hasbrouck's Kettleborough farm, but these stones are a veneer over concrete block walls. Beneath the church is a secure, climate-controlled manuscript room or archive resting on a concrete slab.

The building begun about 1717 and dedicated in 1720 was built of stone, was square in plan, and had a cupola. According to a sketch on a 1760 New Paltz Patent survey map, the building had a simple gable roof. The hipped roof of the reconstruction may have been suggested by the hipped roof of the First Reformed Dutch Church built in Albany in 1715 and demolished in 1806. The interior, like an early New England Puritan meetinghouse, avoids all Roman Catholic elements—no long aisle leading to a central altar, no stained glass, no sculpture, no organ, nothing to distract from the preaching sent down to the people clustered around the minister in the central pulpit. Significantly, early documents referring to the building can be translated as "this house" or "this house of prayer," and not as "church," since the Huguenots, like the New England Puritans who worshipped in meetinghouses, avoided both the forms and words associated with Roman Catholicism.

Remnants of the old Huguenot burying ground lie next to the reconstructed church and are well cared for. In 1862, however, the burial place was sadly neglected, and a new rural cemetery was opening on Plains Road (see XI–27). The *New Paltz Times* lamented that:

> the old burying-ground ... around each of whose graves so many tears have been shed by our parents, and grand-parents, and in which the honored remains of our Hugue-

not ancestors lie, is in a sad, reproachful state of repair! The ancient wall covered with the moss of a century and a half is tumbling down ... the fence and gateway at the entrance is dilapidated and admits the entrance of swine to root up and befoul the sacred graves, and weeds cover the venerable memorials that mark the spot wherein our dearest friends repose!

Among the remaining gravestones and perhaps the finest in design is Elsie Hasbrouck's (died 1764), with arched top and carved winged head of an angel or soul of the deceased. Its inscription is in English, and the design of the carving follows English tombstones in the colonies, an indication that the Huguenots were becoming absorbed into the larger colonial culture.

XI–4 Deyo-Brodhead House
c. 1700 (1894 alterations and additions by William J. Beardsley).

Fans of Victorian architecture need not avoid Huguenot Street. For them, the nearly complete engulfing of the stone Pierre Deyo house (begun about 1700) with Victorian, Queen Anne–style additions was an improvement over the original, plain house.

Abraham Deyo Brodhead (1863–1926), a devotee of tennis and horse racing, married Gertrude M. Deyo on December 17, 1890, and the same day the New Paltz newspapers announced that Brodhead had inherited about $150,000 from a great uncle in Milwaukee. Abraham's mother Cor-

XI-4. Deyo-Brodhead House (c. 1980 photo)

nelia owned the old stone Deyo house in 1890, but ownership had passed to Abraham by 1894 when he sought plans to enlarge the homestead and make it a suitable residence for one of his newly acquired wealth and social ambition—he enjoyed giving parties. Brodhead discussed his needs with Poughkeepsie architect William J. Beardsley (1872–1934), and it was undoubtedly Beardsley who designed the expanded Queen Anne house. At the time, Beardsley was in his early twenties and beginning his architectural practice after being employed in his father's sash and blind factory. (In 1894 the young architect was also creating another impressive house in New Paltz, the James P. Hayden house on Main Street; see XI–15.) Beardsley would become Poughkeepsie's most successful architect of the early twentieth century, designing the Dutchess County Courthouse (1903) and other courthouses and government buildings across the state.

Abraham's wife Gertrude by 1902 demonstrated her pride in her colonial ancestry by joining the Daughters of the American Revolution. The couple clearly wanted to occupy, after all the improvements, what was still a Deyo ancestral homestead, thanks to the old stone walls that were retained as the first story walls to south, west, and north. But even these walls were subjected to changes; a bay window was added on the west, and other windows and doors were repositioned. The first story was expanded to the east, and a full second story was built, surfaced with shingles that overhang the lower stone and clapboard walls in good Queen Anne fashion. A porte-cochere and hipped roof complicated with dormer and projecting gables also fit into the Queen Anne mold. Some Queen Anne details had Colonial origins— here the semicircular windows facing east and west above the porch are enlarged Georgian Colonial fanlights. Consequently Brodhead could believe that his additions were in the spirit of the colonial past. The interior, with its new carved oak staircase and carved wood and tile mantel, was just as radically transformed as the exterior.

The transformation was controversial from the outset and inspired the creation of the Huguenot Patriotic, Monumental and Historical Society in 1894 to spare at least one ancestral landmark

from such modernization so that future generations would understand how their ancestors had lived—the Jean Hasbrouck house was acquired and opened as a public museum in 1899 (see XI–2). Brodhead was a founding member of the society—perhaps to make amends for bastardizing the Deyo house.

In 1952, when a taste for things Victorian was just reemerging, *The New York Times* reported that the house begun by Deyo and altered by Brodhead "has been firmly ruled out of the historical roost by the Huguenot Historical Society as a hybrid 'monstrosity.'" However, in the 1970s the society adopted a broader view and acquired the house, which subsequently has been returned to its c. 1915 appearance.

Another fine example of the Queen Anne surviving in New Paltz is the Jacob and Gertrude Deyo house (1886–1887) at 24 Church Street, designed by Poughkeepsie architect Arnout Cannon, best known for his transformation of Wilderstein (1888) in Dutchess County. The similar house at 20 Church Street (1887–1888), built for Gertrude Deyo's father Jesse Elting, was undoubtedly also designed by Cannon.

XI-5 Bevier-Elting House
c. 1699–1735.

Built for Louis and Marie Bevier and expanded for son Samuel before being purchased by Josiah Elting after Samuel's death in 1761, this house remained in the Elting family until donated to the Huguenot Historical Society in 1963. With

XI-5. Bevier-Elting House (DeWitt photo, c. 1940)

XI-5A. Bevier-Elting House hardware (blueprint of measured drawings by Teller for HABS)

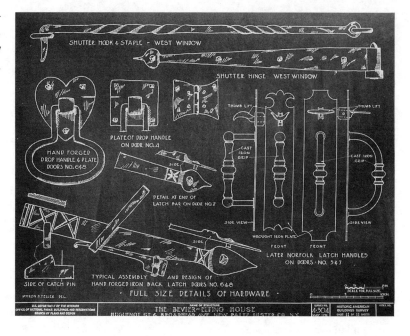

its west gable end facing the street, the Bevier-Elting House represents a common house type in north European urban settings, but very few early gable-to-street houses survive in the Hudson Valley. Also distinctive are the long porch along the north side and, within, a low subcellar beneath the partly-below-ground kitchen. A 1795 inventory suggests "Negroes bedstead and bedding" were in the kitchen.

Like the nearby Abraham (Daniel) Hasbrouck House, this has three rooms on the main floor, built in three stages in a linear fashion. Helen Wilkinson Reynolds wrote that the middle room, cellar, and subcellar belonged to the earliest part of the house, while the east room was from 1735, the date cut in the chimney but no longer visible. She thought it probable that the west room, like the east, was built after the middle. When Kingston architects Myron Teller, Charles Keefe, and Augustus Schrowang made measured drawings of the house in 1934 for the Historic American Buildings Survey (HABS), they determined that the west or front room was the earliest, followed by the middle room in 1735, and finally the east room. Teller was responsible for the measured drawings of the house's old hardware. His admiration for the house led to his use of photos of the west entrance door with transom sash above and of an "old window with batten shutters fitted with hand forged iron strap hinges and sill hooks" to illustrate his 1959 booklet on the county's early stone houses. More recent studies also indicate that the house grew from west to east. The 1934 HABS drawings include one of a romantic feature, the "Old well and sweep as restored"—the well curb or wall then being of wood, not the present stone.

Since 2008 the Archaeological Field School at SUNY New Paltz, led by Dr. Joseph E. Diamond, has discovered, in the land between the Bevier-Elting and Deyo-Brodhead houses, "a pattern of postholes indicating a seventeenth century post-in-ground or earthfast house ... [as well as its] hearth and probably an oven."

XI-6 Abraham or Daniel Hasbrouck House
c. 1721 and later eighteenth century.

The street façade of this house is nicely disordered, the windows and doors of differing levels, just as the three rooms composing the first floor are of various heights. Historians have long speculated about which of the three rooms was built first. Helen Reynolds believed it to be the northernmost, while recent structural analysis indicates that the middle room is the earliest, followed by the north room, and finally the south with its relatively large windows and high ceiling.

Ivar Elis Evers (1866–1955), an artist, architectural designer, illustrator, and antiques dealer, owned the house from 1918 until his death in

ily Association acquired the house for the Huguenot Historical Society, which carried out a series of restorations, including removal of dormer windows and a wooden wing to the rear, as well as rebuilding the jambless fireplaces in the south and middle rooms. A fireplace in the north room of the cellar is served by the brick chimney, which is unusual locally in extending beyond the north wall. This cellar fireplace also provided heat for the room above.

XI-7 Reformed Church
1838–1839. Abel Saxton (transepts added 1871–1872 by J. A. Wood).

The white cupola, classical portico, and red brick walls of the nineteenth-century Reformed Church rise high above Huguenot Street's eighteenth-century stone houses. Because Americans have long confused the Greek Revival style of the church with architecture of the colonial period, the church has often been accepted as a part of the historic colonial street, while remaining an active place of Christian worship independent of the nearby museum houses. The 1839 building replaced a smaller, gambrel-roofed, stone church built a few feet to the south in the early 1770s—itself a replacement of the first stone house of prayer dedicated in 1720, demolished a little over fifty years later, and reconstructed in 1972 (see XI–3). In a practical and sentimental gesture, stones from the 1770s church were incorporated into the side wall of the steps leading to the porch of the 1839 building—note especially the datestone 1772 with the initials of men involved in the building of

1955. He was the first person without Huguenot ancestry to own the house, and at first older inhabitants feared the Swedish-born newcomer would disfigure the venerable house, but Evers soon proved himself an admirable preserver and even restorer of the place, which he filled with antiques, mostly American. He did a number of finely detailed and evocative watercolors of old stone houses in the Wallkill Valley, but especially of his own house and the flower garden he developed around it. In July 1948 the *National Geographic* published a color photo of the interior with the genial Evers seated in a colonial armchair with four young women ("local girls") attentively gathered around. The photo gives a nice sense of the cozy charm of the house during his stewardship. Evers's son Alf spent some of his boyhood here, and went on to become the distinguished historian of the Catskill region. Also in the 1940s, the interior of the Freer-Low house, just north of Evers's place, was updated according to Colonial Revival taste for the Rev. John W. Follette.

After Ivar Evers's death there was profound concern that a new owner would "modernize" the landmark, the fate that had befallen the Deyo house in 1894 and a fate purists of 1957 believed "worse than destruction." In due time the Hasbrouck Fam-

*XI-7. New Paltz Reformed Church
(c. 1980 photo)*

the second stone church. Additional foundation stones came from the LeFevre house, which had stood on the site of the church.

Minutes of the church's governing consistory reveal that in 1838 the building committee traveled to New Hackensack, Dutchess County, where "the new brick church" impressed them as a "suitable house of worship," and so it was recommended "in the main as a model" for New Paltz. Spurred by the pastor, the Rev. Douw van Olinda (remembered as a man of "executive ability" who in 1833 had presided over the construction of the nearby Academy [see XI–23]), the consistory reviewed such design questions as the inclusion of a portico. Some argued, "the portico will cost more than it is really worth." Even more controversial was the matter of building in stone, brick, or wood. Wood appealed to some because a wooden church "in plain style" could be built for $5,000, but others said wood was "impermanent" and would soon require "expensive repairs." Stone was readily available and was sanctioned by local custom and tradition. But stone was too expensive, and brick was finally chosen after its advocates raised the $1,500 cost difference between it and wood.

In January 1839 the consistory entered into a contract with a member, Abel Saxton, to build a brick church of dimensions similar to New Hackensack's and with brick pillars. He was to be paid $8,100. As was common in the 1830s in communities like New Paltz, the services of an architect were not required. Saxton finished his work on time, and the building was dedicated December 17, 1839. The fine new church was the stateliest building in the nineteenth-century village. With its portico of four Doric columns supporting a pediment and two-stage cupola fitted with corner pilasters, it was more purely Greek than the New Hackensack church, whose essentially Grecian appearance was mixed with pointed-arched, Gothic cupola openings and side windows. At New Paltz, doors, windows, and louvered openings in the cupola were uniformly rectangular—Greek. No

one objected to the fact that Christians would be worshipping in a building reminiscent of a pagan Greek temple.

The main room for worship, called the "Lecture Room" in the 1840s, was nearly square, with a central pulpit as focal point on the west side. Leaders of the church and those able to afford the most expensive pews sat near the pulpit. A three-sided gallery rested then, and now, on simple Doric columns. The least desirable pews in the gallery were set aside for Academy students and "colored people."

In 1871–1872 un-Grecian transepts designed by architect J. A. Wood were added to the west. The windows are round-arched (like those of the Presbyterian Church in Marlboro by Wood in 1868), not rectangular, and inside the transepts the curving brackets with industrial-looking pegs belong to the free eclecticism of the 1870s. At the same time clear glass windows were replaced with the simple stained glass that still fills most windows. In the early 1900s the church installed in the south transept two pictorial stained-glass windows, one portraying Christ as the Good Shepherd and the other Christ in the Garden at Geth-semane. The beautiful figures no doubt caused distress in the Huguenot spirits who had opposed images of Biblical figures and were responsible for the utterly plain 1720 House of Prayer.

Members of the New Paltz church have usu-ally resisted the temptation to allow its interior to be surfaced with plaques honoring individuals or their ancestors. The first such memorial, placed in memory of the Rev. Philip Peltz, was accepted in 1885. Adorning the narthex, this brass plaque with Gothic lettering was made by Cox and Buckley of London and New York. In 1933 a larger bronze tablet was unveiled on the back wall of the sanc-tuary, one which Judge Alphonso T. Clearwater had commissioned to honor his Huguenot and Dutch ancestors and, not least, himself. Designed by Maxfield Keck, the tablet was cast by Gorham Company of New York. Judge Clearwater, a lead-ing citizen of Kingston, past president of the Hol-land Society, and a vice president of the Huguenot Society of America, was proud of his forebears' "heroic devotion to the faith and to this church." Writing in the 1928–1929 Holland Society *Year Book*, Judge Clearwater claimed that his com-memorative idea was shared by, if not inspired by, President Theodore Roosevelt:

Sitting on the south veranda of the White House ... with President Roosevelt one rare morning in June, he said to me: "I think we should erect a monument to our Dutch ancestors, either at Kingston, New Paltz or Shawangunk. They were real Dutchmen and would not be bossed ei-ther by old Stuyvesant or that old Patroon Van Rensselaer so they went to Esopus and founded your Dutch church, the mother of those at New Paltz and Shawangunk and many others."

In the early1950s Dominie (Pastor) Gerret Wull-schleger and architect Bernard Guenther collabo-rated on remodeling the west end of the interior. Two tall, wooden, fluted shafts were purchased from a demolition firm, split in half, and applied to the wall behind a new central communion ta-ble. With new Doric capitals, these half columns gave the interior a classical aura matching that of the exterior portico. A new pulpit was constructed to one side of the communion table and a lectern (later removed) on the other. A sound-muffling acoustic tile ceiling with recessed lighting was un-fortunately built below the original plaster ceiling.

In 1983 the bell from the 1772 church was retrieved from the cupola of the van den Berg campus school (where the bell was unused) and mounted near the baptismal font in an effort led by Richard Hasbrouck with the assistance of the author. The bell has the cast inscriptions "I. Bai-ley" and "N. York." John Bailey was a brass found-er and cutler most famous for making a battle sword for George Washington in 1778. After the demolition of the 1772 church, the bell—proba-bly dating from the 1780s or '90s—had a number of homes, including two village schoolhouses and a racetrack across the Wallkill River, before arriv-ing at van den Berg in the 1940s.

Village of New Paltz (beyond Huguenot Street)

XI–8 New Paltz School (former)
15 North Front St. 1812 and c. 1881.

Although disguised by Victorian additions, this building, originally the first public school building in New Paltz, is among the village's most venerable antiquities. The stones of the first-story walls once formed the walls of the Huguenot House of Prayer (1717) that stood near the site of the reconstructed French Church on Huguenot Street (see XI–3). When the House of Prayer was demolished in 1773, the stones were left unused until 1812, when they were relaid for this school. Both the place of worship and the school were, in plan, about thirty-three feet square. Initials, presumably of members of the DuBois and Hasbrouck families who were among those responsible for constructing the House of Prayer, can be seen on stones on the side of the building facing uphill toward Main Street. Were the finely cut stones forming quoins at the corners of the school building also from the House of Prayer? The second story was built by 1828 when the building began to be occupied by the Classical School (the forerunner of the New Paltz Academy, which was built near the Wallkill River in 1833). About 1856 a cupola was added (no longer extant) to hold the bell originally used in the Reformed Church's second stone building (see XI–7).

By 1873 school commissioner (and *New Paltz Independent* editor) Ralph Le Fevre reported efforts to have the old school condemned. "From the records it appears that the village school house has

XI-8. New Paltz School (stone) (1975 photo)

been standing sixty years. Having performed its part in the education of two generations it is about time that the old landmark should be compelled to give way before the march of improvement." Some were suggesting that the old landmark become "an elegant lockup." Were they mindful of the sturdy stone walls, or of the children whose freedom had been restrained within its walls?

In fact, the former school was sold at auction to John Drake and became his residence. In 1881 Drake hired John L. Rosencrans to make "repairs." These may have resulted in the appearance of the building in a photo, reproduced in Le Fevre's 1909 history, showing symmetrical, two-story, bay windows projecting toward the street, as well as decoratively patterned shingles and brackets beneath the low-pitched hipped roof. Today the building remains outwardly much as it was during Drake's ownership, although the right-hand bay has been altered.

XI–9* New Paltz School (demolished)
Church St. 1874 (demolished 1960s).
Lewis B. Van Wagenen.

"Now does our village school boy gaze at the comely proportions of the new school house fast approaching completion with the feeling of the heir apparent to the throne," wrote Ralph Le Fevre, school commissioner and editor of the *New Paltz Independent*. The old schoolhouse (1812) on North Front Street was obsolete and destined, some supposed, to be "an elegant lock-up" (see preceding entry, XI–8).

Lewis B. Van Wagenen of Kingston was paid $20 for drawing up plans and specifications for the Italianate-style building. Characteristic of that style were its paired brackets, segmental arched windows and doors, and classically detailed two-stage cupola. The cupola held the historic bell that first rang out from the second stone Reformed Church, later from the North Front Street school, and currently within the brick Reformed Church

XI-9. New Paltz School (brick) (DeWitt photo, 1955)

on Huguenot Street. The schoolrooms had high ceilings "to keep the air pure."

Van Wagenen was paid for the plans, and so should be considered the school's architect. He is listed in the 1871 county directory as a maker of window sash and blinds, but also associated with J. D. Stevens as Van Wagenen & Stevens, "architects and draftsmen." In this period the separation between the professional architect and the carpenter-builder-contractor was not yet clear. Editor Le Fevre, after citing the school as "the neatest and most tasteful of any in this Assembly District," called Jesse Steen, Jr., "a good architect," despite the fact that Steen was here simply the contractor. Steen did advertise himself as "Contractor and Carpenter. Builder and Architect." He later was a builder of the similar Italianate schoolhouse in Alligerville (see XIV–11), and built (and probably designed) his own house (1885–1886), which still stands at 6 Wurts Avenue.

The New Paltz school served only fifteen years as the village school and was subsequently used by the Normal School and for community meetings. It was wholly abandoned after World War I and demolished in the 1960s. (A porch had been removed earlier.) Dominick's Restaurant (1966, Gionta & Loedy, architects), now the Jewish Community Center, and an apartment house were built on the former school grounds.

XI–10 Henry L. Griffis House
19 North Chestnut St. 1892–1893.

This is a remarkably well-preserved example of the Shingle Style, a picturesque composition of shingled and stone walls, triangular gables and round-arched openings, delicate Colonial balusters and oval windows. The eclectic approach of the late nineteenth century is fully in evidence; the Colonial (actually Federal style) forms are successfully juxtaposed with rustic stonework and broad Richardsonian arches. Oddly, the cobblestone chimney on the south façade disappears behind shingles and a narrow slit window on the second story and attic levels. The cobblestones Griffis used to face the foundation walls were drawn from the nearby mountainside. The local press thought it noteworthy that the cellar was dug and stone walls laid by (unnamed) Italian workers. However, the chimney, said to be "the largest in the village," was erected by Irving Mackey, and Kingston mason Abm. C. Brundage put in the fireplaces. Work on the interior continued into the summer of 1893, when the house was declared "unquestionably, the finest finished of any in our village."

The original owner, Professor Henry L. Griffis, may also have been the designer of the house. Griffis had studied science at Lafayette College and had charge of the science department at the New Paltz Normal School. That he also functioned as village engineer and superintended construction of the iron truss bridge over the Wallkill in 1891 suggests that he had the ability to design his residence, perhaps with the aid of a pattern book.

XI-10. Griffis House (1975 photo)

XI–11* New Paltz Savings Bank
29 Main St. 1891–1892 (not extant).
Andrew F. Mason.

When nearing completion in November 1891, the New Paltz Savings Bank was named "the handsomest edifice in our village" by the local press. Its façade was the most imposing on Main Street—three stories tall with a mansard roof, it was faced with red pressed brick and red Massachusetts sandstone. Thanks to the Wallkill Valley Railroad, it was no longer necessary to use local stone. The ground story was treated with great blocks of rusticated or rough-surfaced stone as popularized by the Boston architect Henry Hobson Richardson. Also Richardsonian was the central stone gable rising over the sloping mansard. The banded stone cylinders topped with finials, found at the corners of the third story and, in smaller form, at the corners of the central stone gable, again stem from Richardson, but here appeared dangerously detached from the wall.

Andrew F. Mason was a Kingston architect whose own showily picturesque Queen Anne–style house (c. 1893) on Downs Street, Kingston, burned in 2007. His Savings Bank succumbed to modernizations in stripped classical style in 1935–1936 and 1950, the former, at least, by Tilghman Moyer and Co., the architectural and engineering firm that had recently designed the new Huguenot National Bank, also on Main Street (see XI–13).

XI-11. New Paltz Savings Bank (early-twentieth-century postcard)

XI–12 Solomon Elting Homestead (Elting Memorial Library)
93 Main St. Late eighteenth or early nineteenth century (library additions 1962–2006). NR

The Elting Memorial Library reflects the community's pride in its early history. Since 1920 the library has been located in "the old Elting house," a stone house of uncertain date but on property purchased by Solomon Elting in 1817. The community has also understood the needs of a progressive library and has supported a series of additions, the latest and largest designed by Schoenhardt, a Connecticut architectural firm, and completed in 2006.

The Elting house is of the often-encountered, story-and-a-half, five-bay type. Its central doorway is framed with sidelights and a transom, while a distinctive porch of four slender columns and central elliptical arch stands before the doorway. The delicate grace of the porch belongs to the Federal style of the early nineteenth century. Neil Larson has suggested that the benches along the side of the porch indicate the survival of the Dutch stoop, here combined with newly fashionable Federal elements. He also has proposed that the house as a

XI-12. Elting Memorial Library (DeWitt photo, 1947)

whole should be dated c. 1820. Attached to the west of the stone house is an early but undated frame section fronted with a charming porch and retaining an early fireplace and Dutch oven.

Philip LeFevre Elting (1866–1929) was born in the Abraham Elting stone house (1759) just north of the village of New Paltz, but became a wealthy paint manufacturer in Chicago. He maintained a second home in New Paltz at 169 Huguenot Street, an 1872 house altered by Myron Teller for Elting in the 1920s. In 1909 women of the New Paltz Study Club had established a public library in commercial buildings on Main Street, but a decade later the library had no permanent home. This was rectified when in 1920 Philip Elting purchased the old Elting house on Main Street and donated it to the community "as a public library to be known as Elting Memorial Library." Myron Teller restored the building in 1920, "with trifling alterations to accommodate its use for the library." Later, in 1928, Teller and Halverson restored and added to the 1759 Elting homestead for Howard Elting, a distant cousin of Philip and also a Chicago paint manufacturer. (Still later this became the Locust Tree Restaurant at 215 Huguenot Street.)

Leon H. Smith, a New York architect who married Elizabeth LeFevre Elting, had been asked to design the 1920 alterations, but declined because too busy. Forty-two years later, Smith had the time to serve as architect of a low, Colonial Revival wing of white-painted clapboards with green shutters. The wing, based on a rough sketch by Professor James Van Derpool of Columbia University, was compatible with the old stone building,

but also related to the Greek Revival house occupied by Smith and his wife Elizabeth (see XI–33). Bernard Guenther was responsible for the design of a similar but larger wing in 1978. The 2006 expansion succeeded in greatly increasing the space of the library while preserving all but the 1978 wing. Schoenhardt designed the new entrance porch as an enlarged version of the Federal-style porch of the old Elting house.

Next door at 101 Main Street, an old garage was rebuilt by Teller & Halverson in 1936–1937 to become a "Colonial style" Shell gas station operated by Raymond Terpenning. The owner was Miss Helen Hasbrouck. The architects aimed to create a gas station "in harmony with the library next door and the Huguenot bank" across Main Street. Dormers in the gable roof were intended to match those of the library (which had been added in the late nineteenth century). Oak beams from the old garage were reused as door lintels and ceiling beams in the office. In 1962 the Shell station was purchased by Peter J. Savago, Town Supervisor, and altered for use as his insurance office and rentable office space. Harry Halverson designed the 1962 alterations.

XI–13 Huguenot National Bank (JPMorgan Chase Bank)
2 Plattekill Ave. at Main St. 1935. Tilghman Moyer Co.

The Huguenot National Bank was opened in 1853 by descendants of New Paltz's founders. In the 1930s the bank's leaders were still of the old families; the president was Frank J. LeFevre. During the Great Depression, bank failures were common, but the Huguenot Bank was sound and in 1935 took advantage of low construction costs

XI-13. Huguenot National Bank (c. 1948 photo)

to replace its undistinguished wooden building with a new stone landmark whose construction would provide employment for local men desperate for work. According to bank publicity, stone was chosen to represent the character of both the New Paltz Huguenots and the bank. "There is just one material that is symbolic of the stalwart, rugged character of the Huguenots and representative of the stamina of the Huguenot Bank, more imperishable than New Hampshire granite, a local product uniquely appropriate for this edifice—Shawangunk conglomerate." The Smileys of Lake Mohonk donated the stone, which was chosen not only for its durability (and impenetrability by burglars) but also for its variety of colors.

The stone mason was Amon Roosa, a thirty-year resident of New Paltz with an old Dutch name who, when he died at age seventy soon after completing his work on the bank, was called "one of the best stone masons in the state." Early in his New Paltz years, Roosa had worked with builder-developer D. C. Storr, and in 1924 Roosa had been the mason for the cobblestone house built for the Mrs. Mary F. Canary family farther up Plattekill Avenue at the corner of South Oakwood Terrace. In 1932 he laid the stone walls of the Rev. John W. Follette's Candlelight Cottage on North Oakwood Terrace, said to resemble "an old stone house remodeled."

The bank announced that the architects, Tilghman Moyer and Co., of Allentown, Pennsylvania, were specialists in bank construction and that "the style is to be colonial French representative of the early French refugees. As the colonial buildings of this part of the state have been modified by Holland ideas the new bank building will be more truly representative of the Huguenot cast than any of them." In truth, aside from the use of stone with brick trim,

the bank has little connection to the old houses of Huguenot Street. Harold Wood, the bank's cashier who in 1940 became its president, related in 1978 that he had admired the stone library in Katonah and asked one of Moyer's men to design the bank in the style of the library. Therefore the bank's arched windows, cupola, and classical porch with balustrade stem not from the Huguenots, but from Kerr Rainsford, architect of the 1928 library.

Atop the cupola is a weathervane "hand wrought of iron by Todhunter, Inc., of New York City." The bank's untrustworthy publicity claimed "the design was taken from weather vanes found on early Huguenot buildings. It is a conventionalized pennant design bearing a silhouette of the *Golden Otter,* the ship on which some of the Huguenot settlers at Hurley came to America." Despite the exaggerated claims for the Huguenot roots of its design, the bank remains, like the Ellenville Post Office, a handsome example of the 1930s revival in stone of colonial architecture. The much-modernized interior retains a stone and brick fireplace in harmony with the exterior masonry and a steel vault grill marked "Huguenot National Bank."

XI-14* George Freer House
106 Main St. 1858 (demolished 1972).

This one-and-a-half-story Greek Revival house was built in 1858 by carpenter Aaron Deyo for George Freer, a blacksmith. A picturesque bay window was added in 1871 by another local carpenter, John C. Deyo, when the house was owned

XI-14. *George Freer House (1972 photo)*

by Elijah Woolsey. The low upper story became more habitable with the addition of a broad dormer in the early twentieth century. Then, in 1972, the house was demolished and replaced by a short-lived Carroll's fast-food restaurant. Professor Hugo Munsterberg had advised his young colleague, the author of this book, to purchase and move this handsome old house, but he declined to do so, merely photographing its demise.

XI-15* James P. Hayden House
3 Prospect St. at Main St. Begun 1893 (destroyed by fire 1991). William J. Beardsley.

Popularly known as "Hayden's Folly," this Queen Anne house was designed by Poughkeepsie architect William Beardsley with a bit of French cha-

XI-15. *Hayden House (1976 photo)*

teau in the cylindrical turret as well as a squared-off turret of uncertain heritage. Wholesale florist James Hayden lacked the funds to complete his house. In 1899 it was sold to New York State, which completed it as the residence for principals of the New Paltz Normal School—the first to occupy the prestigious house being Myron Scudder. The state later sold the house, and its decline was sealed when a gas station was built in its front yard. In 1991 Hayden's Folly, long divided into apartments, was destroyed by fire.

Other large Queen Anne houses were erected across Main Street from the Hayden house. Most have been converted to commercial uses, but 142 Main Street, designed for Luther Hasbrouck in 1902 by another Poughkeepsie architect, Corydon Wheeler, remains a residence.

XI-16* Methodist Episcopal Church (Jewish Congregation of New Paltz)
Main St., later moved to 8 Church St. 1839–1840 (altered 1870, 1884, 1946). Theodore V. Swift and others.

As first erected by Theodore V. Swift of Tuthilltown, this plain, Greek Revival building had no steeple, probably as an economy and also to avoid the architectural example of Roman Catholic and Anglican churches. (The prominent John Street Methodist Church [1841] in New York also had no cupola or steeple.) In 1870 the building was moved a short distance north on Church Street, and the façade was transformed from

XI-16. *Methodist Episcopal Church, 1839–1940 (c. 1869 photo)*

XI-16A. Methodist Episcopal Church, with Gothic additions (c. 1900 photo)

XI–17 Methodist Episcopal Church (New Paltz United Methodist Church)
1 Grove St. at Main St. 1926–1929. Teller & Halverson.

In June 1929 New Paltz Methodists moved out of their uninspiring sanctuary with its makeshift Gothic façade tucked away on Church Street (see XI–16) and into this more sophisticated building prominently located on Main Street. In 1925 the Methodists' Denominational Bureau of Architecture recommended that New Paltz build a Gothic church because of "the historic relationship between the Episcopal and Methodist Churches," and that "collegiate Gothic [be chosen] for the religious educational building in keeping with the educational fame of the town." Architects Teller & Halverson began making plans in 1926, including towered Gothic and Georgian designs. In February 1927 the Gothic—a "simple adaptation of the English Village Church"—was chosen; a rendering shows a low stone church with side tower on Grove Street, and a School of Religion of stone with second story of half timber and brick. However, objections were raised to the elaborate and expensive proposal. The design finally approved and built in 1928–1929 (with Harry Halverson in charge) includes half-timbered and stuccoed gables, casement windows of leaded, diamond-paned, yellow "cathedral glass," and stained wood trusses visibly supporting the roof—all from the late medieval tradition and still described as in the "spirit of the

pagan Greek to a vernacular version of Christian Gothic by the addition of a steeple, arches, and pinnacles, while the side walls remained Greek Revival. The façade's Gothicization, begun in 1870, may have been enhanced by alterations in the mid-1880s.

When the Methodists moved to a new church in 1929, the building was taken on by the American Legion, which was concerned about the building's "ecclesiastical" aura and in 1946–1947 removed most of the façade's Gothic elements to achieve a bland "modernization." In 1960 the Legion Hall was purchased by Redeemer Lutheran Church and again served for Christian worship. The Jewish Congregation of New Paltz began to worship here in 1964, and Congregation Ahavath Achim acquired ownership of the building in 1965. Since that time the congregation has not made major changes to the exterior.

XI-17. Methodist Episcopal Church, 1926–1929 (1978 photo)

English village church." But there is no tower—only a modest cupola and spire rising from the ridge of the gable roof—and stone walls were eliminated in favor of wide clapboard siding. Rather than make a bold statement on Main Street, as the big Reformed Church with its Greek Revival portico continued to do on Huguenot Street, the Methodists opted for a low building with siding stained "to blend with the surroundings. The whole appearance will be that of having grown into its place." This could also be said of Teller's 1913 Shokan Reformed Church (see XII–7).

A rock garden (1930) along the Main Street sidewalk, designed by the Scottish-born New Paltz landscape architect Samuel McKeand Kevan, enhanced the entrance and helped give it a sense of rootedness. (Kevan had earlier designed the landscaping for the Howard Elting house on Huguenot Street, another Teller & Halverson project.)

The architects donated hand-wrought hardware worth $350 to the church, and devotees of Teller's hardware can readily examine marked examples on the front and side doorways. The front door hinges, with their multiple curving patterns, depart from Teller's standard Colonial designs, which are found on other doors at the church. While the building is not overtly Colonial, its simple lines and natural materials allow the Colonial hardware patterns to seem entirely appropriate.

XI–18 Iver Miller House
15 South Oakwood Terrace. 1929.

This is a well-preserved example of the so-called "Dutch Colonial" house built by the thousands across the country in the 1920s. Sinclair Lewis's middle-class businessman George Babbitt was a proud owner of one in the Midwest. While the Miller house looks nothing like early Dutch houses in the Hudson Valley, its gambrel roof was considered Dutch in the twenties. The porch may originally have been fitted as a Dutch stoop with benches to either side of the door. A feature unknown in colonial America, the long dormer emerging from the lower slope of the gambrel was common in Dutch Colonials of the twenties and allowed what would otherwise be merely at-

XI-18. Iver Miller House

tic space to become a useful second floor of bedrooms and bath.

Miller's house relates to designs published and sold by several companies, including Standard Homes of Washington, D.C., which sold blueprints and specifications for a house like Miller's for $10. Iver Miller purchased this house from the New Paltz Lumber Co., with which he was associated. When new in June 1929, it was opened to the public as a model house. Miller had visited the Northwest and incorporated features "in vogue" there, notably a "natural cool air refrigerator especially for use in fall and winter."

XI–19 Storr Houses
26 and 28 North Oakwood Terrace. 1907.
David C. Storr, builder.

These two similar houses (originally both had flat roofs) display the richly molded cornice, two-story polygonal bay, and columned piazza usually associated with the Victorian period's Italianate style. Yet the houses were obviously and unusually built of concrete blocks—not only the walls, but also the cornices and chunky piazza columns and balusters—and so belong to a later period. They were put up by David C. Storr (1852–1924), who eventually resided at #28. Storr was born in England, but by 1870 was a store clerk in Massachusetts, where he became a furniture manufacturer in the 1880s. In 1894 Storr resided in Boston, but was president of the Storr Furniture Company of Oshkosh, Wisconsin. Then, around the turn of the century, he headed the New York Couch

XI-19. 26 North Oakwood Terrace

Bed Company, maker of novel "steel couch and sofa beds." From Manhattan he moved to New Paltz in 1905. Two years later he began to manufacture concrete blocks from Portland cement and sand in a former coal shed belonging to A. P. LeFevre. Amon Rosa (or Roosa), who managed the factory, was said to have had experience in making blocks in Middletown. The 16-x-8-x-8-inch blocks were "figured in front, so that a house built of them will look like a house of rough dressed stone." Storr was part of a nation-wide fad for concrete block houses that began about 1900; in 1908 the Sears general catalog advertised "handsome nine-room concrete" houses and "concrete block building machines" for fabricating their walls and porches at two-thirds the cost of a stone house.

Storr purchased and developed land on the hill east of the old village. He laid out streets, put in water and sewer lines, and erected at least twenty houses in the vicinity of the pair on Oakwood Terrace. Most are of conventional wood-frame construction, although some of these have incongruously heavy concrete piazzas. Storr became "the largest property owner and taxpayer in New Paltz." At his death he was praised as a civic leader; he had served as a village trustee, president of the board of trade and of the Liberty Loan Committee, and had been a generous contributor to worthy causes—though not a member, he donated land for building the Episcopal Church on Main Street at North Oakwood Terrace. His business associates included Elting Harp, whose son Peter Harp remembered Storr in 1975 as an "English Jew ... polished and intelligent." In conservative New Paltz, where the descendants of the early

Dutch and Huguenot inhabitants dominated the community into the twentieth century, Storr was remarkably successful in working with the deeply rooted leaders of the village. While his experiment with concrete block construction in New Paltz was short-lived, these two houses can serve as reminders of a good citizen of the village.

XI–20 O. Lincoln and Virginia Igou House
43 North Manheim Boulevard. 1950–1951. Henry F. Miller.

Dr. O. Lincoln Igou, a professor of music at SUNY New Paltz, commissioned this house, a rare and refreshing example of modern design in conservative New Paltz. Even Woodstock had few comparable modern houses in 1951.

Dr. Igou earned a Ph.D. at Northwestern University and studied in Vienna, Salzburg, and Basel before marrying Virginia Florence Wegener in 1947. For the design of their home, he perused various house magazines and sent letters to a number of architects inquiring whether they would be interested in designing the New Paltz house. At Northwestern, and especially under Professor Carl Beecher, Igou had studied a wide range of the arts and had been drawn to modernism. He wanted his house to "look forward, rather than back as

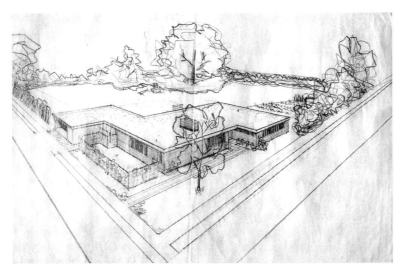

XI-20. Igou House (drawing by Miller, c. 1950)

modern lines. In 2001, shortly after Miller's house in Orange was placed on the National Register of Historic Places, the retired architect recalled that fifty years earlier he (like many architects and critics) had imagined that the International Style would become widely accepted in the U.S. and throughout the world. Instead, Miller found that, "While the style did become somewhat popular ... during the 1950s, it never caught on the way I expected—I guess because most people are used to living in cozy capes or large colonials and never quite embraced this more unique and modest style." Dr. Igou embraced the progressive style of his house and occupied it nearly sixty years, until his death at age 101 in 2010.

In 1951 the Igou house shared the distinction of being a pioneer of modernism in New Paltz with a house at 70 Prospect Street built for art professor Larry Argiro and designed by his brother Nicholas Argiro.

a Cape Cod or Colonial would." Noted architect Edward Durell Stone and others associated with the modern movement were uninterested in the job. Fortunately, Henry F. Miller, a 1948 graduate of the Yale School of Architecture who had served as an artillery officer in World War II, was interested at the beginning of his architectural career in Connecticut. A modern house Miller designed and built in 1948–1949 for his own family in Orange, Connecticut, had appeared in *House Beautiful*'s series on "The New American Style."

For the Igous, Miller planned a low, flat-roofed, one-story house with horizontal windows, free-flowing interior space, and no historical ornament—a design influenced by Frank Lloyd Wright's houses and the International Style. Built on a concrete slab, the house is sited close to the street intersection, and the low massing of the house protects the pleasant backyard garden from street noise. The living room and dining room are joined as one space and together are united with the garden via a glassy wall. The screened terrace was oriented to the southwest to admit the heat of the sun in the winter, while the terrace roof shields the interior from the direct summer sun. As Wright advocated, all living is done on one floor—no basement, no attic.

While the novel house was generally well received in New Paltz, the flat roof of the International Style struck some neighbors as impractical in snowy winters, and some disliked its stark,

XI–21 Judge A. V. Dayton House (Hanmer House, Geography Department, SUNY New Paltz)
Mohonk Ave. East at South Manheim Boulevard. 1937. Oscar Parliman, contractor and builder.

This modest house appears to be one of what architectural historian Daniel D. Reiff calls "houses from books." Essentially a cozy Cape Cod cottage with sun porch to the west, there is added to the front a projecting, steeply pitched gable and an over-scaled fireplace chimney that cuts through the curving roof. The lines of the projecting gable were to give an English accent. This slightly eccentric

XI-21 Dayton House (threatened with demolition)

façade compares closely to "The Maplewood" advertised by Sears, Roebuck & Co. in its 1932 and 1933 catalogs, as well as the "Ridgeland" from the 1933 to 1939 catalogs. The tiny window to the left of the doorway and in front of the chimney is a delightful bit of whimsy, although the rectangular door frame of the Dayton house is more prosaic than the arched top of "Maplewood." (The Dayton house does have an archway cut into the wall extending eastward from the façade.) The Sears design called for shutters, a batten door with ornamental strap hinges, and an "English" lantern above the door. A photo of the house in the 1950s, when it was owned by Lee and Mary Hanmer and nicely landscaped, shows dark-painted shutters and a rectangular door with a Colonial fanlight. The plan of the Dayton house's living room, dining room, kitchen, bathroom, and bedroom on the first floor resembles, but is not identical to, the Sears plan.

XI-22* Elting T. Deyo House
Mohonk Ave. 1870–1871 (demolished by New York State, c. 1966). Elting T. Deyo.

The expansion of the SUNY campus brought on the demolition of this mansard-roofed, Second Empire–style house with tower adorned with overscaled finials. It had been built by and for Elting T. Deyo (1831–1907), who was trained as a carpenter by Tobias Elting and established himself as "a boss carpenter" and builder of barns and houses in and near New Paltz. In 1869 Deyo received the contract to enlarge the Mountain House at Paltz

Point (Mohonk), and in 1872 he would win the contract for the carpentry and painting of the substantial addition to the New Paltz Reformed Church, of which he was an active member.

The editor of the *New Paltz Independent* (May 11, 1871) reported that he had been told that Elting's house was:

> a great ornament to our village. To satisfy our curiosity, we visited the place ... and found that it was quite as elegant as it had been represented to us. Mr. Deyo is a very superior architect [it is not clear that Deyo called himself an "architect"] and has spared no pains to make his own residence an exponent of the perfection of his art. The first floor contains five large rooms, the parlor being furnished off with wood of three different kinds—oak, chestnut and black walnut.

Fourteen additional rooms were on the second and third floors. "The building is surmounted by a tower about eight feet square, from the summit of which a view of the village and of the country for miles around may be obtained." The house was clearly designed for boarders, and in 1873 Deyo advertised that there were rooms for about twenty in his residence "at Prospect Heights." Boarders would find "a tower ... commands a very extensive view of the Catskill and Shawangunk Mountains, and of the Wallkill River and the beautiful country though which it flows." The railroad depot was only a half mile away; attractions included Lake Mohonk and the Rosendale railroad bridge. However, Deyo's timing was unfortunate—the economy was depressed when he opened—and by July 1874 he was bankrupt. The resilient Deyo did recover, but abandoned carpentry in favor of farming, fruit growing, and an undertaking business. He was a village trustee, and in 1885 became a member of the New Paltz Academy's board of trustees.

In 1947 the property was acquired by the state and used as a dormitory and later as offices. It was probably during this period that Ruth Mack Havens (died 1961), a teacher of English and kindergarten at the college, used its Victorian form

XI-22. Elting T. Deyo House (John Jacobson photo, 1966)

in her bookplate, an indication of the nostalgic appeal things Victorian were beginning to exert at mid-century. When the house was demolished, the college's information office described a demolition photo of the "Victorian style residence" as emblematic of the passing of an era—"An Era Topples." In its place would rise a modern steel, concrete, and glass Science Building by New York architects Davis, Brody and Associates. But the old did not succumb without a struggle: "With almost half the ground floor ripped from under it by a bulldozer, the tower and cupola twice broke the machine's cable attached to pull it down. The picture was taken as it tottered and fell with the bulldozer tearing at it from the back."

XI-23 New Paltz Normal School (Old Main, SUNY New Paltz)
Near intersection of Plattekill Ave. and South Oakwood Terrace. 1907. George L. Heins.

For the New Paltz community, Old Main's appeal resides in its status as the first building erected on the campus of what is today SUNY New Paltz.

The college developed out of the New Paltz Academy, a private school quartered in a plain classical building with central cupola that stood near the Wallkill River from 1833 until it was destroyed by fire in 1884. (North and south wings were appended in 1840.) The Academy was quickly rebuilt in the Queen Anne style according to a design by New York architect Charles W. Romeyn (1854–1942). The new building was turned over to New York State in December 1885, and the Academy became New Paltz Normal School. Albany architect Albert W. Fuller designed a large, austere, Richardsonian Romanesque brick addition (1888–1889), but the Romeyn-Fuller building was destroyed by fire in 1906.

State officials were then confronted with arguments that the school should move to a larger, more accessible town, such as Kingston or Newburgh, or should remain in New Paltz. And if it remained, should it be built on the original, riverside site, or on a new, higher one. With the strong support of Lake Mohonk proprietor Albert K. Smiley, chairman of the school's local board, and of Judge G. D. B. Hasbrouck of Kingston, an Academy graduate and local board member, New Paltz residents succeeded in convincing the state to keep the school in the village. The *New Paltz Times* argued that, "New Paltz bears a high reputation for health, cleanliness, and morality, as well as education. Here young men and young women could be safe from temptations which would assail them in larger towns. We are a village of churches … Besides the village is free from illiterate foreigners." Moreover, the paper pointed to the village's low-cost places of room and board, its accessibility by steamboat and train, its pure drinking water, and its freedom from malaria. The rival *New Paltz Independent* chimed in that Lake Mohonk's "magnificent grounds" and its conferences attracting "the best minds and the most advanced thinkers" made New Paltz more appealing as a Normal School location than were larger cities.

Sentimentalists with links to the old Academy and Normal School pleaded for rebuilding on the site of the ruins, but there were objections to the noise and smoke of the trains on the nearby Wallkill Valley Railroad. Those with a larger vision

XI-23. New Paltz Normal School (1907 postcard)

of the future, led by Albert Smiley, pushed for more spacious grounds allowing for the school's expansion, and an elevated site on the hill east of the village would provide a panoramic view to the west toward Mohonk, where Smiley had created a highly successful mountaintop resort. Smiley's forces carried the day, and at the 1907 ground-breaking ceremony he remarked that "from this site we have the finest view of any place in this vicinity, except from the hill over yonder, Mohonk"—which brought forth laughter from the crowd. While no one referred to Thomas Jefferson and his plan for the University of Virginia at Charlottesville, that was the great American precedent for the campus on elevated ground with a fine landscape vista.

The new building was designed, with little obvious regard for the elevated site, in the Albany office of the State Architect, George L. Heins (1860–1907). Appointed to the post by Governor Theodore Roosevelt, Heins was well known as the original architect (with C. Grant LaFarge) of the Episcopal Cathedral of St. John the Divine in New York, as well as the Bronx Zoo and IRT subway stations. After Heins's death on September 25, 1907, following a nervous breakdown from overwork, supervision of the school's construction passed to his successor, Franklin B. Ware, who was very familiar with New Paltz. He was a member of the firm of James E. Ware & Son, which had designed sections

of the hotel at Lake Mohonk for Albert Smiley.

An early design by Heins was put on view in John Schmid's show window in the village. It called for a cupola, but by December 1906 the cupola had been eliminated. What Heins and Ware finally produced—the building occupied and dedicated in 1909—was a dignified but unremarkable classical design where historical precedent and architectural refinements were less important than practicality and economy. The classical details are few: the central doorway is set off with paired Doric columns and pilasters of Indiana limestone with triglyphs in the frieze above; a metal cornice crowns the three-story central block and two-story wings; and light-colored bricks at the corners of the wings are laid like quoins. The composition of the façade is markedly symmetrical and horizontal—classical attributes—in contrast to the Romeyn-Fuller designs of the 1880s. The roof is nearly flat and hidden behind a low parapet above the cornices. The windows topped with low, segmental arches and keystones appear French classical in origin, but there is also a good deal of no-nonsense, turn-of-the-century America in the façade. The double-hung sash windows (originally in wooden frames) admitted much daylight and could be thrown open for fresh air—abundant daylight and fresh air were considered essential for schools of the time. Like contemporary commercial buildings, the two stories of the wings and upper two stories of the central block are joined by the "pier and spandrel motif," where brick piers project and rise without interruption over the two stories while the metal spandrel, like the window above and below it, is recessed. Given the fires of 1884 and 1906, fireproofing was clearly desirable. The exterior walls were of stone and brick, and the internal structure was of concrete, iron, and steel. Still, the floors, window frames, and other interior trim were wooden.

Expense was reduced by reusing some of the brick and stone from the ruins near the Wallkill. (Much handsomely cut stone composes the basement walls.) Ornament was kept to a minimum. No one would confuse this state normal school with the Gothic halls of elite private institutions, like Vassar College across the Hudson, where the conspicuously expensive carved stone and figurative stained glass of Thompson Memorial Library (Allen & Collens, 1903–1905) provided an aura of academic tradition and prestige rooted in Oxford and Cambridge. A large, ornamental glass window above the main entrance was planned from the outset for the Normal School, but the window (with the dates "1916" and "1917" in the glass) has no figures and tells no inspiring story, although the fleur-de-lis may refer to the French origins of the community. (The motif's royal connotations, however, seem inappropriate.)

The interior of the Normal School was always plain, and has not been well treated in recent decades. Its most intriguing element, the former gymnasium's elevated running track, suspended from the walls of the south wing, was off-limits for many years and has disappeared in the current overhaul of Old Main. The school's 1909 Circular of Information advertised that, from the Art Rooms on the third floor, "the view of the western hills is more inspiring than any picture that could be hung on the walls." Albert Smiley must have been delighted with this affirmation of his belief in the value of the view toward Mohonk.

The contractor for the new Normal School was Morris Kantrowitz of Albany, a native of Russia who immigrated to the United States as a boy. His highly successful career included the rebuilding of H. H. Richardson's Albany City Hall and

the construction of Roberts Hall (designed by George Heins) for Cornell University's College of Agriculture. The unskilled construction workers hired by the contractor for the New Paltz project were primarily Italian immigrants. A local newspaper commented that they were "men of good character who have done their work well and created no disturbance," but concluded, with apparent relief, that "all are now gone."

The building was dedicated in January 1909. By 1916 plans were being made under the direction of Lewis Frederick Pilcher, State Architect, for an addition to the north. Largely completed in 1919 and dedicated in 1920, the addition contained a 1,200-seat auditorium. High on its façade, three small stained-glass windows furnish tenuous links to traditions of classical education—a pair of windows with a torch of learning bears the Latin motto "Sit Lux 1921" (Let There Be Light), while the third, with the date "1922," represents a classical lamp of learning.

XI-24 Lawrence H. van den Berg School of Practice (van den Berg Hall, SUNY New Paltz)
Tricor Ave. at Hasbrouck Ave. 1929–1932. William H. Haugaard.

By 1927 Lawrence H. van den Berg, principal of the Normal School, was pushing for a second building to accommodate the expanding student body; in March 1927 there were 595 students (only 15 of whom were boys), while in September 1928 there were 740. Led by banker-businessman Bruyn Hasbrouck, New Paltz civic leaders lobbied the state for the new building; Hasbrouck met several times with Governor Franklin D. Roosevelt in 1929. Both men were active in the Holland Society, open only to men of long Hudson Valley Dutch ancestry. The State Education Department at first did not support a second building. The department was annoyed that New Paltz's frugal citizens would not pay a school tax, instead relying on the state to educate New Paltz children at the Normal School. Moreover, Westchester County was lobbying for a new normal school in White Plains. In the end, New Paltz citizens agreed to build a central union

XI-24. Van den Berg School of Practice (c. 1975 photo)

high school (now the middle school), while the lower grades would attend the new practice school built by the state.

Governor Roosevelt broke ground for the practice school October 25, 1930, at the end of a day of campaigning for reelection. Earlier in the month he had been attacked by his Republican opponent, Charles H. Tuttle, for his administration's slowness in carrying out construction projects—New Paltz Normal's promised building being cited as a prime example. Moreover, Roosevelt had recently had to defend himself against critics who contended that his inability to walk unassisted diminished his ability as governor. A local newspaper reported that when the governor arrived at the site by car, it was almost dark. The scene was illuminated by car headlights and powerful lights mounted on a steam shovel. Roosevelt did look weary and, as always, he needed help to reach the speaker's stand. But "plucky son of Holland that he is, he has made his way to the leadership of the state in spite of the handicap of lameness. On the platform was another good son of Holland, Dr. van den Berg." FDR remarked that he had been making political speeches throughout the day, but "in New Paltz he had come to wield the shovel, not the hatchet," and he commented on his "friendliness" to the New Paltz Normal School. Before turning the first shovelful of earth, the governor read the inscription on the ceremonial shovel, which referred to his role in the ceremony. The shovel was intended for preservation within the building, and it is preserved by SUNY New Paltz as a reminder of the campus's link to a great leader of the state, the country, and the world.

The design of 1929–1930 was the responsibility of State Architect William H. Haugaard,

who had been trained at Pratt, MIT, and the École des Beaux-Arts in Paris. Construction was completed in 1932, and the building was dedicated in 1934 as the Lawrence H. van den Berg School of Practice. It stands 100 feet west and down a steep grade from the earlier Normal School (now Old Main), and it looks out upon the village's Hasbrouck Memorial Park, which the village agreed to lease to the state as a playground.

By 1929 the free, vaguely French classicism of the 1907 Normal School design was passé. Like many schools and government buildings of the 1920s (including Haugaard's Administration Building at the State College for Teachers at Buffalo, begun in 1928), van den Berg's exterior belongs to the Colonial Revival, in this case reviving and expanding upon eighteenth-century Georgian and Federal-style forms found on college and public buildings of the earlier era. The center of the long, red-brick façade is accented by a pedimented doorway within a three-bay, three-story pedimented pavilion that in turn is crowned with a cupola resting on a square base. Clock faces emerge from the square base, while urns top its corners. The cupola, an arcaded belfry surmounted by a hemispherical dome, descends from those gracing colleges since colonial times—Harvard Hall (1675), the College of William and Mary (1699), the College of New Jersey (Princeton, 1756), and King's College (Columbia, 1760).

Haugaard, however, felt no need to create an

accurate reproduction of a colonial college. The volume of van den Berg exceeds any eighteenth-century college structure, and individual parts (such as the windows) are over-scaled. Beyond the central pavilion, the windows are grouped in threes to meet the demands of the time for daylight and fresh air in the classrooms. The huge, chimney-like forms on the end walls are fitted with louvers indicating additional efforts at air circulation. The underlying structure of the building is modern concrete and steel.

The popularity of the Colonial Revival in the 1920s and '30s was based on several factors. It was less expensive than the Gothic Revival, which typically required skilled craftsmen in stone, wood, and glass. It was also a distinctly American style, growing out of American social, political, and architectural traditions; was not the nation founded in Independence Hall, a red-brick building with a Georgian cupola? The Colonial Revival did not have obviously foreign connections, an advantage in a time when many Americans claiming long American ancestry feared the influx of foreigners with radical, seemingly irrational ideas and agendas. In the 1930s, New Paltz Normal School catalogues and speakers at ceremonial occasions routinely referred to the valuable inspiration provided by the colonial settlers of the region. Judge Gilbert D. B. Hasbrouck proposed at the dedication that the early Dutch and Huguenot inhabitants and their descendants in 1934 held firmly "to the high ideals of industry, thrift, temperance, religion and education; that here [in New Paltz] the surroundings of youth find the best examples of citizenship and everything to induce the foundation of high character." While such pronouncements seem innocuous, they were silently linked to a corrosive bigotry that resulted in van den Berg's exclusion of Roman Catholics from the Normal School's faculty—a policy that the local board, led by Kingston businessman Vincent A. Gorman, criticized in 1932.

In the 1940s the bell, originally located in the cupola of the 1772 stone Reformed Church on Huguenot Street and subsequently used at a number of locations, was placed in van den Berg's cupola. Fortunately, this bell, made by John Bailey

in New York, probably in the 1780s or '90s, was formally returned by the college to the church in 1983, and so escaped destruction when the cupola was destroyed by fire in 1990. The roof remained without its distinguished accent until 2005, when a fine recreation of the original was lifted into place and the college once more had its crowning emblem of American tradition. Perhaps sometime in the future the unpleasant electronic chimes sent forth half-hourly will be supplanted by a genuine bell rung less frequently.

XI-25 Library (Old Library, SUNY New Paltz)
Plattekill Ave. at South Oakwood Terrace. 1948–1954. Robert J. Reiley. (See XI–26)

XI-25. Library (former) (1976 photo)

XI-26 College Hall (SUNY New Paltz)
Plattekill Ave. at Ridge Rd. 1946–1952. Teller & Halverson.

New Paltz Normal School became New Paltz State Teachers College in 1942, but buildings expressive of the expanded ambitions of the college had to await the end of World War II. After the war, college catalogues abandoned references to the conservative, Huguenot-inspired culture of the village and embraced more progressive ideals. Architecturally, the more progressive spirit is found in hints of modernism in designs retaining strong elements of the Colonial Revival for the college's first buildings dedicated to library and dormitory use. The library, designed by Robert J. Reiley (Reiley and Thorn, Architects, New York City), was described in the *New Paltz Alumni News* as "of traditional design to harmonize with other buildings on the New Paltz campus," although the equipment and facilities within were "most modern." Also modern is the north façade on Plattekill Avenue with its glass bricks once providing soft illumination for the multi-tier book stacks.

The dormitory and student union, College Hall, was commissioned in 1946, ground was broken in 1949, the cornerstone was laid in 1950, and in 1952 Governor Thomas E. Dewey dedicated the building. The architects were nominally Myron Teller & Harry Halverson of Kingston, although by this date Halverson was fully in command. Teller & Halverson were noted Colonial Revivalists, but here Halverson produced a stripped Colonial diluted with modern simplicity. Spartan red-brick wings are joined to a centerpiece faced with heavily rusticated Shawangunk grit and fitted with very thin pilasters and modern steel doors (now replaced). Here was the last gasp of historically inspired traditional architecture.

Only in the 1960s, under Governor Nelson Rockefeller, an enthusiast for modern art and architecture, would New Paltz and other SUNY campuses receive examples of modern design worthy of a very good state university. Davis, Brody & Associates' Wooster Science Building completes the quadrangle formed by Old Main, the Old Library, and College Hall. Seen from the quadrangle, the long, low, concrete and glass building has been compared to a sleek transatlantic liner. However, the projecting form of the staircase on the west end was not sleek, and reminded one critic of the useless tailfins of a Cadillac. The science building earned the Davis, Brody firm a design award from *Progressive Architecture* in 1966, despite a debate within the jury (which included the architect Kevin Roche and the historian Vincent Scully) as to whether its sculptural form was suited to its functional requirements. In 2010 the sturdy concrete modernism of the 1960s is out of fashion, and there are plans to rework Wooster into something softer, more harmonious with its brick neighbors.

XI-26. College Hall

Town of New Paltz (beyond the Village)

XI-27 New Paltz Rural Cemetery
81 Plains Rd. Begun 1861. B. F. Hathaway.

The villagers of New Paltz joined the rural cemetery movement in 1861, acquiring land on the plain south of the village, near the Wallkill River, and leaving the old Huguenot burying ground in dilapidated condition (see XI–3). In the 1850s the Poughkeepsie Rural Cemetery and Kingston's Wiltwyck Rural Cemetery and Montrepose Cemetery were laid out as picturesque parks with plantings and drives placed irregularly according to the naturally rolling contours of the land. The New Paltz cemetery, however, was sited on flat land, and most of the drives and plots conform to a rectilinear grid.

The initial design was by B. F. Hathaway of Connecticut, described in cemetery publicity as "an experienced Civil Engineer and Landscape Gardener" whose "Engineering taste" assured that the cemetery would be both practical and beautiful. (Hathaway also designed Laurel Grove Cemetery in Port Jervis.) The term "Landscape Gardener," used earlier by renowned tastemaker Andrew Jackson Downing, offered further assurance that the grounds would be planted to create an attractive park. It was announced that "the avenues, paths and plots are being artistically laid out" with the intention of "adorning the plots and walks with evergreens, shrubbery and trees so disposed as to give an air of pleasant variety to the grounds." In 1861, before the cemetery opened, trees were planted along "Entrance Avenue or the carriageway to the Cemetery ... An ornamented gateway is to be erected at the entrance with separate passages for carriages and those on foot." Today Entrance Avenue is still lined with stately, tall trees, but the picturesque Gothic gateway has been moved to the rear of the caretaker's house and altered to serve as a maintenance building. The gateway's central carriageway has been enclosed and most of the picturesque details removed.

Perhaps more significant than the designed improvements to the landscape, the natural background—the Wallkill River and Shawangunk Ridge—provided markedly picturesque qualities. At the time of the cemetery's dedication in 1861 by Reformed Church clergy, the *New Paltz Times* endorsed the venture, finding "the soil ... excellent" and "the location ... most appropriate," since it was away from "the noise, bustle, and dust of the town ... yet sufficiently near for convenience." But most appealing was the view from the cemetery of the river, ridge, and Catskills beyond, which lent itself to poetic and spiritual interpretation: "On the West and North the gently flowing Wallkill silently rolls onward toward the sea, while in the distance the white battlements of the Shawangunk and the misty blue of the Catskills meet the eye suggestive of the River of Death (ever near) and the dimly descried but gorgeous hills of immortality."

The dead would be remembered thanks to monuments that should outlast those erected earlier in New Paltz. The *Times* asked, "'where do the ... forefathers of the hamlet sleep?' Where are the eight generations of your Huguenot Ancestry? Not

XI-27. New Paltz Rural Cemetery, Boyce monument

half of them have a record or a remembrancer to tell they lived or died. No storied urn or ... marked monument with historic inscription stands to tell the traveler the history and virtue of these noble sires." The remedy was obvious: "Let the cherished and honored dead have their written memorial among you, let these virtues live in marble."

Elting T. Deyo (1831–1907), the New Paltz architect, builder, and undertaker whose mansarded residence does not survive (see XI–22), rests beneath a marble monument capped with a classical urn. Some earlier nineteenth-century marble monuments in the classical taste with shallow carvings of weeping willows over classical urns, such as those for Roeliff Hasbrouck (died 1842) and Jemima Eltinge (also died 1842), were brought in from other burial places. The Richard B. Davis and Lydia Maria LeFevre Davis monument (1895), a shrouded obelisk of Massachusetts granite twenty-five feet high, was designed and executed by B. W. Van Wyck of Van Wyck & Collins of Poughkeepsie. It was said to be "by far the largest and finest" monument in the cemetery, and so a conspicuous and everlasting demonstration of wealth and power (the monument's carved oak branch was "emblematic of strength"). It was in fact taller than the Quincy granite obelisk erected by the predecessor firm of Miller & Van Wyck in 1870 to commemorate New Paltz's heroic Civil War dead. (The firm's name is incised at the base.) Davis, a successful merchant and real estate speculator, had lived in Carmel and Fishkill Landing, but his wife Lydia was a sister of Congressman Jacob LeFever of New Paltz (LeFever is variously spelled).

The McKinstry mausoleum with a pair of classical columns and rough-hewn blocks of stone for walls and roof looks as if it will stand for eternity. It was apparently built for the remains of David McKinstry (1853–1919), son of Floyd S. McKinstry—Wallkill Valley Railroad president and creator of Gardiner hamlet—whose obelisk memorial is nearby. The younger McKinstry went west and became a wealthy Oklahoma businessman. He was known for his "strong force of character" and was proud of his "fine and costly" house (1908) in Oklahoma City. His final New Paltz home exudes strength and looks costly.

Joseph Boyce (1835–1915) lives on in a stone portrait bust (signed "By Wands"[?]) as an alert old man with full mustache. Boyce was, according to his obituary, "a well-known stone cutter ... For a number of years Mr. Boyce was employed on the stone dock at Wilbur and was a most efficient workman." Portrait busts of the deceased in stone are extremely rare in Ulster County, but it seems highly appropriate that a worker in the stone industry should be thus memorialized.

The Linderbeck monument (c. 1900) looks like stone hung with tassels, but is actually cast metal. Twentieth-century monuments to members of the Smiley family of Lake Mohonk are appropriately and honestly of Shawangunk grit. Oscar Tschirky, the famous "Oscar of the Waldorf," maître d'hôtel of the Waldorf-Astoria Hotel in New York, erected a monument to his parents and himself, while nearby are dozens of small markers over the graves of residents of the Culinarians Home that he founded (see XI–34). When the cemetery opened, burials of "the African race" were not permitted, but within a few years African Americans were allowed to bury their dead in the western section and erect modest monuments—see, for example, that of John Hasbrouck (1806–1879) and his wife Sarah (1806–1892).

XI–28 Josiah DuBois House
181 Libertyville Rd. 1822. NR

This federal-style, two-story, brick house represents a repudiation of the informally composed, low houses of irregular stone built a few decades

XI-28. Josiah DuBois House (1975 photo)

earlier in the village of New Paltz and elsewhere in the town. The house is distinguished by a fine doorway with sidelights capped with an elliptical arch and keystone in marble. The arch is carved with the name of the original owner, Josiah Du-Bois, and the keystone with the date, 1822. The window lintels and sills are also of marble. Sheltering the doorway is a wide, gable-roofed stoop with side benches, described by Neil Larson as "a signature element of the [houses of the] rural elite." Josiah DuBois in 1822 was the former son-in-law of Col. Josiah Hasbrouck, the owner of the elegant but wooden house built in 1814 and later called Locust Lawn. (DuBois's wife and Hasbrouck's daughter, Elizabeth, had died in 1815, and Du-Bois remarried.) In the later nineteenth century, the roof of the DuBois house was altered to extend beyond the walls, and paired brackets were added as decorative roof support.

XI–29* Ulster County Poor House
Libertyville Rd. 1888, 1904, 1920 (demolished 1985). Albert Mauterstock and others.

This county institution was established in 1828 and provided for those who were poor, sick, handicapped, or homeless. In 1860 French's *Gazetteer of the State of New York* described the poorhouse, located on a 140-acre farm, as "poorly constructed, not ventilated at all, and ... entirely unfit for the purposes for which it is used." The main building, a frame structure with low ceilings probably erected about 1853, continued to subject residents to "foul air" in the 1870s. A new, three-story brick building with mansard roof was built in 1886 with separate spaces for men and women, and for the poor and the insane. This building, designed by architect A. M. Russell of Ilion (apparently Archimedes Russell [1840–1915], a prolific architect in Syracuse), and modeled after his Herkimer County asylum, was destroyed by fire in 1904.

Kingston carpenter-builder-architect Albert Mauterstock (1851–1923) designed a two-story brick poorhouse (1888) with arched lintels and simple brick ornamentation under the cornice. It stood 300 feet south of the 1886 building, which

XI-29. Ulster County Poor House (1975 photo)

at that time was reserved for the insane. The committee that oversaw completion of the new poorhouse proudly reported that it was "constructed in a durable manner, well ventilated, heated by steam, amply provided with water-closets and bath-rooms, and all modern improvements, and with ample room ... for at least one hundred inmates, and that the sexes are kept separate from each other."

In 1904–1905 three new buildings were put up—a women's building replacing the 1886 structure, an administration building between the women's building and the 1888 structure (now reserved for men), and a laundry/heating plant behind the administration building. The buildings were connected by a roofed passage whose east wall was of glass to allow "sun baths" for the health of the inmates. The centrally sited administration building, which resembled a Georgian mansion, lent an air of dignity to the institution. A hospital designed by Myron S. Teller was added in 1920 to the poorhouse complex. Closed by the state in 1977, the county institution was demolished in 1985 and the site was absorbed into the Ulster County Fairgrounds.

In 2004, thanks to the efforts of Susan Stessin-Cohn, the mostly unmarked graves of some 2,500 people on the poorhouse grounds were commemorated with a statue and monument. The tombstone of Rebekah Maclang, who died in 1862 at age thirty after being admitted to the poorhouse in 1849 for "insanity," bears a long poem, "Who'll Weep for Me?" and stands at the eastern edge of the fairgrounds.

XI-30. David Hasbrouck Barn (1978 photo)

XI–30* David Hasbrouck Barn
Butterville Rd. After 1797 (altered 1980s).

David Hasbrouck erected his stone house in 1797, and then put up a sturdily framed Dutch barn nearby, directly on Butterville Road. The barn's form was characteristic of Dutch barns in the Hudson Valley—a broad, gently sloping gable roof over a rectangular structure with low side walls, wagon doors centered under the triangular gable, a pentice, or roof, of one slope projecting over the wagon doors, and narrower doors to either side of the wagon doors. The interior typically was divided into a central "nave," where wagons could unload onto the threshing floor, and side areas for housing animals. The barn was extensively altered for human habitation in the 1980s. Another Dutch barn, on Route 208 in Gardiner, was enveloped in a new skin for the use of Cathgro Industries.

XI–31 Smiley Testimonial Gateway
Gatehouse Rd. 1907. James E. Ware & Sons.

Today this monumental structure of Shawangunk grit and reinforced concrete stands isolated and shorn of its original function as an impressive marker of the east entrance to the vast Smiley estate. (It is no longer the entrance and, standing on private property, it must be viewed from Gate-house Road.) Through its great arch runs the road formerly used by guests to ascend to the Shawangunk ridge and the renowned Mohonk Mountain House (see IX–21). The gateway was erected by some 1,300 donors, mainly guests of the Mountain House, to honor the fiftieth wedding anniversary of Albert and Eliza Smiley, who had presided over the hotel since 1869. Among the donors was Napoleon LeBrun, whose architectural firm had designed part of the Mountain House itself.

The gateway's architects, James E. Ware & Sons, had already designed the great stone-arched east and west porte-cocheres (1899) of the Mountain House. For the gateway they added a four-story tower that served as a beacon identifying the estate's entrance from afar. The fourth story was treated as a "loggia" with balconies providing vistas over the surrounding countryside. Quarters for the gatekeeper were designed at the base of the tower. Stairs, partitions, and floors are of reinforced concrete, but the exterior is composed of great blocks of Shawangunk grit quarried on the Mohonk estate. Master mason John Lawrence directed the placement of boulders, while the elderly Albert Smiley took boyish pleasure in watching the heavy stones lifted by steam power. Architect James Ware made periodic inspection visits. On one inspection he found the stone "too regular and smooth" and urged that Lawrence achieve "a more rugged effect." The combination of boul-

*XI-31. Smiley
Testimonial Gateway
(c. 1980 photo)*

der masonry and big round arches over the drive must stem from Boston architect Henry Hobson Richardson's gateway (1880) to the Ames estate in North Easton, Massachusetts. (A close observer writing for a New Paltz paper noted, however, that the "arch is slightly horseshoe shaped, something in the Moorish or Saracenic style.") The colorful Spanish tile roof (the architects specified "Akron vitrified tile") resembles the tile the Wares used on towers at the hotel, but is also a Richardsonian touch. However, the stepped gable over the arch is not Richardsonian but Dutch, alluding to the early Dutch settlement of the region. The Wares had already designed Mohonk's powerhouse (1900) in the Dutch Revival style (see IX–21).

At the 1907 celebration of the wedding anniversary and the 1908 dedication of the gateway, Judge George G. Perkins and J. Edward Simmons, a New York banker and former president of the city's board of education, spoke for the committee of guests overseeing the project about the significance of the gateway's materials and forms. Employing very hard "Shawangunk grit" meant that the testimonial gateway would be "enduring." It was "high and broad, strong and imposing" like the ridge to the west. At the 1907 event Albert Smiley himself allowed that the gateway's "chaste and artistic design," chosen by the committee, was "the finest of its kind I have ever seen! Its lofty tower and massive archway are supremely attrac-

tive. It is to be built of Shawangunk grit, one of the hardest stones in existence, firmly cemented together and fitted to endure the storms for innumerable ages." Clearly Smiley welcomed the idea of an enduring monument to the founders of Mohonk, although the architecture and landscape of Mohonk already bore his stamp. As the Latin text on the bronze tablet over the archway tells us, QUAERE MONUMENTUM CIRCUMSPICE ("If you seek a monument, look around you").

XI–32 Albert K. Smiley Memorial Tower (Sky Top Tower)
Sky Top, above Lake Mohonk. 1920–1923. Allen & Collens.

Visible from great distances as a small but distinctive silhouette rising above the profile of the Shawangunk ridge, this tower was erected as a memorial to Albert K. Smiley (1828–1912), the founder of Mohonk Mountain House. Because Smiley was influential in the siting of the New Paltz Normal School on the hill east of the Wallkill River, it is appropriate to gaze upon the distant tower from the New Paltz campus. However, to experience the tower up close and take in the awe-inspiring panoramic view (said to encompass parts of six states) from its summit, obtain a walking pass at the Gatehouse on Mountain Rest Road and enjoy reaching the tower on foot.

The cost of construction was borne by 879 of Smiley's admirers, a number of whom had already contributed to the Testimonial Gateway down in the valley that honored Albert and his wife Eliza on their fiftieth wedding anniversary in 1907 (see preceding entry, XI–31.) The gateway included a four-story tower, and some friends had argued that the testimonial should take the form of "a great tower on one of the heights," rather than the gateway. Albert himself had long hoped to have a permanent observation tower at Sky Top from which his guests could absorb the natural grandeur of his estate and its surroundings.

This tower at Skytop was preceded by three others built of wood, which were destroyed by wind or fire. In 1872 Albert's twin brother Alfred designed the second, a three-story "observatory" whose flat roof, which served as the observation platform, projected beyond the walls and was supported by ornamental brackets. When this tower was nearly complete, Alfred exulted that the "ob-

XI-32. Albert K. Smiley Memorial Tower (drawings by Allen & Collens)

servatory will be a grand success. It is magnificent to watch storms and sunsets from." However, in 1877 it was destroyed by fire. In 1919 New York State proposed a standard-issue, steel-frame, forest-fire watchtower for the site, but Albert's family and friends had something more distinctive and monumental in mind—a structure that would appear to be "growing out of the rock that nature has placed there," and not a foreign intrusion. The Smiley Memorial was built to be in harmony with the natural site and to endure, like the Testimonial Gateway, and both tower and gateway were constructed of roughly textured blocks of local Shawangunk grit. Albert K. Smiley (son of Daniel, a brother of Mountain House founder Albert K.) supervised construction. John Lawrence served as master mason, as he had for the gateway. The stone in this case was quarried from near the base of the tower, the quarry later serving as a reservoir. Reinforced concrete forms the interior staircase of 100 steps to the observation platform.

The architect was Francis R. Allen, a Mohonk guest who donated his services in designing the tower. Allen headed the Boston firm of Allen & Collens, well known for their collegiate Gothic buildings at Vassar College in Poughkeepsie and later for Riverside Church in New York, also in the Gothic style. Allen did not have a free hand in designing the memorial. A limited budget required the elimination of diamond-paned windows, a large terrace, and Gothic-arched loggia or covered stone porch on each side of the tower, all of which had appeared in blueprints from November 1920. Moreover, Allen disliked the big, rough blocks of stone used at the gateway and favored an exterior of small stones that would make the tower look taller, but he was overruled by the Smiley family, which supported John Lawrence's preference for large blocks of Shawangunk grit.

Gothic was the inspiration for the tower, drawn from fortified towers with buttresses at the corners, narrow slit openings in the walls, and battlemented tops without visible roofs. Allen turned, at least initially, to the square stone towers of medieval Ireland. At the laying of the cornerstone in 1921, Daniel Smiley recalled seeing "the castle of Pfaltz" on the Rhine in the Palatinate, where the

Huguenot founders of New Paltz had found refuge before coming to America, and he noted that New Paltz's early settlers called the memorial tower's site "Paltz Point." Allen, however, did not adopt the more complex forms of the castle of Pfaltz.

The tower furnishes an elevated platform for guests of Mohonk and other walkers to absorb the panorama, and the glassy, steel-framed top of the corner turret originally accommodated a State Conservation Department forest fire watchman. (In 1924–1925 sketches were made for a "Fire Warden and Picnic Parties' Lodge" at Sky Top in "California Bungalow style," but the bungalow was never built.) On the tower's entrance level there is a large fireplace, little used, although Allen envisioned it as making the space "a more livable room," especially with an "old fashioned settle with high back" on either side of it.

The stone tower was intended as a permanent memorial to Albert Smiley and an elevated observation platform. It seems also to have been emblematic of Mohonk's status as a moral citadel. Under Albert Smiley, the Mohonk resort forbade alcohol, dancing, and gambling, while endorsing Christian worship and humanitarian causes (including international arbitration, and Negro and Indian education), and was described in 1911 as a "citadel—morally embattled and fearless of the foe." Although Smiley, as a Quaker, worked for peace, the image of the fortress tower was still appropriate for Smiley's memorial, sturdily defending Mohonk against the onslaught of the dissolute world beyond.

XI–33 Josiah P. Lefevre House and Barn
454 Rte. 32 North. 1850.

Greek Revival farmhouse, weathered barn, and idyllic landscape—all flash by as one drives past on Route 32. In the 1850s it would have been easier to stop along the roadside and admire the place developed by Josiah P. Lefevre (1811–1893), a leading citizen who had grown up nearby in the stone house of his father, Peter, and grandfather, Daniel Lefevre. One of Josiah's sons, Ralph Lefevre, was editor of the *New Paltz Independent* and observed that his father built this house in 1850,

XI-33. Josiah P. Lefevre House

resided there the rest of his life, and "always tilled the ancestral acres." For son Ralph, "there never was a place quite as pleasant as the old home, when we sat on the broad piazza in the summer evenings and talked about everything." Josiah had around seventy first cousins through his mother, an Elting, and the last survivor of these was Tobias Elting, said to be the leading "boss carpenter" in the locality in 1850 and possibly responsible for Josiah's house (see XI–37 for Tobias Elting's own house).

After Josiah's death, the property became his youngest son Simon's. In 1941 Simon LeFevre sold the farm to a cousin, Elizabeth LeFevre Elting Smith (1882–1970), wife of Leon Hills Smith (1881–1981), a 1904 MIT graduate and New York architect who designed Long Island country houses. In 1962 Smith planned the first wing of New Paltz's Elting Memorial Library. In its white-painted clapboard it relates easily to the old stone section of the library, but also to Smith's own New Paltz home. The Lefevre farm remains in the hands of the Smith family.

XI–34 Oscar Tschirky Estate (The Culinarians' Home)
71 Old Tschirky Rd. c. 1901, 1941.

Swiss-born Oscar Tschirky (1866–1950) arrived in New York in 1883 and rose to renown as "Oscar of the Waldorf," maître d'hôtel of the Waldorf-Astoria in New York. He claimed "to know more people from all over the world than any other person in America," but foreign royalty and American presidents were his special prizes.

XI-34. Chalet Oscar (watercolor by unidentified architect, c. 1900)

In 1898 Tschirky purchased the John R. Wood place, four miles north of New Paltz on the east side of the Wallkill River. This property became known as Oscar's Farm, or The Oscar Farm. In 1901 he put up a large addition to the existing house. Photos dated 1902 show the mansion picturesquely gabled and with rustic stone veranda and porte cochère. Tschirky took pleasure in making sketches and wood models inspired by the chalets of his homeland, and about this time a New York architect at 315 Fifth Avenue produced (and signed illegibly) a handsome watercolor perspective of a Swiss-style "Chalet Oscar / New Paltz, N.Y.," probably based on Oscar's rough sketches, but never built. Chalet Oscar may have been the building intended in 1899 "for summer guests" that was to rise on the hill east of the highway.

A record of the many buildings standing on the estate in 1916 is furnished by a monochrome picture by T. S. or S. T. Landis and reproduced as a postcard showing the mansion with turrets added after 1902. The grounds are attractively landscaped: a small lake lies just east of the house, garden pavilions stand at water's edge, and the entrance drive crosses the lake on an arched bridge. A boathouse overlooks the Wallkill River, and

there are many agricultural and service buildings. The small cottage on the road in the lower left corner (today this is Old Tschirky Road) is probably what is described as the small Swiss chalet that Tschirky used in winter. In 1941 he gave his eighteen-room turreted house and other buildings on the 320-acre property to the Societé Culinaire Philanthropique as a residence for retired chefs. Tschirky then occupied the small chalet and apparently added its western section with Swiss-inspired roofs and porch parapets according to his own design.

Most of the outlying buildings have been removed, and the exterior of the main house has been much altered in recent years, but the interior retains a strongly Swiss-Germanic quality in its dark woodwork, ornamental iron light fixtures, and leaded glass windows with coats of arms in stained glass. In the basement, behind a

XI-34A. Oscar Tschirky Estate (picture by T. S. or S. T. Landis, 1916)

heavy wooden door with carved bird-on-a-spring door knocker, the Germanic aura culminated in what Tschirky called "a spacious rathskeller ... for the entertainment of our friends. I brought in large barrels and kegs of wines and beverages ... and gave the place a genuine Swiss atmosphere." Not surprisingly, the host dressed in "quaint Swiss costume." The rathskeller was fitted with massive tables and benches, and its walls were painted with scrolls bearing German texts. (In the same space, Tschirky's wife set up a dairy room and storage for canned foods.) Tschirky, who considered the day Prohibition took effect in 1919 as the saddest day in his career, no doubt took advantage of the privacy this windowless room offered.

Oscar Tschirky's proclamation of his Swiss roots in the design of his country place must have made perfect sense to his neighbors, proud of their own Dutch and Huguenot ancestry and their old stone houses.

XI–35 Jerome Le Fevre House
238 Main St. c. 1918.

Now surrounded by New Paltz's commercial strip, this is a good example of the American bungalow of the 1910s and '20s, which characteristically is less than two full stories, has a broad front porch sheltered by a low-pitched roof joined to the roof covering the main block of the house, and has sturdy porch piers of no traditional design. Like many bungalows the Le Fevre house has tapering piers, a large dormer with gable roof, widely projecting eaves with diagonal braces, and a bay window projecting from the dining or living room. The low lines and projecting roofs were intended to give a feeling of homey, friendly shelter, which today is diminished by the surrounding parking lot.

The Le Fevre house probably derives from a book of plans put out by a company such as Standard Homes of Washington, D.C., or it may have been erected from factory-prepared lumber, millwork, hardware, and other building products shipped by rail and assembled on the site. Sears, Roebuck was the best-known seller of such ready-cut houses, but others included Aladdin Homes of Bay City, Michigan, and Gordon–Van Tine Homes of Davenport, Iowa.

Its absence of obvious historical references aligns it with the modern movement, but the bungalow appealed to many middle-class Americans who had no interest in radical breaks with the past. Jerome Le Fevre (1889–1943) was a member of the New Paltz Dutch Reformed Church and of the Holland Society.

Another bungalow, built in 1932 for Robert Atkinson, an employee of Central Hudson Gas & Electric Corporation, stands at 30 Center Street in New Paltz. It remains a private residence and is in essentially original condition.

XI–36 Villa Locascio or Lo Cascio (Villa Cusa)
125 South Ohioville Rd. 1920 and later.

Italian Americans in the early twentieth century were employed in fruit farming and on the construction of the Catskill Aqueduct of the New York City Water Supply, while others came to

XI-35. Jerome Le Fevre House (1986 photo)

XI-36. Villa Locascio (1975 photo)

New Paltz as summer visitors. The Joseph Locascio family moved from New York City to New Paltz in 1913 and, in 1920, established a boardinghouse that expanded into the several buildings pictured in a postcard written in August 1933 to Miss Nora Calciano in Brooklyn. The writer, Rose, was "having a tranquil time" and found "the air ... so fine and pure that it makes one forget it's ever warm in the city."

The appearance of the Villa and other houses newly erected by Italians on South Ohioville Road attracted the interest of the New Paltz press. This "Italian colony" was identified by the cobblestone walls of its "large and substantial" buildings. "The peculiar style of architecture is, no doubt, Italian. The only objection is the scarcity of windows." At the Villa, the windows do not seem scarce. The writer who found the architecture peculiar also suggested that the Italian people, though "noted for their industry," lived differently from others in New Paltz—several families were believed to occupy each house, and they had "large families of children." The Italian character of Villa Locascio can be compared to the Swiss quality of Oscar Tschirky's estate, but longtime residents of New Paltz apparently welcomed more warmly the financially successful Tschirky with his Germanic roots than they did their Italian neighbors.

XI–37 Tobias Elting House
71 Old Rte. 299, Ohioville. c. 1850.

This modest Greek Revival house, with corner pilasters and low second-story windows fitted into the frieze of the finely detailed entablature, was the residence of Tobias Elting (1815–1894). Listed in the 1871 county directory as "carpenter and farmer," Elting probably designed and built this house sometime after his marriage in 1843.

His obituary in the *New Paltz Independent* noted that "in his early life and until middle age, Mr. Elting was a boss carpenter, and almost all the houses and barns put up in this vicinity were built under his supervision. His charges were always reasonable and the work was honestly and carefully done." Elting was the "contractor" and probably the designer of the former parsonage (1848–1849) of the Reformed Church at 153 Huguenot Street. Now missing its porch with four squared piers, the parsonage resembles Elting's Ohioville residence. Although born the same year as Andrew Jackson Downing, Elting clearly had no desire to adopt the newly fashionable picturesque approach to house design. He is buried nearby in the Lloyd Cemetery, but his bulky stone monument has no sign of the Greek Revival, which by the 1890s had long passed out of fashion.

XI-37. Tobias Elting House (1975 photo)

XII
Town of Olive

Formed from part of the towns of Shandaken, Marbletown, and Hurley, 1823.

Population: 3,099 in 1870, 4,579 in 2000.

The forests of mountainous Olive were harvested by lumbermen and tanners in the early and mid-nineteenth century, and their products could reach Kingston over the Ulster and Delaware Turnpike, which opened in 1832–1833. General Henry A. Samson (1818–1869) operated a tannery at Samsonville, a hamlet of some thirty houses and a church in 1871. His fine Italianate house (c. 1858) stands at 32 West Chestnut Street in Kingston. By 1871 lumbering and tanning were in decline. The Samsonville tannery was no longer functioning in 1880, but Sylvester reported that there were new sources of wealth in the town, and both were dependent upon the railroad. On the one hand, "quarries of bluestone [are] now yielding their inexhaustible resources." Hewitt Boice was a prominent dealer in stone at Boiceville (where earlier Lemuel Boice had built a tannery), and he had a stone yard and planing mill at Brodhead's Bridge. The mansarded Hewitt Boice house remains at 110 Fair Street in Kingston. In addition there were the "summer tourists" attracted by "the trout streams, the ice caves, the mountain gorges, and the wild depths of the primeval forest," and who were leaving behind money "with the hotels, the boarding-houses, the guides, the liverymen, and others."

In 1853 the Hudson River School painter Asher B. Durand portrayed a fisherman and his helpful wife along the Esopus Creek with the bold profile of High Point in the distance (*High Point: Shandaken Mountains*, Metropolitan Museum of Art). Early in the next century, New York City dammed the Esopus to create the Ashokan Reservoir, thereby inundating hamlets like Brodhead's Bridge and transforming the landscape that had inspired Durand. Still, the new, vast sheet of water provided another picturesque ingredient in the mountainous landscape that sophisticated builders of country houses found appealing.

XII–1 Upper and Lower Gate-Chambers, Screen Chamber, and other structures

Ashokan Reservoir. 1905–1915. J. Waldo Smith, chief engineer; Herbert Lincoln Rogers, architect (York & Sawyer, consulting architects; Charles Wellford Leavitt, Consulting Landscape Engineer).

The creation of the twelve-mile-long Ashokan Reservoir for the City of New York was an enormous engineering project that dammed the Esopus Creek and submerged more than 8,000 acres, destroying farms and hamlets in large parts of the towns of Olive and Hurley, as well as a corner of Marbletown. In 1911 *The New York Times* looked upon the impending destruction with a mixture of "regret ... at the approaching doom of the countryside" and wry detachment: "In all probability the buildings will be deliberately burned, which should give a splendid opportunity for the moving picture men." By 1914 some 500 houses, 35 stores, 10 churches, and 8 mills had been removed, as well as 2,637 bodies from cemeteries and family plots on farms. Although property owners were compensated financially, a century after these events some in Ulster County still resent the taking of the land by the heartless big city to the south.

In exchange for the rural vernacular buildings that disappeared, the city erected vast engineering works, two or three parts of which the *Times* declared "promise to be beautiful in themselves" and would offset the lost buildings. "The engineers are throwing across the valley a mighty curtain of masonry." The Olive Bridge Dam "will tower in stern abruptness

XII-1. Lower Gate-Chamber (c. 1980 photo)

210 feet above the old bed of the creek, and on either side banks covered with verdure will slope across its face." A less intimidating source of visual delight would be the oval aerator basin, its 1,518 bronze, four-inch nozzles justified by the need to kill waterborne microorganisms by exposing them to oxygen. The aerator, however, was also to be a beautiful fountain: "The water will be thrown heavenward and will be twisted into dozens of different shapes. ... the effect is likely in beauty to outrival the glories of the gardens of Versailles and other European palaces." (In the 1980s the installation of a small hydroelectric plant caused the removal of the old aerator and its replacement with a new fountain. Aeration was replaced by other methods of purification.)

The façade of the Lower Gate-Chamber provided a suitably formal backdrop for the Versailles-like aerator-fountains whose water was controlled by valves in the Lower Gate-Chamber. Board of Water Supply architect H. Lincoln Rogers (1876– or 1878–1944) was evidently inspired by the classical façade of the Boston Public Library (1888) designed by the great American Renaissance architect, Charles F. McKim. Rogers's training included study in the Atelier Masqueray in New York and so, like the Paris-trained McKim, he designed with the Renaissance-inspired approach of the École des Beaux-Arts. Rogers revised McKim's design to be less ornamental and more solid—thanks to the big blocks of rusticated, rough-surfaced,

XII-1A. Upper Gate-Chambers and Ashokan Bridge (c. 1920 postcard)

concrete-stone with boldly defined joints—as befits a building housing not books but, in 1917, electrically driven valve-stands, vertical generators, an overhead traveling crane, and machine tools. Over the central doorway Rogers placed a French classical cartouche with the arms of the city—the four sails of a windmill with two beavers and two flour barrels. The cartouche and arms are repeated over the doorway of the Screen Chamber, whose façade resembled the Lower Gate-Chamber and also looked out upon the aerator. (The windows of both buildings have been altered, although the change was less detrimental at the Screen Chamber.) Also Renaissance-inspired are the twin superstructures of the Upper Gate-Chamber (their arched windows have been filled in). For all the architectural elements of the headworks, the city rejected a picturesque style such as the Smileys had adopted at Lake Mohonk, and instead unapologetically imposed a simplified version of urban classicism upon rural Olive. In a witty drawing of 1909, Rogers has a shirt-sleeved designer indicating the water's route to a gentleman in eighteenth-century costume—the city's Father Knickerbocker, not the Catskills' rustic Rip van Winkle.

Rogers was also responsible for the architectural enhancement of the reservoir's dams and bridges—the major ones became the subject of popular postcards. The fifteen-arch, reinforced concrete Ashokan Bridge, integral with the weir separating the east and west basins and connecting the Upper Gate-Chambers to the north shore of the reservoir, was embellished with a cartouche at the top of each arch. (The concrete-stone cartouches and adjacent

balustrades have been removed and metal railings substituted.) Located in a forest setting, the Traver Hollow Bridge, built with three hinged, reinforced concrete ribs, was sufficiently graceful without a cartouche. This bridge seemed functional and modern, its forms determined by the properties of reinforced concrete and not by the traditions of stone-arched bridge building. In 2008 work began on a $36 million project to reconstruct seven of the reservoir's historic bridges.

Rather than allow the reservoir to overflow its banks after heavy rainfall or melting snow, engineers designed a "safety valve" in the form of "a weir 1,000 feet long ... over which the reservoir may spill its surplus into a broad sloping channel, shut in on either side by masonry walls. Down this the flood will dash till it falls 200 feet to the creek." The *Times* predicted that periodically "the waste weir ... will display a rush of water that will be superb." Woodstock painter Arnold Wiltz, conscious of the Surrealist movement in art, in his *Spillway, Ashokan Dam* (1934, Smithsonian American Art Museum) captured the eerie stillness and emptiness of the stepped spillway when there is no flood, as well as the enigma of the phallic stone shaft jutting through the arched cavity of the Spillway Bridge.

More prosaically, countless motorists have, like John Burroughs (see XII–6), been drawn to drive around the reservoir on what was once called "the boulevard" to take in the spectacle of the sheet of water set before mountains to the west and north. Adding to the spectacle are the works of Rogers and the engineers that restrain the water and prepare it for the journey by aqueduct to New

XII-1B. Spillway (1981 photo)

York. Here and there along the route to the city are lesser versions of the gate-chambers at Ashokan—superstructures for gauging, drainage, siphon, and blow-off chambers (for one in Gardiner, see III–7).

While the architectural elements of the Ashokan water system are themselves monumental, it was thought fitting to perpetuate the names of the men who led the project on a tall stone monument now set within a wooded area southwest of the Lower Gate-Chamber. (The monument can be reached by parking in the lot on Route 28A just west of its intersection with Route 213, then walking on a paved road [closed to motor vehicles] in a northerly direction along the edge of the reservoir, and finally taking the first road on the right for a short distance.) Known as the Triangulation Tower, it replaced a wooden tower used by the engineers as a starting point in running levels. The stone version was dedicated in honor of Mayor McClellan in 1908 at a ceremony where the mayor called the monument "beautiful" and defended the controversial and far-from-complete reservoir project. Several stones are engraved with the names of officials, but most prominent is a memorial inscription with bronze portrait medallion of chief engineer J. Waldo Smith (1861–1933) created by sculptor Anton Schaaf in 1936. In 2010 the monument, with its great blocks of masonry and sealed doorways, appears to have been put up by some ancient civilization and, like other ancient monuments, its walls are weathered and trees and vines grow from them.

XII–2* "Old Stone House"
West Shokan. Early nineteenth century? (not extant).

This postcard was mailed from West Shokan on July 7, 1910. The writer, a woman named Laura, believed the building was 200 years old and "one of N. Y. state's old land marks which will soon be torn down in order that the valley may be flooded for the new reservoir." With the destruction of the old came not only the new Ashokan Reservoir, but also new Colonial-inspired structures—for example, the residence of Jules Breuchaud, a contractor in building the reservoir (see next entry, XII–3).

XII-2. "Old Stone House" (c. 1905 postcard)

XII–3* Jules Breuchaud House (High Point Springs Farm)
Olive Bridge. 1911 and later. Myron S. Teller.

Jules Breuchaud (died 1934) was a contractor and engineer involved in the construction of the Ashokan Dam and headworks of the Catskill Aqueduct. He was responsible for the construction of several of the most important architectural elements—the Lower Gate-Chamber, the Screen Chamber, and the Aerator. His house at Olive

XII-3. Breuchaud House (cover, House Beautiful, Nov. 1914)

Bridge overlooks the Ashokan Reservoir and is an early example of Myron Teller's adaptation of the county's modestly scaled old Dutch stone houses to the grander needs of wealthy businessmen establishing country estates in the early 1900s. Teller's work for Breuchaud, which includes Teller's hand-forged hardware, was well publicized in the October 1913 issues of *Arts and Decoration* and *Architectural Record*. It was also featured on the cover of *House Beautiful* (November 1914), although in that instance Teller was not credited with the design.

Breuchaud was a business associate of Hannibal Choate Ford, serving as "the first president of the Ford Instrument Company, makers of anti-aircraft and other precision instruments used by the United States Navy." Ford's country place in Olive Bridge also has hardware by Teller (see next entry, XII–4).

XII–4* Hannibal Choate Ford Estate
Olive Bridge. 1918 and 1930.

XII-4. Tower, Ford Estate

Although the buildings of the Hannibal Ford estate are not documented as the work of Myron Teller, some of the hardware bears his mark, and the shingle-sided house (1918) shares some bungalow characteristics with Teller's Watson Hollow Inn, which once stood nearby. Ford (1877–1955) was an electrical engineer and inventor, credited with "the first mechanical brain for controlling gunfire" and developing "the world's first automatic tracking bombsight and the first time-of-flight clock." During the summer he and his wife Katherine kept open house for their many Woodstock friends. The *Woodstock Press* reported in 1931 that Ford "has built a fine observation tower" at their "wonderful summer home overlooking the entire Shokan reservoir" and that "he will this year add a number of instruments made by himself, making it a real observation point, capable of many uses." The tower, dated 1930, is reminiscent of a tapering cylindrical lighthouse, but it is faced with irregularly shaped local stone and was equipped with electrically powered spiraling steps and rotating windows.

XII–5* Watson Hollow Inn
Rte. 28A, West Shokan. c. 1915 (not extant).
Myron S. Teller.

The Watson Hollow Inn was a charming, old-fashioned-looking place for automobilists on excursions into the Catskills to refresh themselves while enjoying views of the Ashokan Reservoir. The proprietor was Jane Crosby Teller, wife of the architect Myron Teller. She sought the automobile trade by advertising in the 1920 *Automobile Blue Book*, and her postcards of the inn show a touring car standing on the road. Surviving postcard messages indicate that her clientele was predominantly female. In August 1925 "Elizabeth" enthused to a woman friend that she and Jane Ryder had spent the night there, with "breakfast & supper on the porch. A lovely spot. Very old house & furniture. Candle light! We had a two-day drive thru the Catskills." In 1960 the inn was under different ownership, but comments by a postcard writer suggest it was functioning as it had for more than

XII-5. Watson Hollow Inn (1916 postcard)

forty years: "We went to this Inn ... for tea, never have had more dainty delicious tea sandwiches and dessert ... a very beautiful spot." The novelty in 1960 was the frequent presence of Mary Margaret McBride, the radio personality, who lived "just up the hill" and chatted with each table of guests.

Tea rooms in a quaint Colonial setting, run by refined women mainly for other refined women, were fashionable in early-twentieth-century America (see also Sarah Lounsbery's Sally Tock Inn, IX–2, and Katharine Hasbrouck's Shop in the Garden, IX–10, both at Stone Ridge). However, in an era when female architects were virtually unknown, the buildings usually were designed by men. Here Myron Teller merged the forms of old Ulster County farmhouses with those of the early-twentieth-century bungalow, as he had at the nearby house of Jules Breuchaud. A broad, stone-flagged porch and adjacent pergola added a Mediterranean touch for enjoyment of the panorama of the Ashokan Reservoir. The interior was more obviously Colonial with its big hearth, simple white paneling around the hearth, and black strap hinges—the latter probably made by a local blacksmith to Teller's specifications. In the glow of candlelight, the rooms must have seemed "very old," although actually created by architect Teller using oak from an old barn frame and material salvaged from houses demolished for the creation of the reservoir.

In the 1920s Jane and Myron Teller divorced, and she married William Jay Robinson. At that time she became an important figure in the revival of colonial handcrafts in New York City, as well as the sale of antiques.

XII-6 Tongore Cemetery
Rte. 213 (County Rte. 4).

This is a lovely rural cemetery on a low hill providing views over fields to the east. A number of the graves were reinterments from cemeteries inundated by the Ashokan Reservoir. In August 1909 John Burroughs and his wife Ursula came to Olive to arrange for the removal and transfer of her parents' bodies to the cemetery at Tongore, near the school where the youthful John Burroughs had taught. He noted in his journal that "the big water-works [is] spoiling all this part of the country." Later, in 1918, he would revise his opinion and himself lead an automobile excursion for author T. Morris Longstreth around the new reservoir, pointing out its natural and engineered beauties, before stopping at the burying ground at Tongore and mourning over the grave of Ursula, who had died in 1917. Her tombstone is modest, like her parents'. Clara Barrus, John Burroughs's biographer and companion, observed that Burroughs chose the simple tombstone, but she believed that Ursula would have preferred a more imposing one.

XII-6. Ursula North Burroughs Monument, Tongore Cemetery

XII-7 Shokan Reformed Church
4 Church St., Shokan. 1912–1913.
Myron S. Teller.

The Ashokan Reservoir consumed the previous site of the Shokan Reformed Church. The pres-

XII-7. Shokan Reformed Church (1976 photo)

ent cornerstone, laid in 1912, also indicates the year 1799 when the church was founded. Teller was much more a designer of houses than churches. He designed this Gothic Revival church with some of the Arts and Crafts qualities—its low lines and robust simplicity of stonework—also seen in his slightly earlier Breuchaud house (see XII–3).

XII–8 Emile Brunel House and Sculpture
Rte. 28, Boiceville. c. 1933. Emile Brunel, architect and sculptor. NR

This roadside curiosity was created by Emile Brunel (1874–1944), a portrait and motion picture photographer and proprietor of a photography school in New York. In 1914 Brunel identified himself in a *New York Times* ad as "an artist painter and graduate of the art schools of Paris," but currently "The Photographer in Town," with seven studios in New

XII-8. Brunel House (c. 1935 postcard)

York as well as others in Paris, Boston, and Philadelphia. He compared his portraits to paintings by Rembrandt and French academic masters Bonnat and Carolus Duran. "An atmosphere of chic" surrounded his images of such celebrities as Grand Duke Alexander of Russia, Enrico Caruso, and Mark Twain, but his photographers also turned out inexpensive portraits of the general public.

Brunel published a postcard of his stucco-walled bungalow in Boiceville, calling it "La Maison des Brunels" and naming himself as its architect. Apparently self-trained as an architect and sculptor, the house is adorned with a long sculptured frieze, said to represent an Indian festival, and a smaller circular relief of the sculptor and his wife Gladys. These sculptures overlook the driveway, which is entered through posts resembling Indian totem poles. Near the house, Brunel put up a number of naively eccentric sculptures, several of Indian subjects. One, described as a figure of an "Indian maid facing the Wittenberg Range in supplicating gesture," was said to be "symbolic of a princess of the Moonhaw tribe" that once inhabited the locality. Brunel asserted that his Indian-themed works were "a Token of admiration of the Beauty of the Catskills Mountains and in memory of the Travelers to the Happy Hunting Grounds." However that may be, "The Great White Spirits," a thirty-five-foot-high white column, with heads of Buddha, Moses, Christ, and Mohammed at the top and, at the base, the "Evil Spirits" (Satan, Bellona, Bacchante, and Cleopatra), eschewed the regional in aiming for the universal. Although not far from Woodstock, Brunel and his creation nevertheless remained outside the orbit of Woodstock artists.

XII–9 Ulster & Delaware Railroad Station (former)
Coldbrook Rd., Cold Brook. 1911. Vaux and Emery.

Immaculately maintained by a hunting club and located in a beautiful, parklike setting, this is a classic example of the small, hip-roofed, Shingle Style station well suited to its Catskill forest surroundings. It is one of the standard or prefabricated stations designed for the U & D by Downing

XII-9. Cold Brook Station

Vaux and Marshall L. Emery. A larger version, the former U & D station in Phoenicia, is now the Empire State Railway Museum (see XVII–2), and the former Ashokan station (1904; originally at Brown's Station) was moved and now is a store on Tinker Street in Woodstock.

XII–10 Nissen Road Bridge
Over the Esopus Creek, near Rte. 28, Boiceville (Cold Brook). 1895. Owego Bridge Co.

Once common, late-nineteenth-century metal truss bridges are disappearing, and one survivor, the Nissen Road Bridge, is in poor condition and closed even to pedestrians. Photographed in 1977 when still open to traffic, the bridge was made by the Owego Bridge Company in 1895, according to a plate above the roadway at each end of the bridge. This company, founded in 1892, was one of many manufacturers of metal truss railroad and highway bridges in the late nineteenth and early twentieth centuries. (An iron truss bridge that

XII-10. Nissen Road Bridge (1977 photo)

spanned the Wallkill River in New Paltz from 1891 to 1941 was made by the Groton Bridge & Manufacturing Co. of Groton, New York.) Typically the individual members of such bridges were fabricated and riveted at the shop of the manufacturer, then shipped to the site where the trusses would be assembled. Presumably the parts of this bridge were brought to the site by the Ulster & Delaware Railroad, whose tracks are only a few feet away and whose Cold Brook station is visible down the line. The linear play of the bridge's structural members is appealing, even without the decorative grill that crowns each portal or entrance. This grill is reminiscent of the iron grills atop many mansarded houses.

In the 1890s iron and steel bridges replaced wooden covered bridges, which were more susceptible to destruction by fire, flood, and ice. These old metal bridges, however, seem to lack the romantic appeal of wooden covered bridges, whose admirers have succeeded in preserving Perrine's Bridge and others in the county.

XII–11* Richard Hellmann Lodge (Onteora Mountain House)
96 Piney Point Rd., Boiceville. 1928–1930 (altered later). Julius Gregory.

At the core of this inn with its expansive view of the valley of the Esopus Creek is the rustic lodge of Richard Hellmann (c. 1877–1971), the German-born "mayonnaise mogul" who emigrated to the U.S. in 1903 when in his twenties. The living room, or great room, retains its original massive stone fireplace with andirons of matching scale. Door hinges and chandeliers are also formidable in black iron, and bear the marks of handcraftmanship.

Blueprints for the main lodge do not survive, but a 1928 blueprint of the multifunctioned "garage building" identifies the architect as Julius Gregory of 2 Park Ave., New York. Gregory (1875–1955) designed fashionable suburban and country houses featured in professional journals and home magazines such as *House and Garden*. He presumably planned Hellmann's main lodge, named BOB/RAY after Hellmann's two sons. While its exterior has been altered to serve the needs of

XII-11. Garage Building, Hellmann Lodge

the Onteora Mountain House, the north side of the garage building, looking out upon a swimming pool, remains much as it was designed by Gregory with its rustic porch posts, cobblestone chimney, and Colonial windows and shutters. Gregory's preference for the rustic and handcrafted relates to his hobby; *Time* magazine reported in 1932 that at the "first Architects Hobby Show" at Knoedler's Gallery in New York, Gregory revealed that he "took time off from designing country homes to hammer out a pair of silver sugar tongs," in contrast to most architects whose hobby was recording their travels in watercolor.

XII–12* Civilian Conservation Corps, Camp P–53
Boiceville. 1933 (not extant).

The only Civilian Conservation Corps (CCC) camp in Ulster County was located in Boiceville

between Route 28 and the Esopus Creek, across the state highway from today's Onteora Central School. Under Franklin Roosevelt's New Deal, the CCC provided young men unemployed during the Great Depression with shelter, food, and useful employment. Corps enrollees wore uniforms and were subject to quasi-military discipline from their commanders, who were regular and reserve Army officers. FDR took office in March 1933, and the Boiceville (or Olive) CCC camp opened in June 1933, the first of about a dozen CCC camps in the Catskills. The young men of the Boiceville camp hailed from greater New York City and were assigned the task of destroying "forest pests," particularly the gypsy moth. However, when this effort proved unproductive, the men were put to work planting trees and building trails and campgrounds.

Diane Galusha has described the typical CCC camp as "little villages, usually with five 40-man barracks buildings, a mess hall, tool house, a garage ... water and sewage facilities, streets and sidewalks, a recreation hall, a camp store, and an education building." Except for the occasional cobblestone chimney, the wood-frame buildings appeared more starkly utilitarian than comparable New Deal buildings in the county—the handsome stone National Youth Administration buildings supported by Eleanor Roosevelt at Woodstock and the rustic caretaker's cabin, probably built by the CCC, at Woodland Valley Campground (see XXI–18 and XVII–8). Still, this social experiment stirred public interest, and the *Kingston Daily Freeman* predicted that the camp "will prove a drawing card for ... sightseers [in Ulster County] second only ... to the great Ashokan reservoir." Then, in 1935, CCC enrollments declined nationwide, and the Boiceville camp

XII-12. Morning muster at Boiceville CCC Camp (c. 1935 postcard)

XII-12A. Boiceville CCC Camp with cobblestone chimney (c. 1935 postcard)

was closed in January 1936, with its 125 workers sent to other camps. Today no trace of the camp remains in Boiceville.

XII–13 Van Kleeck Blacksmith Shop (former)
Upper Samsonville Rd., Samsonville.
Flourished c. 1910–1940.

In 1930, the *American Architect*, a leading professional journal, used a photo of this old-fashioned rural blacksmith shop to illustrate an article on Myron Teller's hand-wrought hardware. While by then much of Teller's Colonial Revival hardware was produced in the city of Kingston, this small frame building, set on a hillside along a dirt road and sheltered by trees, assured Teller's architect-customers that his hand-wrought hardware had its roots in the independent craftsman working in a setting and under conditions very similar to those of the colonial blacksmith.

About 1910 architect Teller, unable to find hardware suitable for his Colonial restorations and revivals, decided to find a blacksmith who would make accurate reproductions. Traveling by auto he searched the Hudson Valley for weeks before finding "in the foothills of the Catskill mountains some twenty-five miles from the city of Kingston, an old country blacksmith shop that time and progress had not as yet effaced—a dusty, dimly lighted shop with wide swinging doors ... equipped with the primitive tools of bygone days." This was the Samsonville shop of the Van Kleeck family. For Teller, finding the building and tools was important, but "most important of all—[this was] a shop that was presided over by a journeyman of

the old school, just as his father, and his grandfather too, had presided over it before him." Teller and the smith "worked patiently at forge and anvil for many days" until Teller was satisfied that the journeyman was making hardware "that embodied the character and spirit of the old time ware." The architect, proud of his early Hudson Valley Dutch ancestry, was a member of the Holland Society, and so the ancestry of his blacksmith was a key ingredient in achieving the desired character and spirit; the Van Kleecks belonged to "an old Dutch family, in which the smith's art is a tradition." Not surprisingly, Teller had acknowledged the Italian roots of brick manufacturer Joseph D. Mayone when he designed Mayone's Saugerties residence (1915) in the style of the "Italian Renaissance."

Teller's hardware enterprise became so successful that it outgrew the little Samsonville shop and he was obliged to open a larger shop in a nondescript industrial building in Kingston. Still, George Van Kleeck was among the smiths, and there was no large force of unionized workers and no factory floor filled with machinery.

XII-13. Van Kleeck Blacksmith Shop

XIII
Town of Plattekill

Formed from part of the Town of Marlborough, 1800.

Population: 2,031 in 1870; 9,892 in 2000.

In 1813, Spafford's *Gazetteer of the State of New York* thought well of the town's farming land and found "the inhabitants are principally farmers, of plain economical habits, and much of their clothing is the product of the household wheel and loom." By the 1870s, apples and grapes were extensively cultivated in the town, and today apple orchards are still found in abundance. According to the *Gazetteer*, "a very large proportion of the inhabitants of this Town are Friends." Today the 1818 Friends Meeting House is preserved as an historic site on Old Mill Road while, in Clintondale, Quaker buildings are in use as the Clintondale Friends Christian Church.

XIII-1 Methodist Episcopal Church (former)
Rte. 44–55 and Maple Ave., Clintondale.
1894. John Ireland, builder.

Methodist services were last held here in 1969, but this weathered, gallant, old Gothic church remains rooted in place—although shorn of its corner tower.

XIII-2. Shuart–Van Orden House

XIII-1. Clintondale Methodist Episcopal Church (1975 photo)

XIII-2 Shuart-Van Orden House
41 Allhusen Rd. c. 1773. NR

The appealing combination of brick façade and gable ends with stone foundation, side and rear walls is unusual in the county, as are the gambrel roof and brick relieving arches above the one-story façade windows. Harrison Meeske and Ken Walton suggest that these features derive from New Jersey practice; the builder-owner of the house was Johannes Shuart, who came from New Jersey and in 1772 purchased 500 acres on which he built

this house. In 1799 he sold the house and land to Peter Van Orden. The low stone wing to the west was added in 1982–1983.

XIII-3 Modena Rural Cemetery
Rte. 32, Modena. Begun 1869.

This rural cemetery, organized in June 1869 and dedicated in July 1870, retains its picturesquely cross-gabled (and now vinyl-sided) gatehouse that defined the boundary between the business of the road leading north out of Modena and the quiet contemplation of visitors to the cemetery. The gatehouse of the New Paltz Rural Cemetery (begun 1861; see XI–27), now moved and altered, would have functioned similarly.

South of the gatehouse is the Hasbrouck monument; Joseph E. Hasbrouck (1850–1934) presided over the hamlet of Modena from the Cole-Hasbrouck house a short distance down Route 32 (see next entry, XIII–4). In the northwest corner

XIII-3. Gate House, Modena Rural Cemetery (1977 photo)

of the cemetery, a tall marble shaft is ornamented with a garland of roses and bears the name of its maker, "Miller & Co., Po'keepsie." Around this nineteenth-century monument are buried members of the Brodhead family, including Abraham Deyo Brodhead (1863–1926) and his wife Gertrude Deyo Brodhead (1868–1954), who in 1892 were responsible for transforming the plain stone Deyo house on Huguenot Street, New Paltz, into a stylish Queen Anne place (see XI–4).

XIII–4 Cole-Hasbrouck House (Delamater House)
Rte. 32, Modena. Begun c. 1820. NR

Just north of the crossroads in the small hamlet of Modena, this stately brick house appears as something of a surprise. Impressive are the Federal-style doorway with expansive, elliptical-arched transom, and the tall gable ends with twin chimneys and round-arched and quarter-round windows. Front windows have sandstone lintels carved with Greek key motifs. In 1917 the doorway and first floor windows were made to recede in shadow cast by the addition of a classical porch whose stocky piers and nearly flat central pediment have something of the simple sturdiness of an Arts and Crafts bungalow porch, but also seem harmonious with the mostly unadorned brick walls of the earlier house.

The large and dignified house was appropriately the center where John Cole, a lawyer and landowner, directed activities on some 1,000 acres, including a home farm of 200 acres. Cole—and subsequently members of the Hasbrouck

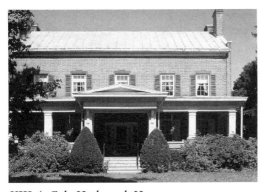

XIII-4. Cole-Hasbrouck House

family—dominated the hamlet of Modena into the 1920s, renting houses to tenants and sponsoring institutions including the church, cemetery, and fire company.

At the nearby crossroads of Route 32 with Routes 44/55, the two-story wood-frame building painted yellow was built about 1825 as a hotel. Around 1900 it was known as the Modena Hotel, and a Carpenter Gothic porch overlay the simple classical composition of windows and central doorway. In the late twentieth century, housing Modena's post office and without the Carpenter Gothic porch, it seemed a nostalgic reminder of small-town America. Sadly, the post office has moved outside the center of the hamlet.

XIII–5 Reformed Dutch Church of New Hurley (New Hurley Reformed Church)
1145 Rte. 208. 1835. NR

This prime example of the Greek Revival as interpreted for a rural church stands close to traffic on Route 208 but is partly insulated by the regimented stones of its tranquil graveyard. The church's south-facing front portico was loosely derived from ancient Greek temples—here four, short, fluted Doric columns support a two-part entablature (the upper part, the frieze, lacking the triglyphs expected in the Greek Doric), with triangular pediment above. The cupola or bell tower, common in American Greek Revival churches but unknown to the ancients, was originally fitted with Doric pilasters framing the louvered openings and with un-Greek pinnacles rising at the very top. Overall, the south front can be compared to contemporary portraits by Ammi Phillips that are both naïve and somehow appealing to the modern eye in their distortions of human form. To the classically trained eye or to professional architect Alexander Jackson Davis (who designed the façade of Newburgh's Dutch Reformed Church [1835] closely following a Greek Ionic temple), the cupola's considerable height and bulk and the pediment resting on such low columns would have been the subject of criticism. Sophisticated Europeans from

XIII-5. New Hurley Reformed Dutch Church (1976 photo)

antiquity and the 1830s would have ridiculed the wooden walls painted white to imitate marble.

The interior retains the historic centrality of the pulpit and communion table, although these furnishings are not the original ones. The four Doric pilasters on the north wall behind the pulpit accord with the Doric of the portico and may be from the original construction of the church. Eleven colorful stained-glass windows, made by Pittsburgh Plate Glass Co. and designed by F. J. Grenier, were added in 1905. The stained glass, especially when depicting Biblical figures, would have been frowned upon by the Reformed faithful of the 1830s.

XIII–6 Friends Meeting House
Old Mill Rd., near Rte. 32. 1818.

This example of Quaker architecture is one of the county's undervalued landmarks, in part because of its location on a side road near the Orange County border. The meetinghouse is also absolutely sim-

ple—a two-story rectangular box with a gable roof and no ornament—in line with Quaker insistence on plainness in all things including speech and dress. Originally there were separate doors for men and women on the broad east side (traces of the openings remain), and men and women sat on opposite sides within. Elders sat in a row facing those assembled; there was neither minister nor pulpit. Later the entrance was shifted to the narrow north end, through two closely spaced doors, and a raised platform at the south end of the interior made for a more churchly orientation.

In 1880 the building was described as "neat," but the society was said to be "not specially strong." Declining membership led to the cessation of meetings about 1948. In the 1970s the Gerow Family Association, affiliated with the Huguenot Historical Society, undertook preservation of the building.

In Clintondale, at the northern end of the town, two Friends meetinghouses survive in altered form on Crescent Avenue. A small and plain meetinghouse built in 1811 was moved down the hill to Maple Avenue to make room for its larger and more church-like replacement, completed in 1889 with Gothic arches and tower. After serving as a temperance hall, funeral parlor, and residence, the 1811 building was moved back up the hill in July 1983 to the grounds adjacent to the 1889 building and partially restored. It is now the Clintondale Branch of the Highland Public Library.

XIII-6. Friends Meeting House

XIV

Town of Rochester

Incorporated by patent, 1703; organized as a town, 1788.

Population: 4,088 in 1870; 7,018 in 2000.

The rural Town of Rochester, named for the Earl of Rochester, retains important landmarks from the eighteenth-century period of settlement and the nineteenth-century era of the Delaware & Hudson Canal followed by the New York, Ontario & Western Railway. Historian and preservationist Harry Hansen has recorded these early structures, but also ones from the twentieth century when summer visitors came first by railroad and then by auto. The Shawangunk range furnished rock for "Esopus millstones," formed with hard labor, but also provided scenery for restful contemplation by guests at Lake Minnewaska and Lake Mohonk—the former wholly in Rochester, the latter shared with Marbletown. As elsewhere, much has been lost—the waterpowered mills themselves (some from as early as 1703), the early buildings of the Reformed Church (the first, c. 1700, said to have been of log, then stone in 1743 and 1818, followed by frame in 1860 and 1902), as well as the mountain houses at Lake Minnewaska. Historically inclined motorists on Route 209 can, however, pull over at the present Reformed Church (1924) and return briefly to the eighteenth and nineteenth centuries via monuments in the burial ground near the church.

XIV-1 Hillside Restaurant (Friends & Family II Hillside Restaurant)
4802 Rte. 209, Accord. 1940.

This rustic cobblestone restaurant was built on the premise that automobile travelers would welcome a meal in pleasant, homey surroundings suggestive of a cozy Arts and Crafts bungalow. The great stone chimney implied cheerful conversation around a generously scaled hearth. Frank Seaman's earlier Hut, not far away at Yama Farms, projected a similarly hospitable spirit, but the Hut was open only to a limited, elite clientele (see XX–9).

   Originally the restaurant occupied the north side of the building, and a store the south side. Gas pumps stood near the highway. The owners, George and Maud Stokes, had been employed at Lake Mohonk, he in the blacksmith shop and she in the Mountain House. Stokes later operated a forge, store, and auto repair garage on this property on Route 209. According to Marie Blank, the Stokes's granddaughter, George Stokes was probably himself the builder of the cobblestone structure. He also built several rental cabins, one with slab sides across Route 209 that is described in the Stokes diary as "the log cabin." While the gas station, garage, and cabins have long been discontinued, a series of proprietors have successfully maintained the restaurant.

XIV-1. Hillside Restaurant (photo c. 1950)

XIV-2 Dirck Westbrook House
18 Old Whitfield Rd. Eighteenth century and mid-nineteenth century. NR

As the traveler approaches this house from Route 209, the paved Whitfield Road splits off to the left while the traveler takes the unpaved right fork

XIV-2. Dirck Westbrook House

onto Old Whitfield Road and briefly has a sense of shedding a century of progress. The house, in a locust grove, looks out upon the dirt road, and just beyond is the steep bank down to the North Peterskill. The property once included a gristmill. It is still possible to see why Helen Reynolds described the location as "one of true rural beauty." The front of the house is a handsome combination of stone wall and classically treated central entrance with roof raised in the fashion of the Greek Revival of the mid-nineteenth century. Around the right corner of the house, but not easily visible, is a stone wing, the oldest section of the house and little altered when studied by Reynolds, who remarked upon its eighteenth-century Dutch oven, doorway, small windows and shutters, and roof overhang.

XIV-3 Krom House and Barn
286 Whitfield Rd., Whitfield. 1790s (barn). NR

The stone house is undated and has been altered at various times, but Harry Hansen points to the west "gable end wall entirely of stone from the ground level to the roof ridge" as unusual and probably the earliest part of the house. The more common clapboard peak is found on the later, east, gable. Of still greater interest is the Dutch barn, located just to the side of the road. It is in poor condition, but highly visible to motorists, including those making their way to the nearby Accord Speedway. The massive timbers of the barn's H-frame separate the central aisle from the two side aisles of the main floor. Built into a hillside, the barn's lower story includes an enclosed area

XIV-3. Krom Barn

for livestock. The barn may have been built in the 1790s, then disassembled and moved to the present site in the 1830s.

XIV–4* Benjamin Schoonmaker House (Howard C. Sykes Estate, Appledoorn Farm)

Rte. 209, Accord. 1758 (restoration and expansion of estate by Teller & Halverson, 1930s).

Sheltered by a long driveway from Route 209, the Benjamin Schoonmaker house is a colonial-era stone house at the core of a gentleman's country estate developed in the 1930s by Howard C. Sykes (1893–1966) with his architects, Teller & Halverson. The south front of the stone house is a symmetrically composed arrangement of central doorway with two windows on either side, suggesting a late-eighteenth-century construction date, but a stone to the left of the door is dated 1758 with the initials BS (for Benjamin Schoonmaker) and other initials. (Tradition has it that the house was begun by Benjamin's father, Jochim Schoonmaker, about 1722.) In the Victorian period the stone house received a number of wooden additions.

Howard Sykes was a wealthy New York broker (president of the New York Curb Exchange, predecessor of the American Stock Exchange) and a Schoonmaker through his mother, Alice Adele Schoonmaker Sykes. In 1931 Sykes and Teller & Halverson began to transform the Schoonmaker property into a Colonial Revival showplace. The eclectic Victorian additions to the house were replaced or altered with simply detailed Colonial porches, dormers, and white-painted clapboard wings. Internally, "the old beamed ceilings and wide board floors, long concealed, have been uncovered and brought back to light, fitted with hinges and latches hand forged in iron [by Teller's blacksmiths] as in the Colonial days."

Sykes was no idle antiquarian, for he and others of the family were dedicated hunters of big game in Africa and around the world. His father, Walter Henry Sykes, was English-born, and Howard, born in New York, was educated at the Hotchkiss School and Yale. He then worked for Standard Oil in the Far East and enlisted in the British Army in 1917, but became an artillery officer in the AEF when America entered World War I.

For this adventurer, Teller designed a new stone Recreation Building, or Trophy House (1937), whose front looked much like the eighteenth-century Schoonmaker house farther down the drive, but expanded with a stone wing and given non-Colonial board-and-

XIV-4. Recreation Building, Sykes Estate (1990 photo)

batten siding in the gable end. Stone for the new building was taken from the decaying Jacob De-Witt house on Route 209 on land adjoining Sykes's. Sykes purchased and demolished that house to obtain its stone for the new building, and timbers from an old barn were also reused.

The interior was laid out as a dormitory for sportsman guests of the family, and as a party place (what Harry Halverson called "Whoopee Rooms") with bar and two-and-a-half-story-high trophy room, illuminated by a 12-by-14-foot studio window at the back of the building. The uninitiated must have been surprised—as Teller intended—to open the front door, pass into the entrance hall, and find, not a series of compact, low-ceilinged rooms, as expected in the Dutch Colonial tradition, but a balcony overlooking the spacious trophy room rising to the visible roof trusses (composed of the old oak beams from the neighboring barn and "finished off with artistic iron"). Also eye-opening, the knotty-pine-paneled walls were dotted with the taxidermist's art—culminating in the front half of a giraffe—and the great stone fireplace was equipped with andirons in giraffe form. As was Teller's custom, hardware was "fashioned and hand forged by local craftsmen in the old manner."

Teller was an architect dedicated to the revival and restoration of his county's colonial houses and their hardware. At the same time, as his grandson Dirck Teller recalled, he was "sociable and enjoy[ed] a good party." Dirck Teller retained a bar guide authored by his grandfather and "titled in the manner of his architectural proposals, 'Specifications for Restoration of the Spiritual Builder-Ups after the Manner and Form of Original Antique Receipts of the Ancient Hoffman House Bar, Once on Broadway, In Little Old New York.'" The disjunction between the prosaic exterior and trophy-party room interior suggests that in the 1930s he retained the sense of humor that in 1903 allowed the rising young architect to perform in a "circus" in the Kingston Armory as "Mlle. Onanag, the famous young lady bareback rider ... with streaming curls and fluffy pink abbreviated skirts."

That Sykes was a Schoonmaker descendant may have impressed Myron Teller more than it did Sykes himself, as Teller took special pleasure in re-

XIV-4A. Trophy Room, Sykes Estate (1930s photo)

storing early Ulster houses for the offspring of their builders. The Sykes family did not embrace modern architecture, but they had no objection to modern machinery. They, like most Colonial Revival clients, had their place designed for autos—here an old wagon shed was made over into a three-car garage with attached shop. But highly unusual was their airstrip with hangar, still visible from Airport Road.

XIV–5 New York, Ontario & Western Railway Station (former), at Accord
Accord. 1902. Jackson, Rosencrans and Canfield.

Despite the presence of a bright red caboose resting on rails as a stationary artifact, the Accord station is stranded in the midst of the hamlet—tracks no longer connect it to the metropolis to the south. The building has been converted to living quarters, yet it still calls up images of a century ago when tourists and local residents could sense the pride the railway took in its trains and stations. The picturesque complexity of gables and dor-

XIV-5. Accord Station (1990 photo)

mers in the roof, the accented rafters at the eaves, the half-timbering of the gable above the agent's trackside bay window—all suggest that Downing's taste for the picturesque in rural and mountainous places was still flourishing in 1902. The second story served as a four-room residence for the stationmaster and his family.

South of the station are abandoned buildings from Charles Anderson's feed, coal, and farm supply business, which was served by a rail siding. Anderson's stucco-walled house (c. 1920) is next door to his business.

XIV-6 DeWitt House
582 Old King's Highway, Accord.
Eighteenth century.

Beautifully sited on a quiet road with a weathered shop building just across the road, this old stone house charmed Helen Reynolds in the twenties and it continues to do so in our day. Despite the raising of the roof in the nineteenth century, the front retains its early doors, windows, and hardware. The

XIV-6. DeWitt House

pure symmetry of the façade is currently enhanced by the pristine white of the walls and trim.

XIV-7 New York, Ontario & Western Railway Station (former), at Kyserike
County Rte. 6, Kyserike. 1902. Jackson, Rosencrans and Canfield.

As seen from the road, the narrow south façade of this station resembles the picturesque assemblage of board wall, grouped windows, and multiple roof slopes that distinguishes the nearby station in Accord. In fact both stations were built from the same set of plans, with dwelling for the agent on the second floor. An early photo shows awnings at the dwelling windows and the grounds near the station neatly landscaped. The April 1929 O & W schedule listed four trains in each direction on weekdays taking six minutes to run the three miles between Accord and Kyserike. To the south, just across Route 6, is a former creamery distinguished by its tall brick chimney. The O & W's Cottekill station also resembled the Kyserike station and, while altered, still stands on the O & W Rail-Trail at the intersection with County Rte. 26.

XIV-7. Kyserike Station (1990 photo)

XIV-8 Cross House
217 Kyserike Rd. (County Rte. 6), Kyserike. Begun 1914. Attributed to Sears, Roebuck & Co. (1938 altered and enlarged by Albert Edward Milliken).

The prefabricated parts making up the first form of this house, which stands between the county

XIV-8. Cross House

road and Williams Lumber (formerly Cross Lumber), were shipped by the O & W on a gondola to Kyserike and assembled by local carpenters. The house served as the home of Virgil and Margaret Cross, who started the lumber yard, which originally was a coal yard and grocery store. This compact and economical kit house was square in plan, with a hipped roof, front roof dormer, broad front porch, and one-over-one window sash. Having few references to historical tradition, it was a very popular house type in the early twentieth century; today it is called a "box" or "four-square house." Several companies produced this form of kit house; John S. Cross, Jr., believes his family ordered theirs from Sears Roebuck.

In 1938, when four-square houses were out of fashion, the talented young Kingston architect Albert Edward Milliken was employed by Virgil's and Margaret's son, John Sanford Cross, to enlarge and transform the Sears house into something Colonial with sufficient space for three generations of Crosses. J. Sanford Cross and his wife Marjorie Tillson Cross were friends of the relatively untried Ned Milliken and his wife—this was Milliken's job No. 6. (In 1942 Milliken again served as J. Sanford Cross's architect in the complete rebuilding of an eighteenth-century stone house on Clove Valley Road.) The hipped roof was replaced with a gable roof, the single-pane-sash windows were removed in favor of old-fashioned sash having numerous small panes, and a rear wing and Colonial porches were added. John S. Cross, Jr., grew up in the house and recalls that his father "loved colonial architecture" and believed that much new "residen-

tial architecture ... [was] 'cheap' and temporary, just a fad, [while] Colonial is a style that never goes out of style." John and his brother Wess set up a Lionel standard-gauge electric train that ran around the perimeter of the attic playroom, not far away from the full-size tracks of the O & W whose trains announced their arrival with a "cheery steam whistle."

XIV-9 Jacobus Van Wagenen House
2659 Lucas Turnpike, at intersection with County Rte. 6. c. 1751 and later. NR

This attractive stone house derives its appeal not only from the original eighteenth-century stone structure, but also from early-twentieth-century Colonial Revival alterations. It was probably begun about 1751 by Jacobus Van Wagenen (1729–1790), who was married in 1754, signed the Articles of Association at the beginning of the Revolution, and served as a private in the Ulster County Militia. The house remained in the family into the twentieth century. By 1880 it was treasured as a family heirloom by John Hardenberg Van Wagenen (1821–1902), who had his house and farm, then called Maple Lawn, pictured along with his biography in Sylvester's *History of Ulster County*. In that biography Van Wagenen revealed his ancestral pride, citing the arrival of Van Wagenens in Ulster County as early as 1642. His education included a year at the New Paltz Academy, and he went on to be a teacher and principal in Pennsylvania and New York until 1876, after which, according to Sylvester, "he has given his entire attention to his farm, which is ancestral, and has come down to

XIV-9. Jacobus Van Wagenen House (1992 photo)

him in a direct line through several generations, the proprietorship never having passed from his family name from the original purchase or grant ... The house, which is his birthplace, is unique in appearance, is constructed of rough blocks of stone broken from a neighboring limestone quarry, and is in a good state of preservation."

From the lithographic illustration, it is apparent that the current front of the house facing Lucas Avenue was doorless in 1880, having only three windows in the stone wall in the position they retain today. The present door, porch, and dormers are tasteful Colonial Revival additions. The lithograph also depicts the nineteenth-century barn, in which John Van Wagenen evidently also took pride, and the observation tower atop the Shawangunk ridge to the east at Paltz Point, or Skytop.

XIV–10 Westbrook-Brodhead-Kortright House (Dreamland Farm; Epworth United Methodist Camp & Retreat Center)

Lucas Turnpike (Ulster County Rte. 1) and Epworth Lane, Kyserike. Eighteenth century; mid-nineteenth century.

Now on the grounds of Camp Epworth, a Methodist Church camp that acquired the property in 1959, this house has had a variety of uses and has undergone a variety of architectural transformations. Harry Hansen has found that its origins lie in an eighteenth-century stone house, although the first verifiable owners were the Westbrook family in the mid-nineteenth century. In 1854 Richard Brodhead (1815–1865) moved to Kyserike and operated a distillery on the farm, which was continued by his son-in-law, Philetus Kortright. Brodhead or Kortright were probably responsible for the picturesque and Gothic Revival elements added to the house as it appears in the lithographic illustration in Sylvester's *History of Ulster County* (1880)—a cross gable with prominent chimney rising from the center of the façade, concave diamond-shaped vents in the cross and end gables, as well as scrolled brackets at the eaves and other ornamental brackets at the porch posts. Visible now are paired Gothic colonettes flanking the sidelights of the central doorway and a Gothic scroll-sawn screen in front of the transom over the door. The artist of the lithograph drew what appear to be stone walls rising a story and a half, the rectangular stone blocks oddly alternating between light and dark. Today these walls are stuccoed, and there are remnants of incisions to give the effect of rectangular stone blocks. Perhaps the stucco was colored in 1880 to imitate multicolored masonry.

From 1925 to 1955, what had been the Kortright place was operated as Dreamland Farm by the Kristeller family. According to Alice Westbrook Cross, this was a working farm with 30 dairy cows and 200 chickens, but also a summer resort with facilities for 150 boarders drawn by its reputation for lively social activities such as dancing. The old stone house, pictured in Dreamland postcards and called the Manor House, was the center of resort activities. A large, utilitarian frame addition attached to the rear of the Manor House was removed in 1986. In the early 1900s the nearby O & W Railway facilitated the shipping of milk and travel of boarders from the city.

XIV-10. Westbrook-Brodhead-Kortright House (print in Sylvester, 1880)

XIV–11 Alligerville School (Alligerville Fire House)

Creek Rd., Alligerville. 1878. Jesse Steen and John Hess, contractors (1966 addition attributed to Albert Edward Milliken).

In 1878 this brick schoolhouse, crowned with a cupola and ornamented with paired Italianate brackets, would have stood out in rural Rochester as a source of pride for the community. Jesse Steen of New Paltz was one of the contractors. In 1874 Steen had acted as contractor for a school in New Paltz of similar design, down to the shape of the panel for the school's name and the central circular panel with four small circular openings. Lewis B. Van Wagenen was the architect of the New Paltz school (see XI–9). Van Wagenen may also have designed the Alligerville school, although in 1875 Steen advertised himself as "Contractor and Carpenter, Builder and Architect," and therefore competent to do his own designs.

Albert (Ned) Milliken is said to have donated his services as architect of the fire truck garage added to the front of the school in 1966. Many architects of his time had little sympathy for the ornamental flourishes of Victorian architecture. (It was determined, however, to preserve the lines of the cupola by placing the siren within it.) In 1954 another Kingston architect, Harry Halverson, had stripped away what was considered Victorian excess from the Ulster County Savings Bank in Kingston.

XIV–12 Catherine Harnden House

County Rte. 6, Alligerville. Mid-nineteenth century.

The Harndens were a merchant family in Alligerville along the Delaware & Hudson Canal, and the 1875 Beers *Atlas* identifies this as the residence of "Mrs. C. Harnden." It stands on a slope above the Rondout Creek and the former canal bed. From the east the house appears as a one-and-a-half-story brick house in the Greek Revival style with low windows fitted into the frieze, but the sloping ground allows the basement to emerge on the west front, which is graced with a two-story porch oriented toward what would have been a landscape combining quiet nature and busy commerce. (The east porch was added after 1992.) While the house generally conforms to the Greek Revival mode, the decorative brackets beneath the eaves belong to the picturesque reaction against the Greek Revival led by A. J. Downing. Were the brackets a later addition?

Directly across County Route 6 is a nineteenth-century frame house, unusual in the county for its picturesque board-and-batten walls and Gothic drip moldings over the windows. This house also belonged to the Harnden family. East of the Catherine Harnden house, off Church Hill Road, is the former Dutch Reformed Church of Alligerville (1858–1859), which resembles her house in being built of brick and mostly in the Greek Revival style, but with later stylistic touches—the church façade has round-arched windows

XIV-11. Alligerville School (Fire House)

XIV-12. Harnden House

as well as a small Gothic rose window. The Dutch Reformed Church in High Falls (dedicated 1867; now the High Falls Community Church) closely resembles the Alligerville church and was organizationally linked to it.

XIV–13* Minnewaska Mountain House

Cliff House (opened 1879, enlarged 1880–1881, destroyed by fire 1978). Wildmere (opened 1887, enlarged 1911, destroyed by fire 1986). Lake Minnewaska. Alfred H. Smiley, proprietor and designer.

The mountaintop resort at Lake Minnewaska was founded in the 1870s by Alfred H. Smiley (1828–1903), the twin brother of Albert K. Smiley, proprietor of the Lake Mohonk resort begun in 1869. In Mohonk's early years, Alfred Smiley managed the hotel for his brother and also had charge of constructing several additions. While Mohonk continues to flourish, Minnewaska failed as a privately owned resort in the 1970s and hardly a trace remains of its buildings. Enthusiasts of fine architecture may speculate that one reason for Minnewaska's failure and Mohonk's success lies in Mohonk's grander design by well-regarded New York architects, while Alfred, confident of his own ability in architectural design, believed that to hire an architect added unnecessary expense to any building project (see IX–21). Alfred had studied surveying, road building, and architecture, but he was not a professional architect. Joseph M. Wilson, noted architect and engineer from Philadelphia, and his family were longtime guests at Minnewaska, but there is no evidence that Wilson played a role in its design.

In September 1875 Alfred informed his brother of his intention to purchase a vast tract of land at Minnewaska. Alfred borrowed the name "Minnewaska" from the distant Dakota (Sioux) language, according to Marc Fried, while Mohonk had the benefit of stemming from an Indian word appearing in the 1677 Indian deed for the New Paltz tract. By the spring of 1877, Alfred was bringing lumber by the D & H Canal to Kerhonkson and then up the mountain to the hotel site. The Hudson River School painter Jervis McEntee described in his diary in August 1878 "a most delightful excursion to Lakes Minnewaska and Mohonk" and found the mountain house then under construction at Minnewaska "in a remarkably fine situation with fine views from every room." Two months later a New Paltz paper reported that five carpenters from New Paltz, with others from Clintondale and Highland, were among the forty men at work on construction, and the first mountain house at Minnewaska was completed in time to be open for summer guests in 1879.

Early publicity for Minnewaska focused on the magnificence of the natural landscape, rather than on the design of the hotel:

> Minnewaska Mountain House, opened in 1879, is located on Minnewaska Heights, a picturesque crowning ridge 150 feet above Lake Minnewaska. The lake is surrounded

XIV-13. Cliff House, Lake Minnewaska (print by Elias J. Whitney, c. 1885)

XIV-13A.
Wildmere
House, Lake
Minnewaska
(photo 1975)

by extraordinary bluffs and piles of tumbled rocks, and all around there are masses of trees and shrubbery. ... The House is on a commanding height, 1800 feet above tide water ... and from every room in the Hotel there are magnificent valley and mountain views. ... The whole region abounds in strange and picturesque places.

The only exterior features of the hotel thought worthy of note were the many "private balconies" for taking in the landscape views. A cupola, numerous gables, bargeboards, and finials gave the hotel, soon enlarged and called Cliff House, a picturesque quality suited to the rugged setting. Guests were encouraged to ascend into the cupola and there gaze out over six states.

In July 1879 the artist McEntee was an overnight guest and rowed on the lake. He was impressed that "Mr. Smillie [*sic*] recognized me and was very polite." Other artists among the early guests were Daniel Huntington of New York and James R. Lambdin of Philadelphia (both also guests at Mohonk), and somewhat later, John Ferguson Weir, painter and professor at the Yale School of Fine Arts.

A second, larger hotel called Wildmere House was put up in 1887 on the west side of the lake. Its lake front was a rich display of cupolas, dormers, balconies, and porches providing vantage points for enjoying the scenery. Moreover, by 1889 some

seventy-five rustic seats and summerhouses had been built around the lake and beyond.

Alfred and Albert Smiley were both Quakers and operated Minnewaska and Mohonk with similar ideals. Alfred advertised Minnewaska as a place for "the refined and moral classes, where they could enjoy the splendid scenery without molestation from the fast and rougher elements of society." No alcohol, no dancing, no arrivals or departures on Sundays. In the early twentieth century, health concern led to forbidding tubercular guests. Automobiles and electric lights were slow in being accepted at Minnewaska. As late as 1920 the main access was by Ontario & Western train to Kerhonkson, then a horse-drawn stage to the mountaintop. Electric lights came in the early 1920s with power from a hydroelectric plant walled with Shawangunk grit. At Mohonk, electric lights had been installed earlier, in 1893.

Minnewaska passed from Smiley family ownership, and its long period of financial and physical decline culminated in the closure of Cliff House in 1972 and its awful but spectacular destruction by fire on New Year's Day 1978. Wildmere ceased operation as a hotel in 1979 and burned in 1986. Great steel water tanks that once forcefully punctuated the skyline have been removed, as have the modest rustic seats and summerhouses. Between 1969 and 1987 the state acquired the property for Minnewaska State Park.

XV

Town of Rosendale

Formed from part of the towns of Marbletown, New Paltz, and Hurley, 1844.

Population: 3,625 in 1870; 6,352 in 2000.

"Rosendale" derives from the Dutch term for "rose valley," which appears in a 1685 document for land on the Rondout Creek. The town was organized in 1844 and, while some earlier stone houses remain, its most distinctive landmarks belong to the nineteenth century when the Delaware & Hudson Canal operated and cement manufactured in Rosendale was nationally renowned. Hydraulic cement (that would harden underwater) was needed for construction of the canal, and by happy chance cement rock of the right sort was found in 1825 in High Falls during construction of the canal. By 1870 a number of companies were mining and processing cement between High Falls and Rondout. A large producer in Rosendale was the Newark & Rosendale Lime and Cement Company, whose works at Whiteport had a capacity of about 1,000 barrels a day and employed about 180 men. The cement-rock was quarried through tunnels, some 200 feet long and 130 feet deep. The rock was heated in fifteen kilns and ground in a mill whose three-foot grinding stones were turned by a waterwheel and two steam engines. A horse railroad carried the barrels of cement to the navigable waters of the Rondout Creek. Cement made in Rosendale by various companies was shipped for use far and wide, including for the Croton Aqueduct, Brooklyn Bridge piers, Statue of Liberty pedestal, and wings of the U. S. Capitol.

While industry is often considered the enemy of the natural landscape, Sylvester's *History* recorded how, for "the traveler and the practical geologist" in Rosendale, one could reinforce the other: "The quarries, with their long tunnels, piercing deep into the mountainsides; the sharp precipices; the beautiful lakes; the rough, craggy hillsides; the secluded glens, and the wild ravines—have a thousand attractions. The busy scenes of labor, the hundreds of workmen, the frequent explosions in the blasting of the rocks echoing along the mountain-sides, the ceaseless clang of the mills ... all add to nature's pictures, and continually blend the 'useful with the ornamental,' the works of man with the works of God."

In the early twentieth century, Rosendale cement fell from favor, replaced by Portland cement. Today the quarries and some stone and brick cement kilns remain, but there are no cement workers, no explosions, and the clanging mills have disappeared.

XV-1* Lawrenceville Cement Co.'s Works
Formerly along the Rondout Creek and Delaware & Hudson Canal. Pictured in 1880 (not extant).

The utilitarian cement mill buildings housed a 225-horsepower steam engine and were dominated by a tall smokestack shown by the artist about 1880 as belching black smoke that dissipated so quickly that the countryside on the far side of the Rondout Creek was unsullied. While the Wallkill Valley Railroad had reached Rosendale, the cement works were still dependent on roads and wagons to bring cement-rock from nearby quarries to the kilns on the hillside above the mill, and on the canal to bring in coal for the kilns and carry out barrels of cement from the works. (Up to 700 barrels could be produced in a day.) In 1854 the kilns were connected to the cement mill (converted from an old stone gristmill) by a short, man-powered railway. Only in the design of the office, distinguished by a classically inspired cornice and cupola (with bell and

XV-1. Lawrenceville Cement Co. Works (print in Sylvester, 1880)

weathervane), did the art of architecture enter modestly into play. The art of signage was more striking—the parapet above the eaves proclaimed LAWRENCEVILLE CEMENT and OFFICE. This office building stood near today's entrance to the Snyder Estate. Ruins of the kilns on the hillside above the mill can still be seen from this entrance.

XV-2 Snyder Estate (Century House Historical Society)
Rte. 213. 1809 and later. NR

Visitors to the ancestral estate of Andrew J. Snyder (1889–1975) should not miss the gateposts, topped with light fixtures in the form of miniature Brooklyn Bridge piers. Snyder's family was long active in the Rosendale cement industry, which produced cement for the piers of the Brooklyn Bridge. Once inside the gate, head for the estate's barn and carriage house with museum exhibits on the local cement industry, as well as Snyder's carriage collection. Rosendale's leadership in the industry was such that natural cement—no matter what its source—came to be called Rosendale cement. The industry supported hundreds of workers until around 1900, when faster-setting Portland cement came to be favored over natural cement. Motorists can still see ruinous kilns, once used for roasting cement rock, between Rosendale and Kingston.

Andrew J. Snyder (sometimes known as Andrew J. Snyder II) was the proprietor of the last cement works to operate in Rosendale; it closed in

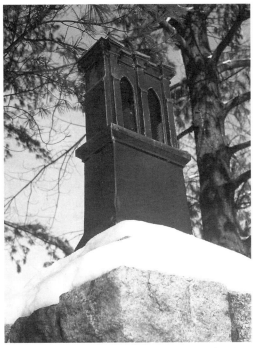

XV-2. Gate post, Snyder Estate (c. 1980 photo)

1970. Andrew occupied the stone house built in 1809 for Jacob L. Snyder by Jacob's father, Christopher Snyder. The house (not open to the public) was altered for Andrew and his wife in 1941, at which time they purchased Colonial Revival furniture from W. & J. Sloane in New York. Albert E. Milliken drew a handsome watercolor elevation (1941) of proposed alterations, but it is not known whether those actually carried out were designed by him.

A short walk from the barn and carriage house leads to the Widow Jane limestone mine, from which natural cement was extracted and which now is an enormous cavernous room, one of Ulster County's great man-made spaces.

XV-2A. Snyder House (watercolor elevation by Milliken, 1941)

XV-3 Andrew J. Snyder House
Rte. 213. c. 1880 (1954–1955 alterations by Harry Halverson).

In 1954 Victorian architecture was admired by few Americans. Harry Halverson was among the many who preferred the restrained good taste of the Colonial to the exuberance of the Victorian, and here he designed the transformation of a mansarded Second Empire–style house into a gable-roofed Georgian with new Palladian window above a new doorway with fanlight and sidelights. What he did not erase— and what make the Georgian façade eye-catching if not unique—are the glazed polychrome bricks marked Ingham & Sons, Wortley, Leeds, England. The segmental arches of the windows are another holdover from the nineteenth century. Halverson's client, Andrew J. Snyder, was the owner of the last incarnation of the Rosendale cement industry.

XV-3. Andrew J. Snyder House

XV-4 Wallkill Valley Railroad Bridge (Wallkill Valley Rail Trail)
Mountain Rd. 1895–1896. King Bridge Co.

This former railroad bridge crossing a deep gorge formed by the Rondout Creek now looms high above motorists on Route 213, as it did above canal boats during the final years of the Delaware & Hudson Canal. Pedestrians and bicyclists on the rail trail can (or will soon) traverse the bridge and enjoy the view railroad passengers and crews once had of the creek and village far below—or they can experience "something like a feeling of terror" that first-time passengers felt in the early years of the bridge. The present steel bridge was fabricated by the King Bridge Co. of Cleveland to bear the substantial weight of trains of the 1890s. It replaced a lighter, wrought-iron bridge built 1870–1872 by the Watson Manufacturing Co. of Paterson, New Jersey, which used a diagonal truss system patented by S. S. Post. Post's truss was first used in 1865 on the Erie Railway. The original Rosendale bridge, 988 feet long and 150 feet above the creek, was hailed at its completion by *The New York Times* as "the highest span bridge in the United States." Paterson photographer John Reid captured a train of box cars and coaches crossing the bridge in celebration of its opening on April 6, 1872. Reid also recorded daredevils standing on the bridge trusses, locomotive, and tender—the train had stopped mid-bridge to be recorded by the official photographer. In 1875 the bridge was even recommended to guests at Albert Smiley's Lake Mohonk as an excursion destination, apparently on the assumption that Mohonk itself did not provide everything required by lovers of the picturesque: "The village of Rosendale has always been famous for its picturesque position, and this characteristic

XV-4. Wallkill Valley Railroad Bridge (1985 photo)

The American Hotel,
Rosendale, N. Y.

AMERICAN HOTEL.

XV-5. American Hotel (early-twentieth-century postcard)

has been much increased by the building of a light and lofty iron railroad bridge, spanning the Rondout Creek, and Delaware & Hudson Canal."

Another high, steel-truss railroad bridge is still in use (by CSX freight trains) across the Rondout Creek between the City of Kingston and Town of Esopus. The present bridge was built in 1904 for the West Shore Railroad as a replacement for an earlier West Shore bridge.

XV–5 American Hotel (Astoria Hotel)
435 Main St., Rosendale. c. 1870.

Although a porch has been enclosed and another added since the American Hotel was pictured in an early-twentieth-century postcard, the brick façade retains much of its original Italianate character. The segmental arched windows and richly bracketed cornice resemble commercial buildings from the same period in Rondout.

XV–6 St. Peter's Catholic Church and Rectory
1017–1021 Keator Ave., Rosendale. 1875–1876. Arthur Crooks.

An imposing building on a commanding site overlooking the Rondout Creek and the village of Rosendale, St. Peter's Church stands as an expression of the important roles immigrants and

the Roman Catholic Church attained in Ulster County by the 1870s. Workers for the Delaware and Hudson Canal and in the cement industry had created a parish of some 1,400 members to be served by Irish-American clergy. The church was described with enthusiasm at the time of its consecration: "The new church is 'a thing of beauty' of which all our citizens are proud, and 'a joy forever' to the souls of the generous people of whose faith and zeal it is an enduring monument. The site … is the finest in Rosendale. The ground is so elevated that the spire rises monument-like above the village."

The architect, Arthur Crooks, was English-born but had served in the Union Army in the Civil War. After the war, Crooks was employed as a draftsman in the New York office of the great Gothic Revival architect Richard Upjohn. Then, practicing independently, Crooks designed more than a hundred churches in the city and surrounding region. He was an outspoken advocate of recent immigrants such as those that worshipped at St. Peter's; as the elected quartermaster of a national guard regiment in New York that was disbanded by the state in 1882, Crooks angrily attributed the state's decision to its bias against German-Americans. He told his men that "although our lips may be twisted by foreign dialects we are as good as any other man who has a vote."

St. Peter's reveals the hand of a designer skilled in the Gothic. The tall nave, lower side aisles, and corner bell tower are clearly articulated masses. Pointed Gothic arches with plate tracery abound, and these justified the identification of the church design as "Early Decorated Gothic"—from English churches of the early

XV-6. St. Peter's Catholic Church and Rectory (print after drawing by R. W. Rallray for Crooks, c. 1876)

fourteenth century. In the windows of the side aisles, the plate tracery takes the form of a panel pierced by one small and two larger circles and a cusped version of the quatrefoil. The front (which faces north, not west; the lay of the land and the need to face the village overruled Christian tradition) has, at the apex of the gable, a large circular panel with plate tracery, a simple variation on the Gothic rose window. The circular panel is penetrated by three small and three larger geometric windows.

The real glory of St. Peter's arises from its rich coloration, not only in stained glass, but also in the permanent polychrome of its exterior. The red brick walls (of North River pressed bricks) are vividly contrasted with light-colored Amherst sandstone and bands of yellow (Perth Amboy) and black brick, as well as with yellow-painted wood trim. (In the 1970s the polychrome walls were hidden under a coat of paint, later removed.) Rather than follow the monochrome Gothic of England, Crooks here turned to the polychrome Gothic of Italy celebrated in the writings of the nineteenth-century English critic John Ruskin. The rectory, also by Crooks, has similar polychrome effects in the brick and stone walls. Both the church and rectory originally had slate roofs of at least two colors. The geometric cutouts in the panels of the rectory's gable ends and porches echo those of church windows' plate tracery.

As originally designed, the church's interior was dominated by a nave of seven bays defined by white pine columns that supported the clerestory and nave roof, and also differentiated nave from side aisles. The architect noted that the interior had not yet been "decorated in polychrome." (Subsequent polychrome decoration extended to murals in the chancel and below the clerestory windows.) The clerestory and roof were constructed "of white pine, all of which is exposed, wrought, chamfered, and ornamented with geometrical tracery." Crooks's mentor Upjohn had sometimes been guilty of concealing the true wooden frame of the roof with imitation Gothic vaults in cheap plaster. The focal point of the interior—the sanctuary—lies at the south end of the nave and is separated from it by a pointed arch. For the sanctuary Crooks allowed a rib-vaulted ceiling.

The polychromatic Gothic of Italy that was championed by Ruskin has two large-scale examples in Ulster County—Kingston's City Hall (1873–1875) and St. Peter's Church, both designed by Arthur Crooks. Badly damaged by fire in 1927, City Hall was repaired, but details the 1920s considered Victorian and ugly were eliminated. Fortunately, St. Peter's retains much of its original character. Crooks's perspective drawing of the church published in the *American Builder* (August 1877) and a view of the church and its surroundings published in 1880 in Sylvester's *History* do, however, confirm that the tower roof was once more decorative and was surmounted by a slender turret, and that the church and rectory were roofed with broad, alternating bands of black and lighter-toned green slate, enhancing the Italian polychrome effect. Crosses that were both symbolic and ornamental rose atop the turret and both ends of the nave roof, and helped define this as a Catholic church.

The 1880 view also shows to the right of the rectory a small cemetery (in 1872 St. Peter's initiated its larger, parklike cemetery on high ground some distance south of the church), and still farther to the right a plain, classical building identified as the church hall, but actually built in 1850 as Rosendale's first Catholic church. The iron bridge (not extant) over the Rondout in the foreground appropriately had Gothic tracery at its entrance.

XV-7 Friends Meeting House (Tillson Community Church)

Grist Mill Rd., Tillson. c. 1895.

Like the Clintondale Friends who completed a church-like meetinghouse in 1889, the Friends of Rosendale Plains (Tillson) turned away from Quaker plainness and adopted the principal architectural emblem of Christianity, the steeple. The Gothic arch, however, was still not accepted, and ornament here is minimal.

XV-7. Tillson Friends Meeting House (1982 photo)

XV-8 James Henry Elmendorf House and Barn

Rte. 213 at 1 Dutch Barn Drive, near High Falls. c. 1850.

A fine example of the Greek Revival, the Elmendorf house harked back to ancient Greek temple porticoes in its four, fluted Doric columns supporting a horizontal entablature and triangular pediment. Unlike Greek temples, which had a central doorway and no windows, this American house required a doorway to one side opening to

the staircase and allowing a spacious front room lit by generously scaled windows positioned between the columns. Strict classicists would also be puzzled by the asymmetrical wings and the wooden walls, even if they were painted white in imitation of marble. The one-story wing to the left of the portico is more in keeping with the Greek Revival, as its sloping roof and horizontal cornice has the appearance of the left side of a classical pediment.

Elmendorf's barn, beautifully maintained, lies 200 feet southwest of the house and is a late and unusually large example of the Dutch barn. Its west front—with central wagon door, a smaller door at each corner, and several windows (the latter uncommon in early Dutch barns)—stretches over fifty-six feet in width. The name, J. H. Elmendorf, and date, 1851, is painted under the peak of the west gable, while the name Josephus Elmendorf and the date 1857 is found penciled on an interior board.

XV-8. Elmendorf House

XV-8A. Elmendorf Barn

XV-9 Colonial House, Sozialistischer Unterstütz.-Verein, Socialist Relief Society (Cottekill Village Apartments)
County Rte. 26 at County Rte. 7, Cottekill.
c. 1932.

Colonial House was an expanded version of the simple Colonial Revival houses being put up around the country in the 1920s and '30s—"Colonial" most obviously in the doorway with elliptical fanlight and narrow rectangular side lights. It may seem surprising that the Socialist Relief Society, which provided a retirement home for its aged, German-American members, would adopt an old American style rather than something Germanic. However, in the early twentieth century, immigrant groups often chose to build something Colonial as an expression of their desire to be Americanized, to become part of the mainstream American society through learning the English language, as well as American history, government, and culture.

Despite its socialist connection, the Relief Society was subjected to a strike by the carpenters putting up its new building. Described as "apparently foreigners" and "apparently Germans," the six men were working ten hours a day for 60¢ an hour, while the Ulster County union scale was 90¢ an hour for an eight-hour day.

Before building Colonial House, the Socialist Relief Society occupied several buildings on what had been the Pine farm, and it continued farming operations in order to serve products from its farm. A brochure, "Town of Rosendale Resort Accommodations," (c. 1944) lists the S.R.S. Home having room for 100 guests at $22 a week, with amenities including the use of the Williams Lake Beach.

XV-9. Colonial House, Socialist Relief Society (c. 1933 postcard)

XVI

Town of Saugerties

Formed from part of the Town of Kingston, 1811.

Population: 10,456 in 1870; 19,868 in 2000.

"Saugerties" stems from the Dutch "Zagger," meaning a sawyer, and it was named for a sawmill built on the Sawkill Creek. Early settlement was probably by the Dutch but, during the winter of 1710–1711, Palatine German Lutherans built three villages at West Camp before most moved on to Schoharie or the Mohawk Valley. The present Lutheran church at West Camp stands on the site of the Palatine church (said to have been organized in 1708), although the building has been entirely transformed over the years.

The village of Saugerties, incorporated as the village of Ulster in 1831, was renamed Saugerties in 1855. It is located on the Esopus Creek at falls near where the creek joins the Hudson, and was the site of a very early gristmill. As late as 1813 the hamlet had only about a dozen houses. In 1825–1826 Henry Barclay, a New York City businessman, purchased land with the intention of creating "a model village." He also purchased the water rights of the Esopus Creek, which he dammed and began operation of a paper mill (1827) and the Ulster Iron Works (1828). According to Sylvester, "Under the impulse of these extensive works ... the hamlet of a few houses developed [by 1880] into a place that rivaled the shire towns of this side of the river north and south." After Barclay's death in 1851, J. B. Sheffield and his son William R. Sheffield continued and expanded the manufacture of paper—building a new brick mill (1872) and William's fine Queen Anne–style residence (1882). Brickyards were located along the Hudson; Glasco was a brick-making center in 1880, with one firm, J. T. & R. C. Washburn, turning out 100,000 bricks a day. At the same time, bluestone quarrying was an important industry to the west of Saugerties village in the aptly named hamlet of Quarryville and elsewhere. Bluestone was transported from around the county to the mill and yard of John Maxwell in Malden. Maxwell's bluestone was used in building William H. Vanderbilt's Fifth Avenue mansion, designed by Richard Morris Hunt, as well as for window and door sills, curbing and sidewalks, in many towns and cities in the eastern United States and Canada. In the early twentieth century the influence of the Woodstock art colony spilled over into Saugerties, notably in Harvey Fite's wondrous Opus 40, an abandoned bluestone quarry transformed into a work of environmental art.

Village of Saugerties

XVI–1 Du Bois–Kierstede House (Saugerties Historical Society)
119 Main St. 1727 and later. NR

In 1929 Helen Reynolds described the Du Bois–Kierstede house as "one of the most attractive homesteads in Ulster County," not only for its architecture, but also for its beautiful, parklike setting of locust trees. The place remains just as attractive today, thanks in part to the grove of black locusts some 270 years old. Two stones on the front (south) wall are marked 1727 with initials of unknown significance—they do not relate to the earliest known owners, Hezekiah Du Bois, followed by his son David Du Bois, who sold the house to Dr. Christopher Kierstede in 1773. By 1880 Sylvester recognized the house as a landmark, "the old family homestead" of the Kiersteds (variously spelled), built in 1727. There is clear evidence in the building that it was added to over time—seams in the stone walls, changes in wall heights, and differing levels of finish in the stonework, including the window lintels. The oldest part of the house may be the small, low, "old kitchen" at the east end. Or the oldest section may be at the west end. The beams of this west room run parallel to Main Street, and it has been proposed that the original, one-room house had its gables facing north and south—south being the street front—and only later were the gable ends shifted to face east and west.

Reynolds thought the half-oval, sunburst window in the dormer over the nineteenth-century porch (the present porch is from c. 1990) was early, but in fact it was added after 1900. In the west gable the finely cut stone frame of the low arched window is said to have been brought from Fort Sumter, although details of the fort do not resemble this arch. In the rear, the northwestern porch with stone piers and the shed-roofed dormers are probably from the early twentieth century. Reynolds, in her 1925 field notes, observed that it was thanks to its owner

XVI-1. Du Bois–Kierstede House (early-twentieth-century postcard)

at that time, Mrs. P. J. Ehrgott, that the house had been "reclaimed and repaired." The fact that Mrs. Ehrgott, although a resident of Brooklyn, belonged to the Kiersted family made the homestead all the more appealing to the ancestry-minded Reynolds.

The Saugerties Historical Society purchased the house in 1999 and has acquired the frame of a Dutch barn that stood on Tissal Road, Saugerties, before its disassembly in 2003. It will be appropriate to reconstruct the barn behind the Du Bois–Kierstede house, because in 1790 the house was part of a forty-nine-acre farm with a barn (long destroyed) believed to have been similar to the one awaiting reassembly.

XVI–2 Saugerties High School (L. M. Cahill School)
Main St. at Washington Ave. 1907. Wilson Potter.

The Main Street front of the former high school has a kind of weighty dignity befitting a place of learning. In broad outline it resembles the Normal School erected in New Paltz about the same time (see XI–23). Influenced by classical designs of the Renaissance, the lowest story of the Saugerties school is treated as a sturdy brick-walled basement with small windows. The main entrance is accented with a terra-cotta frame with segmental arch

XVI-2. Saugerties High School (c. 1907 postcard)

and keystone whose simplified classicism stems from French, Beaux-Arts taste. A wide band of hard, cream-colored brick separates the basement from the next two stories. These stories are unified by three vertical bands of the cream-colored brick, and are defined as classroom areas by their broad bands of windows. At the time educators believed abundant daylight and fresh air were required for effective classrooms. The slightly projecting central section of the façade has a broad but plain entablature and cornice, with low attic and hipped roof above.

A postcard reproducing the architect's proposed design for the school indicates that he had intended a more ornamental treatment of the façade, notably in the entrance door frame and cornice of the central section. No doubt taxpayers pushed for a less expensive building. In the end it cost $71,000, or 13.5¢ per cubic foot. This allowed a fireproof building, except for the floors, described as "slow-burning." The architect, Wilson Potter (1868–1936), practiced in New York City and designed high schools in Poughkeepsie (1911–1914, a Gothic design), Peekskill, Geneva, and Fulton, as well as schools in Pennsylvania and Connecticut.

During the Depression, Woodstock artists Petra Cabot and Edward Dries were commissioned by FDR's New Deal to paint murals placed in the school. In 1934, with the sponsorship of the Public Works of Art Project, Cabot painted a panoramic view of Saugerties. Dries used a twenty-eight-foot canvas to create an idealized depiction of Saugerties papermaking.

XVI-3 Saugerties Public Library
91 Washington Ave. 1914–1916 (altered and expanded 2010). Beverly Sedgwick King.

The library and the adjacent 1907 high school (now Cahill Elementary School) established the nucleus of a classically designed civic and education center. At the library's dedication the president of the school board cited the two fine buildings as proof of the "enlightenment of [the] community." Such was the vision of many communities around 1900 under the influence of the Chicago World's Fair of 1893. Kingston had opened its classical library on Broadway in 1904, with its high school following, 1913–1915. Both the Kingston and Saugerties libraries were built with funds from Andrew Carnegie; Kingston was granted $30,000 in 1902, Saugerties $12,500 in 1914. Between 1886 and 1917 Carnegie grants were used in building over 1,600 libraries. Most were designed, like Kingston's and Saugerties's, in a formal, classical style. Although by different architects (Kingston's was by Raymond F. Almirall), the façades of the two libraries were similar: a central entrance is approached by a flight of steps with the doorway framed with columns supporting a pediment; the basement is raised above ground level and fitted with three windows to either side of the central stairs; the main story with bookshelves and reading areas is defined by its three generously scaled windows to either side of the entrance; a low hipped roof crowns the whole. However, where the Kingston library proclaims Greek classical sources, Saugerties's is based on American eighteenth- and early-nineteenth-century buildings, broadly called "Colonial" at the time. The library belongs to the Colonial Revival thanks to its red brick walls, white wood trim, double-hung sash windows with small panes, and especially the white classical portico with columns called "colonial" at the dedication. The books in the library, but also the dignified American-rooted building, would aid the cause of creating good American citizens in Saugerties. The locally made brick and the native bluestone trim and steps helped tie the building to the town.

The original interior layout (later altered) had the delivery desk facing the entrance and in front

XVI-3. Saugerties Public Library (c. 1916 postcard)

of book stacks for ease of supervision by the librarian—readers were permitted in the stack area. The Adult's Room and reference area were to the north, the Children's Room and librarian's office to the south. As late as 1941 the plan was recommended by the American Library Association to those intending to build new libraries.

The south wall of what was the Children's Room is still enhanced by an important work of art, a fireplace faced with tiles illustrating Washington Irving's tale of Rip Van Winkle, designed by Henry Chapman Mercer and made at his Moravian Pottery and Tile Works in Doylestown, Pennsylvania. The fireplace, often a feature of Carnegie library children's rooms, gave the room a friendly, homey quality, especially as the librarian in charge of the room, typically a woman, was to take on a nurturing, motherly role. The Saugerties librarian, Miss MacAdam, was instrumental in the successful completion of the building, and she anticipated the pleasure of the children of Saugerties in their new space. Abigail Van Slyck points out that progressive educators of the time advocated storytelling to stir the imaginations of young children, and the amusing story of Rip as told on the tiles (really low-relief sculptures) would have encouraged such storytelling (while probably downplaying the alcoholic catalyst of Rip's sleep). As Mercer wrote, "if tiles could tell no story, inspire or teach nobody, and only served to produce aesthetic thrills, I would have stopped making them long ago." Mercer designed the tiles for the Saugerties library in June 1915 and was surely aware that Saugerties was close to Rip's legendary home. Later, he produced several other versions of the story, but only one other for a public space—the John A. Howe Library in Albany. Few American libraries possess a work of art and craft as distinguished as this one by Mercer.

The library retains the watercolor rendering of the building by its architect, Beverly S. King (1879–1935), who practiced in New York City. In 1905 King and his partner, Henry D. Whitfield, had designed a garage on East 90th Street for Andrew Carnegie's electric autos, using an eighteenth-century Georgian style in red brick and white marble. Whitfield was the brother of Carnegie's wife Louise. Whitfield and King were the architects of a number of other Carnegie libraries including Eaton Memorial Library (1908) for Tufts College in Boston and the White Plains Library (c. 1909). The 2010 expansion of the Saugerties library by Butler Rowland Mays Architects is sensitive to the original building, although its four-column portico has been encased in glass as a reading porch, while the entrance has descended to the ground level of the addition.

XVI-3A. Rip Van Winkle Tiles by Henry Chapman Mercer, Saugerties Public Library

XVI–4 Reformed Church
173 Main St. 1852. James Renwick, Jr. NR

The architect of the Reformed Church, James Renwick, Jr. (1818–1895), was among America's foremost designers of the period. Renwick by 1852 had produced the elegant Gothic Revival Grace Episcopal Church and Rectory (1843–1847) on Broadway in New York, as well as the stolid Romanesque Smithsonian Institution (1847–1855) in Washington. Later he would acquire even greater fame as the architect of New York's St. Patrick's Cathedral (1853–1888) derived from several European Gothic cathedrals. In the mid-Hudson Valley, Renwick was also responsible for the Parisian-inspired, mansard-roofed design of Vassar College (1861–1865) in Poughkeepsie.

The tall spire, rose window, and quatrefoils of the Saugerties façade stem from the Gothic Revival, but Renwick included key elements of the pre-Gothic, Romanesque period of the Middle Ages—round-arched doorway and windows (with drip moldings), and round-arched corbel tables in the tower. The Romanesque was typically less ornamented than the Gothic. Renwick had turned to the Romanesque for his Church of the Puritans (1846–1847; destroyed) on Union Square in New York. This was a Congregational church, and Renwick may have wanted to express the simpler forms of Reformed and Congregational worship by employing the simpler architectural forms of the Romanesque. Renwick would again mix Romanesque and Gothic in his Clinton Avenue Congregational Church (1854–1855) in Brooklyn, as well as in two designs for Congregational churches in *A Book of Plans for Churches and Parsonages* (New York, 1853).

The lithographic view of the church in Beers's *Atlas* shows the façade apparently composed of rectangular blocks of masonry. Instead of today's smooth walls of stucco-over-brick, the stucco was probably originally inscribed to imitate stone blocks. In contrast to Gothic Revival churches by Richard Upjohn, where the side aisles are clearly evident as being quite low in relation to the central nave, here the twin gables flanking the taller central gable of the nave rise higher than necessary, higher than the aisle roofs—a little like the false commercial fronts of new settlements in the West. A. W. N. Pugin, England's fervent Gothic Revivalist, had railed with overheated zeal against just such "deception" in his *True Principles of Pointed or Christian Architecture* (1841): "We should never make a building erected to God appear better than it really is by artificial means. These are showy worldly expedients, adapted only for those who live by splendid deception, such as theatricals, mountebanks, quacks, and the like."

The main worship space of the Saugerties church is plaster vaulted and, unlike Upjohn's and Renwick's Episcopal churches, this space is not on the ground level, but raised up, allowing a basement lecture room. (In 1868 and again in 1879, J. A. Wood made plans— never executed—to

SUNDAY SCHOOL & LECTURE ROOM JOHN ST.

XVI-4. Saugerties Reformed Church (lithograph, Beers, 1875)

lower the main floor to street level to ease access for old worshippers.) The central placement of the pulpit (and according to the present arrangement, the organ) also represents a departure from Episcopal and Catholic practice. The church is excellently preserved, and whatever Pugin might criticize, it adds distinction to the center of the village.

The construction of the church, according to Sylvester, "gave rise to a difference in the congregation, the result of which was that a portion of the people withdrew from the church, and afterwards organized the Congregational Church of Saugerties." The Dutch Reformed Church (Old Dutch) in nearby Kingston had endured its own division when Second Reformed Dutch Church broke off from Old Dutch and built a Gothic Revival sanctuary on Fair Street in 1850 designed by New York architect Thomas Thomas, Jr. A more prominent New Yorker, Minard Lafever, was then called upon for classically based plans for a splendid new Old Dutch (1850–1852). It may well be that leaders of the Saugerties Reformed Church were trying to keep up with Kingston by erecting an imposing church designed by a notable New York architect.

The parsonage next to the church in the Beers lithograph was built in 1858 (architect unknown). Sometime in the 1860s or '70s the parsonage was made more ornamental with new iron window lintels, a more elaborate main cornice with paired brackets, and expanded porch with similar brackets. A Sunday School and Lecture Room or Chapel was erected in 1875 on John Street, to the rear of the parsonage. Although not prominently sited, this building is a handsome and sophisticated work, possibly by New York architect J. Cleveland Cady, who designed two buildings on William Sheffield's Saugerties estate (see XVI–17). The chairman of the chapel's building committee was J. B. Sheffield, William's father. When new, the chapel was described as "a magnificent building of Gothic style, beautifully adorned and painted interiorly." Intricate cut-out patterns in the gable over the entrance recall Eastlake and Queen Anne residences of the 1870s. The honest, undisguised use of unpainted, unstuccoed brick (in contrast

to the stuccoed brick church) with harmoniously painted wood trim (surely not white originally) and stained glass in geometric patterns suggests the more refined taste of the Aesthetic Movement of the period. The great six-pointed star within the circular window is a reminder that the Star of David was a biblical image used by both Jews and Christians.

XVI–5 I. Lazarus Clothier (former)
110–112 Partition St. c. 1898. Mesker Brothers Front Builders. NR

This façade's freely adapted Renaissance classical forms were manufactured by Mesker Brothers Front Builders (also known as Mesker Brothers Iron Works) of St. Louis, Missouri. The firm produced thousands of sheet-metal façades for commercial buildings across the country between the 1880s and about 1910. At the Lazarus building, pedestrians can find three small identical panels identifying Mesker Brothers as the maker of this façade. Each panel also bears the patent

XVI-5. I. Lazarus Clothier

date, apparently "Oct. 4, '97"—although the year is hard to decipher. The customer ordered a design from the firm's illustrated catalogue, the galvanized sheet-metal parts stamped with architectural motifs were shipped by rail, and then the storefront was assembled at the site quickly and inexpensively—more quickly and less expensively than a similar façade of masonry or cast iron. J. A. Wood, architect of the Seamon Brothers Building (see XVI–8), must have regretted that a potential client like Lazarus turned to a mail-order operation rather than commissioning one of his distinctive designs. Mesker Brothers may also have manufactured the front of the commercial building at 241–243 Main Street, which resembles the Lazarus façade, although the Main Street building has no panel stamped "Mesker."

XVI-6 Saugerties Municipal Building (Saugerties Village Hall)
43 Partition St. 1940–1942. Harry Halverson of Teller & Halverson.

This municipal building rose on the site of Fireman's Hall (1873), an Italianate-style building destroyed by fire in May 1940. The new Colonial Revival building included village offices, a kitchen, and fire and police departments on the first floor, while a spacious auditorium occupied the second. Harry Halverson's design derives from American brick buildings in the Georgian or Federal style of about 1800 with classically treated pedestrian doorways, second-story arches, and cupola having a marked sense of graceful refinement. However, modern fire trucks would exit the three garage doors (now altered), and the brick walls and slate roof concealed a modern, fire-resistant structure of steel and concrete. Washburn Brick Corp. of Glasco furnished the brick. *The Saugerties Daily Post* noted that the bell in the new cupola had hung in the tower of Fireman's Hall—it had been cast by Meneely in Troy in 1850—and the 1873 datestone of the hall had been placed at the southeast corner of the Municipal Building, thereby "preserving a sentimental connection with the old and the new buildings on the site." The 1941 cornerstone is at

XVI-6. Saugerties Municipal Building (1978 photo)

the southwest corner and is boldly inscribed with the name of the architectural firm.

The New Deal had already bestowed a new brick post office upon Saugerties (see XVI–9), and the WPA contributed $63,000 toward the cost of the Municipal Building; the Village spent $60,000 of its own funds. The Municipal Building resembles many brick Colonial Revival town and village halls built across the country in the 1920s and '30s. Architects Teller & Halverson were best known for their revival of the region's eighteenth-century Dutch fieldstone architecture, but for schools and public buildings they recognized that brick was less expensive, hence favored by taxpayers, especially in Saugerties with its long history of brick-making. The Georgian-Federal category of the Colonial Revival was understood by the New Deal and by previous administrations as a style rooted in the culture of the nation's founders, hence a fine, patriotic choice for a local government building.

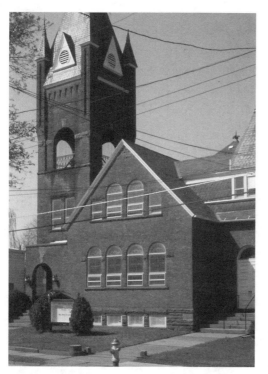

XVI-7. Saugerties Baptist Church (1993 photo)

XVI-7 Baptist Church (former)
32 Partition St. 1890.

The round-arched Romanesque style as interpreted by Boston architect Henry Hobson Richardson
was faintly echoed in the design of this church.
Like Richardson's designs (and unlike the Romanesque adapted earlier by J. A. Wood), the broad,
smooth surfaces of brick are contrasted with
rough-textured stone trim. Also Richardsonian is
the rounded turret with conical roof. The main
tower's hipped roof and corner pinnacles resemble
the top of the tower formerly crowning the Methodist Church (1894) in Clintondale (see XIII–1).

XVI-8 Seamon Brothers Building (former)
Main St. at James St. 1882–1883. J. A. Wood. NR

The Seamon Brothers Building, an important
component of the Victorian streetscape of central
Saugerties, was designed by J. A. Wood, the architect
much in demand by Ulster County clients of

the era. Although the first-floor storefront has
been altered, the upper windows filled in, and
the name panel—"Furniture. Seamon Bro's."—
removed above the third-story cornice, enough
remains to get a sense of Wood's inventive re-
working of traditional Renaissance forms. Red
Philadelphia pressed brick is contrasted with
lighter-toned Ohio granite trim. (Curiously, Ulster County bluestone was not used.) Four tall
brick pilasters join the second and third stories of
the left and right bays. The central windows are
framed not with conventional columns or pilasters, but with double and triple stacks of bricks
interspersed with horizontal granite blocks. Windows are topped with bricks in segmental arches
(with keystones on the third-story front, without keystones in the many windows facing James
Street), or granite mechanically incised with
stylized plant motifs. The date of construction,
1882, still appears below the Renaissance Revival
cornice.

An engraving made of the new building
shows the original form of the first story on Main
Street, primarily large windows to display stylish
furniture in harmony with the intricately wrought
façade. Wood was able to minimize structural
supports that would interfere with the show

XVI-8. Seamon Brothers Building (c. 1885 print)

windows by using iron, including a 4,300-pound girder. The two aspects of the Seamon Brothers business are named on the closed awning and are represented in the two vehicles—at the left, with top-hatted attendants, is the hearse of the undertaking establishment while, at the right, two workmen load a light wagon with furniture that has been lined up along the James Street sidewalk. A writer for the *Saugerties Telegraph* was enthusiastic about the "handsome ware-rooms" first opened to the public one Saturday evening in March 1883: the "good taste of the firm" was evident in a front show window displaying a "walnut chamber suite consisting of a bedstead of the latest design with fine carvings, a French dressing case with full marble top, and a French bevel plate glass." Inside the store, however, Victorian morbidness drew the writer to "a child's beautiful white casket, upholstered in satin and lace of the finest texture, with mountings of silver and blue velvet-covered handles."

Wood also designed the Cornell Building (1881–1883) in Rondout in a similar style. While the Cornell Building has been demolished, the former Newburgh Free Library (1876) and Vassar Brothers Institute in Poughkeepsie (1881) survive with brick and stone trim in freely adapted Renaissance forms akin to the Seamon Brothers Building.

XVI–9 Post Office (former)
Main St. 1934–1936. Louis M. Simon, supervising architect. NR

At first glance this building resembles hundreds of other one-story, brick post offices with white classical entrances built across the country in the 1930s by the federal government. Its Georgian or Colonial Revival style was widely adopted, especially for post offices in the East, out of respect for traditional design in the region. However, a closer look at the walls and a reading of the design correspondence reveal that President Roosevelt and the local citizenry made an effort to tie the building to the region, especially by selecting specific types of brick and stone.

In the depths of the Depression, Roosevelt's New Deal used federal construction projects to

XVI-9. Post Office (c. 1936 postcard)

put people to work and bolster the economy. Roosevelt personally enjoyed planning and overseeing construction when he was assistant secretary of the Navy and governor of New York. As president (1933–1945) these interests continued, and his modest involvement with planning the Saugerties Post Office in 1934 was a sign of his later, more serious involvement with the design of four post offices in his own Dutchess County, as well as the Ellenville Post Office in Ulster.

Frederick E. W. Darrow, an attorney and a Republican with old Hudson Valley Dutch ancestry and an interest in local history, lived in New York City and in Saugerties 200 feet from the site of the proposed post office. In April 1934 Darrow wrote to the Procurement Division of the Treasury Department, which had charge of post office design and construction, urging its officials to call for bluestone walls since Saugerties was "the home of the blue stone industry." He further recommended that Henry Corse, who had designed houses in Saugerties, be hired as consulting architect. Corse (c. 1886–1949) was a native of Saugerties, had an office in New York, and completed grand houses on Long Island and in Hobe Sound, Florida, as well as the Steenken Estate in Saugerties (see XVI–16), but did not secure the consultancy for his hometown post office.

Over the next months government architects completed drawings and were about to announce awarding of the construction contract when, in November 1934, Darrow wrote a postcard to FDR's secretary requesting presidential intervention to secure "native stone or brick" for the walls of the new building. Senator Royal Copeland was also lobbied by influential Saugerties residents who wanted local bluestone, which would boost local employment, rather than generic cast concrete. By November 19 the Procurement Division had agreed to substitute bluestone for the façade's cast concrete watertable, windowsills, and key blocks.

The president himself entered the fray on behalf of local materials, sending a memo to Admiral Christian Joy Peoples, Director of Procurement: "it would be a fine thing if this building could be built of stone which is the natural building material used by the earlier settlers. Perhaps it would not add greatly to the cost. If it does, would it be possible to use a local brick instead of one made at a distance?" Peoples sent an engineer to Saugerties and passed along to Treasury Secretary Morgenthau his report that "there are no quarries available for the production of blue stone in quantities sufficient to construct this building entirely of stone and further there are no buildings in this city that have been built entirely of this stone." In the end Saugerties citizens, who feared that further insistence on bluestone might seriously delay the whole project, had to be satisfied with local brick and, on the façade and two side elevations, bluestone trim. Darrow was pleased with his partial victory and thanked the White House for its role, going so far as to write: "As a Republican I ... have trouble in defining the latitude and longitude of the N.R.A. [National Recovery Act] but that it might result in the National Religious Awakening." The brick chosen was made by the Washburn Brothers Brick Co. of Saugerties, while the bluestone was supplied by the Adam Ross Cut Stone Co. headquartered in Albany.

Although no longer a post office and shorn of its double-hung window sash with small 12-over-12 panes, the brick walls (with corners treated as quoins) and bluestone trim remain as reminders of FDR's and the New Deal's dedication to regional traditions.

XVI–10 First Congregational Church
333 Main St. at First St. 1853–1855. NR

This Congregational church, the first of the denomination in Ulster County, was organized in 1853 by members of the Reformed Church who disagreed "over the building of a new house of worship and the sale of the old property." The division would be made evident in the façades of the two churches—the Reformed church is a mixture of the Romanesque and Gothic of the Middle Ages, with an asymmetrical tower and spire (see XVI–4), while the Congregational church is symmetrical and classical, with Renaissance brackets, pediment, and keystoned arch marking the central doorway, and the broad roof gable treated like a classical pediment. The central tower houses the village clock (still operating with weights and pendulum), and early photos show it was once crowned with a balustrade. Below the clock faces, the arched openings are filled with four stacked circles, not usual in classical design. The circular motif is repeated in the frieze below the main cornice. The church's walls are of brick covered with stucco inscribed to resemble granite blocks, as was customary in Saugerties churches but condemned

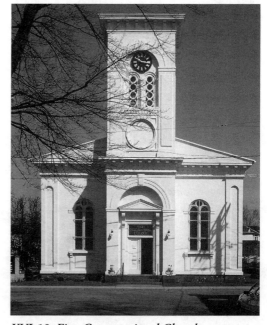

XVI-10. First Congregational Church

as a "deceptive contrivance" by an 1853 Congregational committee on church planning.

The main space for worship, known to Congregationalists of the time as the "audience room," is a simple, boxy auditorium with a gallery (enclosed c. 1960) above the entrance and supported by thin iron columns. Broad arches define the exterior façade, while the face of the gallery parapet is handsomely ornamented with narrow-arched panels. Ten large, round-arched windows, always with colored glass (although the present glass is apparently not the original glass) illuminate the audience room. The church planning committee allowed colored glass so long as it did not distract worshippers, as figurative stained glass surely would have. The ceiling is flat, not vaulted or trussed in the Gothic manner, but originally panelled and stuccoed. The clear focal point of the interior is the central and elevated pulpit. There is no deep chancel, no ritualistic altar.

Congregational churches had their roots in New England Puritanism and were treated by some nineteenth-century New Yorkers as unwelcome usurpers from the outside. Because of their Puritan origins, a number of Congregational churches turned away from the rich ornament and liturgical plan of the Gothic and instead embraced simpler forms, round arches, and the unified space of a Protestant preaching box. A committee of Congregationalists in 1853 argued for the primacy of the pulpit and preaching, which must not be "lost amid the labyrinthine intricacies of clustered pillars and groined arches, leading hither and thither" as was the case with the enormous Gothic cathedrals of Roman Catholics and Anglicans. Saugerties's Congregational church adhered to Congregational planning principles, as did a later church in the region, Poughkeepsie's First Congregational Church (1859–1860, by James H. Dudley).

XVI–11* George W. Washburn House
Washburn Terrace. 1873 (altered c. 1929).

Brick manufacturer George W. Washburn's wood-frame house was among the most exuberantly ornamented mansarded Second Empire designs in

XVI-11. George Washburn House (photo in Hassinger, 1911)

XVI-11A. Washburn House altered (1980 photo)

the county. Early-twentieth-century Americans claiming good taste could not stomach what they considered the crude vulgarity of this Victorian style, and the Washburn house, like others of its kind, was subjected to a radical paring away of its ornament and a restyling in a manner probably thought Colonial by its then-owner. Nearby on Washburn Terrace is the Frelich and Washburn Block (by 1875)—five brick row houses whose Italianate brackets and cast-iron lintels and sills have fortunately remained intact.

XVI–12* West Shore Railroad Freight Station (former)
Near Rte. 32 and the CSX tracks. 1883.

Partly hidden within a gas and oil business, this bracketed, shingled, and board-and-batten building advertised itself by the decorative cutouts in the panel set into the gable facing the road— "Freight/ NY WS & B R Co"—indicating that it was the freight house of the New York, West

XVI-12. Saugerties Freight Station (1978 photo)

Shore & Buffalo Railroad. The West Shore station surviving in Milton is very similar (see X–11). The Saugerties West Shore passenger station stood nearby, but was demolished in the early 1960s.

XVI-13 St. Mary's Church (St. Mary of the Snow Roman Catholic Church)
Cedar and Post Sts. 1833–1852 and 1891. Michael Quigg, builder.

The first Catholic church built between New York and Albany, St. Mary's was completed slowly over some nineteen years—its working-class parishioners, mainly Irish, were hard put to find the necessary funds—but for more than a century and a half its Gothic tower and spire have been a strong presence. In 1880 the church was described as occupying "a commanding position, overlooking the village of Saugerties, the harbor with the adjoining mills and iron-works, the valley of the Hudson, and the surrounding country ... for many miles. ... Its tall and graceful spire may be seen from many distant points."

Construction began in 1833, but two years later the roof, floor, windows, and doors were still unfinished. A Catholic paper of the time, *The Truth Teller*, beseeched donors, "Who will deny a few shillings for the completion of such an object." The bell tower and spire probably date from the end of the construction period (the bell, by Jones & Co. Founders, is dated 1863) and are distinctly Gothic in the pointed arches, corner but-

tressing, and ornamental tracery of the window over the main doorway. (About the same time, the Saugerties Reformed Church was erecting its own Gothic façade; see XVI–4). Similar Gothic tracery marks the windows to either side of the tower—windows that, oddly, are of different heights—but the low pitch of the gable roof and the classical details of the raking cornice of the gable indicate that the c. 1833 design was at least partially classical. As in other Saugerties churches the brick walls are surfaced with stucco.

St. Mary's has withstood a number of fires. In 1854 fanatical anti-Catholics set fire to the building, but failed to destroy it. The mid-1850s saw the rise of nativism and anti-Catholicism in the United States and in Ulster County. Native-born Protestants opposed to immigrants and Roman Catholics united as Know Nothings, and in 1855 they carried Ulster County. In 1891 the church was gutted by another fire and quickly rebuilt, with a taller addition to the north for transepts and chancel. The corner of the west transept has a cornerstone carved "1833 1891."

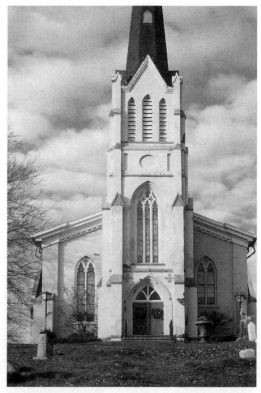

XVI-13. St. Mary's Church

The awkward break between the high roofs of the transepts and the lower roof of the old nave is clear evidence that the intention was to rebuild the nave with a roof matching the profile of the 1891 addition.

The handsome interior is enriched with stained glass. The large window in the east transept, the Donovan Memorial Window by Tiffany, is of appropriately pale colors as it depicts the Virgin Mary at the time of the Immaculate Conception. In 1989 the church again suffered a serious fire and was once more rebuilt.

The brick Gothic rectory east of the church was built in 1885; its south façade has been altered unsympathetically. (An earlier rectory became the home of the first school and sisters' convent.)

In 1880 visitors found, "around ... [the church] upon all the grassy slopes are buried the Catholic dead ... The graves are almost numberless, but well marked with memorial stones. Some have the tall and handsome shaft wealth has been able to lavish upon the beloved dead; others the simple slab which poverty has struggled to place above the departed. All bear the holy symbols of faith." Many of the simplest slabs have been lost over time or their inscriptions have become illegible. The tall shaft of Patrick Curley, a native of Ireland who died June 2, 1860, at age seventy-eight, still stands not far from the church's main entrance. Of similar origins, John Glennon died July 6, 1865, at age forty-six and rests beneath a modest, arched-topped stone. Among the finest monuments is John Kearney's shaft, signed by its maker, "W. J. Nicholson [lettering indistinct]/ Hudson." Kearney was born in Dublin in 1788 and died in Saugerties, January 20, 1846, having served as bookkeeper of the Ulster Iron Works.

XVI–14 Saugerties Lighthouse
Hudson River at the mouth of the Esopus Creek. 1867–1869 (rebuilt late 1980s). NR

This is a fine but not extraordinary Victorian brick house with segmental arched windows and multigabled roof of polychrome slate. What makes this house worth a detour is its site on the Hudson River and the cylindrical glassy lantern of its riverside tower, announcing that here lived the keeper of the light. Originally fitted with a sixth-order Fresnel lens, the light was fueled by kerosene and guided boats into Saugerties harbor during the years when it was a major river port with passenger boats to Manhattan and Albany and ferries to Tivoli. The light was automated in 1954, and the building was subsequently abandoned by the Coast Guard. It deteriorated to a roofless ruin, but local preservationists rallied, and it was rebuilt in the late 1980s. In 1990 the light was restored to operation with a fourth-order solar-powered light. The lighthouse is open at scheduled times, and it is even possible to stay overnight by advance reservation with the Saugerties Lighthouse Conservancy. There are panoramic views of the river and the Catskills. The conservancy maintains a nature trail (flooded at high tide) to the lighthouse from a parking area on Lighthouse Drive.

XVI-14. Saugerties Lighthouse

XVI-15 Trinity Episcopal Church

32 Church St. at Barclay St. 1831–1832
(Chancel furnishings, 1873–1874, by Edward
T. Potter, with stained-glass window by
Morris, Marshall, Faulkner & Co.) NR

Here, tucked away in a church whose Grecian exterior resembles many in the Hudson Valley, can be found a beautiful and important stained-glass window by William Morris's London firm, the first such window to be commissioned by an American client. A writer for *Scribner's Monthly* saw the window when it was exhibited in New York early in 1873, while ice on the Hudson delayed its final shipment to Saugerties, and admitted, "We envy the people of Saugerties their new possession."

Trinity Church was established and built thanks to "the zeal and liberality of Henry Barclay [1778–1851] and John Watts Kearny [died 1850]." A round-arched marble plaque near the pulpit commemorates the accomplishments of Barclay and Kearny, and of Barclay's wife Catharine (or Catherine, 1782–1851) in founding the parish and erecting the church. (The two men had married sisters; Henry, John, and Catharine died within a few weeks of each other in December 1850 and January 1851.) Henry and Catharine Barclay had strong links to prestigious Trinity Church on Broadway in New York, and Trinity in Saugerties may be considered an offspring of that church. Catharine erected a pedimented marble plaque to memorialize her parents; her mother Mary Watts died in December 1831 and was buried beneath the chancel of her daughter's church.

Beginning in 1825 Henry Barclay undertook the industrial development of Saugerties, which led to the rapid growth of the community. Barclay envisioned "a model village" and, as he was an Episcopalian "of deep religious temperament," Trinity Church was given a prominent site on the hill on the south side of the Esopus Creek and on the Kingston-Saugerties road. (The church was near Barclay's residence, Ury, which was demolished in 1854 and replaced by J. B. Sheffield's house.) Barclay encouraged his "English iron workers" and their families to worship in the church he founded. There they would find a

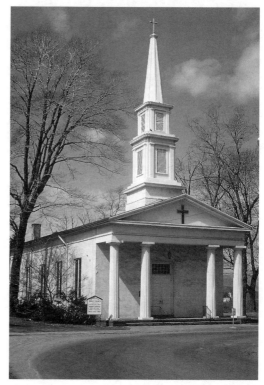

XVI-15. Trinity Episcopal Church (1972 photo)

tranquility remote from the drama of iron production. In 1880 one spectator compared the "stirring scene" of "workmen, naked to the waist, running about with great red-hot bars of iron; the flames shooting out of those tall chimneys; the weird shadows falling grotesquely around" to "scenes of Dante's 'Inferno.'"

From the church's grounds, nineteenth-century worshippers could take in magnificent vistas: "The Hudson rolls majestically by in the view from the portico ... while from the grounds in the rear one of the grandest views in the locality unfolds itself ... the calm and silvery Esopus, the quiet country village, and on beyond towering heavenward rise the glorious Catskills, soul-inspiring monuments to Him who made them."

Trinity, said to have been designed by Ralph Bigelow who, in 1840, built a covered bridge across the Esopus Creek for Henry Barclay, was among the first churches in Ulster County to revive the form of an ancient Greek temple. Four fluted Doric columns support a two-part entabla-

XVI-15A. Morris Window, Trinity Episcopal Church (1978 photo)

es required bells to call the faithful to worship, and towers to hold the bells. Bell towers were unknown to the Greeks, and to join such a tower to a revived Greek temple "is a most glaring absurdity."

By the 1860s the Greek Revival was dead, and Pugin's beloved Gothic Revival dominated the American church designs of his followers, notably Richard Upjohn. In 1873, after Trinity was damaged by fire, Edward Tuckerman Potter (1831–1904), a prominent Gothic Revival church architect trained in Upjohn's office, was called upon to create a new chancel. While the church was enlarged in 1917–1918, the furnishings designed by Potter mostly remain, although the pulpit (at the congregation's left) is a memorial to a longtime rector, the Rev. Thomas Cole (the artist's son), who died in 1919. Potter felt obliged by the existing Greek Revival church to use a semi-classical style in designing the Italian marble altar and carved mahogany furniture of the chancel. The lectern or slender stand for the Bible at the congregation's right has finely worked images of the four evangelists—St. Matthew as a winged man, St. Mark as a winged lion, St. Luke as a winged ox, and St. John as an eagle—who were also represented on the pillars supporting the communion rail. A narrow brass plaque above the altar identifies, in Latin, Judge Aaron Vanderpoel (1799–1870) and other members of the Vanderpoel family who were memorialized by the judge's widow, Else, in Potter's furnishings and Morris's glass.

The crowning glory of the chancel and the church as a whole is the stained-glass window located over the altar and obtained by Potter as part of his redesign of the interior. The window was produced in the renowned workshop of Morris, Marshall, Faulkner & Co. of London. William Morris, poet and chief proponent of the Arts and Crafts movement, designed the eight stained-glass panels depicting angels holding scrolls, and he supervised the making of the window as a whole. The central and largest panel, designed by Morris's friend and colleague Edward Burne-Jones, represents Christ on the Cross with the Virgin Mary and John at the foot of the cross. Burne-Jones also designed five of the six panels portraying events in Christ's life; the sixth panel, at the

ture and then a triangular pediment. Like an ancient temple, a high door is centered at the front, and the front has no windows. Unlike an ancient temple, the columns are not regularly spaced—they are spread apart at the center (to ease access to the doorway?)—and there are windows along the flanks of the building (worshippers did not enter ancient temples, and so windows were not required). About 1840 a two-stage tower and tapering spire were added above the pediment. (The church has lost its tapering spire—not a loss according to lovers of the classical.) An early-twentieth-century postcard shows walls not of Greek marble, but smooth stucco, the stucco worn in patches to reveal brick beneath.

The English architect and polemicist A. W. N. Pugin was unable to fathom how good Christians could revive the forms of the Greek temple, intended as they were for the worship of pagan gods. "These temples were erected for idolatrous worship, and were suited only for the idolatrous rites which were performed in them." Christian church-

lower left and showing the Agony in the Garden, is by Ford Madox Brown. The artists were influenced by the English Pre-Raphaelite Brotherhood to shed the artificiality of Renaissance art and aim for the truthfulness thought to reside in the earlier fifteenth-century art of Italy and northern Europe. Stained glass as a medium flourished in the Gothic period, and the willowy grace of the figures by Morris and his associates instill a late-medieval aura surprising the visitor who is familiar only with the Grecian exterior of the church.

XVI–16* Anna M. Steenken House
Burt St. c. 1920. Henry Corse of Butler & Corse.

The architect Henry Corse was a Saugerties native who trained under the renowned Gothic Revivalist Bertram Grosvenor Goodhue and went on to a successful career in New York. (At Christmas 1916 Goodhue inscribed C. Matlack Price's *The Practical Book of Architecture* to Corse and described himself as Corse's "chief.") After World War I, Corse designed this Tudor-style country house for Miss Anna M. Steenken. The families of client and architect were close; in November 1925 Miss Steenken sailed with Miss Jeanette Corse, the architect's sister, on the White Star liner *Majestic*.

The east front of the house (now a bed and breakfast) is set well back from the busy street, while the west façade, with terrace and originally a fountain, looks out over what the architect called "the winding course of the Esopus [Creek] and the misty blue Catskills in perspective." In a well-illustrated article in *Arts & Decoration*, Corse wrote that his aim was to create "an English house of the small manor type that is eloquently expressive of

XVI-16. Steenken House (c. 1920 postcard)

its friendly alliance with American soil." He sought accuracy in designing the house in the Tudor mold, studying books on the subject and spending "many months in England seeking inspiration ... to faithfully translate ... the best English country house tradition." In the end he was content that, "built low to the ground of soft-hued local brick and a slate roof of variegated tones, the house with its clustered chimney stacks and leaded casements has seemed as authentic an adaptation of Tudor days as we could conceive it." Yet this American architect was pleased that the Tudor merged easily with some aspects of the American Colonial; for example, "the simplicity of the dining room treatment, still English in feeling, has a hint of our own Colonial in it, which as always exerts a certain heart appeal."

XVI–17 William R. Sheffield Estate, Cloverlea (Dragon Inn)
Burt St. 1878–1883. J. Cleveland Cady; Alfred H. Thorp.

Once a fine Victorian mansion, later made over into a Chinese restaurant, and now fire-damaged and derelict, the Sheffield house was designed by New York architect Alfred H. Thorp. Thorp, who had been Edward T. Potter's junior partner in the design of Mark Twain's well-known Victorian Gothic house (1873–1874) in Hartford, produced one of Ulster's most complexly picturesque houses. The great pyramidal roof is fitted with many shed-roofed dormers on three levels, while

*XVI-17. Cloverlea
(1980 photo)*

two not-quite-identical gables project from the roof toward the highway. Slender brick chimneys rise high. Gothic (or Stick Style) trusses are fitted into the peaks of the two front gables, and diagonal braces support the projecting south gable. The Queen Anne style appeared in the variety of materials—patterned wood-shingled walls above brick walls—and broad bands of glass in the bay windows. Bluestone from local quarries was used in the foundation and window trim, while brick was furnished by the Lent brickyard in Glasco. The Sheffield house resembled the design for Mark Twain's in having balanced, but not symmetrical, front gables and ornamented brackets at those gables. However, the Saugerties house reveals its later date in its less vividly colorful walls and use of wood shingles for parts of the upper walls according with the Queen Anne style.

William R. Sheffield (1848–1913) was his father's partner in J. B. Sheffield & Son from 1869 to his father's death in 1879. The firm, with several hundred employees, made a wide range of paper goods in buildings along the lower Esopus Creek in Saugerties. The younger Sheffield acquired land for this estate on Barclay Heights in 1878, and the same year employed the prominent New York architect J. Cleveland Cady, best known

for the original section of the Museum of Natural History, to design a gate lodge and stable. The well-preserved gate lodge stands just north of the main house. Before undertaking construction of the house in 1882, Sheffield also arranged for the fine landscaping of the grounds. In her history of the estate, Karlyn Knaust Elia notes that originally there were views from the house to the mountaintop hotels of the Catskills.

Why Sheffield chose Cady is not known, but his selection of Thorp to design the main house probably came about through his active membership in nearby Trinity Episcopal Church. Potter had designed alterations to the church in 1873, but retired from active practice in 1877, no doubt leading some clients to his former partner Thorp. Little is known about Thorp's accomplishments in New York. His Racket Court Club (1876) on 6th Avenue, a Romanesque design with inventive iron brackets supporting the cornice, was demolished in the 1990s.

Sheffield was prominent in the Republican Party and, in 1888, held what *The New York Times* described as a "big reception" at his "handsome home" for party leaders in the region. Samuel D. Coykendall brought the Kingston contingent by special train.

Town of Saugerties (beyond the Village)

XVI-18 Seamon Park
Malden Ave. 1909.

Retired Saugerties businessman John Seamon (one of the Seamon brothers whose 1882 building stands on Main Street; see XVI–8) purchased the Egbert Cooper property in 1907, paid for its improvement and beautification as a place of public recreation, and then deeded it to the village in 1909 "for use as a park, a breathing place, open and free at all times to every person." Some had speculated that Seamon the entrepreneur was planning "an amusement enterprise, conducted along business lines," but the donor's only demand was that the park be named "Seamon Park."

By 1907, a prosperous and progressive community needed a public park; New York famously began to develop Central Park in the 1850s, and Newburgh's Downing Park was laid out in the 1890s. In Poughkeepsie, Matthew Vassar and George Eastman, businessmen like Seamon, had opened the landscaped grounds around their residences to the public in the 1850s and 1860s. Kingston Point Park had been opened as a commercial enterprise in the 1890s, but the city of Kingston was slow in embracing the municipal park movement—land for Academy Green Park was only deeded to the city in 1918.

Central Park and Downing Park were laid out by Frederick Law Olmsted and Calvert Vaux, the foremost talents of their day. Seamon Park's designer is unknown, but early photos suggest the hand of one less talented than Olmsted or Vaux. Cobblestone piers and walls flanked the main entrance which, since the park was to be "open and free at all times," had no gate—it still has none, and the park is open from dawn to dusk. Near the entrance and just behind the iron fence separating the park from Malden Avenue was the Children's Fountain (donated by schoolchildren) in the form of a boy and girl under an umbrella. The children stood within a circular pool rimmed with a circle of cobblestones, with two square or rectangular pools also rimmed with a layer of cobblestones framing the central, circular pool. Just above these pools is the custodian's residence. Formal, geometric flower beds were interspersed among informal landscaping. Pleasant walks led up a gentle grade to a hilltop cast-iron fountain (again encircled with cobblestones), formal flower beds, and an open-sided pavilion resembling a primitive classical temple but providing a sheltered lookout for the magnificent view west and north to the Catskills.

Changes made to the design of the park over the past century have generally been in the spirit

XVI-18. Seamon Park (c. 1909 postcard)

of the original park. The Chrysanthemum Festival in October and Christmas lights in December are current highlights of life in the park.

XVI-19 West Shore Railroad Depot (former)

160 Malden Turnpike (County Rte. 34), Malden. c. 1910.

Moved from its original location, this survivor from the golden age of rail passenger service resembles several early-twentieth-century stations in the county, including Marlborough's West Shore Railroad Depot (not extant; see X–6) and New Paltz's Wallkill Valley Railroad Depot (1907–1908; altered)—the sheltering hipped roof projects well out from the wooden walls and is supported by large brackets, while the projecting rafter ends provide a decorative frieze. The bay window, which originally gave the station agent a view up and down the tracks, seems to rise through the roof, and the resulting low dormer has its own picturesque hipped roof. To the right of the bay window was the passenger waiting room, while to the left was the baggage or express room with wide door facing the tracks.

XVI-19. Malden Depot

XVI-20 Katsbaan Reformed Church

1800 Old Kings Highway (County Rte. 34). 1732, 1816, 1867.

This beautiful stone church has a complex construction history. The church was organized about 1730; some of the founders were Dutch, others

were Palatine Germans. In the north wall of the present building are several stones, originally on the east wall of the building, that bear the initials of the builders of the church. The uppermost marked stone has the initials "CM," for Christian Meyer, perhaps head of the building committee, and the date "1732." Although the dated stone is not in its original location, a portion of the north wall may have been laid in 1732, predating the more extensive surviving walls of the Reformed Church of Shawangunk erected in the 1750s (see XVIII–1). The 1732 place of worship, a meetinghouse, probably resembled a story-and-a-half, gable-roofed stone house. It had no steeple, and differed from a residence primarily in the elaborate frame of the door—not under the gable, but in the east side wall.

In 1816, to expand seating capacity, the walls were raised to a full two stories, and galleries built within. Two doors were placed in the south side, with the pulpit on the opposite, north, wall. A steeple with bell was also added over the south front. A photo of the church taken before 1867 records these changes and dark stones on the east

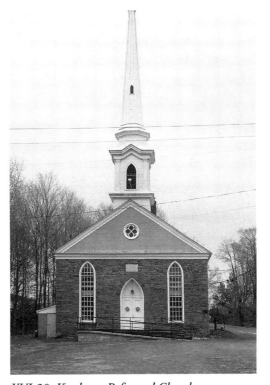

XVI-20. Katsbaan Reformed Church

side (now on the north wall) carved with the initials of the builders of the church.

In 1867 the church was largely rebuilt, and it is this version we see today. The inclusion of tall Gothic windows on the west and east walls required the moving of the initialed stones from the east to the north wall. At the same time the church was enlarged by seventeen feet to the south. The handsome front of the church, from 1867, combines a Greek Revival gable treated as a classical pediment and classical pilasters at the corners of the belfry, with Gothic Revival arched door, windows, and louvered opening in the belfry, as well as a Gothic quatrefoil-within-circle in the pediment. If the church had been wholly new in 1867, the façade probably would have been more thoroughly Gothic, but the stone over the doorway, carved with the dates 1732, 1816, and 1867, indicates that the 1867 congregation valued the work of their predecessors.

An early-nineteenth-century three-manual organ, apparently made and first used in New York City, was given to the Katsbaan church in 1892 by the Saugerties Reformed Church. It is a rare survivor of its type and is currently being restored.

XVI–21* Elijah Lemuel Crawford House
Kings Highway (County Rte. 34) at Wilhelm Rd., Asbury. c. 1870 (altered later).

This Victorian house, now shorn of its bracketed eaves and Gothic porch, was surrounded by a delightful yard of lawn, flowers, and trees when

XVI-21. Crawford House (painting by Lucy Weeks, c. 1902)

recorded about 1902 in Lucy Kendall Sanford Weeks's painting. A farmer, Elijah Lemuel Crawford (1821–1897), resided here in the predominantly Methodist neighborhood of Asbury in the 1870s. Just west of Crawford's house on Wilhelm Road stood the West Camp (later Asbury) Methodist Episcopal Church, which was under construction in 1807 when Francis Asbury (1745–1816), first Methodist bishop in the United States, visited the locality and prayed with the carpenters building the church. The plain, steepleless building no longer stands, but Elijah Crawford's tall monument can still be found in its graveyard.

XVI–22 Wynkoop House (Schoentag's Colonial Tavern)
Rte. 32 near Thruway entrance. c. 1740 and 1790. NR

One stone on what is now the rear wall of this house is dated 1740, but Peter Sinclair's inspection indicated that the structure is essentially from 1790, the date found on bluestone lintels above the front windows. Initials and symbols (possibly Masonic) are also found on these datestones. The kitchen portion of the house (the door and window to the right in the drawing) therefore would be contemporary with the more formal section of the house—two windows to either side of a doorway leading to a stair hall. Sinclair suggests that rafters, beams, paneling, and some window sash may have been reused from a 1740 house.

In 1932 the house was acquired by Mrs. T. Donovan and Mrs. E. Williams, who operated it as Schoentag's Colonial Tavern, marketed as an "old Dutch inn." Their menu was illustrated with a drawing (signed "Johnson '40") of the old stone façade. In front of the house, an iron pot and tripod called up visions of Revolutionary camps, but why is the spinning wheel standing outdoors? Unlike Sally Tock's Inn at Stone Ridge or the Old Fort in New Paltz, this tavern run by women offered not only food but also alcohol. Among the cocktails was an exotic Cuba Libra, but from the list of highballs and whiskies one could select Catskill Apple.

In 2003 the threatened demolition of the Wynkoop house galvanized local preservation

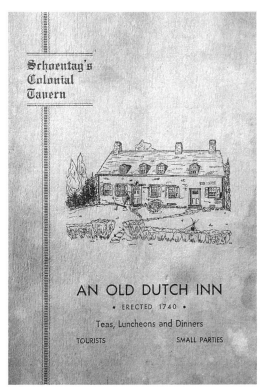

Schoentag's
Colonial
Tavern

AN OLD DUTCH INN

• ERECTED 1740 •

Teas, Luncheons and Dinners

TOURISTS   SMALL PARTIES

XVI-22. Wynkoop House (menu cover drawing by Johnson, 1940)

Over the years Fite labored to create organically curving stone terracing and pedestals to serve as a setting for his figurative stone sculptures. In the end, however, the stone setting itself became the work of art, and Fite moved his simplified, carved-stone figures to the lawn at the edge of the nearby woods. Working mostly alone, Fite used traditional stone mason's hand tools—hammer and chisel, winch and boom—to assemble, without mortar, irregular pieces of stone left by the quarriers into beautiful, tightly knit walls and terraces. Maria La Yocona's iconic photo of Fite at work shows the handsome, muscular former actor stripped to the waist and lifting a capstone into place with his bare hands. He believed the resulting construction could last 10,000 years, far longer than modern steel-framed skyscrapers clad in stone, such as Rockefeller Center. The sculptor was killed in an accidental fall in 1976 when his masterwork was nearly completed. Fite, who disliked the pretension of the name "acropolis" that had been applied to the site, preferred the historically neutral term "Opus 40," which referred to the forty years he expected completion of his work to require.

Visitors have long been able to enjoy the adventure of walking the ramps, stairs, and terraces surrounding the monolith, peering down into moat-like cavities or out over pools, while avoiding the hazards of abrupt drops to lower regions. Fite conceived his creation, however, not as a playground, but as a work of art susceptible to a variety of interpretations. A guide to Opus 40 written before Fite's death suggests that "to some, it has a profound religious significance; to others, it is a magnificent theater. It is solid by day, ephemeral by night. It is one thing in a summer rain, and another covered with a frosting of snow."

In 1934 Fite had built himself a cabin at Hervey White's Maverick art colony, near another abandoned quarry. Frustrated by White's refusal to sell him property, Fite left the Maverick and purchased the quarry in High Woods. He put up a combined bachelor's residence and sculpture studio at the edge of the abandoned quarry in the late 1930s. Just as he formed the new sculptural environment from stones in the old quarry, he constructed the house and studio partly with

sentiment. The house was saved, and the town established an Historic Preservation Commission chaired by Barry Benepe to prevent the loss of other important landmarks.

XVI-23 Opus 40
**50 Fite Rd., High Woods. 1939–1976.
Harvey Fite. NR**

Opus 40 is Harvey Fite's magnificent transformation of an abandoned bluestone quarry at High Woods into an endlessly fascinating work of environmental sculpture surrounded by trees with Overlook Mountain in the distance. Here the visitor is invited to admire Fite's sculptural sensibility—also his craftsmanship and endurance—while ascending stone ramps toward a culminating nine-ton, vertical monolith.

Fite (1903–1976), a self-taught sculptor and professor of sculpture at Bard College, began work at the rubble-strewn quarry in 1939.

XVI-23. Opus 40
with Fite House
(1984 photo)

old barn timbers. The exterior of that studio-residence remains little changed, although in the mid-1950s Fite built a separate studio in the woods and, with the large doors of the former studio removed, the onetime studio became a living room. (After about 1950 the sculptor's wife, the former Barbara Fairbanks Richards, whom he married in 1944, was responsible for major decisions regarding alterations to the house.)

While the sculptural stone heart of Opus 40 is marked by free, organic curves, the house and the Quarryman's Museum Fite built nearby in the early 1970s are wooden and rectilinear. The simple, unadorned walls of the house incorporate, where the studio once was, large windows composed of several sashes grouped to be narrower at the base. This unusual sash grouping, fitted with numerous small panes of glass, is reminiscent of White's Maverick Concert Hall and, like all of White's Maverick buildings, Fite's house blends easily with the surrounding wooded landscape (see V–5 and V–6).

XVI-24 Plattekill Reformed Church
Kings Highway (County Rte. 31),
Mount Marion. 1834, 1850.

This pristine example of the wooden Greek Revival church was built in 1834—the same year the congregation was organized—and altered in 1850. The Plattekill church was linked with the stone Flatbush church until 1838—they shared a minister—and their façades are comparable (see next entry, XVI–25). Both have a tall, sixty-pane

window on each side of the central entrance, and a steeple whose belfry stage is fitted with corner pilasters. However, Plattekill's façade is rigorously Greek in its rectangular openings, while the Flatbush church retains a Federal-style elliptical arch over the entrance to the recessed porch and has a semicircular Roman arch in the belfry.

In 1937 the Plattekill church was in the national spotlight thanks to President Roosevelt's visit to its fair on July 5. *The Kingston Daily Freeman* reported that "the greatest crowd ever to assemble on the grounds of the historic, little, white Plattekill Reformed Church at Mt. Marion gathered there for the annual fair ... when President Franklin D. Roosevelt was the guest of honor." Some 5,000 people greeted FDR, who spoke extemporaneously to the shirt-sleeved crowd while seated on the back of his car. *The New York Times* headlined its story, "ROOSEVELT AFFIRMS NATION'S SOUNDNESS, Bases of American Democracy Unchanged Amid Stress of Today."

FDR used as his "text" the invitation he had received from Mrs. Warren D. Myer, president of the church's Ladies Aid Society. Mrs. Myer had written the President: "You must be weary of great affairs, so maybe this simple invitation will please you." He admitted, "Sometimes I am weary of great affairs, but I would be a lot wearier if it were not for simple parties of this kind." FDR was also moved to quote a passage in Mrs.

XVI-24. Plattekill Reformed Church

standing of American history and architecture, knew that his message was most appropriately given in a setting that proclaimed the traditions of America—the churchyard of an old, white-steepled church. A monument in the adjacent cemetery identifies Mrs. Myer as Ella H. Myer, 1899–1990.

XVI-25 Flatbush Reformed Church
1844 Rte. 32, Flatbush. 1808, 1844, 1866.

This stone church stems from 1808, although the front (south) façade belongs to an enlargement carried out in 1844–1845. The classical cupola resting on a broad pediment and entablature were standard ingredients of a Greek Revival church of the 1840s. However, the elliptical arch over the recessed porch is not Greek, but a characteristic of the Federal style of the period when the church was originally built. The windows are remarkably tall, each requiring four sashes fitted with fifteen panes, and the windows are finely trimmed with stone and brick in quoin-like patterns. In 1866

Myer's letter where she acknowledged that she was not an important personage: "We are a plain, pioneer American family who for eight generations have lived in our Hudson Valley home and tilled the same acres that we wrested from the wilderness. We have been quiet, self-sustaining citizens for 227 years." However, she did proudly assert that "our service during the Revolution, I believe, is unparalleled, as we gave eighteen sons to the service. ... Since we helped then to make July Fourth possible, would it be so unsuitable for our President to grant us a favor on this Fourth of July?" For Roosevelt, Mrs. Myer and her forebears provided exemplars that "we are always going to keep our feet on the ground as a nation in the future, just as we have in the past." The challenges of the modern world were to be met by people with a strong sense of their sturdy roots in the past; FDR told the crowd of his own great-great-great-great-grandfather, in the late 1600s a farmer and member of the militia in Ulster County. FDR, with his keen under-

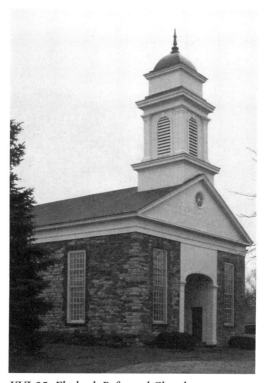

XVI-25. Flatbush Reformed Church

the upper part of the cupola was rebuilt, and the church was extended to the north—the north wall is of brick. Adjacent to the church are carriage sheds (altered), now rarely seen but once common in churchyards.

XVI–26* Boots Van Steenbergh House
Flatbush. c. 1890 (not extant).

The lore surrounding the Catskills is full of stories about hermits and eccentrics. Alf Evers has described Boots Van Steenbergh (died 1898) as a nonfictional hermit and popular entertainer at summer boardinghouses, where he would sing parodies of operatic airs, make nonsensical political speeches, or recite meaningless poetry. Boots—the name from the high boots he wore year-round—fashioned a fantastic shanty in Flatbush that Evers thought anticipated the abstract sculpture twentieth-century artists created out of found materials—"odds and ends of boards rose from the roof. Inscriptions in what seemed like a dead language and in a variety of colors were lettered wherever there was space. Wires coiled round and round the building. Pennants made of strips of newspapers rustled and fluttered." A photo taken about 1896 shows Boots alongside his extraordinary creation.

A later kindred spirit, Clarence Schmidt (1897–1978), a native of Queens trained as a plasterer and mason, arrived in Woodstock in the 1930s and built a cabin of railroad ties near the top of Ohayo Mountain in Hurley. He applied tar to preserve the ties, and subsequently scattered broken glass over the exterior of his home. By 1953 Schmidt had built stone terraces and a multistory, ramshackle wooden house on the mountain slope. Later the eccentric builder incorporated into the labyrinthine structure quantities of thrown-away material including aluminum foil, plastic, and chrome—not the more natural materials favored by Boots. In the 1960s and '70s the media and the art world celebrated Schmidt's "House of Glass" or "Junk Castle" as "an architectural wonder" and "a fine example of American folk art." It burned to the ground shortly after being featured on a special NBC television program.

XVI-26. Boots Van Steenbergh House (c. 1896 photo)

XVII
Town of Shandaken

Formed from part of the Town of Woodstock, 1804.

Population: 2,703 in 1870; 3,235 in 2000.

Like the nearby towns of Denning and Hardenbergh, Shandaken's mountains and ravines made the land little suited for farming, but its forests employed lumbermen, tanners, and makers of shingles and chairs in the later nineteenth century. In 1880 Lemuel A. Chichester owned a chair factory with buildings 464 feet in length capable of making 3,600 chairs and 900 rocking cradles per week; some of his products were shipped to Europe and South America. In 1868 newspapers in more populous and sophisticated towns predicted that the opening of the Rondout & Oswego (later Ulster & Delaware) Railroad would allow "the rustic denizens of Shandaken ... to run their lumber to market behind the 'iron horse.'" The railroad reached Shandaken in 1870, and lumber was shipped, but the coming of the railroad also encouraged stone quarrying for paving and building. The railroad brought large numbers of vacationers from the hot cities to the cooler mountains. No doubt the name Shandaken—of Indian origin and signifying "rapid water"—sounded appealingly romantic to these escapees from the city. Unfortunately, automobiles gradually supplanted rail travel, and the last passenger train ran between Kingston and Oneonta in 1954.

XVII-1 Camp Wapanachki (Zen Mountain Monastery)
Old Rte. 28, Mount Tremper. c. 1930–1936. Victor L. S. Hafner. NR

Since 1980 a Zen Buddhist monastery, this fascinating example of rustic Gothic originally housed Camp Wapanachki, a Roman Catholic camp that in 1938 offered "complete athletic and cultural programs, crafts, nature lore" for boys from eight to sixteen. The name of the camp, Wapanachki—documents from the 1920s and '30s include at least four other spellings—called up visions of Native American camp life, and Native American motifs appeared in the design. The founder of the camp in the 1920s, the Reverend Joseph B. Scully (c. 1882–1956), had been associated with St. Francis de Sales Parish, Phoenicia, before being appointed to the rectorship of St. Mary's Church, Kingston, where he served from 1922 to 1932. Between 1922 and 1924 St. Mary's underwent extensive alterations and new Gothic buildings, a rectory and a convent, were erected.

Father Scully's architect for the camp was Victor L. S. Hafner (c. 1893–1947), an M.I.T. graduate who in 1921 won the prestigious Prix de Rome in architecture, entitling him to three years of study at the American Academy in Rome. Hafner focused on the dome of St. Peter's and caused a stir by announcing that cracks indicated the dome was unsafe. Later, in a private audience with the pope, he urged that statues planned by Michelangelo for atop the dome be carried out. The Vatican declined to take action on either idea. Back in New York, Hafner designed (with engineer Edward Hall Faile) the Goelet Building (1930–1932) at 608 Fifth Avenue, described by Christopher Gray as an "extravaganza in marble modernism." For Robert Moses's Jones Beach State Park, Hafner did murals (1933) of fish moving in their natural element, based on his study of aquaria in Europe and America.

Many of Hafner's blueprints and some pencil drawings for the camp's main building are preserved by the monastery and indicate that his office was variously in New York at 608 Fifth Ave. and in Scarsdale. Notes by Hafner on the prints and drawings are often unconventional and indicate that, for whatever reason, he did not conform to standard drafting-room practice. He did, however, follow the teachings of the Rome Academy by calling for the sculptural enrichment of the camp building—but not in the classical style of Rome. He designed a ruggedly picturesque Gothic building suited for a hillside in the Catskills, and perhaps to the Norwegian heritage of the craftsmen from the Mount Tremper area who are said to have erected the building. A drawing from his office of window details bears the instruction, "Note all muttins [muntins] to be hand widdle [whittled] with jack knive[s]." Local, too, were the bluestone and white oak used in construction.

The section of the building closest to old Route 28 was built first, and an early postcard of this section calls it The Lodge. Soon an auditorium was added on the east to form a T-plan. The south front of the original section, which includes the off-centered main doorway, is secular, north European Gothic in its asymmetrical composition, small-paned casement windows, steeply pitched gable roof, and substantial vergeboards. There are old Norwegian and more recent Norwegian Arts and Crafts precedents for the first story of stone with wood above, the marked overhang of the second story above the first, the gable facing front, the bands of small-paned casement windows, and especially (from old Norway) the lathe-turned posts at the corners of the second story. A 1930s photo shows that the original, unornamented bargeboards were unusual in extending well below and beyond the roof. Hafner's blueprints and drawings called for sinuous linear patterns and grotesque figures to be carved in the vergeboards and the posts centered at the intersection of two vergeboards. Hafner noted that large posts flanking the main door were to follow Native American "totem pole carving painted in colors." This and much of the carving Hafner designed was never carried out.

Most of the intricate ornamentation that was completed takes the form of delightful, highly realistic birds, insects, and animals on pine boughs and oak branches—all in cast metal—that are integral with the strap hinges of the exterior doorways, with additional natural motifs seeming to grow out of the casement window hardware. (Recall

XVII-1. Camp Wapanachki (c. 1935 postcard)

Hafner's study of fish for the Jones Beach murals.) The campers' nature study would therefore be reinforced by the static sculptural renditions, as well as by a stuffed animal head mounted above a gun rack that appears in Hafner's design for the lounge.

The slightly later auditorium/mess hall, attached to the east of the original lodge, resembles an early medieval church with its massive stone walls and relatively small windows. Again the steeply pitched gable roof and the lesser gables above the side windows derive from the Gothic, but the windows have blunt, not pointed. arched tops, and the posts centered on the vergeboards were to be carved like Indian totem poles. (At least one such post survived on the building in 1982, but weathering has forced its removal.) Conventional Gothic buttresses are here transformed into paired triangular walls flanking staircases at the southeast and northeast corners, and cylindrical water spouts project like cannon from the eaves. The stark geometry of the stone walls of the auditorium is only a little less severe than the "cubist" forms of the Goelet Building on 5th Avenue.

The camp building's east façade served as the backdrop for outdoor masses with campers seated in a semicircular amphitheatre facing a stern, larger than life-size, wooden sculpture of the risen Christ inserted in a cross-shaped niche. Above the tall windows to either side of Christ, thin stones were laid vertically and diagonally, evoking candles and their flames. The Christian aura of the east façade would have been diluted had the panel over the central doorway been carved, as Hafner intended, with an American Indian pursuing deer with bow and arrow. For the interior of the auditorium, Hafner designed (but did not carry out) an oak screen at the rear with posts to be carved with representations of "various types of Indians in the world," including "Hindu," "Africa," "American," and "Alaska Indian." The secular nature of these figures indicates that the room was envisioned as an auditorium and not a chapel. (Today it is the meditation hall.)

Not everything at the camp was to be hand-crafted, rustic, or exotic; Hafner designed (but probably did not complete) a paneled wall of "Father Scully's Bed-Study & Private Chapel" for a "built in radio," and the architect called for a spotlight hidden behind the head of Christ to create a "halo effect," reinforcing the radiance achieved in the linear patterns of the stonework surrounding Christ. To visit the monastery, call 845-688-2228.

XVII–2 Ulster and Delaware Railroad Station (Empire State Railway Museum)
Station Rd., Phoenicia. 1899.
Vaux and Emery. NR

This well-preserved Shingle Style station, built for the Ulster and Delaware Railroad, still functions as a train station for seasonal excursions operated by the Catskill Mountain Railroad between Cold Brook and Mount Pleasant. The station also houses the Empire State Railway Museum, with local history exhibits emphasizing the Ulster & Delaware Railroad. The present station replaced the original station constructed in 1870, and is an example of the U & D's "Standard Stations" designed by the partnership of Downing Vaux and Marshall L. Emery. As John Ham and Robert Bucenec reveal in their history of U & D stations, the wooden parts of these buildings were precut and shipped to station sites for quick assembly. Common to American stations of the period, the simple rectangular plan is broken by a projecting bay window on the trackside that allowed the station agent to survey arriving and departing trains. Simplicity also marks the hipped roof and shingled walls that gently curve at their base. Ornament is limited to the curving shapes of the substantial, functional brackets and lighter rafters supporting the roof, extended to shelter passengers as they boarded and alighted. The interior was divided between passenger waiting room, agent's office, and baggage room.

Phoenicia merited a larger station than places such as Cold Brook (see XII–9), for here was the junction between the U & D's main line (from Kingston to Oneonta) and the Stony Clove &

Kaaterskill Branch, which took vacationers up into Greene County to the famous Catskill Mountain House and Hotel Kaaterskill. In 1932 the U & D was acquired by the New York Central. The last passenger train on the Kingston-Oneonta route ran on March 31, 1954, while freight service ended in October 1976. Key to the preservation of the Phoenicia station was its purchase by railroad historian John Ham from the New York Central in 1966.

XVII–3 Methodist Episcopal Church
25 Church St., Phoenicia. 1883. J. A. Wood.

J. A. Wood took Richard Upjohn's staid Gothic Revival church designs and made the wooden forms more complex and exuberant. Note the many spindles—some vertical, some radiating in a quarter circle—fitted into the truss in the front gable of the church, and also found above the first stage of the tower. Wood may also have designed the parsonage next door with its five-sided porch adorned with a frieze of spindles.

XVII-3. Phoenicia Methodist Episcopal Church (early-twentieth-century postcard)

XVII–4* Tremper House
Phoenicia. 1878–1879 (mostly destroyed by fire 1908). J. A. Wood.

Celebrity preacher Henry Ward Beecher opened this summer hotel on June 19, 1879, when he addressed "the assembled company from the grand stairway" on the restorative benefits the mountain region provided "professional men who work

XVII-2. Phoenicia Station

XVII-4. Tremper House (c. 1900 photo)

1895 it was being sold by, surprisingly, architect J. A. Wood. The hotel became the Nordrach Milk Rest and Cure by 1904, and in 1908 it burned. A fountain and other elements of the landscaping survive, as do some of the outbuildings. Especially striking is a U-shaped building with a pair of two-story-high piazzas having a large, round-arched truss fitted into each gable and smaller trusses to the side. These piazzas resemble the splendid one that graced the center of the hotel façade. Twentieth-century apartments emerge on several levels from the historic hotel's basement. While known as Skyrise Apartments, some scarcely emerge above grade.

nearly to the verge of insanity." This theme was maintained ten years later when *The New York Times* recommended the hotel to city residents seeking "amid the grandeur and solitude of the mountain scenery relief from the noise, turmoil, and heat of the town." Guests arrived on the trains of the Ulster & Delaware Railroad, whose station was a short distance from the hotel.

The Tremper House was easy to reach, but it stood on a plateau only a little above the village and lacked the extensive vistas of such rivals as the Hotel Kaaterskill. Still, the pair of mansarded cupolas (added about 1880) and the two-story, arched and latticed piazza at the center of the façade served to advertise the pleasures awaiting guests at the Tremper House. The writer of "Tremper House Gossip" for the Kingston newspaper might have used a photo of well-dressed young women seated on the piazza (FHK collection) as evidence that "outside of Saratoga, Long Branch and a few of the other larger places, there cannot be found a place where more life can be found, or finer dressing." He was of the opinion, however, that, "As to the beauty of the ladies we cannot boast."

J. A. Wood a few years later expanded upon this design in his Grand Hotel above Pine Hill, which was also reached by the Ulster & Delaware (see XVII–14). In the 1890s the Tremper House had financial troubles. Originally built for Thomas and Jacob Tremper, Kingston businessmen, in

XVII–5 St. Francis de Sales Church (Roman Catholic)
Main St., Phoenicia. 1902–1904.

Built of local bluestone with vibrant red brick trim, St. Francis de Sales Church stands as a monument of the bluestone industry. Under the direction of the Rev. M. Julien Ginet, men of the parish quarried and prepared the stone for the walls of this Gothic Revival church. De Lisser wrote at the time that bluestone was "the main stay of Phoenicia in a business way. ... In all directions, high up on the mountain sides, you can see quarries and their dumps, scars on the face of nature." After the hemlock forests had been brought down by the tanning industry, "the denuded mountains now have only their rock to offer for the support ... of the hardy mountaineer ... The work is hard and the pay poor, but this industry is liable to last as long as the county does." In fact the bluestone industry also declined, but this bluestone church remains.

XVII-5. St. Francis de Sales Church (early-twentieth-century postcard)

It stands out from other Gothic Revival churches in the county thanks to the markedly vertical proportions of its façade. Not only is there a three-story stone tower rising from the central entrance, but the tower supports an octagonal spire with cross atop and (originally) four pinnacles at the spire's base. The nave behind the tower is tall and narrow, just a little wider than the tower. And while the side aisles are lower than the nave—allowing a row of clerestory windows— the side bays of the façade fronting the aisles are stretched vertically so that their triangular gables and crosses rise well above the aisle roofs behind them. Architectural moralists might object to this bit of pretense (the façade grander than the reality of the spaces behind the façade), still the practice was fairly common—James Renwick had earlier raised the side bays of the façade of the Saugerties Reformed Church higher than the aisle roofs required (see XVI–4).

Weekday visitors to the church routinely find the front doors unlocked, a rarity in today's security-conscious world. As indicated externally,

the nave is narrow but high, its Gothic vaults obviously of wooden boards in contrast to the plaster vaults of many contemporary churches where an effort was made to disguise plaster as stone. An elaborately ornamented altar and rich stained glass complete the Gothic effect. In addition, murals below the clerestory windows of the nave depict the life of Christ.

Construction of the church began in 1902, the year the La Salette Fathers arrived in Phoenicia. The La Salette Missionaries originated in France in 1852, and in 1892 some ventured to Montreal and then Hartford, Connecticut. French and French Canadian church design of the nineteenth century seem to have inspired the designer of the Phoenicia church—who remains unknown, although Ginet was credited in 1907 with building the "splendid stone church."

XVII–6 Elmer's Diner (closed)
Old Rte. 28, Phoenicia. 1940s. Silk City Diner, Paterson Vehicle Co.

Long out of service, this diner, once named for its owner, Elmer Loveless, has the distinctive hallmarks of diners manufactured by the Silk City firm in the 1940s. These diners resemble contemporary railway passenger cars with a monitor roof and painted metal panels with horizontal bands for a modern, streamlined effect. An earlier type of diner with arched roof is attached to the rear. To experience the interior of a similar Silk City diner, drive to the 209 Diner in Ellenville (see XX–10).

XVII-6. Elmer's Diner

XVII–7 Shandaken Eagle (from Grand Central Terminal, New York)

Intersection of Rtes. 28 and 214, Phoenicia. c. 1898 (dedicated in Phoenicia, August 23, 1986).

From about 1898 to 1913, a number of cast-iron eagles looked down upon 42nd Street from their perches by the towers dotting the top of the Grand Central Terminal that preceded the present landmark. Once coated with white cement, this iron eagle with thirteen-foot wingspread has been given a bronze finish and brought down to earth. The Ulster & Delaware (later New York Central) trains that ran nearby did not reach Grand Central, but remained on the west shore of the Hudson. Still, the Grand Central eagle has become acclimated to furnishing (along with the American flag) a patriotic entry point for Phoenicia. At the time of the American Bicentennial in 1976, the Town of Shandaken adopted the eagle as its logo. Knowledge of this encouraged

David McLane, owner of the eagle and retired *Daily News* photographer, to donate it to the community.

XVII–8 Caretaker's Cabin, Woodland Valley State Campsite (Woodland Valley Campground, New York State Department of Environmental Conservation)

1319 Woodland Valley Rd. Late 1930s.

The caretaker's cabin was built by the Civilian Conservation Corps (CCC), created in 1933 by Franklin Roosevelt's New Deal to provide employment and training for young men who were jobless during the Depression. Many of their projects across the country involved improving forests, streams, and campgrounds that would benefit the general public. Furthermore, it was popularly believed that young men would themselves be improved by working in the great outdoors, free of the troubles and temptations of cities. Diane Galusha, who has thoroughly researched the activities of the CCC in the Catskills, has found evidence that men from the CCC camps in Boiceville and Margaretville (Delaware County) labored to develop the already existing state campground at Woodland Valley. The cabin's rustic wood and stone design is characteristic of buildings put up by the CCC in public campgrounds across the country. However, buildings erected for housing the CCC itself—for example, Camp P-53 in Boiceville (see XII–12)—were more starkly utilitarian.

XVII-7. Shandaken Eagle

XVII-8. Caretaker's Cabin

XVII–9* William L. Beach House (Thomas Bigelow Craig House)
Woodland Valley Rd. 1852.

Landscape painter Thomas Craig (1849–1925) occupied this Gothic Revival, board-and-batten house with intersecting gable roofs and drip moldings over the windows. The house had been built in 1852 by William L. Beach, whose daughter Daisy W. Beach married Craig in 1896. John Burroughs, while staying at the nearby Roxmor in 1907, spent an evening at Craig's where he met "interesting people." The exterior of Craig's house was apparently unpainted, and so took on a rustic quality harmonious with Roxmor and Burroughs's own taste.

XVII-9. Beach-Craig House (c. 1984 photo)

XVII–10* Roxmor Inn
Woodland Valley. 1914–1915.

Roxmor was the creation of Edward B. Miller, a New York City resident who in 1894 came to the Woodland Valley to improve his health and stayed in the Beach house (see preceding entry, XVII–9)

as a paying guest. Miller bought fifty acres of Beach property in 1897 and established the Roxmor colony with a rustic boardinghouse.

John Burroughs stayed at Roxmor in 1907, but already knew the area from earlier camping trips and, in fact, had considered building a log or stone house in Woodland Valley (also known as Snyder Hollow) before putting up Slabsides. Now, in 1907, Burroughs found the place "charming," especially sitting "under the pine trees on the creek-bank" discussing Walt Whitman with two congenial women. No doubt the rustic design of the colony also appealed to Burroughs.

The original Roxmor boardinghouse was destroyed by fire in 1908 and was replaced in 1914–1915. Miller advertised his Roxmor Inn in the *Automobile Blue Book* (1924), hoping to attract motorists to its rustic quarters, "secluded ... [and] charmingly located on the mountainside, commanding fine views." For taking in those views, porches and balconies dominated the exterior of the rustic stone and shingle inn. The rustic note continued inside with the rubble-stone fireplace and bark-covered table legs and stretchers. However, a vintage postcard reveals electric wires and insulators hanging from the ceiling joists, and guests fearful of another fire would be glad to see a fire extinguisher at the foot of the stairs. Miller also placed ads in the *Times* offering furnished accommodations in bungalows, cabins, and camps for those able to present suitable references for admission to this "rigidly restricted" resort. Today Roxmor is a private community.

XVII-10. Roxmor Inn (early-twentieth-century postcard)

Head Master's House, The Mountain School, Allaben, N. Y.

XVII–11* Head Master's House, The Mountain School (former)
Allaben. 1908.

The Mountain School advertised itself in 1913 as "the first open air school for normal boys. No tubercular or invalid cases accepted." Its 300-acre grounds at a 2,000-foot elevation in the Catskills provided the boys with "24 hours a day in the fresh air." The school opened in 1908 and was run by Elias G. Brown, M.D. A 1906 ad for Postum—a powdered roasted-grain beverage—quoted Brown on the harm that coffee and tea drinking inflicted upon children and described him as "the medical examiner of defective school children in the public schools of New York City." Brown was also distressed by the movement of recent immigrants out of the Lower East Side into adjacent districts and the resulting decline of those areas. He urged that "if we are to keep New York clean, wholesome, and beautiful we must start a well-planned and thoughtfully plotted propaganda of clean and fair living."

For parents who doubted that the city could truly be a "clean, wholesome, and beautiful" environment for schooling their sons, Dr. Brown's Mountain School furnished an alternative. The design of the Head Master's House looked not at all urban, suburban, or collegiate, and so helped distinguish the school from other prep schools. Set in the Catskill Mountains, the house was appropri-

ately of rugged log construction from walls to porch posts, with a rustic chimney of cobblestone. Its gambrel roof and long dormer in the gambrel's lower slope, while associated with the period's Dutch Colonial revival, were also common in rustic, Arts and Crafts designs. The log house provided just the right note of sturdiness for the school where "boys with average health are developed into robust health and strength."

XVII–12* Winnisook Club
Oliverea. Founded 1886.

This private membership club was sited in the wilds nine or ten miles from the U & D Railroad and near a trail to the top of Slide Mountain, the highest peak in the Catskills. By 1893 it had several rustic cabins and a clubhouse above a lake created by damming the fledgling Esopus Creek. Chief among its founders was Thomas E. Benedict (1839–1926), a resident of Napanoch who was an authority on Ulster County history and active in the Democratic party in the county and state before being appointed public printer by President Grover Cleveland in 1886. A number of the other founders were prominent Kingstonians associated with the Democratic party and keen about trout fishing, although Winnisook's success over the years may be attributed to its broader emphasis on fun for families. (Republican Samuel D. Coykendall had his own trout-fishing lodge at Alder Lake in Hardenbergh; see IV–1). The club's first president was Judge Alton Brooks Parker of Kingston and Esopus, who was the Democratic candidate for president in 1904 and was handily defeated by Theodore Roosevelt. Another unsuccessful

XVII-12. Parker Cabin, Winnisook (design by Thompson & Frohling)

Democratic candidate, William Jennings Bryan, had visited the club during his 1896 campaign.

While shingle, log, or bark-covered slabs compose the walls of most of the buildings, the ambitiously picturesque "mountain cabin" built in 1910 for George F. Parker (1847–1927) and designed by New York architects Thompson and Frohling has sturdy stone walls and a low cylindrical tower. Parker, a journalist, was closely allied with Grover Cleveland.

In 1893 John Burroughs hiked to the summit of Slide, had "a good time all alone with that sublime view," and "made a nest under the ledge of rocks on the summit." Burroughs, who enjoyed the role of guest at stylish rustic retreats like Byrdcliffe and Yama Farms, accepted several invitations to Winnisook. In 1923 the Winnisook Club placed a tablet in his memory atop Slide.

XVII–13 Morton Memorial Library (Pine Hill Library)
Elm St., Pine Hill. 1902–1903. Wilson, Harris & Richards. NR

This small but monumental and dignified library, given in memory of Henry and Clara Morton, is a reminder of the elite summertime population of Pine Hill around 1900 that included prominent members of the clergy and the academic world. Henry Morton, born and educated in Philadelphia, was president of Stevens Institute of Technology in Hoboken, New Jersey, from its found-

ing in 1870 until his death in 1902. He and his wife Clara established their summer home in Pine Hill at Upenuff, which, according to *The New York Times*, was "a cottage surrounded by secluded nooks and sylvan retreats." There in 1894 they gave a "cotillion," described as "one of the greatest events the little village has seen ... The grounds and house were illuminated, and the floral decorations were elaborate."

Morton was a generous benefactor of Pine Hill, paying for the construction of "good stone roads, bridges, sidewalks ... and planting hundreds of trees along the mountain roads." He also established a village library in a former saloon. Then in 1901 Clara Morton died at Pine Hill, and her husband announced in February 1902 that he would "erect a stone library building, at a cost of $10,000, at Pine Hill ... as a memorial to his wife." However, Henry Morton died later in 1902. A special train carried his body, with mourning Stevens trustees and faculty, to Pine Hill for burial in the mountainside cemetery he had created and where the Morton monuments still stand not far from the library. Happily, Morton's sons, Henry Samuel Morton and Quincy Ludlow Morton, honored their father's wish and donated funds sufficient to build the library of stone—native bluestone trimmed in Indiana limestone—with a red slate roof.

Andrew Carnegie, the industrialist and philanthropist, was an admirer of Morton and of Stevens Institute, and in 1899 Carnegie gave Stevens the Carnegie Laboratory of Engineering Building. Carnegie's fame as creator of public libraries doubtless inspired Morton to provide for Pine Hill's library. Like most Carnegie-funded libraries, including Kingston's (1904) and Saugerties's (1914), Morton Memorial's formal, classical façade projects the library's seriousness of purpose. The category of classical chosen in this instance is the American Georgian style of the eighteenth century; the main façade seems to be a compressed, one-and-a-half story version of a great Georgian house, such as Mount Pleasant (1761) in Henry Morton's hometown of Philadelphia.

The architects of the library, Wilson, Harris & Richards, were successors to Wilson Brothers & Co., the noted Philadelphia firm of engineers and architects who had designed a portion of the Mountain House at Lake Mohonk as well as several West Shore Railroad stations. The senior partner, Henry W. Wilson, was married to a sister of Henry Morton. Like Mount Pleasant, the library has a hipped roof (originally topped with a wooden balustrade), dormer windows, quoins at the corners of the walls, and window lintels with ornamental keystones. Paired Ionic columns accent the library's entrance. The formality of the Georgian exterior continues into the fine, high-ceilinged interior—especially in the classical treatment of the unpainted carved oak mantel of the fireplace that separates the main room from a semicircular alcove. The library's sturdy Windsor chairs, sold by T. G. Sellew of New York, continue the early-American theme of the architecture.

XVII–14* Grand Hotel
Highmount. 1880–1881; west wing, 1884 (demolished 1964). J. A. Wood.

The Grand Hotel was erected during what Alf Evers called the "hotel building mania" of the late 1870s and early '80s in the Catskills that also produced the Hotel Kaaterskill in Greene County, the largest of the great mountaintop hotels of the time. The Grand Hotel was a serious rival of the Kaaterskill. It was grand in scale, 650 feet long with accommodations for 500 guests, grand in its elevated site, some 2,500 feet above tide level, and grand in its view of Slide Mountain and other Catskill peaks from the piazza that extended over 350 feet and was intended as "the

XVII-13. Morton Memorial Library (early-twentieth-century postcard)

living room for the guests." The building was also grand in its architectural adornment, having four richly mansarded cupolas and an intricately arched and latticed two-story-high piazza, as well as grand in its interior, where the central rotunda sheltered a marble fountain flowing with Diamond Spring water whose purity was said to aid digestion.

In designing the Grand Hotel, J. A. Wood went beyond the modest splendor of his Tremper House in Phoenicia (see XVII–4) and, with the backing of Thomas Cornell, proprietor of the Ulster and Delaware Railroad, created a showplace to appeal to wealthy eastern city dwellers. The railroad provided easy access to the hotel via its Grand Hotel Station on the summit above Pine Hill. Rand, McNally's *Handy Guide to the Hudson River and Catskill Mountains* (1897) trumpeted the Grand: "Every means of elegant amusement and fashionable mountaineering is provided for, and wealth and beauty find there the most congenial company and surroundings. The expenditures for fittings and appointments seem to have been practically without limit." Some compared the design of the Grand to the long, mansarded Oriental Hotel on Coney Island, although the Grand lacked the minaret-like spires of the Oriental. Grand Hotel guests seeking something more natural and primitive could hike behind the hotel to a rustic lookout on Monka Mountain (or Knoll) comparable to the rustic shelters still found today at Mohonk.

XVII-14. Grand Hotel (c. 1905 postcard)

XVII-15. Cornish House (early-twentieth-century postcard)

XVII–15* Cornish House
Pine Hill. 1880 (not extant).
James C. Cornish, builder and proprietor.

The writer of this postcard picturing the Cornish House asked in 1906, "Does it look natural?" Surely the answer must be "yes," given the forest-like complexity of the wooden hotel with its abundance of porches with spindled railings and friezes, gable roofs with shed-roofed dormers, and X-bracing in the gable ends. In 1895 *The New York Times* called the proprietor, James Chilson Cornish, "a lover of nature and quiet ease ... [who] has made a beauty spot that is a miniature rival to the scenic grandeur of the surrounding hills." The house was said to be "a favorite retreat for many prominent New-York financial and railroad men."

Cornish, born in New York City in 1829, was trained as a carpenter by his father. For some thirty years James Cornish was a contractor and builder, primarily in New York and in Delaware County, before building his Pine Hill hotel in 1880.

XVII–16* Rip Van Winkle House
Pine Hill. c. 1884–1887 (not extant).

This hotel, operated by the Van Loan brothers, was an excellent example of the Shingle Style, which was first developed in New England in the late 1870s and early 1880s. The style's elements— the broad, shingled surfaces of walls and roofs, the artfully composed asymmetry of gables, dormers, and shuttered windows, and the extensive porches

XVII-16. Rip Van Winkle House (early-twentieth-century postcard

(the view was of Belleayre Mountain)—were all often adopted by architects for summer houses and inns from coastal Maine to the Adirondacks and here in the Catskills. A photo of the Rip Van Winkle House published in the Ulster & Delaware Railroad's *Catskill Mountain Resorts* (1909) shows additional structures to the left and right and indicates that there were accommodations for 175 guests.

XVII–17* Julia Marlowe House, Wildacres
Highmount. c. 1900.

The renowned actress Julia Marlowe (1866–1950) spurned the rustic in favor of a robustly Georgian classical design for her summertime mountain retreat on nearly 400 acres straddling the border between Ulster and Delaware counties. Interestingly, this formal eighteenth-century Colonial style is also found just down the mountain at the Morton Memorial Library (1902–1903) in Pine Hill.

Construction began in 1900 with the $7,766 contract awarded to Frederick Sheeley, but after

more than a year "he became financially embarrassed and abandoned the job." Crosby Kelley was awarded the contract to complete the work, but mechanics' liens and various suits were begun against Marlowe by creditors in Supreme Court in Kingston. In the end Marlowe and her attorney agreed to a modest settlement of $100.

By 1902 the house was sufficiently complete for it to be featured in *Eminent Actors in Their Homes* by Margherita Arlina Hamm. There it was described as "new ... a handsome Colonial structure with shady and generous verandas, large windows, and a door ... marked with the invisible characters of hospitality." Inside, "the feature ... is a great living-room, or hall, which is fairly baronial in its dimensions. At each end is a giant fireplace which will accommodate a score of people in front of the andirons and crane." Extensive murals in this room depicted scenes from Miss Marlowe's favorite plays, including *Twelfth Night, As You Like It*, and *When Knighthood Was in Flower*. There was also a bibliophile's library of over 5,000 volumes (she herself enjoyed practicing bookbinding and illumination). While Marlowe's furniture included some Colonial pieces in harmony with the house's architecture, the furnishings were said to be "largely French and partly Italian." Marlowe had achieved much since her impoverished girlhood in England and the American Midwest. Her summer home expressed her high status and fine taste. It was noted that musically she preferred Beethoven, Bach, Wagner, and Brahms. On the other hand, she had "a deep aversion to ragtime, coon songs, and other forms of cheap and common music."

In 2007 the plan of Belleayre Resort at Catskill Park was to adapt Wildacres as a restaurant.

Julia Marlow Cottage. – Highmount. – Catskill Mountains N. Y.

XVII-17. Wildacres (early-twentieth-century postcard)

XVIII
Town of
Shawangunk

Formed as a precinct, 1743, and as a town, 1788.

Population: 2,823 in 1870; 12,022 in 2000.

Historian Marc B. Fried has found that the name Shawangunk "first appears in the Dutch court minutes of early Kingston, under the date of January 24, 1682," when five Esopus Indians sold "'all their land named Sawankonck.'" Europeans settled along the Shawangunk Kill in the 1680s and '90s, and rural Shawangunk retains notable examples of colonial-era stone houses and an early stone church, the Reformed Dutch Church of Shawangunk. Nineteenth-century industrial development was limited, despite the arrival of the Wallkill Valley Railroad. John Gail Borden's condensed milk factory just across the border in Orange County was responsible for the growth of the village of Wallkill in the late nineteenth century.

XVIII–1 Reformed Protestant Dutch Church of Shawangunk (Reformed Church of Shawangunk)

1166 Hoagerburgh Rd. (County Rte. 18). 1751–1753, 1794–1797, 1833–1834, and later alterations (parsonage, 1751 and later). NR

The antiquity of the stone walls, the novelty of the portico, the beauty of the setting including graveyard and parsonage—all make the Shawangunk Reformed Church a site not to be overlooked. Six acres were acquired for the church, parsonage, and graveyard in January 1751, and by October the parsonage was completed (it was later expanded). Stone was being hauled in January 1752 for laying up the church walls, and in December 1755 the building was completed and pews were auctioned to members to raise funds. The names of those who carried out the construction and their specific skills are recorded; there were four masons, three carpenters and painters, a roofer, a glazier (Nicholas Vanderlyn), a woodworker, and three iron workers.

The 1755 church had a rectangular plan, the north and south walls being fifty feet long, while the east and west were forty feet long. Two arched windows were placed in each of the four walls. The doorway, also arched, was centered in the longer south wall and faced the Albany Post Road (later relocated). Like many colonial churches the Shawangunk church was planned as a meetinghouse, with a short passage from doorway to pulpit, the focal point of the interior, centered on the north wall. Congregational seating took the form of some 59 "benches" accommodating 367 people. On the exterior, between the doorway and a window over the doorway, were five stones with the initials of five members of the building committee. This doorway and window above it have been filled with stone similar to the 1755 wall, but the outlines of the doorway and window are clearly visible. (In 1987–1988 the form of the arched doorway was revealed inside the church.) Two of the five initialed stones—Isaac Hasbrouck's and Gerritt Decker's— remain in place, while a third—Jacobus Bruyn's—was removed and served

as a tombstone in the churchyard. The whereabouts of the other two are unknown. The roof, perhaps originally a gambrel, was crowned with a cupola and finial or cross in wrought iron by Abraham Van Keuren.

Extensive alterations were carried out between 1794 and 1797, including walling up the original doorway and window above. The two west windows were transformed into two doorways. Twin staircases were built on what was now the west front leading to two upper level doorways leading inside to the new U-shaped gallery. Many have referred to this as "the slaves' gallery." While it may not have been exclusively for slaves, slaves and other blacks were no doubt among its worshippers. The narrow, high-backed pews in today's gallery are believed to date from this period and in the 1970s were the model for pews in the recreated Huguenot House of Prayer in New Paltz. As the entrances were now at the west, the pulpit was shifted from the north wall to the east wall, and the congregational seating rearranged to face the pulpit.

During the heyday of the Greek Revival, the 1830s, the church acquired its distinctive classical portico and bell tower. In 1833–1834 five Ionic columns (the capitals having the distinctive scrolls of the Ionic) with triangular pediment were erected to create a porch in front of the west doors. The bell tower, with a pair of columns supporting a full entablature on each of the four sides and Roman (not Greek) classical arches over the louvered openings, has an onion-shaped dome (again not Greek) and a complex wrought-iron finial above all.

While the five columns supporting the pediment present the aura of a classical temple front, Greek and Roman temples always had four, six, or eight columns in this position. Ancient temples had a doorway on the central axis, and a central (odd-numbered) column would interfere with processions through this entrance. The Shawangunk church's classically eccentric fifth column has acquired a charming notoriety over the years with architectural connoisseurs. However, in 1898 the Cragsmoor artist Edward Lamson Henry edited the columns when he painted *Sunday Morning (Old Church at Bruynswick)*, an idealized view of handsomely attired early-nine-

XVIII-1. Shawangunk Reformed Protestant Dutch Church (Smith Studio, Walden, photo, 1922)

teenth-century members exiting the church. The painting and prints reproducing it have helped establish the fame of the church; a fine early print hangs above the rear pew. Henry, skilled in the portrayal of historic buildings, chose to represent the church with four, not five, columns, a fanlight in the pediment, an ornamented central west doorway, a single door into the gallery, and a parsonage said to be inspired by the old Morrell-Gilbert House in Johnstown, New York. Another painting by Henry, *Old Dutch Church, Bruynswick*, 1878 (Parrish Art Museum), takes liberties with the lay of the land and substitutes a tall, Georgian steeple for the lower one in place in 1878. According to Alphonso T. Clearwater, he and Henry worked to preserve "the remarkable shielded outside stairway to the slaves' gallery, a stairway which some of the more youthful members of the congregation thought of destroying." Clearwater and Henry also pushed the preservation of the wrought-iron finial, recasting of the bell, and other church improvements.

While the exterior has been little changed since 1834, the interior has been subject to a number of

alterations. Various changes have been made to the pulpit, culminating in the present commodious Colonial Revival pulpit, designed by Harry Halverson in 1961, which mostly conceals earlier Gothic Revival pulpit chairs. The pews on the main level date from the 1870s. The slender cast-iron columns supporting the gallery were inserted about 1879. In the 1920s William E. Bruyn, whose Brykill estate is nearby (see III–12), paid for stained glass in the tall eastern windows (their elongated form apparently dating from the 1790s) whose earlier clear glass had admitted so much morning sunlight that parishioners had difficulty focusing on the preacher. While the windows portray no religious figures, earlier, sometime after 1890, a painting of an angel was installed behind the central pulpit—no doubt to the chagrin of the spirits of the eighteenth-century members who adhered to the Calvinist prohibition on religious painting and sculpture in churches.

Across the road to the north is the parsonage whose initial form—a story-and-a-half stone house—was completed in 1751. The church and parsonage are remarkable as a surviving ensemble from the mid-eighteenth century. Documentation for the date of the parsonage was provided by a stone marked "K+PD o'1751/2" (the inscribed stone, near a second-story window, is now worn and difficult to decipher), which has been interpreted to commemorate the completion of the house in October 1751 by Cornelius and Peter Decker. The first pastor, Dominie Barent Vrooman, preached his initial sermon September 2, 1753, and formally organized the congregation in October. The addition of the full second story and attic of the present house is not documented, but a date in the 1790s has been suggested. In the nineteenth century several wooden porches and additions were constructed, but these were removed and the exterior subjected to Colonial Revival restorations in the 1930s and 1940s, some involving Harry Halverson as architect and William E. Bruyn as donor. Thermopane windows were installed in 1998.

Two of the church's pastors were buried beneath the church—Dominie Johannes Mauritius Goetschius in 1771 and Dominie Henry Polhemus in 1815. However, the ground to the south and east of the church has served as the principal burial site; the oldest stone has been identified as one inscribed "Ano 1752, ME DEI ISOL EP." William E. Bruyn saw to the righting of old stones and maintenance of the graveyard, and his family tomb, a massive stone mausoleum with a Greek Doric temple front (two columns between two antae, or distyle in antis) perpetuates his role as the twentieth-century version of the lord of the manor. Peering into the mausoleum, one can make out the stone in front of his casket engraved "WILLIAM EDMUND BRUYN 1878–1940" and to the side a window with his coat of arms.

XVIII–2 Schoolhouse, District No. 8 (former)

2146 Bruynswick Rd. (County Rte. 7), Bruynswick. c. 1840. NR

This Greek Revival schoolhouse—note the corner pilasters and front gable treated as a pediment with cornice and entablature broken at the base—has been sensitively transformed into a residence.

XVIII-2. Schoolhouse, District No. 8

XVIII–3* Johannes Decker House

Near Bruynswick. c. 1720 to 1787. NR

Although not visible from a public road, the Decker house is one of the finest and best preserved of the county's houses from the colonial period. Beautifully sited where the Shawangunk Kill flows through meadowland, the house attracted the attention of Helen Reynolds in 1925 when researching her book and was the subject of Mary Anne Hunting's well-illustrated historical article in *The Magazine Antiques* in 1998.

The earliest part of the house, one room at the center of the present house, was built by Johannes Cornelius Decker. Decker was born in 1696 and first married in 1720, which is the approximate date of this part that has a stone inscribed with his initials, ICD. Subsequently, rooms were added to the west, north, and east sides—thus forming a T plan. The front of the house (the top, horizontal line of the T) faces south, with the earliest room at the center. A Dutch oven protrudes from the west wall of the western section, indicating its kitchen function. The only firmly dated section of the house, the addition to the east, has a stone marked 1787 and initials CD, for Cornelius Decker (1732–1812), son of Johannes. This eastern section has the most developed craftsmanship, and so is believed to be the latest in date except for the pleasant front porch, which was added in the nineteenth century, as were the dormers. The north section is more crudely constructed, and Helen Reynolds was told by a Decker descendant that slaves had occupied it. According to the 1790 census, Cornelius Decker, son of Johannes, owned ten slaves. As was her custom, Reynolds romanticized the relations of the Deckers and their slaves, citing "one old mammy, housekeeper for a bride of 1827, who refused to accept freedom under the state act of 1827."

The house remained in the Decker family until sold in 1911. In 1925 Edward B. Edwards (1873–1948), a prominent designer and illustrator of books and magazines in New York, corresponded with Helen Reynolds as the new owner of the property. Edwards, a native of Lancaster County, Pennsylvania, explained in a letter to Reynolds that "my interest in early Americana dates from my seventeenth year ... when I was an architectural draftsman." (In fact, he worked four years in the office of the great New York architects McKim, Mead & White.) He assured Reynolds that "it is not my intention to alter the character of the house, but to restore it, as nearly as possible to its original appearance and to furnish the house with original furniture of the period, from an already extensive collection, to which I am constantly adding." In her book, Reynolds noted that the house remained close to its pre-1800 form, and she congratulated Edwards for his "intention of repairing and restoring the house in harmony with its eighteenth century character." Remarkably, he did not add electricity or plumbing, but he probably did install eighteenth-century paneling in the

north room that was more sophisticated than paneling elsewhere in the house. The current owner purchased the property in 1970 and, while adding modern utilities, has preserved and restored the house and its very early Dutch barn (inscribed with the date "1750") with meticulous care.

XVIII–4 Decker House
(1776 Colonial Inn)
2629 New Prospect Rd. (County Rte. 7), Dwaarkill. Before 1776, 1776 (c. 1940 addition destroyed by fire, 2008). NR

This fine old stone house, near the stream that gave the hamlet of Dwaarkill its name, was subjected to jarring additions some years after it was inspected in May 1925 by Helen Reynolds and her photographer Margaret Brown. A broad porch and small wing partially obscure the south façade pictured by Reynolds. A large addition to the northwest housed a bar, reputedly from the New York World's Fair, within a high-ceilinged, animal-trophy-lined room that was itself a period piece of the 1940s until destroyed by fire in 2008.

Reynolds identified the short western section of the south façade, marked by irregularly placed windows and crude stonework, as the original house of the "pioneer" period. A visible seam distinguishes the earlier section from the longer, five-bay, eastern section, which has more regular stonework and more orderly (though still not symmetrical) placement of windows and doorway. This eastern section is dated 1776 in a stone lintel above the door. The stone also bears the initials of William and Garret (or Gerritt) Decker. (Gerritt Decker's initials appear on the stone wall of the nearby Reformed

XVIII-3. Johannes Decker House (1995 photo)

XVIII-4. Decker House and 1776 Colonial Inn (photo soon after 2008 fire)

XVIII-5. Johannes Jansen House (1983 photo)

Church as a member of its building committee in 1755; see XVIII–1.) When Reynolds visited the house, it retained its eighteenth-century form. She found "as a whole the house has individual character; and its setting, near a stream and bridge, suits it well." She was also pleased—and recorded in her text—that the owner, T. A. Terwilliger, was a descendant, through his mother, of the Deckers. On the other hand, she did not publish a note she wrote to herself: "Mrs. Terwilliger suggests type of pioneer Dutch woman, tall, large bones, large features, fleshy, suggestion of masculinity."

Apparently the bar and restaurant were added by Fred Leonhardt. Its furnishings included a long bar from the F. & M. Schaefer Brewing Co. Pavilion and a smaller one from an English pub, both at the 1939 World's Fair in New York.

XVIII–5 Johannes Jansen House and Barn
505 Decker Rd., Rutsonville. c. 1750 and c. 1803. NR

Here is a handsome grouping of early stone house, barn, and barrack. The two-story portion of the house, with its five-bay Georgian façade, dates from the early nineteenth century, but the small, one-story west wing is believed to be earlier, from about 1750. Preserved in the house is a two-part, eighteenth-century Dutch door with a gouge said to have been made by a tomahawk thrown during a Tory and Indian attack in 1780 upon this, the home of Johannes Jansen (born 1725), a colonel in the county militia during the Revolution.

His nephew, John Jansen (born 1771), inherited the property in 1803, and the Georgian section may have been built soon thereafter. Structural evidence suggests that the barn was put up about 1750, making it one of the earliest in the county, but the walls, interior frame, and roof were raised higher in the nineteenth century. Between the barn and the house is a well-preserved barrack (c. 1800), used for grain and wagon storage.

XVIII–6 J. B. Crowell & Son Brick Moulds
Lippincott Rd., Wallkill. 1915. NR

This is a remarkable survivor from the county's nineteenth-century industrial past. Waterpowered mills have been at this site on the Dwaarkill since the eighteenth century and, as the sign on the main building boldly announces, this Crowell enterprise was established in 1872. (Earlier, in 1870, James B. Crowell founded the Wallkill Val-

XVIII-6. J. B. Crowell & Son Brick Moulds

ley Sleigh Works.) In 2003 the firm was managed by the 4th and 5th generations of the Crowell family and claimed to be "the only independent company in the U.S. manufacturing hardwood brick moulds."

On March 31, 1899, *The New York Times* gave notice: "At Wallkill, Ulster County, James B. Crowell's brick mold factory was burned this morning. Loss $5,000. No insurance." Fires destroyed several mills here. The current building, from 1915, is little changed except for the substitution of purchased electricity for waterpower in 1948.

XVIII-7 Andries DuBois House (Historical Society of Shawangunk and Gardiner)
75 Wallkill Ave., Wallkill. c. 1769, 1815, 1845. NR

A 2005 study by John G. Waite Associates, Architects, including the use of dendrochronology, reveals the complex history of this important house, known for its handsome gambrel roof and unusual use of brick for its front and one side wall, while the rear and other side walls are of wood. Its stone foundations and some timbers date from about 1769, but the main walls and roof of this structure were probably destroyed before 1798. About 1815 the house became a simple example of the Federal style when the present walls were erected, two of brick and

two of wood, with a low-pitched gambrel roof. About 1845 the house was remodeled inside and out in the Greek Revival mode. Externally this involved new, smaller windows, moving the entrance door and adding sidelights, and enhancing the gambrel with a deep cornice. The front was graced with a Greek Revival porch, and small second-floor windows were added over this porch. In 2007 a late-twentieth-century porch was removed. Waite Associates recommend restoration of the Greek Revival porch, along with other features evident in a photo of the house taken about 1940.

XVIII-8 New York Condensed Milk Co. (Borden Condensed Milk Co.) (former)
Rte. 208, Walden. 1880–1881. "Mr. Dutcher" architect.

Mostly ruinous after a fire in 1997, this was one of the factories where the milk condensing process patented by Gail Borden in 1856 was carried out in later years by his son John Gail Borden (1844–1891). While the 520-foot front of the factory is located just over the county line in Orange County, Borden's activities were primarily centered in Ulster's Town of Shawangunk. The factory walls, designed by a Mr. Dutcher, are marked by vivid polychromy in brick and stone (in this case described as "Ulster County marble or white rock"), which appealed to the John Ruskin–influenced architectural taste of the period. Earlier examples of permanent polychrome in Ulster include Kingston's City Hall and Rosendale's St. Peter's Church. The colorfully banded arches over windows and doors are also found in the remaining segment

XVIII-7. Andries DuBois House (2004 photo)

XVIII-8. New York Condensed Milk Co. (1980 photo)

of the Borden condensery (1879) in Brewster, Putnam County.

Borden clearly wanted his factory to present a beautiful appearance through its polychrome walls and other ornamental flourishes like the finials atop pyramids that once adorned the roofline. Landscaping included a cast-iron fountain and urns for flowers, known from early photos. (The fountain may have been the one by the J. L. Mott Iron Works of New York whose ornamentation Borden praised in 1886 correspondence.)

The extra expense of beautification could be justified as demonstrating the high standards of the condensery—whose product was harmful if improperly prepared—and uplifting the morals of the workers, as was also the case in the care taken in designing housing for Borden's workers. Did the red crosses in brick on a section at the south end of the complex refer to the safety of the product, as well as Borden's Masonic enthusiasms as a Sir Knight of the order of the Red Cross? (The "American Society of the Red Cross" was established in 1881 with Clara Barton as president; it was concerned with helping those suffering from war, pestilence, fire and flood.)

Borden sought excellence in the design of all his projects in the community, and used the press to boost his enterprise to the local citizenry. New

Paltz men were among those hired to construct the plant, and New Paltz farmers were urged to submit proposals for supplying milk. The *New Paltz Independent* credited Borden with "erect[ing] beautiful buildings, at an enormous expense" at a "pleasant" site on the Wallkill River. Borden himself gave the editor a tour of the factory where about thirty men and boys made tin cans on the second floor, while boiling and canning was done on the first. A siding connected the factory to the Wallkill Valley Railroad and the larger world. Two women pasted labels on the cans with directions for use printed in English, German, and Spanish. Cuba and South America were good customers, and some cans were even shipped to China. The small, originally one-story building near the highway was the office.

XVIII-9 Borden Housing
Buena Vista Ave., Wallkill. c. 1882.

The village of Shawangunk within the Town of Shawangunk became something of a company town with the opening of the Borden condensery in 1881. John Gail Borden rejected a proposal to rename the village "Borden," and "Wallkill" was chosen instead. A visitor from New Paltz described how many of the condensery workers at 5:30 PM "take their way along the shady road that follows the margin of the Wallkill [River] from the factory to their homes" in the village. The paternalistic Borden was concerned about the appearance of homes in the village and, when offering the Ladies Temperance Union free use of rooms in a house he owned, felt obliged to remind the ladies "that cleanliness & beauty of one house adds to the moral as well as educational condition of our people." *The New York Times* declared that Wallkill—and Green Cove Springs, Florida, where Borden retired in ill health in the 1880s—"are being made the brighter and better for his presence and public spirit."

Picturesque cottages at 3, 15, and 19 Buena Vista Avenue have been identified as housing for Borden workers, although Borden's or his company's role in their design and construction remains unclear. Their designs vary, but decorative porch brackets and trusses in roof gables, as well as varied wall treatments in shingles, and vertical, horizontal, and diagonal boarding all combine for picturesque effect. Similar details are found in the

XVIII-9. Borden Housing: 19 Buena Vista

manager's house (1885) and large barn (1884) on Borden's Home Farm.

XVIII-10 Nelson Smith House
71 Bona Ventura Ave., Wallkill. c. 1896.

This was the residence of Nelson Smith, a superintendent of the Borden condensery who in 1891 had applied for a patent for a bottle-filling machine. It is a good specimen of the Queen Anne or Shingle Style, widely adopted by the 1890s, with its multiple gables and broad, flat surfaces of clapboard and shingle, offset by shingles that swell out over the diamond-paned attic windows.

XVIII-10. Nelson Smith House (1973 photo)

XVIII-11 Wallkill Valley Reformed Church (Wallkill Reformed Church)
Bridge and Church Sts., Wallkill. 1869–1871, 1889–1890.

Built before the ascendancy of the Bordens in Wallkill, this church reflects the rejection of Greek Revival architecture in favor of the Gothic by Reformed churches in the 1860s. Despite the pointed arches, rising wall buttresses, corner bell tower (originally some sixty feet higher), and nave taller than the side aisles, the church appears low and earthbound. Perhaps this was due to the influence of Italian Gothic upon the unidentified architect. The *New Paltz Independent* admired the building "in the Gothic style" as it was being constructed, but reported that the Montgomery

XVIII-11. Wallkill Valley Reformed Church (early-twentieth-century postcard)

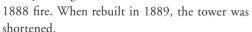

Republican was of the opinion that it "resembles an old Dutch barn of 1609." Perhaps the low walls of the side aisles suggested this comparison. The interior of the church was heavily damaged in an 1888 fire. When rebuilt in 1889, the tower was shortened.

XVIII–12 Wallkill Public Library
7 Bona Ventura Ave., Wallkill.
1935. J. Percy Hanford.

This delightful reminiscence of the old stone houses of the Wallkill Valley slightly precedes Franklin Roosevelt's New Deal post offices in Dutchess County and in Ellenville that were also intended to recall the Dutch colonial houses of the region. The library was built of native, roughly squared stone with private funds provided by the will of Marion Borden (1883–1930), daughter of John G. Borden, who had brought the Borden milk condensing enterprise to Wallkill. During Marion's lifetime, she had given funds for the addition of a community hall (1920) to the Wallkill Reformed Church and for the John G. Borden High School (1921, designed by George E. Lowe of Kingston; her will also provided for an addition to the school carried out in 1935).

Wallkill's proximity to Newburgh and distance from Kingston may explain why Teller & Halverson, experts in the revival of Ulster County's colonial stone houses, were passed over and Newburgh architect J. Percy Hanford selected to design the library. Hanford's design resembles the Elting Memorial Library in New Paltz—an old stone house turned into a library with Teller's professional assistance in 1920 (see XI–12). Both stone

buildings have a white wooden porch with central arch, two dormer windows in the gable roof, wood above stone in the gable ends, and small windows set into the stone of the gable ends. Hanford made minor changes to the New Paltz model for more elegant effect—segmental arches in brick over the first-story windows, an arched fanlight over the main door (originally a Dutch door), and arched dormer windows. Underneath the old-fashioned skin, however, Hanford designed a modern, fireproof frame—steel trusses support the roof, and the main floor is of reinforced concrete with oak boards laid on top.

The library displays a handsome watercolor of the building and its landscaped park setting; Hanford is identified as the architect, although the artist or delineator was "C.D.R." A stylish couple exits the library with a book, and they, the building, and the landscape combine to create an aura

XVIII-12. Wallkill Public Library

of idyllic refinement. However, in the background, behind a tree trunk, a steam locomotive appears vaguely on the New York Central's Wallkill line (now a rail trail). The machine hardly disturbs the idyll. Hanford's own house in Newburgh at 6 Park Place was a charming Tudor cottage overlooking the Hudson and above the railroad.

XVIII–13* Wallkill Diner
Bona Ventura Ave. Flourished 1940s (not extant).

Ollie Burgess, in her charming little book *Hometown Memories*, pictures the exterior of this barrel-roofed diner (a type made from c. 1910 to 1935) and adjacent gas station in their heyday on Bona Ventura Avenue near the railroad crossing. She

XVIII-13. Wallkill Diner (1983 photo)

also pictures herself as the cheery, pretty waitress at the counter with shiny coffee urns behind. The caption, "I loved working in the diner," seems apt. Sadly, by the 1980s the diner had been moved a short distance and stood derelict, though the coffee urns were intact.

XVIII–14 Hasbrouck House and Borden Home Farm (partly the School of Practical Philosophy)
Borden Rd., near Wallkill. Eighteenth century to c. 1906.

In 1881, John Gail Borden built a new milk condensery just over the Orange County border (see XVIII–8) and nearby purchased a fine country place centered around a century-old Hasbrouck house. When illustrated in Sylvester's *History of Ulster County* (1880), the property belonged to John P. Andrews. The old house is shown expanded with a substantial, one-story, mansard-roofed structure, while several farm buildings stand nearby. (Andrews had been a leader in organizing and building the Reformed Church [1868–1871] in the village of Shawangunk, later Wallkill; see XVIII–11.)

Borden occupied the Hasbrouck-Andrews house, adding a mansard-roofed tower, and built a small brick office a few yards away. It is flat-roofed, as was the office building at his condensery (see XVIII–8), but its walls lack the striking polychrome effects of the condensery buildings. The bracketed cornice (originally topped with a low, ornamental parapet) and geometric pattern of small and larger window panes enliven the exterior, while within, Borden (known as a patron of the arts) was surrounded by rustic

XVIII-14. Office, Borden Home Farm

XVIII-14A. Marion Borden House

farm scenes in the form of Minton tiles designed by William Wise and dated 1879. The office has been preserved with little change by the Hoyt family, although the house was altered about 1950 and heavily damaged by fire in December 2009.

Borden's estate, named Home Farm, by 1888 had grown to 1,100 acres and was cited by *The New York Times* as the county's largest farm. (Eventually the Home Farm included about 2,000 acres.) The 354-foot-long, board-and-batten barn (1884), with Gothic trusses in the gables of the dormers and cupola, still stands (as part of the School of Practical Philosophy), but unfortunately a round barn (1886), some 365 feet in diameter, no longer remains. Sheep and dairy cattle grazed in a pastoral, parklike setting under the watchful eyes of shepherds, "as in olden times." A sign was posted: "Visitors and strangers welcome to every part of the Home Farm." From their carriages polite visitors admired "what has been done by the large-hearted proprietor to make this place an attractive one for people to view."

Borden died in 1891. About 1906 his daughter Marion put up a large, picturesque Queen Anne/Tudor Revival house (now a part of the School of Practical Philosophy) with half-timbered gables, located on the site of an old wooden farmhouse demolished in 1894 and not far from her late father's house and office. John Gail Borden, his wife Ellen L. (1845–1928), and daughter Marion (1883–1930) are memorialized on a bronze plaque set into a boulder at the family's informal burial ground, a site chosen by JGB and a short walk from his home.

When the Bordens occupied the Home Farm, its pastoral qualities were celebrated. From the "manor house" there were picturesque views of the Shawangunk range, and surrounding the house was "a gentle undulation of forest and field, dotted here and there with the homes of the natives, cottages of the workmen, barns, outbuildings, and herds of cattle—a scene of perfect rest and quiet." While this language from the early twentieth century may appear too evocative of Old World aristocracy, in the twenty-first century this scene of rest and quiet continues to inspire local residents to preserve the fields and forests from the improving hands of developers.

XVIII–15* Wallkill State Prison (Wallkill Correctional Facility)
Rte. 208, Wallkill. 1931–1933.
Alfred Hopkins and Associates.

Signs along Route 208 announce that the public is prohibited from stopping to look at this site. Built as a medium-security facility without a wall or fence (today there are fences), Wallkill State Prison was planned to overcome the crowded conditions in state prisons that led to riots in 1929. It was designed by New York architect Alfred Hopkins (1870–1941), who had developed a reputation as a designer of prisons as well as of farm buildings on upper-class estates. Hopkins's earlier Westchester County Penitentiary (1916) was designed in the collegiate Gothic style of Oxford, Princeton, and Yale, and the architect was emphatic that his intention was to "express in its design the educational side of the prison."

The prison at Wallkill was meant to resemble multigabled Gothic college dormitories, and the wooden doors to the cells, each occupied by just one inmate, were unlocked. According to a 1934 state inspector, "the inmates are allowed to have pictures in their cells, install electric lamps, which some of them create in the shops, and many of the cells presented a neat and rather artistic appearance." The high-ceilinged assembly room–gymnasium rises on one side of a central courtyard like a chapel above a collegiate Gothic quadrangle. A sculptured relief on one wall of the courtyard represents an idealized but exhausted male figure supported by an heroic female, with Gothic lettering below referring to the Biblical "furnace of adversity." Admittedly, Ivy League dormitories have larger windows without the steel grids that bar the prison windows, and the expensive stonework of the elite universities was replaced here by concrete-block walls with cast-stone trim. From the beginning the goal at Wallkill was to educate inmates to prepare them for a better life as productive citizens after serving their sentences, and Hopkins's collegiate Gothic provided an appropriate setting for learning. It was the architect's belief that "beautiful architecture" exerted a "beneficent influence" upon both prisoners and prison personnel in achieving the "regeneration of the prisoner." Hopkins himself lived in Princeton in the 1930s, enjoying the academic tone of that town; in 1939 he and his wife entertained Albert Einstein at their home.

XVIII-15. Wallkill State Prison

Governor Franklin D. Roosevelt took an active interest in shepherding the construction of the prison through the state bureaucracy, and he attended its opening in 1932. When president in 1934, he and Eleanor Roosevelt went by auto from Hyde Park to inspect the completed institution whose slogan, "rehabilitation through education," would have appealed to both Roosevelts. *The New York Times* described their visit to "the institution, constructed in the Norman style ... [where] three hundred and five honor prisoners devote themselves to agriculture and work in the crafts." The presidential party was welcomed by the institution's drum and bugle corps and escorted through the grounds by mounted state troopers. On display were prize corn and vegetables grown on the prison farm, as well as items made of wood or iron. After a long talk with Warden Leo J. Palmer, "the President was driven through the recreation yard, where the men, who were gathered for dinner, stood in lines, virtually unguarded, within only a few feet of the path of his car, much closer to him than crowds are permitted to stand on city streets. As he left they applauded him heartily."

In 1944, when the war precluded almost all construction unrelated to the war effort, Wallkill inmates were able to create St. Peter's Episcopal Chapel in the low attic of one cell block. They were responsible for hand-carved Gothic details in the 100-foot-long chapel whose stained-glass rose window was radiant above the altar. Destroyed by fire in 1986, this Protestant chapel was soon rebuilt. A Catholic chapel was dedicated in 1948. Understandably (but incorrectly), a Web site intended for people visiting inmates advises: "When you arrive at the prison you have to take a second look because it does not remind you of a prison. It is in fact an old monastery with incredible architecture."

XIX
Town of Ulster

Formed from the Town of Kingston, 1879.

Population: 2,806 in 1880; 12,544 in 2000.

The Town of Ulster, until 1879 part of the Town of Kingston, surrounds two sides of the City of Kingston. The rural character of the town was altered in the nineteenth century by the cement and brick industries that grew up along the Rondout Creek and Hudson River. In the 1950s the area just to the north of Kingston was transformed by construction of an IBM plant, which was vacated by IBM in 1995. Today most visitors to the Town of Ulster are simply going to the Hudson Valley Mall, which opened in 1981, or another store in the pedestrian-unfriendly commercial strip of Ulster Avenue that has drained much of the vitality from the shopping districts of the city.

Lovers of early architecture can still see several noteworthy stone houses in the town. Also, ruins of the cement works and brickyards can be found along State Route 213 and County Route 28 in Eddyville and in East Kingston near the Hudson. The late George V. Hutton, historian of Hudson River brick making, foresaw that natural forces and new construction would soon obliterate nearly all signs of the once extensive brickyards. Nevertheless, he hoped that the "graceful nineteenth-century brick boiler flue" visible in a c. 1885 etching and still standing at the former Charles A. Shultz brickyard in East Kingston would be "treasured as the sole remaining industrial artifact of ... the great Hudson River brick industry."

XIX-1. Osterhoudt House

XIX-1 Osterhoudt House
35 Lohmaier Lane, Lake Katrine.
c. 1691 to 1740.

This stone house is among the oldest to survive
in the county. A stone on the east wall bears the
date 1740 and the initials of William Osterhoudt
and Sarah Hasbrouck (grandchild of Abraham
Hasbrouck, the New Paltz patentee), who married
in 1737. According to Helen Reynolds, this east
portion of the house was the last to be built. The
west section is often dated 1691 because of an inscribed stone, said to have been covered over by
a frame addition. The middle section then would
date between the 1690s and 1740. The windows
of the long south front are smaller to the west, as
might be expected in a very early house. The single
doorway on this south front is fitted with sidelights and leads to a hall with stairs between the
east and middle rooms. Dormers are of the early,
shed-roofed variety.

As early as 1880 the house was valued as an
ancestral home. The biography of Tunis P. Osterhoudt in Sylvester's *History of Ulster County*
relates that Tunis was born in 1814 in this "old
stone house" and that he farmed its land as his
father, grandfather, and great-grandfather had
since 1796. Before that year another branch of the
Osterhoudts had owned the property. Tunis's biography suggests that the house was almost 200
years old in 1880, although only the 1740 datestone is mentioned as marking the second of two
additions. The writer notes with pride that the
house "is still in a good state of preservation, and
the beams in the house are twenty by twelve inches
in size."

XIX-2 Benjamin Ten Broeck House
1019 Flatbush Rd. (Rte. 32). 1751, 1765,
c. 1770. NR

Like many eighteenth-century, story-and-a-half
houses in the county, this was built of rubble
limestone or fieldstone with weatherboarded
gable ends. The three rooms on the primary
floor face south and were built one at a time
with windows and doors asymmetrically placed.

The center room is thought to be the oldest; a stone on the south façade is inscribed "IF 1751 MF," the initials perhaps those of the Felton (or Velton) family, German farmers who are said to have worked for the Ten Broecks. However, Robert Sweeney, the current owner of the house and a historian of Hudson Valley vernacular architecture, reports that the eighteenth-century ownership of the property is unclear. The current jambed fireplace in the center room dates from about 1770, but there is structural evidence of an earlier, jambless fireplace. The west room was probably built next; Reynolds noted a stone on this section inscribed 1765, although Sweeney has not found this datestone. He believes the east room was built last, about 1770, as a kitchen with a pent-roofed porch.

When studied and recorded by Helen Reynolds in the 1920s and by Thomas Tileston Waterman for the Historic American Buildings Survey in 1936, this house exhibited a number of features that set it apart from other eighteenth-century stone houses in the region. Waterman focused on three original casement windows, two of which retained their original glazing and shutters, and an original interior door. Reynolds, however, was charmed by the occupants, Steve Chmura (believed to be the figure in a 1936 HABS photo) and his family, East European immigrants who had "whitewashed the stone walls, and painted the exterior woodwork a deep green," generally making the Hudson Valley house into something very like an Old World peasant home. The historian was distressed when early Dutch houses were occupied by Jewish immigrants who failed to meet her standards of housekeeping and decorum, but she found Mrs. Chmura, "gentle, placid, Slavic—sat beneath the shadow of the porch, relaxed in figure as one of Perugino's Madonnas, her youngest clinging to her as the Child by any old-world

XIX-2. Benjamin Ten Broeck House (DeWitt photo, 1951)

master clings to the Mother in the painting." Admittedly, the place was not very tidy. Still, "the artistic quality of their setting fitted them and they fitted it and dirt and poverty were forgotten by the visitor because of the subtle suggestion of race and soil and age-long things."

Reynolds's book drew attention to the house. Waterman documented it for HABS in 1936, but he was also working for Henry Francis du Pont who, with the aid of antiques dealers including Kingston's Fred Johnston, was collecting historic woodwork for his museum in Delaware (see XX-1 for the Hardenbergh rooms Johnston obtained for du Pont in 1938). In 1937 du Pont purchased a casement from Chmura for $100, using Johnston as his agent. Johnston found Chmura, whom he identified as a Polish farmer now employed on the WPA, to be "stubborn"; the impoverished Pole insisted that the replacement window frame be of costly oak. The antique window no longer had its wooden "button" or knob to secure the panels, so du Pont commissioned Johnston to supply one, preferably old, not a reproduction. Du Pont even suggested to Johnston that he should quietly switch an old button (from an unknown source) that Johnston had promised another client, with a new reproduction so that du Pont could attach the antique to his Ten Broeck casement.

At Winterthur the casement was installed in a small space known as the Ulster County Room, whose only Ulster County connection is the window. It is not known whether the button on view is old or a reproduction. The sale and

XIX-3. Watson M. Freer House (photo in Hooper, 1906)

removal of the window damaged the historic value of the house, although du Pont must have believed that he was preserving the window for the ages, while its fate in the hands of an unsophisticated East European peasant was uncertain at best. Worse depredations occurred later in the twentieth century when other windows, shutters, and the original interior door were removed, at least some taken by thieves when the house was vacant.

XIX–3* Watson M. Freer House, Maple Lane Farms
Saugerties Rd. near Kingston City line. c. 1900 (not extant). Wilson Eyre.

This modest gambrel-roofed Dutch Colonial house was designed by the noted Philadelphia architect Wilson Eyre for Watson Marthis Freer (1863–1922) at Maple Lane Farms, a country estate of some 107 acres near the city line. Watson Freer was a brother and business associate of Charles Lang Freer, a railroad freight car manufacturer in Detroit and a sophisticated art collector who created the Freer Gallery on the Mall in Washington. A native of Kingston, Charles made

XIX-4. 9-W Drive-In Theatre (advertisement, Kingston Daily Freeman, *May 27, 1949)*

his fortune in Detroit, but maintained ties with his family in Kingston and was a major donor in the preservation of the Jean Hasbrouck house in New Paltz. Eyre designed a fine house for Charles in Detroit in 1890, a less expensive but still notable Colonial Revival house for his sister Emma F. Freer at 151 Albany Avenue in Kingston about 1896, and this house for their brother Watson and his wife Anna, whose father, Frank J. Hecker, was a partner of Charles.

Watson Freer, born in St. Remy in 1863, was educated at the Kingston Academy but made a career with his brother in Detroit from 1883 to 1899. Returning to Kingston, Watson acquired land on the Saugerties Road in October 1899 from his brother, William H. Freer, and in 1904 photos of the house appeared in Charles Edward Hooper's book, *The Country House.* This suggests a construction date around 1900, although Eyre designed a house for Watson Freer in 1891. Hooper drew attention to the "excellent piazza with flanking benches." The first floor plan reveals some of the elements of Eyre's

larger Shingle Style country houses—a hall with staircase and fireplace, as well as additional fireplaces in the parlor and smoking room.

XIX–4* 9-W Drive-In Theatre
Saugerties Rd. 1948–1949 (not extant).
Leon M. Einhorn.

America's love affair with the automobile and the post-war baby boom converged in the planning of drive-in theatres like the 9-W Drive-In. Designed by Albany architect Leon M. Einhorn for Walter Reade Theatres, Inc., the drive-in with capacity for 700 cars advertised that it would "cater particularly to the family trade. Our Drive-In is a community recreation center as well as a movie theatre. For the entire family we have a picnic area and a spacious playground for the children." In contrast to conventional theatres, babies were welcome—bottle warmers were provided—and smoking was encouraged. The highway-facing rear of the giant screen was "covered with a streamlined shell ... serving as a landmark ... visible for a great distance." This shell functioned as a huge signboard and helped introduce modern design to Ulster County. This was the second drive-in to open in the Town of Ulster; the first opened earlier in the spring of 1949 on Rte. 28. Both represented the movement of business from the city of Kingston to the Town of Ulster, a process that would continue for decades.

XX

Town of Wawarsing

Formed from part of the Town of Rochester in 1806.

Population: 8,151 in 1870; 12,889 in 2000.

"Wawarsing," according to historian Marc Fried, was almost certainly the name recognized by Esopus Indians and European colonists for "the most important settlement of the Esopus Indians at the time the name was first recorded by the Kingston court." Among the first European settlers of Wawarsing were Abram and John Bevier, Huguenots from New Paltz who settled near Napanoch about 1708. Not until 1805 was building begun on the site of Ellenville, and as late as 1823 it still had only about four houses and a tavern, but no mill, no church, and was unnamed. (There was a c. 1745 stone Dutch Reformed Church to the north in the hamlet of Wawarsing.) The naming of Ellenville after a pretty, young visitor in 1823 became a locally celebrated tale perpetuated as a mural in the New Deal post office (see XX–16).

Completion of the Delaware & Hudson Canal in 1828 resulted in the growth of Ellenville and other hamlets along the canal. A glassworks and cutlery factory operated in Ellenville, an ironworks, axe factory, and paper mill in Napanoch, and tanneries in various locations. The Midland Railroad reached Ellenville in 1871, the canal ceased significant operation in 1898, and the Midland's successor, the New York, Ontario & Western, used the former towpath as roadbed for much of its route from Ellenville to Kingston. City residents came to summer at Sam's Point atop the Shawangunk Mountains by 1870 and, nearby, Cragsmoor developed as an art colony with painter Edward Lamson Henry its leading figure. In the twentieth century, huckleberry pickers put up shacks on the mountain, while below, at Napanoch, Yama Farms provided rustic comfort for America's business elite.

XX–1 Johannes G. Hardenbergh House

Rte. 209, one mile southwest of Kerhonkson. 1762 (collapsed 1938; two rooms partially re-erected 1939–1940 at Winterthur, Delaware).

Parts of this stone house, which played a part in the American Revolution, survive in Delaware at the renowned Henry Francis du Pont Winterthur Museum, thanks to Kingston antiques dealer Fred J. Johnston. However, the building's stone walls collapsed after du Pont's crew removed the wooden beams from the much-decayed house in 1938.

Helen Wilkinson Reynolds drew attention to the Hardenbergh house in her 1929 book, citing its role as the safe repository for ten wagonloads of official state, county, and New York City papers when Kingston was threatened by the British in October 1777. Reynolds thought it significant that the house's owner, Colonel Johannes G. Hardenbergh (1731–1812), should be "a leading citizen" and yet occupy such a relatively modest house. There were just three rooms, placed in a line, with each room having a fireplace and a south-facing door. The house's most distinguished feature was its paneling, found in the east room above and on both sides of the fireplace, with lesser paneling next to the chimney in the middle room. The east room door had a stone lintel on the exterior inscribed with monograms (illegible to Reynolds, but found by others to relate to the Hardenberghs) and the date 1762. Winterthur preserves this stone and the paneling from the two rooms.

When visited and sketched by Reynolds in the 1920s, the Hardenbergh house was owned by Mr. and Mrs. Charles W. Osborne, who used it for farm storage while allowing it to deteriorate despite local interest in preserving the house. According to Katharine Terwilliger, "in 1922, with the blessing of Mr. and Mrs. Osborne, a group of ladies from the Town of Wawarsing met ... [at the house] to discuss what might be done" to preserve it. But the ladies, joined by local historian Thomas E. Benedict of Napanoch, were unable to move forward with preservation. At the 1930 annual meeting of the Ulster County Historical Society, Mrs. Rachel McCausland Horton of Ellenville

"pleaded for the conservation and proper marking" of landmarks such as the Hardenbergh house, and over the next several years Olive Brown Sarre of Yama Farms pushed the historical society to purchase the Hardenbergh house from the Osbornes, who were willing to sell the house and a plot of land between Route 209 and the Rondout Creek. Sarre cited the fact that Governor Franklin Roosevelt, when visiting Ellenville, had claimed the Hardenberghs among his ancestors. Cragsmoor's Frederick S. Dellenbaugh joined the preservation cause and wrote an essay, "The Hardenberghs," which he read at a meeting of the historical society in September 1934, not long before his death, urging the society to acquire the decaying building for its association with the Revolution and for its handsome woodwork. He urged quick action: "it is in disrepair and every year makes the redemption more expensive whereas now it still would be comparatively slight."

The preservationists were opposed by the society's president, Judge G. D. B. Hasbrouck of Kingston, who was wary of the cost of purchasing, repairing, and maintaining the house, which was in immediate need of a new roof. Hasbrouck also wondered whether it was of such significance, in relation to other county houses, to justify the cost. Then, too, Kingstonians wanted the society to be quartered nearer Kingston and in a larger building—they may already have had in mind the Bevier house in Marbletown—so this effort also failed.

During this period the Osbornes permitted young people from the Kerhonkson Methodist Church to enjoy Halloween parties among the cobwebs and decay of the historic rooms. Fortunately for posterity, the Osbornes also permitted the WPA's Historic American Buildings Survey to send a field party in December 1936 to measure and photograph the house. This resulted in documentary photos and ten measured drawings, including details of hardware and woodwork, which were completed in June 1937.

By 1938 there seemed to be no hope of saving the house in its original form. At this time it was standard museum practice to remove attractive woodwork from colonial houses, whether the house was endangered or not, for museum dis-

*XX-1. Johannes G. Hardenbergh House, Bedroom at Winterthur
(1962 photo, courtesy Winterthur Museum)*

play. In 1934 the Metropolitan Museum of Art installed, in its American Wing, a Georgian-style paneled fireplace wall that had been removed from a stone house (1752) near High Falls (see IX–18). Four years later, Henry Francis du Pont wrote Fred Johnston in search of "Ulster County woodwork" as part of his quest for old house interiors to serve as settings for his growing collection of American furniture and decorative arts. Johnston replied that "a lovely old building in Ulster County built in 1762 is about to come down. ... It would be an opportunity to get some nice dutch building material cheaply." After du Pont expressed interest, Johnston sent the HABS drawings of the house and further assured his patron that "the paint on the paneling is original, the house is in a ruined condition but the paneling, floor boards, doors, beams etc. are in perfect condition." The house "could be dismanteled [*sic*] very simply and at no

great expense. This house is the finest example of early dutch stone architecture I know of in Ulster county, and I feel it is cheap." The Osbornes would sell the house (without land) for $900, and Johnston asked $100 for himself. The dealer hoped for a speedy answer from du Pont because Gale Carter of Greenwich, Connecticut, was also interested in the house.

Du Pont agreed to Johnston's terms and in August 1938 sent a crew from Delaware to remove everything that might be reused in his museum. Most came from the east and middle rooms; the roof over the west room—the kitchen—had collapsed, and therefore little could be retrieved. Du Pont urged Johnston to check the ruin to make certain that his men missed nothing. In 1939–1940, with the remains safely at Winterthur, architect Thomas Tileston Waterman (1900–1951), an authority on colonial architecture,

XX-2. Nonkanahwa Sanitarium (c. 1910 postcard)

designed two rooms, parlor and bedroom, with wood from the Hardenbergh house. Waterman was obliged to alter and reduce the size of the rooms so they would fit the existing space at Winterthur. By April 1940 the rooms were ready for a visit by Johnston, who enthused to du Pont that "to walk in the Hardenbergh rooms was to walk through the old house but without the dirt."

Today's visitors to Winterthur can admire the "Hardenbergh Parlor" (the original east room), described in a 1963 guide to the museum as having "the planked ceiling, deep beams, and paneled fireplace wall retaining its original gray-blue paint" from the Hardenbergh house. A wrought-iron candle stand from the Hermanus Myderse House (built 1743) in Saugerties is among the few furnishings from an Ulster County source. Open cupboard doors reveal two exterior and two interior photos of the Hardenbergh house before its fall. Forming an L with the Hardenbergh Parlor is the "Hardenbergh Bedroom" (the original middle room), which incorporates woodwork from the old house as well as the 1762 lintel stone, although most visitors will focus on the rare grisaille-painted Hudson Valley (but not Ulster County) Dutch kas. Johnston gave du Pont a printed copy of Dellenbaugh's

The Hardenberghs which, bound in leather, was once tucked into the bedroom. (Today it can be found in Winterthur's Rare Book Collection.)

XX-2 Nonkanahwa Sanitarium of Dr. Andrew Green Foord (Soyuzivka Ukrainian National Association Estate)
216 Foordmore Rd., Kerhonkson. c. 1906.

Andrew Green Foord graduated with honors from Long Island College Hospital in 1897, spent four years as a resident at Mount Sinai Hospital, and founded this sanitarium in 1906 on some 1,100 acres on the lower slopes of the Shawangunk ridge. At the time of his death in 1950, he was praised for successfully treating patients "worn down by the stress of modern life." Contact with nature was part of the "rest cure" at Nonkanahwa ("by the side of the stream"); a 1915 postcard from the sanitarium to Mr. and Mrs. Gray expressed the hope that they "both feel benefited from your visit to 'Nonkanahwa'" and reported that birdhouses were being made in the shop.

The one-story segment of the sanitarium was faced with rugged stone, but most of the building was designed with unadorned stucco walls, casement windows, and picturesque gables and dormers belonging to the Arts and Crafts movement—not the cobblestone-and-log variety of the Hut at Yama Farms built by Frank Seaman and Olive Sarre (though in 1940 the Foords sent a Christmas card to Olive, their "dear, wonderful neighbor"), but the less rustic kind associated with the British architects C. F. A. Voysey and M. H. Baillie Scott. Dr. Foord's father, John Foord, originally from Scotland, became editor-in-chief of *The New York Times*, but never relinquished his pride in his Scottish ancestry. The doctor, too, was remembered as being of Scottish descent, and the design of his sanitarium is in line with the semi-modern geometric simplicities of Voysey and Baillie Scott.

Dr. Foord's sanitarium closed in 1942, and ten years later the Ukrainian National Association purchased it from his estate for use as a resort. Today it is maintained by the Soyuzivka Heritage Foundation, Inc., "an educational and cultural institution for all Americans/Canadians of Ukrainian descent."

XX–3* Arthur S. and Adelaide Lyon Estate, Lyon Lodge

Rouge Harbor Rd. c. 1923. Francis A. Nelson; Vitale, Brinckerhoff & Geiffert, landscape architects.

The region's one-and-a-half story, fieldstone house of the colonial period was here revived, expanded, and given an air of sophistication suited to the taste of 1920s Manhattanites. The client, Arthur St. Clair Lyon (c. 1877–1952), was captain of the U.S. Olympic fencing team in 1924 and president of the Lyon Furniture Mercantile Agency on Broadway. His wife, Adelaide Tietjen Lyon, granted a divorce in 1933, was residing at Lyon Lodge when she died in 1964.

Myron Teller might have designed something simpler and more in the spirit of the old Dutch Colonial; he would have avoided the symmetry of the long wings and the refinement of the arched dormer windows and classically treated wooden segments joining the stone central block and stone appendages. For architect Francis Nelson (1878–1950), a graduate of Columbia in 1900 who then went on to study in Paris at the École des Beaux-Arts, the local vernacular must have seemed awkward and in need of improvement. The gambrel roof of Lyon Lodge is more common in colonial New Jersey than in colonial Ulster. Nelson would have been familiar with New Jersey gambrels, as he lived in a house he designed in Upper Montclair. His wife, Helen Ackerman Nelson, descended from a Dutch family that settled near Allendale in 1662.

In addition to the main house, this large estate included a barn, piggery (later housing pheasants), springhouse, icehouse, slab-sided cabin, and log boathouse on man-made Lyon Lake. Blueprints by the noted landscape architects Vitale, Brinckerhoff & Geiffert of New York are dated May 31, 1923, and indicate that all of these buildings had been erected by then, except for the boathouse.

XX-3. Lyon Lodge (1985 photo)

Napanoch and Vicinity

XX–4 William Doll House and Southwick Store (former)
Main St. 1810, 1833. NR

The Southwick Store (1833), built for Richard and George Southwick, is one of the county's best examples of Greek Revival commercial architecture from the period of the Delaware & Hudson Canal's ascendancy. Notable is the long, L-shaped file of Doric piers of the porches facing Main and Clinton streets. The William Doll House (1810), standing closer to Main Street, predates the store and is a good example of the five-bay house from the Federal period. The short segment connecting the house and store was added about 1837 when Doll acquired the Southwick property, while the second-story porches are twentieth-century additions. Thanks to research by Neil Larson, the house and store (along with other nearby buildings, including the Napanoch Female Seminary [1841]) are listed on the National Register of Historic Places as the Hoornbeeck Store Complex, named for the family that owned the store from 1867 to the 1970s.

XX-4. Doll House and Southwick Store (1972 photo)

XX–5* Reformed Church
Church Street. Begun 1836 (demolished 1982). Samuel Reynolds, contractor.

Perhaps the finest of the county's Greek Revival churches, the wooden Napanoch Reformed Church had a well-proportioned Doric portico with finely executed Greek details, notably fluted column shafts with entasis (a slight convex swelling) and, above the columns, a frieze of triglyphs. One Napanoch resident wrote in 1866 that "but for an uncouth looking box on top, called a cupola, this would be the finest specimen of the Doric order of architecture in the county." Greek temples had no cupolas. How Samuel Reynolds, the contractor from nearby Port Ben on the D & H Canal, learned his Greek architectural vocabulary is not known. The building contract did state that the balcony at the rear of the interior should be similar to one in Welton's Church in Poughkeepsie—which was the Second Presbyterian Church (1835), a Greek Revival building at the corner of Mill and Vassar streets.

Completion of construction was delayed by the financial panic of 1837, which led to the failure of the firm of A. R. & G. Southwick, financial backers of the church. The Southwick residence, also Greek Revival (see next entry, XX–6), adjoined the church property; the Southwicks had sold a portion of their land to the church. In 1840 the church building was sold at a sheriff's sale. It was eventually redeemed by its congregation, but regular services ended in 1908, summer services in 1962.

Although the derelict church was razed in 1982, the parsonage survives close by the site of the church. Built in 1855, the parsonage demonstrates the fading of the Greek Revival and the rise

XX-5. Napanoch Reformed Church (early-twentieth-century postcard)

XX-6. Southwick House (1972 photo)

of the picturesque Gothic Revival in the 1850s, especially for buildings associated with churches. The parsonage, built by Nathaniel Blake and William Brock, has a Gothic-arched window facing the site of the church, the gables are fitted with Gothic bargeboards, and the windows with Gothic drip moldings.

XX-6* Adna H. Southwick House
c. 1835 (destroyed by fire, 1973).

The Southwick house was probably put up during a period when the family's axe-manufacturing and tanning businesses flourished in Napanoch—after the opening of the Delaware & Hudson Canal in 1828 and before the financial panic of 1837. With its four-column Ionic por-

tico, this house was a handsome example of the adaptation of the marble Greek temple to the wood-frame American dwelling. The Southwicks were supporters of the Reformed Church (begun 1836), also Greek Revival in style, which stood on an adjoining lot that they sold to the church (see preceding entry, XX–5).

The portrait painter Mme. Elizabeth Shoumatoff, best known for her 1945 portrait of Franklin Roosevelt, lived in this house when it was owned by Frank Seaman of Yama Farms, and she executed watercolors and miniatures of Seaman's guests.

XX–7* Eastern New York Reformatory (Eastern New York Correctional Facility)
1894–1900. John Rochester Thomas.

While readily seen through windshields of moving vehicles on public roads, this enormous landmark (the west façade is some 700 feet long) can only be visited or photographed with official permission. Like many earlier nineteenth-century prisons, it presents itself as a turreted medieval fortress, a grim reminder of the austere life awaiting those who commit criminal deeds. While originally to be constructed of local stone from the Shawangunks, Ohio sandstone was substituted because it was more easily worked. Canal boats transported stone to the site until through traffic on the canal ended in 1898. Construction went slowly; ground was broken in October 1894, but the main building was not complete when the reformatory received its first prisoners on October 1, 1900. Prisoners were used in completing construction, and a 200-foot-long Work House was erected in 1903 for breaking and cutting stone.

State Reformitory, Napanoch, N. Y.

XX-7. Eastern New York Reformatory (c. 1905 postcard)

The architect, John Rochester Thomas (1848–1901), designed some 150 churches in his relatively short career, but also developed a reputation as planner of prisons and armories with the aura and actuality of a fortress. In 1874 he was appointed architect of the State Reformatory in Elmira, which was followed by designs for the New Jersey State Reformatory in Rahway, the combined 71st Regiment and Second Battery Armory, and the 8th Regiment Armory (1887–1890), both in New York City. He was also responsible for the Squadron A Armory (1895) on Madison Avenue, mostly demolished, although its castellated façade survives. The Napanoch structure is well preserved except for the ill-designed addition of an administration building to its front in the 1960s.

XX–8* New York, Ontario & Western Railway Station (former)
1902. Jackson, Rosencrans & Canfield. NR

Travelers lulled by the beauty of the Shawangunk Mountains can be surprised to come upon the enormous castellated prison that is Eastern Correctional Facility, and then find just west of the prison a railroad station in the Spanish Mission style of the American Southwest. Not much attention was paid to regionalism by the architects of these apparent intruders. Characteristic of the Spanish Mission style are the station's smooth cement-on-metal-lath walls, round-arched windows and doorways, and small domed tower with (originally) "Spanish tile" in harmony with the red, tile-like slate of the roofs. The O & W's Kerhonkson station (not extant) was an identical Mission-style building. By the 1920s and '30s many hotels in Sullivan County and nearby Ulster had adopted the style—so many, in fact,

that the term "Sullivan County Mission style" is found in several histories of the region. The Mission style had been revived in California in the 1890s, and communities in Sullivan and southern Ulster hoped to entice city folk as summer visitors with buildings suggesting the pleasures of sunny southern California.

The architects, Jackson, Rosencrans & Canfield of New York, designed a number of other O & W stations in a picturesque half-timbered style (see XIV–5 and XIV–7). Architect B. K. Canfield has been identified as the son of the O & W's superintendent, Edward Canfield. Canfield's partners, together or individually, designed YMCAs in Poughkeepsie (1909), Kingston (1912; destroyed by fire 1991), and Newburgh (1912) with Renaissance or Georgian façades.

From its opening in 1902, the station served inmates arriving for Eastern Reformatory, but it also served the general population, notably highly respectable guests of Frank Seaman at Yama Farms. The station was built adjacent to the recently abandoned D & H Canal, yet the railroad was to have a shorter life than the canal. Passenger service ended in the early 1940s, and freight in the 1950s. Now a part of Eastern Correctional Facility, the station—and especially the long-gone domed tower—has been restored by the correctional facility with community support.

The Port Ben station (NR), next up the line to Kingston, is small, boxy, but well preserved in the half-timbered manner used by Jackson, Rosencrans, and Canfield for the O & W.

O & W Depot, NAPANOCH, N. Y.

XX-8. Napanoch Station (early-twentieth-century postcard)

XX-9. Tea House, Yama-no-uchi (c. 1915 postcard)

XX-9* Yama-no-uchi
(Yama Farms of Frank Seamon)
Rte. 55. c. 1906–1913. Olive B. Sarre.

Yama-no-uchi is today mostly ruinous, and "no trespassing" signs are strictly enforced, but in its heyday its 1,300 acres included a remarkable group of buildings and garden structures influenced by Japanese design and the Arts and Crafts movement. At first the country estate of Frank Seaman (1858–1939), a leading advertising man in New York, its Japanese character reflected the enthusiasm he and his companion, Olive Brown Sarre (rhymes with "far"; 1873–1954) had for Japanese culture. (Seaman, who was separated from his wife about 1903, had a relationship with Sarre for some three decades before they could marry in 1934.)

Seaman and Sarre traveled to Japan sometime between 1902 and 1906. According to a 1907 newspaper account, Sarre sailed first to Japan and was later met there by Seaman; both then toured "several gardens to get ideas." In Japan Seaman felt honored to have the statesman Marquis Ito Hirobumi provide the name "Yama-no-uchi" ("home in the mountains") for his country place on the

hill above Napanoch, which some wags came to call "Nipponoch." As Seaman wrote in his unpublished memoirs, it was in Japan that he decided to give buildings he was planning "a Japanese atmosphere." After failing in his effort to bring a carpenter from Japan to design and oversee construction, and failing as well to convince a New York architect (probably Francis A. Demeuron) to design the buildings with the aid of "two elaborate books on Japanese architecture" that he had brought from Japan, Seaman followed the architect's advice and assigned the task to Sarre. It appears that Sarre had attended the Art Students League, but had no formal architectural training. Seaman expressed surprise that a woman could function as an architect, but he was assured that "her genius as a designer and an interior decorator, and her special knowledge of things Japanese" would allow her to succeed. After inspecting the property, Sarre agreed to serve as designer if Seaman would build a house for her, her son, and her mother. Sarre apparently established herself at Yama in 1906, and by 1910 she had completed a number of Japanese-inspired structures. Carlyle Ellis credited her with the estate's "detail plan and its fulfillment," while describing her as "an authority on Japanese architecture and landscape gardening and Japanese arts and crafts."

Sarre's first Japanese design built for Seaman was probably the stable and garage, now a ruin. Its splendid curving mass of cobblestones is visible from Rte. 55, especially in winter. Local masons, unaccustomed to the masonry forms of Japan, required the diligent supervision of Olive Sarre. The stone wall appears to be a bastion, originally with what Seaman called "a graceful [wooden] superstructure of delicate Japanese lines." The effect was that of a Japanese castle, like Kumamoto Castle as pictured in Ralph Adams Cram's *Impressions of Japanese Architecture* (1905), although the Japanese did not use cobblestones.

Closer to Rte. 55 are the cobblestone walls of the small, tower-like structure that once housed a waterpowered dynamo to generate electricity for the property. The Japanese curved and flaring roof has not survived. Seaman and Sarre apparently saw no conflict between Japanese tradition and modern American technology. Out of sight is the ruin of the Japanese teahouse, a wooden structure with—unlike Japanese examples—a cobblestone base. The height of the cobblestone base gave the structure a tower-like form, and a vintage postcard fittingly identified the structure as the "Pagoda," as it resembled the taller tower-shrines of the Far East. (In 2007, members of the Roebling Chapter, Society of Industrial Archaeology inspected the smooth concrete core of the base and suggested it may have functioned as a cistern.) The wooden teahouse itself was described by Carlyle Ellis as "wholly Japanese in design," although "built of native chestnut by American workmen all recruited from the village below."

XX-9A. Entrance Gate, Yama-no-uchi (c. 1915 postcard)

The gateway to the property closely resembled a Japanese gate, and early photos show a Japanese woman in traditional costume standing by the gate, which is long gone. In vintage postcards the gate lies behind a lantern stand with curved roof over a glowing, flesh-colored lantern bearing the Japanese ideographs "Yama-no-uchi." Sarre apparently took proper pride in her design, and a photo of the gate is captioned "Olive B. Sarre Architect" in an advertisement in the March 1915 issue of Gustav Stickley's magazine, *The Craftsman*.

Parts of Seaman's property were landscaped with "the best collection of Japanese iris outside of Japan" and ornamented with Japanese vehicular and pedestrian bridges. One was "a small facsimile of the famous one at Nikko, glowing a wonderful crimson against the green." A Japanese tea garden was designed along the shady side of one of the estate's several ponds.

Seaman's spacious log residence, modestly called the Hut, was built about 1906 and probably was designed by Sarre—she initialed a drawing of the Hut printed on the cover of her booklet, *The Pottery and Porcelain at the Hut* (1918). (The Hut, set back on high ground some distance from Rte. 55, in 2010 is an inaccessible ruin retaining its outer walls and chimneys.) Seaman had in mind building a Japanese "bungalow" as his residence, and at first conceived the Hut merely as a smaller, temporary home. The Hut's fine site, with a view overlooking a wooded ravine toward the Shawangunk ridge, led him to alter the Hut's plans by

Entrance Gate to Yama-No-Uchi, Napanoch, N. Y.

enlarging the rooms and adding a stone servants' wing, described as a "Swiss chalet." While the Hut is not overtly Japanese, its low, horizontal lines and spreading roof are in harmony with Japanese taste. Seaman had a passage from Kakuzo Okakura's *The Book of Tea* carved on the living room mantelpiece: "Let us linger here in the beautiful foolishness of things." Tea might be served here by Seaman's butler, himself Japanese.

The Hut's sturdy log construction, casement windows, and cobblestone chimney—its base flowing out and joining the house organically to the land—belong to the Arts and Crafts movement. The rustic log house suggestive of a pre-industrial era had entered the vocabulary of sophisticated Arts and Crafts architecture in the Catskill region in the 1880s at Onteora Park and Twilight Park in Greene County, both private summer colonies for New Yorkers escaping to the cool, rural mountaintop. John Burroughs's rustic retreat, Slabsides (1895; see II–9), at West Park was probably a direct influence on the Hut, although Seaman did not visit Slabsides until September 1908. From 1908 to 1920, Burroughs was a frequent guest of Seaman at the Hut, and in 1914 Burroughs called the Hut "a larger, finer Slabsides, with open fires, radiators, electric lights, and walls lined with books." Once, Burroughs arrived unexpectedly and told Seaman, "I come here to find myself; it is so easy to get lost in the world." Seaman had Burroughs write out and sign this endorsement (in 1913 paying guests began to come to Yama Farms Inn), which was then reproduced on a copper panel over the Hut's living room fireplace. (The panel is now preserved by the Ellenville Public Library and Museum.)

Seaman's and Sarre's fine library included several books written by Burroughs and inscribed by him to Sarre. Seaman subscribed to Stickley's *The Craftsman* magazine from at least 1906. (Many of Seaman's issues of *The Craftsman*, as well as Sarre's Burroughs volumes, are now in Sojourner Truth Library at SUNY New Paltz.) Stickley, the most important advocate of Arts and Crafts design in America, was clearly an influence upon Yama Farms and is known to have visited by September 1914. Many house designs with the low, broad shape of

the Hut appear in *The Craftsman*, and Stickley was attracted by the strong simplicity and American roots of the log cabin. In June 1906 *The Craftsman* praised a log house called "the hut" and built in Montana for Joseph Sharp, a painter of Indians and "an artist deeply in sympathy with Craftsman aims and purposes." Stickley's own log house (originally intended as a clubhouse) at Craftsman Farms, near Morristown, New Jersey, resembles Seaman's Hut, but its design was not published in *The Craftsman* until December 1908. Sarre's drawing of the Hut focuses on its cobblestone chimney flowing out over the ground. This chimney is a type sanctioned by *The Craftsman* (August 1908) as "connecting a house with its surroundings" and giving "the appearance of massive strength and solidity."

An office and lodge building near the Hut also was bound to the earth by a spreading cobblestone chimney. Its walls, however, were not log, but horizontal boards with an overlay of vertical wood strips that Clay Lancaster identified as of Japanese inspiration. The large shingled lodge (also called the Grill, heavily damaged by fire in June 2010) on Rte. 55 at today's entrance to Yama Farms corresponded closely to Craftsman architecture in its gently sloping gable roof that extended beyond the shingled walls, as well as in the horizontal grouping of windows, and cobblestone foundation allied with nearby cobblestone walls defining the roadside.

Yama-no-uchi was also known as Yama Farms, and Seaman was proud of its commercial ventures—an elaborate trout hatchery, as well as poultry and dairy production. In 1913 he opened Yama Farms Inn, which occupied additional buildings erected not far from the Hut. The inn's main structure, a rambling frame building with extensive porches and balconies and a great cobblestone chimney, no longer stands. For an extra charge, guests were offered "tent-houses (of the gay colored oriental sort) with electric lights, telephones, baths and open fire places." The Yama Farms Theatre, a shingled building with a rustic stone chimney, survived into the early twenty-first century. Its function was announced by a wooden panel below the eaves with a passage from Shakespeare—"I hold the world a stage

XX-9B. The Hut,
Yama-no-uchi

where every man must play a part"—lettered in the archaic, fifteenth-century style sometimes favored by the Arts and Crafts movement.

Seaman oversaw a remarkable list of paying guests, a list that included captains of industry and notable musicians, naturalists, and socialites. Cragsmoor's Frederick Dellenbaugh and George Inness, Jr., were among the favored guests. Seaman announced through *The New York Times* that May 12 to 18, 1914, was "John Burroughs week" at the inn, with Burroughs as "guest of honor" and Thomas Edison among the Burroughs admirers in attendance. In 1920 the *Times* publicized that Edison, Burroughs, Henry Ford, and Harvey Firestone were giving up their usual summer automobile trip in favor of a "reunion" at Yama Farms. Vintage postcards reveal, however, that curious strangers were confronted at the gate with a sign: "NO ADMITTANCE."

Seaman recognized that exclusivity, when properly publicized, would add to the inn's appeal for America's elite, especially since Wawarsing and nearby Sullivan County were well known for Jewish resorts catering to the lower half of the social and economic ladder. Ironically, in 1944, five years after Seaman's death, Yama Farms Inn (which included a nine-hole golf course) became Ravin Country Club, a Jewish resort conducted by Nat J. Ravin, who had previously operated resorts in Sullivan County. This and other attempts to operate a resort on the property failed, and the inn was eventually destroyed by fire.

In contrast to the Smileys at Lake Mohonk, Seaman seems to have discouraged, or at least not sought, the presence of straight-laced Christian clergy. Alcohol was forbidden at Mohonk, but was served at Yama. During Prohibition, Seaman somehow managed to stay within the law and produce his own wine for consumption by his guests. A door of one of the outbuildings long bore the playful wording, "YAMA GRAPE JUICE FACTORY." Seaman and Sarre were very discreet about their relationship, but it, like alcohol, would have unsettled many clergy of the time.

Olive Brown Sarre Seaman resided at the Hut after Seaman's death until her own in 1954. She and Seaman deserve to be remembered for creating a rare example of the harmonious union of the natural landscape with architectural forms drawn from Japan and the Arts and Crafts movement. The admirable book by Wendy E. Harris and others, *Yama Farms: A Most Unusual Catskills Resort* (2006) preserves a wealth of information about this landmark whose near loss is tragic.

Ellenville and Vicinity

XX–10 Charlotte's Diner (209 Diner)

8073 Rte. 209. 1952 (exterior resurfaced 1990). Silk City Diner, manufactured by the Paterson Vehicle Co.

Within this diner's currently prosaic shell is a handsome and well-preserved interior from the classic era of modern diner design. The glistening surfaces of chrome, stainless steel, tile, and Formica assure customers of the diner's cleanliness and efficiency. The low arched ceiling and band of windows in metal frames would have reminded customers in the 1950s of fast railroad cars. But the long file of stools, counter, narrow passage for waitresses, and food and drink visible on the back wall could only mean roadside diner, that all-American institution. Traditionally men would sit at the counter, women and families in the booths. As democratic places to eat, diners catered to all classes, but no doubt Frank Seaman and Olive Sarre, of an earlier generation at nearby Yama Farms, would have dismissed this eatery as beneath their culinary and social standards.

Over the front door is the small metal label identifying this as a factory-made Silk City Diner from the Paterson Vehicle Co., in operation from 1927 to 1964 in New Jersey, the center of diner manufacturing. The assembled diner would be shipped by rail and/or truck from factory to its roadside foundation and could later, if necessary, be transported to another location.

XX-10. Charlotte's Diner (1982 photo)

The diner's pre-1990 exterior resembled steamlined, stainless-steel passenger railroad cars of the 1930s, '40s, and early '50s. The horizontal treatment of the stainless-steel wall panels, the windows, and the low monitor roof all suggested potential speed and little wind resistance. The narrow blue band of porcelain enamel set the tone for the largely blue interior. The kitchen and bathrooms occupy a second rectangular unit whose ends received the same streamlined treatment as the front and ends of the dining section. Charlotte's acquired a certain fame when its vintage exterior was reproduced on a commercial note card in the 1980s (Paper House Productions, Woodstock; photo by Jeff Milstein), but this did not save it from the common late-twentieth-century practice of resurfacing the aging exterior. At least it escaped the fates of the Colonial Diner, a c. 1949 Silk City Diner on Broadway in Kingston, which was removed from its site in 1985, or another Silk City product closed for many years outside Phoenicia (see XVII–6).

XX–11 Fantinekill Cemetery

Rte. 209. 1871 and later.

Ellenville's picturesque, parklike cemetery was laid out in 1871 to take advantage of its hilly site and views across the valley of the Rondout toward the Shawangunk ridge. Before the coming of car and truck traffic on the state road, it must have been a place of rural tranquility.

The cemetery's most striking feature was the small Gothic Revival chapel that stood (until natural forces brought it down in the winter of 2010–2011; it is being rebuilt) in front of a hillside receiving vault. Details were Gothic—the pointed arched window above the doorway, as well as the small quatrefoil window to either side, the diamond panes, and the timber framing—while the overall effect was of a glassy porch to a Gothic church whose nave is absent. Gothic was a sensible choice—it was associated with the Christian church, and this was a Christian cemetery; it

XX-11. Chapel, Fantinekill Cemetery (1996 photo)

XX-12. Scoresby Hose & Hook & Ladder Co. Clubhouse (c. 1915 postcard)

was also considered by Downing and others to be the style suited to hilly, picturesquely landscaped grounds like the cemetery's. (A similar Gothic building stands before the receiving vault of the Poughkeepsie Rural Cemetery, also picturesquely landscaped.) The chapel and receiving vault were given in 1891 by Jackson S. Schultz (1815–March 1, 1891) in memory of his father Abram, or Abraham, Schultz. Jackson Schultz was a rich leather merchant, but also civic-minded and a key figure in bringing down Boss Tweed. The Schultz family's main residence in Leurenkill is Italianate (see XX–23), but another house nearby (the "brown house") is Gothic Revival.

XX-12 Scoresby Hose and Hook and Ladder Company Clubhouse
North Main St. at Liberty St. 1911–1912. George Young, Jr.

Arts and Crafts architecture is represented in Wawarsing not only at rural Yama Farms and Dr. Foord's sanitarium, but also in the village of Ellenville by the Scoresby Clubhouse, designed by Napanoch native George Young, Jr. A colored rendering of the building, signed by Helen Binkerd Young, its delineator and the architect's wife, remains in the clubhouse. Like an expanded Arts and Crafts bungalow, the clubhouse is low, one and a half stories, with a tile roof that is fitted with broad dormers and flows down over the expansive veranda. Walls are of concrete and stucco and, like the veranda piers, are flat and unadorned. Solid simplicity is the keynote. When new, the style was

called "semi-colonial," but little aside from the elliptical arch over the doorway seems early American. The wood-paneled game room retains a landscape frieze painted by O. W. Krause. A memorial window was emblazoned with the coat of arms of the Scoresby family, long prominent in Ellenville.

The three faces of the façade were planned to take advantage of its prominent site on North Main Street. The creator of the sophisticated design had earned his B. Arch. degree from Cornell University in 1900. In 1899 *The New York Times* hailed George Young, Jr., as "the little quarterback" who kicked the decisive goal giving Cornell a 5–0 victory in football over Princeton, leading to a celebration the likes of which had never been seen in Ithaca. After graduation Young worked as draftsman and superintendent for several firms before becoming assistant professor of architecture at Cornell in 1909. He was promoted to professor in

XX-12A. Game Room, Scoresby Clubhouse (c. 1912 photo)

1914, later served a period as dean, and retired in 1946. Young was named a Fellow of the American Institute of Architects in 1934. His wife Helen was his classmate in architecture at Cornell when few women entered the profession. She designed houses in Ithaca and wrote magazine articles on home planning and design, but taught home decoration and home arrangement in Cornell's College of Home Economics.

XX–13 Methodist Parsonage (former)
83 North Main St. 1870. J. A. Wood.

J. A. Wood was the region's leading architect in 1870, and the former Methodist parsonage is a fine example of his work in the mansarded Second Empire mode, with the main and porch cornices accented by substantial brackets. As in the case of Wood's Reformed Church parsonage (1872–1874; not extant) on Canal Street, a low, mansarded tower interrupts the roof line.

XX-13. Methodist Parsonage (1970 photo)

XX–14 George Deyo House (Terwilliger House Museum)
40 Center St. 1895. Alfred Grimley, builder.

Ellenville's finest surviving house from the turn of the twentieth century was built for George Deyo (1862–1920), a Republican town supervisor and county treasurer, as well as one of the

XX-14. George Deyo House

building commissioners for Eastern New York Reformatory at Napanoch in 1894. Deyo then served a stint as warden of Clinton Prison before returning to Napanoch in 1907 to take charge of the reformatory. Deyo's house would proclaim his high standing in the community; it was up-to-date in style and designed with striking details of more-than-average cost.

Its style is Queen Anne, eclectic, with touches of the Richardsonian Romanesque and American Colonial. The round arch of great blocks of rough-textured stone marking the entrance is Richardsonian (although Richardson preferred brownstone, while this appears to be local Shawangunk stone of lighter tone). The three-part Palladian window of the second story stems from the Georgian Colonial, and the oval windows from the Federal period of early America. To observers of the 1890s, the shingled walls, gables and dormer projecting from the hipped roof, and the delicate railing atop the roof, would all have evoked the old Colonial. But the whole is Queen Anne of the Victorian period. The busily picturesque composition of many projecting parts in a variety of materials was unknown in American architecture before 1830. The interior, which houses an excellent museum and archive of local history, is finely appointed with chestnut paneling, tiled fireplaces, stained-glass windows, and a handsome staircase.

Alfred Grimley, the builder of the Deyo house, was the grandson of John Grimley, who had a large farm near Ellenville and owned and operated a chair-turning factory. Alfred enlisted in the Union Army at sixteen, was severely wounded at Winchester, Virginia, and after the war became a contractor and builder in Ellenville. The designer of the Deyo house is unknown, but whoever drew the plans probably also designed the house at 87 Mansion Street in Coxsackie, Greene County, whose façade is very similar to the Deyo house.

XX–15 George and John R. Hunt Memorial
Liberty Square. 1917. Frank E. Estabrook. NR

The paired Ionic columns of the Hunt Memorial lend a dignified air to the west side of Liberty Square, as the Dutch Colonial Revival post office (1939) does to the north, and the Tudor Revival Wayside Inn (1907, H. King Conklin, architect) did to the east until gutted by fire in 1967. Ellenville businessman John R. Hunt provided funds in his will for the local Women's Christian Temperance Union to erect this building with space for WCTU meetings, civic gatherings, and the public library, as well as rental office space. Hunt's wife had been active in the WCTU, and the frieze above the Ionic colonnade was emblazoned with the Union's name. Large letters above the pedimented doorway on the Canal Street side announced the presence of the public library, although the library did not occupy space in the building until 1928 and has since departed to a modern building on Center Street. Readers benefited from daylight admitted through the tall arched windows. The asymmetrical Canal Street façade also has a lesser doorway and two stories of small rectangular windows indicating the location of the rental offices.

Hunt Memorial's architect was Frank E. Estabrook of Newburgh, best known for that city's Broadway

XX-15. Hunt Memorial (c. 1920 postcard)

School (1908), whose classical portico looms above the thoroughfare. For the Hunt Memorial, Estabrook freely adapted the Federal style of Charles Bulfinch's Massachusetts State House (1795) in Boston with its paired columns and Palladian windows recessed behind the broad, brick wall surface.

XX–16 Post Office
1 Liberty Square. 1939–1940.
Rudolph Stanley-Brown. NR

Thanks to the vigorous lobbying of Ellenville citizens, President Franklin D. Roosevelt prevailed upon his New Deal bureaucracy to provide Ellenville with a handsome stone post office in the Dutch Colonial manner. While FDR ordered four such post offices for communities in his native Dutchess County, Ulster County would receive only this one in Ellenville. In 1934, for their new post office, Saugerties citizens had requested bluestone from the president, but his mild enthusiasm for their cause resulted only in bluestone trim on a brick exterior (see XVI–9). In 1938 New Paltz and Highland were listed among communities eligible for new post offices, but no other New Deal post offices were built in the county.

The site of the new post office was announced in December 1937 as the Eaton property, whose mid-nineteenth-century temple-porticoed house would yield to the post office. By April 1939 people in the county were aware that the Procure-

XX-16. Ellenville Post Office (c. 1940 postcard)

ment Division of the Treasury Department, which had charge of all post office design and construction, was planning to put up a brick building with bluestone trim. This combination had satisfied Saugerties, brick was standard for post offices across the country, and the nearby Hunt Memorial was brick. Nevertheless, Kingston lawyer and city court judge Bernard A. Culloton objected to brick; Procurement replied that the local residents wanted the building to be harmonious with others on the village square, none of which was of stone. The "Colonial design" was said to be "in keeping with the tradition of the vicinity." Community leaders were not placated and mounted a campaign to obtain a design more accurately reflective of local colonial tradition.

On May 1, 1939, while FDR was dedicating the new Rhinebeck Post Office, built at his command of stone from the ruin of an early Dutch colonial house and in the form of that house, Tuthill McDowell, supervisor of the Town of Wawarsing, wrote to the president requesting that the Ellenville Post Office be constructed of fieldstone. Ellenville Mayor Benjamin S. Parks and other community leaders followed with a telegram to the president on May 9:

Since reading Rhinebeck dedication our Dutch settled community upset about new brick office planned for Ellenville. Village lies twenty-eight miles up Rondout valley from Kingston on King's Highway from which are visible ninety-nine pre-revolutionary stone houses. We wish replica of one and there is available stone for incorporation in it from house used as state capitol during burning of Kingston. ... Please make possible.

FDR also heard from his Hyde Park rector, Frank R. Wilson, and assured him on May 10, "I will stop that brick right away!"

The mayor, supervisor, and community leaders received more formal word from the president in a letter of May 19: "I have requested the architects of the Treasury Department to redesign the façade of the Ellenville Post Office in keeping with the traditional architecture of the Rondout

Valley, and making use of native stone." FDR had conferred with Procurement and gave Ellenville much of what was requested. But he did not insist upon a replica of an early house, and he did not specify stone from any particular source. The source recommended by Mayor Parks—the Johannes Hardenbergh house in Wawarsing (see XX–1)—had not in fact been the temporary state capitol, but had served as a repository for state papers. Moreover, Ellenville was too remote from Hyde Park and the homes of his ancestors to stir FDR to strive for the level of historical accuracy he had demanded for the Rhinebeck Post Office.

Rudolph Stanley-Brown was the architect assigned by Procurement to handle the revision of the post office design. He had excellent credentials: grandson of President James A. Garfield; educated at Yale, Columbia's School of Architecture, and the École des Beaux-Arts in Paris; and a successful practitioner in Cleveland before the Depression made him turn to government work in 1934. Most important, when designing the Rhinebeck Post Office, Stanley-Brown had managed to satisfy FDR's exacting historical demands. By May 24 Stanley-Brown could report on a quick tour from Kingston to Ellenville, by way of Old Hurley and Stone Ridge, "stopping to inspect and photograph the stonework of many of the old pre-Revolutionary houses along that route" and examining "possible sources of stone supply." Those sources were quarries, not derelict houses. (Ulster County bluestone had in fact recently been used in building the porch and fireplace of Top Cottage, the Dutch Colonial–style retreat FDR designed for himself in Hyde Park. The *Kingston Daily Freeman* proposed that the Ulster bluestone "will stand as a monument to an area industry.")

On June 2, FDR was shown Stanley-Brown's drawing for the revised exterior and was told that it reflected his study of pre-Revolutionary houses in the Rondout Valley. "The walls are to be of native limestone, fairly regularly coursed on the front and laid random on the sides as seems to be the custom in the old houses. The entrance door, windows and trim are in character with the dutch work and the whole design, while not a replica of any one building, is in keeping with the traditions of the Rondout Valley." FDR wrote, "Very good," and the project proceeded without further presidential involvement.

Some local citizens had feared that the lobbying against brick would seriously delay or even cause cancellation of the new building, but publication of FDR's May 19 letters set these fears to rest. Still, detailed drawings took time to revise, and construction bids were not requested until November when Stanley-Brown's attractive perspective drawing and a description of the building appeared in the *Ellenville Journal*. It was pointed out that the walls would be of native stone, except for the gable ends of wood, as in early Dutch colonial houses in the valley. The cupola and its bell, according to the *Kingston Daily Freeman*, gave "the building the appearance of America's old town meeting halls of a century or more ago." New Deal post offices ordinarily do not have bells—perhaps the Liberty Square address suggested its inclusion here. The bell was cast by McShane in Baltimore, and the "artistic weathervane" crowning the cupola's spire was wrought by Eastern Iron Works of New York City. The cupola with weather vane may have been inspired by one atop a new stone bank in New Paltz that Stanley-Brown had admired (see XI–13).

The building was completed in October 1940 and opened with little fanfare. The president expressed no interest in attending a ceremony, Supervisor Tuthill, a Democrat, had been defeated in November 1939, and the local citizenry were apparently content to have no formal opening.

The design of the interior remained much as it had been in the original plan for a brick building. The L-shaped lobby is surprisingly spacious—what appears on the outside to be a building of modest residential scale turns out to be much larger. The lobby is paneled in white oak, but its most distinctive feature is Louis Bouché's mural depicting the naming of Ellenville in 1823.

Ellenville citizens began pushing for a mural just as construction of the building was getting under way in January 1940. Deyo W. Johnson, president of a local lumber and coal company, wrote his friend Olin Dows, the artist of the Rhinebeck

XX-16A. Post Office mural study (drawing by Bouché, 1941)

murals and a family friend of the Roosevelts, to express the hope that Dows would paint murals in the Ellenville Post Office. Dows had his hands full painting murals for FDR in Rhinebeck and then Hyde Park, but he wrote Edward Bruce, head of the Treasury's mural program, urging a mural for Ellenville.

Bruce's office selected Louis Bouché, and in January 1941 invited him to submit sketches for their review. He would be paid $1,000 for a panel some fourteen by five feet, painted on canvas. Bouché accepted the commission and, following customary practice for post office muralists, went to the site, interviewed local people about a suitable subject pertinent to the area, and began to research that subject. Reporting to Washington on April 6, 1941, Bouché, in good humor, described his discussions in Ellenville with Tuthill McDowell, now postmaster, and "another official ... who is an Irishman and violently anti-British." That official wanted Bouché to paint "a massacre by the Indians led on by the vicious red-coats." McDowell and Bouché were not keen on this subject, and the artist's supervisor in Washington, Edward Rowan, agreed that "massacres are out. This office is not interested in taking any part in continuing or abetting any racial prejudice."

McDowell was probably responsible for suggesting that the mural depict the tale of the naming of the place, as recounted in Child's *Gazetteer and Business Directory* (1871–1872) and Sylvester's *History of Ulster County* (1880). Bouché proposed

that his mural retell "the story of the meeting at the old corner store when it was decided to ask the Federal government for a Post Office. The village had no name and apparently no one could think of one—but a name was necessary before asking for a P. O.—finally someone was dispatched to ask the women about it and a belle of the village whose name was Ellen said why not call it after me—Ellenville." According to Katharine T. Terwilliger, the Ellen in question was Ellen Snyder, an attractive young visitor whose death in 1882 was mourned in the village named for her.

The subject was quaint and mildly amusing, just the thing for a noncontroversial mural paid for by taxpayers. New Deal muralists treating historical subjects were expected to do historical research to achieve a level of historical accuracy—especially if President Roosevelt might decide to look over the sketches with a sharp eye for anachronisms. Bouché was frank—he had been unsuccessful in finding old prints of the area that could serve as the basis for his mural. So he was obliged to rely on his sketches of the current landscape, particularly the "mountain background." Since the original site was now crowded with stores, the artist sketched from atop the library, WCTU, and mayor's office. Because portraits of the 1823 participants were not known, Bouché proposed using the faces of current post office staff. Costumed models would also be used. No word reached Washington about the source of the store building that appears in the mural—a wooden building with simple classical details, it is an appropriate backdrop for an 1823 scene, but it is unrelated to the president's Dutch colonial enthusiasms.

The front of the store is populated with three seated men, idle personages of the sort commonly associated with nineteenth-century country stores. More dramatic are the well-dressed men standing in the center and approaching from the left, several with uplifted arms. Bouché represents the moment when Charles Hartshorn, the store owner and soon-to-be postmaster, returns from meeting with ladies of the community and announces that one of them, Miss Ellen Snyder, has offered her own name as the village's. As recounted in Sylvester's *History*, Hartshorn "reported at the store," where "the name was accepted with a shout." Unfortunately, the scene chosen is populated only by men, and so young Ellen (who was living in Dutchess County in 1880) is not herself portrayed.

Bouché was a New York artist with a national reputation. He could be condescending about Ellenville; he told Rowan, "I've met nearly all the big shots of the town and they really don't catch on very quickly." And, like many artists, he found the New Deal's preference for artistic realism annoyingly restrictive. He wrote Rowan sarcastically on another occasion that his sketch of the landscape "looks very much like Ellenville which I think is most important for the future stamp and money order purchases of the community." FDR never scrutinized the sketches, but Rowan quickly approved a color sketch in June 1941. In February 1942, after the attack on Pearl Harbor, Rowan wrote admiringly of the just-completed mural (the mural is signed "Louis Bouché 1942"), which he knew only from a photo. He judged it "a very amusing and entertaining painting with a good deal of life and quiet charm that seems particularly fitting to the time of the scene. ... There is a sweet note of good fellowship and nostalgia ... and I am sure it will be well liked in Ellenville." McDowell considered the mural "beautiful" and told the artist that it "fits perfectly with the style of the building." He and others in town wanted Bouché to paint additional murals in the lobby, but no more were done—Roosevelt's administration was focused on winning the war.

Ellenville's principal historian, Katharine T. Terwilliger, was no fan of Roosevelt and concluded in 1972 that the mural stemmed from the artist's "imagination" rather than historical research. Nevertheless, the Ellenville Post Office and its mural are the outstanding examples of New Deal architecture and public art in Ulster County.

XX-17 Ellenville Reformed Church
188 Canal St. 1852. Augustus Truesdell.

How Augustus Truesdell of Rockville, Connecticut, came to be the architect of Ellenville's Reformed Church remains a mystery. Truesdell (1810–1872), a builder-turned-architect, designed in a variety of styles, including Greek and Italianate. The Avery Library of Columbia University preserves his plans for "a church in the Grecian Style" (1837), but his best-known work is the Jedediah Wilcox mansion (1868–1870) in Meriden, Connecticut, whose grand rear parlor in the Renaissance Revival style is preserved in the

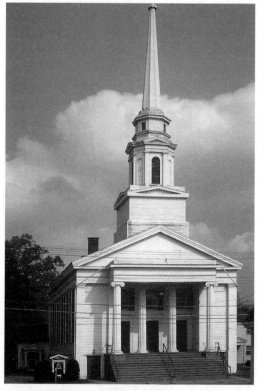

XX-17. Ellenville Reformed Church (1970 photo)

American Wing of the Metropolitan Museum of Art. Perhaps Kingston's Old Dutch Church (1850–1852; see VI–3), designed by New York architect Minard Lafever, stirred Ellenville to seek an architect from beyond the community.

Like Old Dutch, the Ellenville church is crowned with a tall, tapering spire. Ellenville's façade is more closely aligned with the Greek Revival—its broad pediment visually supported by corner pilasters, with two fully rounded Ionic columns placed before the three doorways and arranged in the distyle in antis pattern also found at the Marbletown Reformed Church. The projecting portico (with entablature, but without pediment) is supported by two additional Ionic columns. This portico was apparently added or modified in 1868. The London classical churches of Christopher Wren and James Gibbs, and the American Georgian churches of the followers of Wren and Gibbs, influenced Lafever in designing Old Dutch, while the octagonal pedimented belfry at Ellenville harks back to Georgian towers like St. Paul's Chapel in New York. The Cragsmoor artist E. L. Henry, something of a connoisseur of Georgian architecture, included the tower of the Ellenville church in a number of his paintings, including landscape views where the church was not in fact present.

Unfortunately, many of the wooden classical details have been obscured by the application of siding, and the manse next door, by J. A. Wood, (see next entry, XX–18) has been demolished.

XX–18* Ellenville Reformed Church Parsonage
Canal St. 1872–1874 (extant 1980, not extant 1996). J. A. Wood.

J. A. Wood's mansarded, wood-frame, Second Empire–style parsonage with a small mansarded tower stood alongside the (mostly) Greek Revival church built in 1852 and still in use. Wood's treatment of the parsonage's main bracketed cornice with a series of shallow arches was inventive. Also inventive (or odd) was his use of truncated pilasters with circular motifs in the middle of the second-story walls. By eliminating the lower part

XX-18. Ellenville Reformed Church and Parsonage (lithograph, Beers, Atlas, 1875)

of these pilasters, he denied them their customary function of providing visual if not actual support. His brick Second Empire–style parsonage (1870) for the Methodists of Ellenville survives on Main Street (see XX–13), although no longer housing their pastor.

XX–19* St. Paul's Chapel (St. John's Memorial Episcopal Church)
Market St. 1866 (later altered).

This small Gothic chapel, built of stucco-surfaced stone, is said to have been designed by a "Mr. Upjohn"—either Richard Upjohn or his son, Richard M. Upjohn—although it is not listed in Everard Upjohn's catalogue of their works. It resembled the Episcopal Church of the Holy Trinity (1870–1873) in Highland (see VIII–12). By 1874, Episcopal services moved next door to the new wooden Gothic building of St. John's

XX-19. St. Paul's Chapel (1996 photo)

Memorial Episcopal Church, whose fine interior survives. After years of neglect, St. Paul's Chapel was rebuilt in 2000.

XX–20* Synagogue of the Congregation of the Hebrew Aid Society
Center St. 1909–1910 (not extant).

This building quietly revealed its function by the six-pointed star high on its façade, while the round-arched windows and curved lines of the front gable were also characteristic of early-twentieth-century synagogues in the region. The stuccoed walls and curved gable gave the building something of the flavor of the Mission style of the Southwest. A surviving synagogue in similar style is the Kerhonkson Synagogue at 26 Minnewaska Trail, established in 1922.

At the cornerstone-laying ceremony on April 27, 1909, Morris I. Lewin of New York represented the Hebrew Aid Society and spoke about the history of Jewish synagogues. Another speaker was the Rev. Madison C. Peters, a Protestant minister and author of such works as *Justice to the Jew* (1899), *The Wit and Wisdom of the Talmud* (1900), and *The Jew as a Patriot* (1901). Joseph Slutsky, founder of the Nevele Hotel, was also the founder of the Ellenville Hebrew Aid Society.

XX-20. Synagogue of the Congregation of the Hebrew Aid Society (1980 photo)

XX-21. Ellenville Station, 1892 (Wright photo, 1892)

XX–21* New York, Ontario & Western Railway Station
c. 1891 (not extant). Bradford Lee Gilbert?

This photograph, signed "Wright" and dated "Jan. 27th [18]92," shows New York, Ontario & Western engine No. 66 with passenger coaches behind and the engineer, fireman, conductor and trainmen posing for the photographer. Also posing is an assembly of men and boys at what appears to be a newly built station. The station can be identified as the second O & W station at Ellenville. It was probably designed by Bradford Lee Gilbert (1853–1911), a prominent architect with many railroad stations to his credit, including the Illinois Central Station in Chicago and a remodeling of the Grand Central Terminal that preceded today's terminal in New York. Gilbert was responsible for the Shingle Style O & W station (1892) in Liberty, Sullivan County, that resembled the building pictured by Wright. The latter building can be linked to Ellenville in part by the light-toned blocks of stone below the dark, shingled walls—stone doubtless drawn from the nearby Shawangunks.

When the railroad was opened north from Ellenville to Kingston in 1902, an expanded version of the station served Ellenville. While much altered, this building survives on the north side of Canal Street.

*XX-22. English Lodge
(c. 1940 postcard)*

XX-22* English Lodge at The Fallsview
c. 1940 (not extant).

Ben Slutsky (c. 1900–1974), son of Russian immigrants, was the founder and owner of The Fallsview, one of the renowned Jewish resorts of the Catskills. In 1940 he published this postcard alerting "Smart Vacationists" to the availability of "all seasonal sports on the premises," as well as accommodations in the "English Lodge," a picturesque, multigabled and half-timbered building set apart from the larger and more conventional hotel. The English character of the Lodge might have appealed to those guests who favored assimilation into Anglo-American society and who occupied half-timbered Tudor houses and apartments in and around New York.

XX-23 Schultz House
Oak Ridge Rd. at Rte. 209. 1850s.

The Schultz house, probably built for the wealthy tanner Abram (or Abraham) I. Schultz within a few years prior to his death in 1853, is a fine example of the Italianate style of picturesque architecture. The round-arched windows and doors, mostly grouped in twos and threes, and the low-pitched hipped roof, with bracketed eaves and a low central gable, are characteristic of the style. The octagonal cupola or belvedere, bay windows, extensive veranda, and tall windows opening onto the veranda on the first story, all suggest a house for summer occupation and delight in summer breezes and landscape views. The dark-painted, louvered shutters could be closed when necessary. The Italianate house often had a symmetrical front, as in this case, but retained picturesque qualities in the shadows cast by projecting roofs, in the vertical accents of chimneys and cupola, and in lively details such as the curving cutouts of the brackets beneath the eaves, and the thin boards forming very shallow, hardly Gothic arches between the veranda posts.

XX-23. Schultz House

According to Mary Ann Van Benschoten, Abram I. Schultz owned a successful tannery in Margaretville, Delaware County, in the 1820s, but put it up for sale in 1833. He established a leather store in Manhattan and, by 1837, moved to the Ellenville area. Two years later he purchased land along the Leurenkill, whose water he would use for tanning, and he also purchased land giving him access to the D & H Canal for shipping raw and tanned hides and other materials. His Leurenkill tannery was known especially for its durable and attractively colored "union leather," made by adding oak bark in the usual baths of hemlock bark.

After Abram's death in 1853, his son Judson inherited the Leurenkill tannery and farm and, according to Van Benschoten, "operated the tannery until 1869 when he was forced by a poor economy and depleted hemlocks to move to Wilcox, Pennsylvania," where his brother had a tannery. It was probably in the 1860s, during Judson's ownership, that Conrad Heyd (1837–1912) painted a panoramic view including the white, cupolaed Schultz house and various farm and tannery buildings. Heyd came from his native Germany to New York about 1860 and was active in the city until 1868, when he moved to the Midwest. The painting, which has descended in the Schultz family, portrays the easy transition from forested hills to cultivated fields, to farm and tannery buildings and Schultz's own house. Heyd's view celebrates the harmonious coexistence of nature and civilization, rather than condemning transformations brought on by men like the Schultzes.

Judson Schultz returned to the Leurenkill farm in 1883 and died that year. The Fantinekill Cemetery contains his grave, as well as his father Abram's and a chapel/receiving vault given by Judson's brother, Jackson S. Schultz (see XX–11). Under later owners, the Italianate house became Breeze Lawn, a boardinghouse and then hotel. An advertisement in *The New York Times* (September 12, 1902) sought "boarders ... on one of the finest country places in healthy Ulster County; splendid table, best of service, and large and pleasant rooms; 18-acre farm." Postcards printed thirty or forty years later show the house

at the center of a summer bungalow colony. The Victorian Italianate was downplayed in favor of a "modern bar and cocktail lounge." When sold in 1958, Breeze Lawn Hotel included four main buildings and eight cottages with eighty guest rooms, swimming pool, casino, and eighteen-acre park.

XX–24* Bevier House
Benedict Rd., Leurenkill. Eighteenth century (demolished c. 2005).

When this stone house was demolished, devotees of vernacular architecture regretted its loss as they would any early stone house, but this one had the additional merit of an unusual stone smoke hood. Students of human behavior may remember it as the place whose occupants and condition inspired the historian Helen Wilkinson Reynolds, on the whole a very decent and intelligent person, to fall into a dark state of anti-Semitism when writing her description of the Bevier house, which was occupied by Jews in 1925 when she took a quick look at the exterior. Why so quick? "Like an ant-hill the house and hillside swarmed with the lowest life of the Ghetto and it was tragic to see a once pleasant farmstead in a condition of such indescribable filth and decay that hasty flight from its vicinity was a first thought." (In her travel notes for July 24, 1925, she wrote that the stone house was "in decay, swarming with Jews, house & grounds filthy. No pictorial qualities.")

While exploring Wawarsing, Reynolds found other old landmarks whose decay she blamed on

XX-24. Bevier House (1996 photo)

alien hands. The Coenradt Bevier house in Napanoch was vacant, a "hopeless ... ruin." (It did not survive.) She believed "it is an epitome of life in the Rondout valley from the first settlement to the present time." It spoke of "pioneer" hardships, but also of the comforts enjoyed "in the nineteenth century by native stock, possessed of traditions and a standard of living." Although the house was unoccupied when she visited it, and its owner unknown, she reckoned the "pitiful wreck" had been "abandoned by the fast vanishing native population in the period of the incoming alien." The influx of the alien was accompanied by the allure of "the cheap, frame dwelling, equipped with modern conveniences."

The passing of another stone house, the Jacobus DePuy house in Accord (Town of Rochester), from the good care of elderly DePuy sisters to "a Russian Jew, named Sandak" also distressed Reynolds. Sandak's "youthful summer-boarders from the east side of New York City" surrounded Reynolds's photographer, Margaret Brown. It was "a bit of modern history, sad to those of native stock but full of meaning to be faced and understood." By 1938, Morris Sandak had torn down the old house, except for the foundation on which he erected a new house. (The old house was probably the source of two batten doors, from the "Du Puy House, Accord," sold by Fred Johnston to Henry Francis du Pont in 1936.) Reynolds was more forgiving of the mistreatment of landmarks by "native stock," as when G. Wurts DuBois of New Paltz wrote to her that the Requa house at Libertyville had become quarters for his father's hired men and then declined to a point where the son demolished the house and used its stone as the foundation of a new henhouse.

Reynolds's book was published by the Holland Society of New York, with a foreword by society member Franklin D. Roosevelt. Their pride in their Dutch ancestry was sullied by their prejudice against Jews and immigrants, and especially against those without the education and income to become aware of the value of America's old buildings and with perhaps differing standards of tidiness.

XX–25 Brodhead House
8595 Rte. 209, Leurenkill. c. 1753–1779 and mid-nineteenth century.

Here is a clear example of how colonial-era stone houses might be altered in the Victorian period. Helen Reynolds dated the Brodheads' original L-shaped stone house 1753, and the frame addition to the rear 1842. Sometime during the mid-nineteenth century, the Brodheads applied Gothic Revival elements—especially the lightly curving bargeboards of the several gables. These raised the stature of the house from old and venerable (from long association with one family), but painfully plain, to something admirably picturesque. Calvert Vaux, a leading architect of the time who had strong family links to Rondout, expressed just this belief when he altered the old Thomas Powell house near Newburgh.

The Brodheads owned and occupied the house into the early twentieth century when Henry Brodhead adorned the grounds with a sculpture of *The Boy with a Boot* by the J. L. Mott Foundry

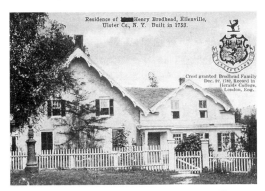

XX-25. Brodhead House (c. 1920 postcard)

XX-25A. Brodhead House with Dowe Shanty (c. 1930 postcard)

and Iron Works, of which he was or had been paymaster. At this time a postcard of Henry's house was printed with the Brodhead crest. In 1925, when Reynolds visited the house, she found a stone on the front or west wall marked "IB AB / 1753 / 1842 / HB 1915". She noted that the two "'eyebrow' windows" set into the roof at the front of the house were its "only noteworthy feature"—apparently she thought them eighteenth century, which seems unlikely. The fact that the exterior had been "altered and modernized" with Victorian additions eliminated the house from inclusion in her book. But worse things were to come. Frank P. Dowe, who owned the Brodhead property in the 1920s, took advantage of the highway that passed directly in front of the old house and operated a sandwich and soda shop in a shanty across the road. Dowe advertised his business with a postcard depicting autos full of hungry motorists stopping at the roadside shanty with the old house and farm buildings made to serve as a quaint background.

Cragsmoor (NR Historic District) and Sam's Point Preserve

XX-26* Edward Lamson Henry and Frances Henry House, Na-pee-nia
1883–1884 (altered later).
Edward Lamson Henry.

E. L. Henry (1841–1919) was the first artist to build on the Shawangunk ridge above Ellenville and was a founder (along with his wife Frances, also an artist, though she rarely exhibited) of what became known as the Cragsmoor art colony. Before 1880 artists summered at scattered points in the Catskills and Hudson Valley, but in the 1880s they began to cluster in colonies, Cragsmoor being among the first in the region. After spending several summers in the Ellenville area as a boarder, Henry purchased land on the ridge in 1883, and the next year his studio-house was under construction, of his own design and built by local carpenter Joseph E. Mance. Henry, a member of the National Academy of Design and an occupant of the Tenth Street Studio Building in New York, was drawn to the summit of the Shawangunks by the grand view—his house had several flat roofs that served as lookouts. But he was also attracted to southern Ulster County by its old-fashioned buildings and people, which he depicted in his widely admired, minutely detailed paintings of historical genre subjects and country life. He collected furniture, costumes, carriages, and harnesses—all to enhance the accuracy of his paintings. He also gathered architectural fragments from old houses being demolished in New York.

Much altered in the twentieth century, Henry's house was originally a fine specimen of the Queen Anne style. Its quaintness was enhanced with old building fragments, including a door, staircase, columns, and mantel sent by boat up

XX-26. Henry House (c. 1900 photo)

the Hudson from New York to Kingston, then through the D & H Canal to Ellenville, and finally by ox cart to the mountaintop. The exterior walls of boards below and shingles above, with a variety of window shapes, ornamental urns, spindles, and balusters, compressed many of the features of a Queen Anne mansion into a building of modest dimensions. According to one account, the local carpenters objected to Henry's design, fearing that, "If you have the rafters show like that ... and stick the roof all over with little gables, you'll make your studio look like one of them old Dutch manor-houses at Kingston." The comment no doubt pleased and amused Henry, but in fact the old Dutch houses were much simpler than Henry's with its abundance of picturesque protrusions. Henry portrayed his picturesque house and its picturesque garden in a small painting, *The Henry Home at Cragsmoor*, dated June 25, 1892 (New York State Museum, Albany). The Queen Anne style was at the time commonly believed to be identifiable with a loosely defined old Colonial style. Henry's house not only echoed his preference for painting antiquarian subjects, but also provided an appropriate setting to inspire his painted recreations of an earlier America.

Like many who were nostalgic for old-fashioned times and ways, Henry was unhappy with the influx of immigrants into New York City and complained about the "enormous sewage of Europe now here." So it seems that Cragsmoor's appeal for Henry included its scarcity of immigrant families as well as its fine vistas, cool breezes, and inhabitants of long American ancestry, whether local people or summer colonists. Cragsmoor, like many other summer colonies of the period, did not welcome Jews. A 1905 brochure for the Cragsmoor Inn advised that "Persons suffering from pulmonary diseases can not be entertained. Owing to neighborhood preferences Hebrews will not be received." The artist's ideal of the simple, quiet life in the country home is perhaps best seen in his painting, *Mrs. E. L. Henry on the Porch* (c. 1914), where neither sublime, overpowering nature, nor the foul city intrude upon his wife's tranquility as she tends the flowering plants that screen her from the world beyond.

XX-27 Mountain Methodist Church (Cragsmoor Federated Church; now Cragsmoor Historical Society)
Cragsmoor Rd. c. 1880 and c. 1908.

The modest design of the Federated Church stands out as a statement for plain, Protestant worship in contrast to the bold Gothic forms of Cragsmoor's Episcopal Chapel of the Holy Name. As seen from Cragsmoor Road about 1915, the low, unpainted, wood-shingle walls (white paint and asphalt shingles came later) of the front of the Federated Church could belong to a house were it not for the low belfry off to the side and the diamond, Gothic panes of the windows.

The Federated Church grew out of the Mountain Methodist Church, which in 1880 held its first service in a simple Greek Revival structure defined architecturally as a church by the low belfry atop the pediment of its façade. It is surprising that the Greek Revival was chosen for new construction as late as 1880. This structure (minus the belfry) survives behind the additions made by the Federated Church in the early 1900s. In 1906 the artist George Inness, Jr., led an effort to find a religious society to serve people of several denominations. Leaders of the Federated Church movement in New York City were consulted, and the Mountain Methodist Church was acquired to become a nondenominational place of worship. The earlier church was extended toward the road for the larger summer congregation and for social events,

XX-27. Mountain Methodist Church (1970 photo)

and a new tower and entrance were built on the north side. The cost of the extension was borne by Mrs. Inness. Among the church elders was artist Charles Curran. Since the 1980s the restoration and reuse of the church has been an important project of the Cragsmoor Historical Society.

XX–28 Cragsmoor Free Library
Cragsmoor Rd. 1922–1925.
Frederick S. Dellenbaugh.

The Cragsmoor Free Library is strongly identified with its architect, Frederick Dellenbaugh (1853–1935). Designer of many buildings at Cragsmoor, Dellenbaugh was not a professional architect but a man of several talents, among them artist, author, and explorer (on Major John Wesley Powell's second expedition down the Colorado River). Not only did Dellenbaugh design the library building (his drawings for the plan and façade of the building survive at the library), but he also gave the land and placed its cornerstone. Dellenbaugh designed the tall, three-arched façade with a freedom not found in his Upjohn-inspired Chapel of the Holy Name. The façade's columns, actually chestnut logs, do not follow standard classical rules, but in their elongation, irregularity of surface, and abbreviated capitals are rustic versions of classical forms, and so suitable to the mountaintop. Also significant of the Shawangunks are the rough stonework of the foundation and the polychrome pebbles of the stucco walls. The cramped spacing of the paired columns and adjacent half-columns seems a sign of Dellenbaugh's amateur status as an architect. Like some nineteenth-century, Greek Revival churches, the original entrance door was to the side of the central recessed porch, but un-Greek are the segmental arches over the windows and joining the columns.

The interior is worth a detour during library open hours. Light is muted through the east window of tinted, translucent glass with three, small, stained-glass panels of subjects appropriate to a mountaintop library—a bird, a flower, and a reader (in this case a reading monk, not inappropriate given the strongly Christian aspect of the colony in its early days). These panels are attributed to the

XX-28. Cragsmoor Free Library (1970 photo)

Lamb Studio, which later was responsible for the rose window Dellenbaugh donated to the Chapel of the Holy Name. Two rows of unpainted chestnut log columns define the alcoves for bookshelves and help support the gallery (added in 1926 or 1927) and roof. Simple trusses rise over paired columns across the "nave." This nave leads not to a chancel, but to a monumental fireplace whose overmantle is a plaster copy of a panel from Luca della Robbia's 1431 marble singing-gallery in Florence Cathedral. Above the overmantle looms a chimney of native stone. Lawrence Keir was the mason responsible for the stonework of this great vertical secular altarpiece celebrating the beauty and vitality of children.

Functioning today as a mural in the nave is George Inness, Jr.'s, large framed canvas, *The Rainbow*, originally placed next door in the Federated Church. Also prominent is Charles Curran's *Blue and Gold* (c. 1929; on permanent loan), depicting handsome local youths atop the ridge. Curran served with Dellenbaugh and Inness's wife Julia on the library's building committee. Small paintings by Dellenbaugh are crowded on the wall of the narrow stairs that rise to the balcony, where there is a cotton wall hanging, designed by Helen Turner and sewed by her sister Laurette (Lettie) about 1910, that depicts Turner's cottage, Takusan (see X–35).

This library has no bright, efficient, and sterile room designed for gazing into computer screens. Rather, it has the aura of both a sacred space and an old-fashioned, wonderfully cluttered historical society (with computers). Its users find a friendly neighborhood center whose hearth still radiates warmth at Valentine's Day festivities.

XX-29 Orchard Cottage
Cragsmoor Rd. at Dellenbaugh Rd. c. 1824 (1902 altered by Frederick S. Dellenbaugh).

Orchard Cottage, one of Cragsmoor's oldest houses, stands at its key intersection, diagonally opposite the architecturally uninteresting post office (dedicated 1960) which, like the nearby library, serves as a center of community life. According to Harry Hansen, an English carpenter by the name of John Whitmore, Jr., purchased the house site in 1824, and the building was probably erected that year. Hansen has also found that: "in 1833 the property was sold ... and ... operated as the 'Mountain House' with a basement tavern for travelers on the Ellenville & Newburgh Turnpike (now Cragsmoor Road). George Bleakley and John Nobel purchased the house in 1862 to run a farm, but soon began to take in summer boarders; among them were some of the later key individuals of the art colony: Mr. and Mrs. E. L. Henry ... and others." In the 1890s Cragsmoor's first post office was built as an extension of the house to the north. This post office was recorded in a painting by LeGrand W. Botsford (at the Cragsmoor Free Library), but was later removed. "In 1902 the land was purchased and subdivided by Frederick Dellenbaugh into what he

XX-29. Orchard Cottage

called 'Bleakley Fields.' ... in 1905 Miss Belle Dellenbaugh, his sister, bought the house and in 1910 extensively remodeled it using her brother as architect." From the time of Belle Dellenbaugh's ownership, the house has been called Orchard Cottage.

The original one-and-a-half-story wood-frame house with hand-hewn beams has received a number of additions, but the early tavern fireplace survives in the basement. Dellenbaugh's hand is apparent in the dormer windows rising from the front wall (as in his own house, Endridge), as well as in the porte cochère to the north, which replaced the post office. Belle Dellenbaugh's bookplate (Cragsmoor Free Library), apparently designed by her brother Frederick, depicts a pleasantly overgrown wall and steps leading from the road to the cottage, and bears the heading, "Over land and water blown, I come back to find my own," which is also inscribed over a fireplace in the cottage.

XX-30 Judge Addison Brown and Helen Gaskin Brown House, The Boulders
Henry Rd. and Schuyler Ave. 1898. Frederick S. Dellenbaugh.

This imposing Shingle Style house has been described by Barbara Buff as "one of Cragsmoor's more fantastic houses." Like a standard Shingle Style house, The Boulders combines lower walls of stone with upper ones of weathered wood shingles, and its picturesque composition includes a variety of roof slopes, window types, and projecting bays and porches. Dellenbaugh was an amateur, not a professional architect, and the composition of the façade seems a little disjointed in comparison to the Shingle Style works of masters like McKim, Mead & White, or William Ralph Emerson. Buff attributed the house's fantastic quality to its "variety of building materials," which Judge Addison Brown (1830–1913) found interesting enough to describe in his autobiographical notes: "The stone work was done by 'Tony' an eccentric Italian, whose treatment of the joints of the rough mason work were [*sic*] new in this region."

Just as curiously, The Boulders incorporates wooden elements from several demolished

XX-30. The Boulders

buildings in New York. Judge Brown himself identified the source of the front door and its surround of delicate Ionic columns and leaded-glass sidelights as "an old building, No. 69 Christie St., New York City, then recently torn down, but originally built about 1825." To the left of the front door is a built-in paneled seat with small oval window above—a charming but incongruous adjunct to the doorway. The dining room's wooden moldings, according to the judge, also were recovered from early New York buildings. The inclusion of bits rescued from demolished structures was not unknown in Queen Anne and Shingle Style work. Such inclusions especially appealed to antiquarians like the artist E. L. Henry, who had initiated the practice locally in 1883 at his house (see XX–26).

Addison Brown was a Harvard-trained jurist who served as a federal judge for the Southern District of New York from 1881 to 1901. A founder of the New York Botanical Garden, Brown's interests in botany and astronomy could be cultivated atop the Shawangunks. The inclusion of fragments of old New York architecture in his house reflected his enthusiasm for the city's history—he was a member of the New-York Historical Society. Also a member of the Sons of the American Revolution, Brown was proud of his early colonial ancestry, counting the Rev. John Rogers, Harvard's president in 1682, and Thomas Dudley, second governor of Massachusetts, among his forebears. Brown and Dellenbaugh were both members of the Century Association, the elite New York club for men active in or supportive of the arts.

After the death of his first wife, Judge Brown married Helen Carpenter Gaskin (c. 1862–1943), a teacher of natural science, in 1893. She, too, was of old Massachusetts ancestry, descending from Governor John Winthrop. She retained the Cragsmoor residence until her death, and descendants of the Browns are to be commended for preserving The Boulders down to the present.

XX–31 Chapel of the Holy Name (The Stone Church)
Henry Rd. 1895–1897.
Frederick S. Dellenbaugh.

The rugged boulder walls of this chapel seem appropriate to the site atop the stony Shawangunk ridge. Aside from the boulder masonry, Dellenbaugh's design resembles Episcopal churches by Richard Upjohn from mid-century. Dellenbaugh's patron was Eliza Hartshorn, a wealthy resident of Providence and Newport who was related to E. L. Henry's wife Frances and Frederick Dellenbaugh's wife Harriet. (Mrs. Hartshorn's summer house at Cragsmoor, Ruhberg [1887], was designed by Dellenbaugh and stands in altered form just west of the church.) She recommended as a model the Upjohn-like design of St. Paul's Episcopal Chapel (1866) in Ellenville. Holy Name Chapel is in fact more similar to Upjohn's Christ Church, Marlborough (see X–2), where a tower is placed at the southwest corner of the nave, which is entered from the base of the tower, and where the chancel is attached to the east end of the nave. Lancet arch-

*XX-31. Chapel of the Holy Name
(c. 1940 postcard)*

es are separated by wall buttresses as in Upjohn's work. But here the massive walls, slit windows, and crenellated battlement of the tower project something of the air of a mountaintop fortress.

The original head mason was the Scotsman John Kier. He died of consumption before the church was completed, and his place was taken by an assistant, Tony Rosa, and Italian masons from New York City. The blocky and rough stone crosses alongside the nave commemorate the Rev. Martin Albert (1833–1913) and his wife Catharine Albert (1840–1904). In New York, Martin Albert served a little-known group of German-speaking Episcopalians as a mission of Trinity Church for more than thirty years.

The interior walls are unplastered and continue the rugged stonework of the exterior, but otherwise the interior resembles Upjohn's churches in its Gothic plan and fine stained-glass windows. The window depicting St. James (with shell on his pilgrim staff) was given in memory of Isaac Hartshorn (1804–1877) by his widow, Eliza Hartshorn. The chapel was intended for Cragsmoor residents, but particularly served the community known as the Ruhberg ("Mount of Rest" or "Mountain Rest"), which Hartshorn modeled on the Hospice of St. Bernard in Switzerland and established next to the church in the house that she had built in 1887 and in other buildings. In 1896 the Brothers of Nazareth, a lay order of the Episcopal Church, maintained at the Ruhberg three cottages and recreation buildings "for young men of moderate means," although the boys and men served by the order seem

to have been both poor and sick. In E. L. Henry's painting, *Vespers* (1892; private collection), the radiant, idyllic landscape is populated with two men in religious garb, while behind them is the chapel. To its left is Mrs. Hartshorn's 1887 house, and to its right a house, Hillcrest (1897), built into the side of the hill as the residence of Father Daniel O'Dell, director of the Brothers of Nazareth, who was brought to Cragsmoor by his friend Mrs. Hartshorn.

The rose window in the west gable of the chapel, designed by Katharine Lamb and executed by J. and R. Lamb Studios in 1932, was donated by Dellenbaugh in memory of his wife, Harriet Otis Dellenbaugh (1855–1930), an actress and dramatic reader. The Dellenbaughs had been married in 1885 in Ellenville by the Rev. Henry Ward Beecher, a friend of the bride's family. The window is inscribed "Her Smile Was Like a Benediction." The chapel has been well restored in recent years, and is understandably a popular site for weddings, fees for which have helped pay restoration costs.

The chapel stands near the edge of a plateau, but not directly above the precipice as Dellenbaugh had hoped. A memorial arch (to Julia N. West, 1931) a few yards from the church is very close to that precipice and frames a magnificent view over Mount Meenhaga, Ellenville, and the Rondout Valley to the distant Catskills.

XX–32 Frederick S. Dellenbaugh and Harriet Otis Dellenbaugh House, Endridge
Schuyler Ave. 1892. Frederick S. Dellenbaugh.

The modest but excellent Shingle Style house Frederick Dellenbaugh designed for himself and

XX-32. Endridge (c. 1900 photo)

his wife Harriet (an actress from a well-to-do El-lenville family) stands on land given to him by Mrs. Hartshorn in recognition of his design of the Chapel of the Holy Name. The house is tightly composed in contrast to the larger and later Brown house he designed nearby. Here, too, local rubble stone lies below and around lighter shingled walls, bays, and oriels. Large windows are placed on the west to take advantage of the vast mountaintop view. (An early photo of Endridge indicates that the window to the left of the bay window replaced an open porch, and there have been other changes in fenestration.)

The combination of local stone and unpaint-ed shingles is common in the Shingle Style and helps integrate the building with its landscape site. Dellenbaugh was conscious of the "moulding ef-fects of the environment ... in the forms and ma-terials of the dwellings" of American Indians. He was also well versed in the local vernacular tradi-tion of log construction. John Burroughs, a guest of the Dellenbaughs about 1905, must have found Dellenbaugh a congenial spirit.

XX–33 Eliza Hartshorn House, The Barnacle
Schuyler Ave. Built c. 1889 as barn (converted to residence c. 1905 by Frederick S. Dellenbaugh).

Eliza Hartshorn, according to Barbara Buff, "built a succession of houses, barns, public build-ings, and roads, using Frederick Dellenbaugh as her architect." This house, originally a barn, was moved to the present site and transformed for Mrs. Hartshorn by Dellenbaugh into a guest or boarding house. With its walls and even its porch posts surfaced with wood shingles, it resembles the coastal Shingle Style houses of Newport where Mrs. Hartshorn also summered. The Barnacle conjures up buildings by the sea, but the word also playfully alludes to the house's barn origins.

Note above the second-story windows the subtle adjustments to the roof slopes and gable end wall. The massive chimney of local stone is charac-teristic of Dellenbaugh's Cragsmoor buildings.

XX–34 Charles C. and Grace Curran House, Winahdin
Hartshorn Rd. 1907.
Frederick S. Dellenbaugh.

This house, built for the painter Charles C. Curran (1861–1942) and his wife Grace, dates from the decade when the art colony and new construction were at their peak in Cragsmoor. In its design, Del-lenbaugh (collaborating with the owners and the builder, Bert Goldsmith) avoided picturesque com-plications in favor of a one-story, shingled rectangle capped with a gambrel roof. Its simple shape can be compared to Arts and Crafts bungalows of the period. The view over the Rondout Valley to the Catskills suggested the inclusion of a broad porch resting on stone piers and set back under the lower slope of the gambrel. Curran's daughter Emily re-called "the large front porch served as part of the living quarters—we sat, rested, played and ate there, even at times slept there." The balconied dormers also are oriented to the expansive vista.

XX-33. The Barnacle (1978 photo)

XX-34. Winahdin

The name of the house, Winahdin, is said to stem from an Indian word for "wide view."

Curran was an advocate of Impressionist light and color, merged with carefully described form. A number of his popular paintings (including *Blue and Gold*, on view in the Cragsmoor library) depict healthy, blond young women in the bracing air at Bear Cliff in the vicinity of this house. The ugly poverty of the city and the blood of distant wars seem remote from this pleasant place, but the artist and his wife supported Red Cross work in World War I, and one of their sons fought in that war. Curran and his sons carved the motto of the house, from Psalm 72, on a flat, square stone over the mantelpiece of the studio-living room: "The mountains shall bring peace to the people."

XX–35 Helen M. Turner House and Studio, Takusan
Dellenbaugh Rd. c. 1910. Helen M. Turner.

Helen M. Turner (1858–1958), an Impressionist painter, designed her small house and studio about 1910. It was built on land purchased from Frederick Dellenbaugh, who may have assisted with the design. She had been introduced to Cragsmoor by fellow Impressionist Charles Curran and his wife Grace, whose house (1907) Dellenbaugh had designed (see preceding entry, XX–34). Bert Goldsmith was Turner's builder, as he had been Curran's.

The front of Takusan is represented in a hand-appliquéd cotton wall hanging (in the Cragsmoor Free Library) designed by Helen Turner and sewed by her sister, Lettie (Laurette) Turner. Here Takusan is shown with red-painted board-and-batten walls as in the house today and as in mid-nineteenth-century cottages by A. J. Downing and A. J. Davis, although Takusan lacks the picturesque adornments favored by the earlier period. "Takusan" relates to the Japanese for "more" or "many," yet perhaps the spare quality of the design also stems from Japan. (The screened pavilion attached to the east side of the house is a later addition.)

Turner's north-facing studio on the second floor could not have been large, but it was called "magnificent" by the local newspaper in 1910. Several of Turner's most successful paintings show handsome young women on Takusan's porch with its white railing and her carefully cultivated flower garden behind. Some of the cheerful porch paintings prominently include her bright green Dutch door—the lower half paneled and fitted with a door knocker, the upper half mostly four panes of glass in sturdy muntins. *Summer* (1913) was created on her porch and won a prize at the National Academy of Design, which elected her an associate in 1913 and a full member in 1921; Turner was only the fourth woman Academician since its founding in 1826.

Before building Takusan, Turner occupied a cottage owned by a Miss Brodhead, who had several rustic cottages on the grounds of the present post office. A rustic building, with vertical logs at the corners and walls of logs or slabs, appearing in an early photo has been identified as Takusan, but probably depicts the Brodhead cottage occupied by Turner before 1910. Other Brodhead cottages were similar in scale and rusticity. Dellenbaugh, whose architectural taste was dominant in Cragsmoor at the time, had published an essay in 1901 on log houses in Russell

Sturgis's *Dictionary of Architecture*, with sketches of a vernacular example he had found in the Shawangunk Mountains.

XX–36 Office of Mary Harley, M.D.
Dellenbaugh Rd. c. 1905?

This one-room, one-story building is now forlorn, but once was the summertime office of Dr. Mary Harley, whose rustic log cabin residence, Windy Hearth, was on this parcel until torn down about 1989. The office, with its rough walls of local stone and its many windows, resembles a sunny garden pavilion more than a forbidding doctor's office. Helen Turner, whose studio-house Takusan is nearby, was a friend of Harley and painted her portrait about 1931. Harley was a physician at Vassar College before going to Sweet Briar College in 1906, where she spent some thirty years as physician and professor of physiology.

XX-36. Harley Office

XX–37* George Inness, Jr., Estate, Chetolah
Vista Maria Rd. Begun 1901.
Howard Greenley. NR

The Inness estate was Cragsmoor's grandest residence, designed by a thoroughly trained professional architect rather than the amateur Frederick Dellenbaugh, who was responsible for so many Cragsmoor buildings. George Inness, Jr., (1854–1926) was the son of George Inness (1825–1894), one of America's great landscape painters, whose subjects included the Shawan-

gunks. The son was himself an accomplished painter of landscapes influenced by his father's late, heavily atmospheric style. Inness, Jr., was married to Julia Roswell-Smith, daughter of a founder of *Scribner's Monthly*.

Chetolah, before being acquired and improved by Inness, was the property of Eliza Greatorex, a painter, member of the National Academy of Design, and early resident of the art colony. Greatorex lived in a farmhouse on some seventy acres that she named Chetolah, said to be an Indian word for "love." Inness eventually expanded the estate to include about 350 acres on Cragsmoor's eastern ridge with views of the Wallkill and Hudson River valleys. In 1903, when construction was still underway, *The New York Times* reported that at his estate Inness "is famed among his friends and fellow-painters for his hospitality and lavish entertainment." When put up for sale in 1929, the buildings included the main house of twenty rooms, and ten cottages with between four and eight rooms.

Today, only the romantically turreted gatehouse (deriving from French châteaux and H. H. Richardson) is visible on Vista Maria Road, but the appearance of the main house and its formal gardens is well known from early-twentieth-century postcards. The main house, with metal roof and walls of shingle, stucco, and cobblestone, consisted of a substantial two-story, hip-roofed block with a wing to either side. The west wing, added in 1905, was devoted to Inness's studio and gallery. In 1906 the *Times* noted that "George Inness, Jr., who owns a palatial studio among the mountains ... has a fine art gallery in his mountain home, containing many of his father's masterpieces." Inness also maintained a studio a short distance from the main house in a shingle-sided structure whose main room rose to a cathedral ceiling, with a balcony and fireplace on the west wall, a broad window facing the valley to the south, and (standard for a painter's studio) a large north-facing window, here about twelve feet wide and eight feet high.

The land sloping down from the main house was reworked into a series of Italian-inspired terraces bounded by rugged stone walls. Near the house were flower beds and a terrace fitted with a white-columned pergola—a setting for refined, upper-class enjoyment of the outdoors, which Frank Russell Green recorded in a painting about 1910. A vintage photo of the interior hallway shows a sequence of paired Ionic columns. While the exterior of the main house is not especially classical, there are enough columns elsewhere and sufficient formality in the plan to suggest the hand of a classically trained designer, as well as the taste of a classically minded patron. Inness had been born in Paris, partly trained there, and maintained a studio in Paris from 1895 to 1899. In 1900 the Paris Salon awarded him a gold medal, and in 1902 he was honored as an officer of the Academie des Beaux-Arts. Chetolah's architect, Howard Greenley (1874–1963), was linked to Inness by marriage in 1903 when Greenley married Inness's daughter Elizabeth. Both Greenley and Inness had experienced success in the Parisian academic system. Greenley worked for the Paris-trained architects Carrere & Hastings in New York before going to Paris in the 1890s for his own training at the École des Beaux-Arts. The French government awarded him an architectur-

al diploma in 1901. About 1902 Greenley began his own highly successful practice in New York, designing the Prince George Hotel (with murals by George Inness, Jr.) in the city, and estates on Long Island and in Newport, Rhode Island.

XX–38 Shacks of Huckleberry Pickers
**Sam's Point Rd., Sam's Point Preserve.
c. 1920–1960.**

A few tumble-down shacks may remain for the visitor to Sam's Point Preserve from the summer community of huckleberry-picking families who came from New York City and urban parts of New Jersey to the cooler elevations of the Shawangunk ridge. In contrast to the mountain-house guests at Lakes Mohonk and Minnewaska and the cottage-dwellers at Cragsmoor, the berry pickers were obliged to work atop the ridge, one person gathering as many as twenty-five to thirty quarts a day. Still, a certain romance has become attached to their lives and these shacks. The Nature Conservancy, in collaboration with the Open Space Institute, announces that it "is committed to preserving Sam's Point and

XX-37. Chetolah (c. 1909 postcard)

the Shawangunk Ridge—the lands the berry pickers once called a home away from home." It notes with regret that "the huckleberry communities of the 20s and 30s may be lost forever." Not that the shacks, or the tents and lean-tos that also made up the community, were architectural treasures, but the lives of these poor city dwellers were somehow better and happier on the ridge, "where budding romances, new friendships, and past reunions rose and fell over the flicker of a campfire and the course of a short, sweet summer."

XX-38. Huckleberry Picker Shack

XXI

Town of Woodstock

Formed from part of the Town of Hurley, 1787.

Population: 2,012 in 1870; 6,241 in 2000.

Alf Evers, the Catskill region's foremost historian, showed how Woodstock was transformed from a rural backwater, lacking both canal and railroad, to an American cultural center (whose importance is not reflected in the small population of permanent residents) thanks largely to Ralph Radcliffe Whitehead's establishment of the Byrdcliffe colony in 1902. Thirty years earlier the village of Woodstock had about fifty houses, three churches, and several commercial and industrial enterprises, notably a tannery able to turn out 16,000 sides of leather annually. But in the 1870s fashionable summer visitors were already being attracted to the Overlook Mountain House, a mountaintop hotel above the village, with the assertion that "the view from the summit is not surpassed in grandeur, beauty and extent of scenery by any other point in the state"—a claim sure to rankle devotees of the Catskill Mountain House in Greene County.

XXI-1 Woodstock Reformed Church
Tinker St. 1842.

The steeple of the Reformed Church rises above Woodstock in Earle B. Winslow's painting, *Tannery Brook* (1928; Woodstock Artists Association and Museum), and many other works of art depicting the hamlet, despite the fact, as *Life* noted in 1938, that "few artists attend." The white steeple and classical portico of the façade on the village green have long stood for the authentic, traditional, American roots of Woodstock, the art colony that sometimes embraced, sometimes challenged, American traditions.

In 1925 the writer of a humorous column for the local paper, *The Hue and Cry*, reported that the Reformed Church was being joined by other examples of the revival of Greek architecture; a new post office and Twadell House, with their own Grecian porticoes, were supposed to be part

XXI-1. Woodstock Reformed Church (Stowell Studios photo, c. 1928)

of an effort to transform the village green into "a modern Acropolis," where "pagan Greece invades Christian Woodstock." The article was illustrated with a sketch of the Parthenon (mis)identified as the new post office, and pious churchgoers, confused by the similar porticoes, were said to be trying to enter the post office on Sunday mornings.

XXI-2 Woodstock Artists Association Gallery
28 Tinker St. 1919–1921. William A. Boring, architect; Griffin Herrick, builder.

In 1920, when planning of the Woodstock Artists Association Gallery was underway, Carl Eric Lindin, a painter and a founder of the WAA, observed that just as Woodstock artists were divided between advocates of "the new and the old, between the realistic the romantic and the decorative," so the gallery's architectural "style [might] be Greek, Colonial, or Soviet." In fact, Soviet or international modernism made no inroads in Woodstock this early in the century, and the artists of the WAA favored a "colonial façade."

The gallery's façade, designed by William A. Boring, appropriately drew upon local mid-nineteenth-century vernacular examples of the Greek Revival (loosely called "Colonial" at the time), since the landscape paintings and prints of its artist members routinely recorded local vernacular buildings, and their own houses and studios were often old or new examples of this vernacular tradition. Then, too, Neilson (or Nelson) Parker—not an artist, but involved with the purchase of the land for the gallery—resided in a stone Georgian–Federal Revival house (again broadly within the Colonial category) he had built about 1912–1914. (The artist Zulma Steele married Parker in 1926, and after his death in 1928 she retained ownership of the house, on Chestnut Hill Road, until her death in 1979.)

Boring's façade is an expanded version of a story-and-a-half, white-painted, Greek Revival house with corner pilasters. He altered the prototype to be appropriate for an art gallery, both by enlarging the overall dimensions and by adding decoration—a classical pediment over the

XXI-2. Woodstock Artists Association Gallery (c. 1980 photo)

XXI-3 Woodstock Town Hall and Fire Station
76 Tinker St. 1936–1938. Albert Graeser.

This unassuming seat of town government resembles countless Colonial Revival town halls across the country, its modest classical portico harking back to the architecture of the early Republic, but with a nod to the local Greek Revival of the Dutch Reformed Church down the street—the distinction between "Colonial" and "Greek Revival" was commonly ignored. As Alf Evers wrote, the 1938 Town Hall had "an acceptable Colonial aspect"— it was in good taste. While the architectural design may be bland, the controversy initially surrounding the building was not.

central doorway—and substituting oval windows for simple rectangular ones above the main story. Interestingly, the Arts and Crafts, or rustic approach, of Byrdcliffe and the Maverick appears to have had no support when the design was under consideration. This would accord with the nationwide decline of the Arts and Crafts and rise of the Colonial Revival after about 1915.

Boring was a well-known New York architect, codesigner of the main building on Ellis Island before becoming head of Columbia University's School of Architecture in 1915. It was thanks to his friendship with Birge Harrison, one of the earliest and most influential Woodstock artists, that Boring agreed to take on this small but highly visible commission. His experience included training in classical design at the École des Beaux-Arts in Paris and work in the office of the great classical architects McKim, Mead & White, and so he was a firm believer in turning to historical precedent within the classical tradition. But Boring also opposed strict imitation of the past. In 1925 he wrote Charles S. Keefe, the Kingston and New York architect, acknowledging receipt of Keefe's book picturing recent American houses, while also spelling out for Keefe the value of freely adapting various types of early-American precedent: "We are so rushed that we must not be held to the restrictions of Colonial days. We lack their good taste, of course, but we have more material wealth and this is bound to come out in our architecture." In this way he could justify modifying homely Greek Revival sources for the twentieth-century art gallery.

The new Town Hall and Fire Station were built without federal funds, a reflection of the suspicion and distrust with which the majority of Woodstock voters viewed Franklin Roosevelt and the New Deal; FDR was trounced by Landon in Woodstock in the 1936 election—817 for Landon and 418 for Roosevelt. That same year Carl Eric Lindin, artist, civic leader, and Democrat, announced a plan to build a community center in Woodstock featuring a Colonial Revival design in bluestone or brick by Teller & Halverson, with most of the $81,000 cost coming from the WPA. The community center would have three major components—an auditorium/theatre, town offices, and a gallery for the exhibit of the Woodstock Artists Association's permanent collection. Fatal opposition arose from Republicans who hated the New Deal, doubted the WPA would fulfill its commitments, and feared federal funds would result in New Deal meddling in town affairs. Firemen also felt left out by Lindin's proposal and wanted something better than their antiquated fire hall on Tinker Street. So, in spring 1937, the town board and firemen put before the voters an alternate proposal to spend $32,000 on a town hall (including town offices and auditorium) and fire station on the site of the old fire hall. There would be no art gallery and no federal funds. The voters backed this proposal by a more than two to one margin.

Lindin also supported a centralized school to be constructed with Public Works Administration

XXI-3. Woodstock Town Hall and Fire Station (drawing by Graeser, Overlook, 1938)

money and designed by Teller & Halverson. Voters again spurned this idea. Judson P. Philips, a backer of Lindin, wrote about how:

> the new Town Hall–Fire House ... came into being. Everyone knows that the local politicians, fearful that the Lindin-proposed Community Center or the Centralized School, or both, might be pushed through ... knowing that either one of these propositions would be in a sense a monument to Democratic or New Deal politics ... knowing that neither one of these propositions would ever reflect any glory on them ... smartly checkmated both schemes by rushing through the Town Hall–Fire House scheme.

Albert Graeser (born 1903), Town Hall's architect, had designed a number of Colonial Revival houses in Woodstock, including Mary and Ernest Early's (1934; see XXI–15). Trained at Pratt and NYU, Graeser and his family were summer residents in Woodstock, and their social life was often mentioned in the local newspaper. Kingston architect Albert E. Milliken submitted a town hall design that was supported by a committee of firemen, but Graeser ultimately won the support of the firemen as well as the town board. Milliken complained that Graeser was merely a summer resident, while he, a full-time Kingstonian, would better supervise the job. The town clerk defended Graeser's selection, as he was the only registered architect who

was a resident taxpayer in Woodstock. Later Graeser designed the "semi-modern" elementary school (1950) across from the golf course; it was to serve only the village of Woodstock, because voters had rejected a central school district.

Dedicated in March 1939, Town Hall lacked the cupola Graeser had designed but for which there were no funds. A weathervane representing a seventeenth-century, three-masted vessel was fashioned by Ned Thatcher, "master metal craftsman" in Woodstock since 1902, and funded by the Federal Art Project. With no cupola to serve as a base, the weathervane was stowed away in the town clerk's vault. Judson Smith, closely associated with the New Deal as a muralist and supervisor of other artists, met with Town Supervisor Albert Cashdollar to discuss the possibility of Smith painting murals in the auditorium and firemen's meeting room. For the meeting room, Smith proposed murals depicting the old fireman's hall and episodes in the history of firefighting in Woodstock. Apparently these murals were never carried out.

XXI–4 Edgar and Kate Eames House (Comeau House, Woodstock Town Office)
45 Comeau Drive. 1911. Frank E. Wallis.

Alf Evers identified the Eames house as "the first in Woodstock to have been designed by an architect of national reputation" and "the first of many to have been inspired outwardly by those of colonial times." Frank E. Wallis (1860–1929) was a well-known ar-

XXI-4. Eames House

chitect, a pioneer in making and publishing measured drawings of old New England colonial houses in the 1870s and '80s. Then, from 1887 to 1897, he was an associate of the dean of American architects, Richard Morris Hunt, in New York. On his own, Wallis designed many buildings in Montclair, New Jersey, where Edgar Eames, a merchant in the silk trade, resided with his family. They established this summer home in Woodstock as a consequence of their friendship with Margaret Goddard, a textile designer who studied landscape painting in Woodstock with John F. Carlson, whom she later married. About 1918 Carlson painted a broad, 90-by-32-inch panel, *Catskill Vista*, which is still set into the woodwork above what was the living room mantel of the Eames house.

The very simple forms of the living room fireplace and of the dark woodwork of the interior belong to the Arts and Crafts movement, already established in Woodstock by the Whiteheads at Byrdcliffe. The unadorned exterior, too, accords with Arts and Crafts principles in its simple geometric forms and plain but sturdy stone piers. There was much overlap between Colonial Revival and Arts and Crafts designs, and here the shingled walls of the gable ends curving out over the first story might be traced back to seventeenth-century New England—or more recently to the Queen Anne style of the 1880s. The roof angling out beyond the first-story walls to form porches was undoubtedly meant to recall the Dutch Colonial houses of the lower Hudson Valley; Wallis included a sketch of such a roof and porch found in an old "Dutch Bungalow, New York State," in

his popular book, *How to Know Architecture*. He believed that such houses represented "the first attack of bungalow fever this country had" and, while amused by them, he also considered "Dutch Colonial ... quite charming in its human expression, and ... peculiarly fit for much of our modern domestic need."

XXI-5 Colony Hotel (Colony Arts Center; Colony Cafe)
Rock City Rd. 1928–1929. Gerard Betz.

The Spanish style of the Colony Hotel's façade—note the stuccoed walls, tile roof and balcony above the central doorway, and ironwork at the windows—stands out as an oddity in Woodstock, but would relate easily to other Spanish-style buildings of the twenties in the New York suburbs and Sullivan County. There is even a touch of the Spanish mission of the American southwest in the beams projecting from the wall near the top of the corner tower.

The Colony's owner was Gabriel Newgold, whose stepfather, Morris Newgold, was building the great concrete Overlook Mountain House above Woodstock (see XXI–12). According to

XXI-5. Colony Hotel

Evers, anti-Semites referred to Newgold's stucco-fronted brick hotel in the village as "the brick synagogue." Others, including devotees of rusticity at Byrdcliffe and the Maverick, would consider it showy, pretentious, and its three stories badly out of place in the quaint hamlet of one- and two-story buildings. It seemed a foreign intruder, yet its artistic ironwork was fashioned by Woodstock blacksmith and community leader Henry Peper; the ornamental millwork was by the Schryver Lumber Co. of Kingston. Architect Gerard Betz was himself from Kingston. Morris Newgold had hired Betz to renovate the old, J. A. Wood–designed Overlook Mountain House, but the plans were never carried out as the building was destroyed by fire in 1923. Betz did complete the façade of the Jewish Community Center (1925) in Rondout in a simple Georgian style. In fact Betz was adept at staid Georgian and English Tudor but, for the art colony's hotel, client and architect may have wanted something more colorful and festive, in the spirit of Latin culture.

When the Colony was being completed during Prohibition in 1928, it was announced that the first floor would function as a tearoom, with space for dancing. Art exhibitions were also planned for the hotel, which would become a center of art colony life. In August 1929 the newly opened building included a basement cafeteria, and "artists were heard to declare that this modern cafeteria was a 'God-send' for small purses." Evers, however, observed that the hotel only operated sporadically and never fulfilled Newgold's ambition of being the center of colony life.

XXI–6* Deanie's Tinker Street Trolley
Mill Hill Rd. and Deming St. 1928
(not extant).

Electric trolleys served Kingston for decades before yielding to buses in 1930. Two years earlier a trolley that had lost one of its front platforms in a collision with an auto was trucked to Woodstock and converted into a "lunch wagon" or diner. Its owner was Albert Cashdollar, called "mechanic to the world at large" by poet and author Henry Morton Robinson. Within a few years it achieved

XXI-6. Deanie's Tinker Street Trolley (advertisement, Overlook, *1938)*

local renown as Deanie Elwyn's Tinker St. Trolley. While the aged and discarded trolley may initially have appealed to Cashdollar as a cheap way to set up a diner, the spectacle of its transformation garnered publicity for the diner via the wit of a writer for *Hue and Cry*—once among the "crack cars" of the Kingston railway system, the trolley not only had lost a platform but been "robbed ... of its wheels." In Woodstock, it:

> settled down to slumber ... by the roadside. Now, sans airbrake, sans farebox, sans everything, it is subjected to sedentary shame; becomes an eating joint, its once proud roof perforated by a chimney, its hallowed platform marred by an ice box, its tattered floor, ancient sanctuary for a thousand weary feet, torn and hacked to fit the needs of a soulless oven!

Although the writer exaggerated, there was at the time a widely felt sense of loss and nostalgia at the passing of the trolley era.

Advertising for the diner soon focused on its trolley origins. The word "trolley" was writ large on its side, and a drawing of the establishment, clearly defining the trolley origin of the structure, appeared prominently in newspaper ads. The eatery was expanded with a wooden building attached to the back of the trolley. Remarkably, the building's roof curved partially over the trolley, giving the impression that it had just arrived under the sheltering roof of a station—identified by a railway-looking signboard as "Woodstock." The town had in fact been bypassed by railway tracks, but now imaginative residents could step aboard the trolley car for any destination.

XXI-7 Woodstock Memorial Society Cemetery (Artists Cemetery)
Off Mt. View Ave. 1934 and later.

While close to the center of Woodstock, this remarkable burying ground, originally established by the Kingsbury family, remains, as they intended, a quiet hillside enveloped by nature. (To reach it from Mt. View Avenue, go uphill through a conventional cemetery to a sign indicating the Woodstock Memorial Society Cemetery.) For those interested in the history of Woodstock and its artists, the place has special appeal as many of the colony's artists lie here, some beneath stones individually designed to tell succeeding generations something about the artist's life.

The popular name for the ground, Artists Cemetery, is a misnomer, as it was never intended to exclude non-artists. The initial burial was of John Adams Kingsbury, Jr., killed in a car crash soon after graduating from Phillips Andover Academy in May 1934. His father, a social worker, was active in a variety of charitable organizations and served on Governor Franklin Roosevelt's State Public Health Commission. John, Sr. (1876–1956), was also a lover of nature, an amateur astronomer and member of the American Meteors Association who hosted all-night "star parties" at his residence, Lavorika, in Shady. In 1935 the young man's mother, Mabel Glass Kingsbury, wrote "The Everlasting Hills," a poem that begins:

> On a hill where one lies buried
> The grass grows rank and free.
> No neatly plotted
> Geranium potted
> Graves for company.
> No somber yew
> To mar the view
> Of those encircling hills.
> No trees stand by
> To hide the sky,
> The wind blows as it wills.

Young Kingsbury was buried near the hilltop with a small boulder marker meant to join with grasses and wildflowers. Soon friends and others asked to have plots, and the Woodstock Memorial Society, Inc., was formed with John Kingsbury as first president. Most of the memorial stones are flat and even with the ground, not affecting the view. One exception is the della Robbia shrine with the ashes of the founder of Byrdcliffe, Ralph Radcliffe Whitehead (1854–1929), which is located at the

XXI-7. Whitehead Memorial, Woodstock Memorial Society Cemetery

edge of the woods near the base of the hillside. The shrine shelters a glazed terra-cotta relief of the Madonna and Child in white and blue with an elaborate polychrome frame including fruit and leaves. The della Robbia family produced terra-cotta relief sculpture in workshops in Italy and France in the fifteenth and sixteenth centuries, and Whitehead's mentor, John Ruskin, had a Luca della Robbia Madonna and Child hanging above the mantelpiece in his Brantwood study. The Woodstock della Robbia was originally an outdoor shrine at Whitehead's home, White Pines, where it served as an "emblem of Byrdcliffe," but was moved here by June 1937 when the Woodstock Memorial Society gathered before the Whitehead memorial and dedicated the grounds. There is also a tall stone slab atop the hillside, erected about 1950, with a text by Dr. James Shotwell indicating that those who "rest here ... added to the beauty of the world by art, creative thought and by life itself." More congenial to the unassuming spirit of the place and to young Kingsbury's stone is another small boulder, in this case sheltered under evergreen trees, carved with the name Bolton Brown, the artist who recommended Woodstock to Whitehead as the site for his art colony. Anita Smith saw Brown, appearing very ill, directing two workmen in placing this boulder a few days

before his death in 1936. Similar stones appear in a number of Brown's landscape lithographs.

Also of interest is the large flat slab of the Kingsbury family, just below the boulder of John, Jr., that is incised with a landscape of mountain peaks and extensive sky—appropriate for stargazers—signed "Rockwell Kent." John, Sr., had been chairman of the American Council on Soviet Relations, while Kent had strong ties with the Soviet Union. A more intimate design—two rose bushes growing toward each other—adorns the marker of Eugene Speicher (1883–1962) and Elsie Speicher (1888–1959) whose marriage, according to Anita Smith, was probably the happiest one in the artists' colony. The marker of George Hamilton Green (1893–1970) and Georgia Ellen Anderson Green (1895–1981?) identifies him as "xylophonist & artist." George Green is credited with many recordings from about 1917 to 1946, when he retired from music in favor of commercial art and cartoons. Their affection for their home is perpetuated in an adjacent marker incised with a picture of a rustic wood and stone cabin identified as "Our home/ 31/ Pine Grove St./ Woodstock, N.Y./ 1945." The cabin itself survives on Pine Grove Street.

XXI-8 Eugene and Elsie Speicher House
Lower Byrdcliffe Lane, Rock City. 1911 (later alterations, including 1935 by Teller & Halverson).

Eugene Speicher (1883–1962) was a prominent American painter in the 1920s and '30s, avoiding controversial abstraction in his critically acclaimed portraits and floral still lifes. As a successful artist and important figure in the Woodstock art colony, Speicher and his wife Elsie enlarged what had been their small frame studio and summer residence into what their neighbor Anita Smith called "an attractive stone and wood cottage with a well kept garden." The low, gable-roofed cottage was picturesquely Colonial without being markedly Dutch. Its white-painted wood and whitewashed stone walls, 6-over-6 window sash, shutters, and dormers declared that here was a quaint Colonial cottage.

XXI-8. Speicher House

The immaculate and largely white interior with its Colonial and Victorian furniture, flowering plants, and bright chintzes struck a cheerful note—the dark, rustic quality of Byrdcliffe was a thing of the past. In 1938 *Life* pictured Elsie, a locally renowned cook, wearing her trademark polka-dot dress and apron while happily turning a hand mixer, with old-fashioned coffee grinder and rows of colorful dishes lining the walls of the cozy kitchen.

Teller's drawings for the Speichers are lost, and so it is difficult to determine exactly what his alterations and additions involved. However, interior photos published in 1939 show his distinctive hardware and cupboards, as well as beams salvaged from an old house in the neighborhood. Speicher valued traditional craftsmanship. In a brief statement prefacing illustrations of his own paintings, he wrote, "I know of no master who is not a master craftsman."

Speicher's house of traditional American forms and materials was related to a category of his painted subjects. He was in great demand as a portrait painter of wealthy Americans, but he preferred to paint noncommissioned portraits of traditional American types from the countryside—for example, *The Mountaineer* (1929; Metropolitan Museum of Art) or *Woodstock Cowboy* (1932), the latter a study of Allen Stoutenberg, whose father, a local stonecutter, helped alter the Speicher house.

The Speichers' artist-friends George Bellows (1882–1925) and Charles Rosen (1878–1950) chose to build white frame houses nearby, on Bellows Lane, "within shouting distance of each other," as Anita Smith put it. Bellows bought land next to the Speichers in 1921, designed a house using the principle of dynamic symmetry that he was also applying to his painted compositions and, enlisting painter John Carroll's help, built the house within a few months in 1922. Bellows showed the completed house to Ralph Radcliffe Whitehead and was offended when the rich Englishman proclaimed that the house would be "very nice" when finished. Bellows retorted, "you mean it's damn beautiful just as it is now!"

XXI–9 Byrdcliffe (Byrdcliffe Art Colony of the Woodstock Guild)
Upper Byrdcliffe Rd. Begun 1902. Ralph Radcliffe Whitehead, Bolton Brown, and others. NR

The buildings of Byrdcliffe, one of America's most important Arts and Crafts colonies, are remarkably intact and many can be seen on a self-guided, one-mile walking tour beginning at the Byrdcliffe Theater, where parking is available. Byrdcliffe was primarily the creation of Ralph Radcliffe Whitehead (1854–1929), a wealthy Englishman educated at Oxford who was a disciple of John Ruskin and admirer of William Morris, two of the initiators of the Arts and Crafts Movement in England. Whitehead met his second wife, Jane Byrd McCall, a Philadelphian and aspiring artist, while she was traveling in Europe. They married in 1892 and, after a short period in Paris, the kindred spirits came to America, intending to establish a community dedicated to the advancement of handcraftsmanship in opposition to the pervasive ur-

XXI-9. White Pines, Byrdcliffe (1979 photo)

ban factory system. The Whiteheads built a white stucco mansion in southern California near Santa Barbara in a Mediterranean style, but no colony arose there. In 1902 Bolton Brown, who had been the first head of the art department at Stanford University, was working on behalf of Whitehead to find a site for his colony when he "discovered" Woodstock. Whitehead wanted to avoid both "the crowded trolley-car of jostling democracy and ... the haunts of the 'fashionables.'" Woodstock offered beautiful mountainside land without factory and railroad on one hand, or the decadent upper-class life of Newport and Saratoga on the other. Yet it was within a few hours of New York. Whitehead purchased seven farms totaling about 1,200 acres and, with the assistance of Brown and Hervey White, a writer and Ruskin-inspired idealist from the Midwest, quickly set about putting up five wooden buildings, with others to come, in 1903.

The colony was named Byrdcliffe, combining his wife's middle name and one syllable of Whitehead's. Their home, White Pines, was designed by Brown and Whitehead and became the center of the community—the Catskills manor house of the lordly Whitehead. Externally it is a picturesque affair of stained pine boards, low roofs, and mostly

XXI-9A. Studio, Byrdcliffe

horizontal lines that allow the house to blend easily with the landscape—in 1902 primarily cultivated fields. White Pines stems from the vernacular traditions of Europe and America—something Swiss, something California 1900 (the adaptations of the vernacular by California architect Bernard Maybeck), maybe something of the rustic Catskills seen in Candace Wheeler's Onteora Park. Whitehead avoided bark-covered log or slab walls, but John Burroughs admired the woody picturesqueness of Byrdcliffe in 1905. Neither the exterior nor the interior of White Pines is ostentatious; the most impressive detail within being the green-blue glazed bricks, made by Jane Whitehead's Pennsylvania cousin and master tile-maker Henry Chapman Mercer, that face the fireplace. The simple geometries of the interior woodwork accorded well with the furniture designed and made in a shop at Byrdcliffe and for sale to the public from 1903 to 1905. In 1906 Whitehead added a workspace he called the Loom Room, joined by a bridge to the main house.

Among the buildings on or near Lower Byrdcliffe Road that accord with White Pine's plain and unpainted rusticity are: the Villetta for student housing; the Studio or School of Art (now the Byrdcliffe Theater) with a wing to house Whitehead's 5,000-volume library; the Forge; the handsome barns complex (based on English medieval manor barns); as well as a number of small cottages, the "cutest" of which is said to be Chipmunk. Many have broad bands of windows; natural light was a necessity for artists and craftsmen, especially as Whitehead disapproved of gas and electric lights. Hervey White took the simplicity of Byrdcliffe a step further toward casual, sometimes ramshackle, design when he departed Byrdcliffe and in 1905 established his own colony at the Maverick, near Woodstock in the Town of Hurley (see V–5 and V–6). While the utopian vision Whitehead had in creating his colony assured its failure in commercial terms, its architecture and the creative spirit embodied in that architecture have continued to have a positive influence on Woodstock as an art center. For a thorough account of Byrdcliffe and its architecture, Tom Wolf's and Cheryl Robertson's essays in *Byrdcliffe:*

An American Arts and Crafts Colony (2004) are highly recommended.

XXI–10 Anita M. Smith House and Shop, Stonecrop
10 Mead's Mountain Rd. 1934, 1938.

Anita M. Smith, best known today for her invaluable book, *Woodstock: History and Hearsay* (1959; second edition, 2006), arrived in Woodstock as an art student from Philadelphia in 1912, became connected with the art colony as a landscape painter but then, in the 1930s, turned aside from painting to develop a commercial herb garden known as Stonecrop Gardens. In 1940 the *Herald Tribune* described her as "the Herb Lady of the Catskills."

Smith erected the story-and-a-half stone cottage facing Mead's Mountain Road in 1934—the date is carved with her initials over an exterior door. The cottage was built of local bluestone and resembles early houses in the county, although here much of the bluestone was cut into regular rectangular blocks. Smith incorporated into the structure a few rafters she had salvaged from an old barn near Cooper Lake that had been demolished by the City of Kingston. She later recalled that she "wept ... because, like poetry, the barn was beautiful in line and color and as rhythmical as the surrounding mountains." Smith's desire to reflect and include local architectural and agricultural traditions fits with her exploration of the region's history and traditions. She read a paper on Catskill Mountain lore at the New York State Historical Association's 1935 meeting at Lake Mohonk. Then, in 1939, she wrote and illustrated *As True as the Barnacle Tree*, a booklet (printed at the nearby Maverick Press) of herbal lore with drawings of her garden and shop, and a chapter on "Woodstock Legends and Cures."

In 1938 a north-facing wing, larger than the original house, was added by Smith's friend Alice Henderson to serve as her residence and antiques shop. Its masonry walls and gable roof are harmonious with the 1934 structure, but its casement windows and dormers recall the Arts and Crafts details of Byrdcliffe, where Henderson had lived.

XXI-10. Stonecrop, 1938 wing

The wooden building at the south end of the property was the shop from which Smith sold herbs, a variety of garden items, and handwoven New England pie baskets. Rafters from the Cooper Lake barn again graced the interior. The front bay window, filled with dried herbs and garden decorations, reminded the *Overlook* of a shop in a Dickens tale. In the 1950s, after the death of Alice Henderson, Smith transformed the shop into her residence, and in this cottage wrote her history of Woodstock. Also on the property, but not visible from the road, is the surviving lower portion of the Woodstock Observation Post that Smith put up in 1942 to assist the Army Air Force by keeping watch for enemy aircraft.

Stonecrop is being carefully tended and restored by Weston Blelock and his sister Julia Blelock, who were introduced to Anita Smith in 1957 when their parents began renting her stone house. In 2006 the Blelocks published a handsomely illustrated and expanded edition of Smith's Woodstock history with biographical information about her.

XXI–11 Church on the Mount (Church of the Holy Transfiguration of Christ on the Mount)
Mead's Mountain Rd. 1890s. NR

This small rustic chapel, perched high on Mead's Mountain Road, was originally built by the Mead family for guests at Mead's Mountain House and was associated with the Episcopal Church. There were other shingled, rustic, Episcopal chapels in the Catskills that served urban sophisticates on summer holiday, including Slide Mountain Episcopal Church in Shandaken (extant in 1912). The Church on the Mount later became an outpost of the Old Catholic Church, which had broken with Rome and was closer to the Episcopal Church, led locally by William Henry Francis (Father Francis). Mrs. Ralph Radcliffe Whitehead purchased the mountain church for Father Francis who, as a woodcarver, was connected with the art colony.

*XXI-11. Church on the Mount
(Louis E. Jones photo, 1920s)*

Today the church is known as the Church of the Holy Transfiguration of Christ on the Mount, and adheres to the Western Orthodox Rite. A weekday visitor finds the door unlocked and the interior arranged according to Orthodox practice with a screen of icons separating the people from the altar.

XXI–12 Overlook Mountain House (ruin)
Overlook Mountain. After 1923 to 1940. Frank P. Amato.

This monumental ruin is a popular attraction for walkers up Overlook on their way to the Overlook Fire Tower (see next entry, XXI–13). To begin the two-mile uphill walk to the hotel ruin, park at the trailhead of the red-blazed Overlook Spur Trail. The trailhead is along Mead's Mountain Road above the village of Woodstock.

New York hotel owner Morris Newgold and his designer, Frank P. Amato, envisioned a great mountaintop hotel of reinforced concrete that would avoid the fate—destruction by fire—that befell two earlier hotels on Overlook in 1875 and 1923. (Lewis B. Van Wagonen of Kingston was the builder of the first Overlook Mountain House, which opened in 1871 and numbered President Ulysses S. Grant among its guests in 1873; J. A. Wood designed the second, which opened in 1878 and later attracted President Chester A. Arthur as a luncheon guest, but was in decline when, in 1921, it was the site of the birth of the Communist Party of America.) Construction of the concrete hotel proceeded slowly and stopped with the coming of the Depression. Moreover, the hotel's never-completed main structure has been gutted by fires; for while the exterior walls are concrete, the interior framing was of wood. Behind the ruinous main building is the ruin of the Lodge with the date 1928 in a panel high above the entrance. Alf Evers noted that this smaller concrete building (which retains its steel casement windows, but not their glass) contained a drafting room for Amato and quarters for Newgold when visiting the site.

Evers argued that Newgold's project was doomed to fail; the big mountaintop hotel (the

XXI-12. Overlook Mountain House (1984 photo)

kind Wood had designed at Overlook and for the Grand Hotel above Pine Hill) was anachronistic in the 1920s. Newgold's financial troubles in the 1930s and his death about 1940 resulted in the abandonment of the project. The state Conservation Department acquired the property, and it became part of the Catskill Forest Preserve. For decades vandals have attacked the buildings, adding to the loss by fire. A porch with paired classical columns and a central, rooftop tower survived until the early 1960s when, according to Thomas Rinaldi and Robert Yasinsac, the roof and tower collapsed and a fire destroyed the remains in 1965.

XXI–13 Overlook Fire Tower
Overlook Mountain. 1927, 1950.
Aermotor Company.

This sixty-foot steel fire tower originally stood on Gallis Hill west of Kingston, but in 1950 was moved by the state Conservation Department to its present site on Overlook Mountain, where it provides a magnificent 360-degree panorama of the Catskills, Hudson Valley, and Ashokan Reservoir. Its manufacturer, the Aermotor Company of Chicago, also made windmills. Aermotor advertised that this model, the LS-40, was suited not only for the observer on watch for forest fires, but also for the public eager to ascend for the enhanced view of the landscape. A cheaper model with ladder to the cab met the needs of the agile observer, but the public would require the internal staircase of the LS-40. Closed as a fire tower in 1988, the Overlook tower was restored for public visitation and reopened in 1999.

The fire tower and nearby rustic ranger cabin are reached after a steep, two-and-a-half-mile hike on the red-blazed Overlook Spur Trail, which passes the ruin of the Overlook Mountain House a half mile before ending at the tower. See the preceding entry (XXI–12) for the hotel ruin and directions to the trailhead.

XXI-13. Overlook Fire Tower

XXI–14 Yasuo Kuniyoshi House
Ohayo Mountain Rd. 1929.

Yasuo Kuniyoshi (1889–1953) left his native Japan as a teenager and by 1929 was a highly regarded and influential American painter. He is said to have designed this, his own house. Kuniyoshi's paintings and prints were influenced by European modernism, and he was active in socially radical artists' organizations, so it is surprising that his house is firmly within conventional Colonial Revival taste.

A partial explanation for his choice of the Colonial may lie in his admiration of the patterns of early American folk art, reflected in his art. Moreover, the Japanese-born artist was keen on being accepted as an American, despite the federally imposed prohibition on American citizenship for those of Japanese birth. In a 1927 *Self-Portrait* (Museum of Modern Art) he presented himself (perhaps with a bit of tongue-in-cheek humor) as an American golfer wearing plus fours. The Woodstock Artists Association had opted for a white, formally composed Colonial building, and Kuniyoshi (who exhibited at the WAA) probably adopted the same style as further demonstration of his American status. He had married an American, Katherine Schmidt, in 1919. They divorced in 1932, and Kuniyoshi later married another American, Sara Mazo. *Life* pictured the couple bringing ice and appetizers from their house to an outdoor (American) cocktail party, Kuniyoshi in American garb, his wife, according to *Life*, looking "Japanese." Oddly enough, the radiating pattern in the elliptical arch over the doorway is both a characteristic of the American Federal style and suggestive of the Japanese rising sun.

XXI-14. Kuniyoshi House (Tom Wolf photo, c. 2000)

XXI–15 Mary and Ernest Earley House
Ohayo Mountain Rd. 1934. Albert Graeser.

New Deal post office muralist Mary Earley and her insurance agent husband Ernest Earley were the original occupants of this Colonial Revival house designed for them by Albert Graeser and pictured in *House and Garden* in 1941. No mention was made of Mary Earley or her role as an artist. Instead, the magazine focused on Graeser's adaptation of the Colonial house for summertime use (the Earleys' main residence was in New York): the second-story casement windows may appear low, but they opened wide for air circulation in hot weather; and a stone terrace was "a perfect setting for a summer lunch." Both the terrace and a picture window in the living room were oriented to the view of the Catskills. Rooms were small, except for the living room, which also served as dining room and combined a Colonial fireplace and exposed joists in the ceiling with a quaint bay window and up-to-date picture window. The Colonial Revival house was also traditional in its furnishings.

Mary Earley's murals dealt with historical and traditional themes and were executed in a conventional realistic style—*Down-Rent War, around 1845*, for the Delhi (Delaware County) post office (1940) and *Dance of the Hop Pickers* for the Middleburg (Schoharie County) post office (1941).

*XXI-15. Earley House (*House & Garden, *June 1941)*

The appearance of her house suggests that these murals were carried out by an enthusiast for the past, not by an artist with avant-garde leanings.

XXI-16* Alfred and Frida De Liagre House
1936–1937. William Muschenheim.

Modern design without visible reference to historical architecture, but instead influenced by such International Style architects as the German designer of the Bauhaus, Walter Gropius, had little impact on Ulster County architecture in the 1930s. Not surprisingly, Woodstock, with its bohemian and progressive culture, was more open to the new in architecture than were other towns. In the 1920s, Alfred De Liagre, a woolen manufacturer, and his wife Frida had followed convention when hiring Teller & Halverson to transform an old stone house and working farm in Zena into what Alf Evers called a "country estate" with "a Colonial quality of an accepted character inside and out."

By 1936, however, the De Liagres had sold their Zena place and their nephew, New York architect William Muschenheim, was designing their modern "vacation house" at Byrdcliffe. (In New York the De Liagres lived on fashionable Sutton Place.) The house was completed in 1937 and received national publicity when published in the *Architectural Record* in April 1938. It was the only

Ulster County building included in the Museum of Modern Art's *Guide to Modern Architecture, Northeast States* in 1940.

William Muschenheim (1902–1990) was a pioneer of modern architecture in America. After studying architecture at MIT, he was exposed to modernism as a student of Peter Behrens in Vienna in the 1920s. In New York in 1931, he joined with other young architects dedicated to the International Style in protesting the popular "modernistic" style now called Art Deco. In 1933 he exhibited designs alongside European masters LeCorbusier and Mies van der Rohe at the New School for Social Research, and Muschenheim worked as a designer for the New School's architect, Joseph Urban.

In the spirit of the International Style, Muschenheim designed the house as a number of flat planes—including a roof of a single gentle slope—with broad areas of glass, and an overall sense that geometry had replaced history as the fundamental element of International Style design. Modern materials—asbestos shingles for exterior walls, plywood for interior walls, steel pipe railing around the second-floor canvas sundeck, and an iron spiral staircase at the corner of the deck—replaced the natural and rustic materials of the Colonial Revival and Arts and Crafts. Vivid colors also distinguished the exterior; a strong green-blue and maroon, as well as cobalt blue, played off against the gray asbestos shingles.

Sited on the mountainside, the house was oriented to take advantage of the view to the southwest. Expanses of glass opened up the generously scaled living room, while the projecting roof restrained the effect of the summer sun. Both the terrace wrapping around the living room and the second-story sundeck outside a tiny bedroom encouraged outdoor living. Consequently the joined kitchen and dining alcove could be made small and tucked into a corner away from the view.

The irregular stonework (drawn from a local source) of the living room fireplace and chimney breast did look back to an earlier era. However, the fireplace was accompanied not by an old-fashioned wooden settle, but by a tubular steel chair created by Marcel Breuer at the Bauhaus, the German school

XXI-16. De Liagre House (Architectural Record, *Apr. 1938*)

of architecture and design. De Liagre remembered his ancestral roots not through revivalist design, but by naming his house "The Pelican" and placing a sculptured pelican on the stone mantelpiece—the ancestral De Liagre home in Lieges, Belgium, was identified with a carved pelican.

The International Style appeared to offer simple, practical solutions to clients wanting inexpensive shelter. However, in practice, the Cape Cod or Dutch Colonial cottage often furnished dryer quarters. During a rainy July 1938 De Liagre complained to his architect, "The rain has just been hell ... No door closes anymore and no drawer and it is the same all over." Still, the owner was pleased to tell his architect: "Professor Moholy-Nagy spoke here—very interesting! He liked your house and wants to meet you. ... He loved your Bauhaus chair in our bedroom!" László Moholy-Nagy (1895–1946) had been a close associate of Gropius at the Bauhaus in the 1920s. In 1933 the Bauhaus was closed by Hitler; in 1937 Moholy-Nagy came to the United States and became director of the "New Bauhaus" in Chicago. He traveled to Woodstock to give a lantern slide lecture at a Byrdcliffe Forum on the principles of Bauhaus design. The reporter for the *Overlook* was bewildered by the student projects described in the lecture; they were reminiscent of "the more outlandish contraptions of Rube Goldberg." Nevertheless, the reporter allowed that "Moholy-Nagy and his

associates hope to revitalize U.S. architecture and design." Muschenheim and De Liagre had already taken steps to do just that in Woodstock.

XXI–17* Marion Greenwood House
1949. Abel Sorenson.

The small, inexpensive studio house, long established as a type in Woodstock, here was designed in the modern idiom, with a nearly flat (gravel) roof, a horizontal band of windows, and overall the insistence on treating walls as flat planes—the house as a box. Marion Greenwood (1909–1970) was a well-known painter and printmaker, yet her budget was very limited. Most of the 734 square feet of the house was given over to her studio, whose north wall was mainly glass. For economy, the studio also served as living-dining room, and the only conventional interior partitions were around the bathroom, while a storage wall of closets separated bedroom from studio. The design shunned traditional Woodstock rusticity, except for the native fieldstone of the fireplace and the terrace "for outdoor living."

Greenwood's house was featured in *Quality Budget Houses* (1954) by Katherine Morrow Ford and Thomas H. Creighton. Identified as an "architect-designer," Abel Sorenson designed modern furniture and fabrics, and was involved with the

XXI-17. Greenwood House (Ford & Creighton, **Quality Budget Houses,** *1949)*

design of interiors at the United Nations Head-quarters in New York in 1949 when Greenwood's little studio-house was built in Woodstock.

XXI–18 National Youth Administration Resident Craft Center (Woodstock School of Art)

2470 Rte. 212. Begun 1939. Albert Graeser and Tomas Penning? NR

Eleanor Roosevelt was the "chief adviser, chief publicist, chief investigator" of the National Youth Administration, a New Deal agency whose Woodstock Training Center taught unemployed youth several craft skills—stonecutting, wood- and metal-working, wool processing—to encourage them to become productive citizens and to continue "the American tradition of fine craftsmanship." Alf Evers observed that the Center struck "many art-colony people" as "an extension of the ideas which had led Ralph Whitehead to found Byrdcliffe." The NYA itself cited the natural beauty of the Catskills and Woodstock's "national reputation" as "the Center of Arts and Crafts for America" to explain the selection of Woodstock as the first and only NYA craft center in the state. Another reason was surely Woodstock's proximity to Hyde Park, where Eleanor Roosevelt had established Val-Kill Industries in 1926 to engage local people in craft-making, but that enterprise ended in 1937.

Most prominent from Route 212 is the low, gable-roofed, native stone–fronted Wood-Working Shop (now the gallery and office of the Woodstock School of Art). The wooden beams

visible within probably derive from the barn near the highway whose wings were dismantled. The shop appears to reflect Franklin Roosevelt's preference for new construction in the regional vernacular of Hudson Valley stone houses, although FDR had no direct connection to this design. The president surely would have objected mightily to the façade's large arched window; FDR had won a battle with architect Henry Toombs, who tried to insert such a non–Hudson Valley Dutch feature in Eleanor Roosevelt's Val-Kill Cottage at Hyde Park. Another arched window graces the stone façade of the NYA's Stone and Metal Shop. The three main buildings—Wood-Working Shop, Stone and Metal Shop, and Textile Building—were constructed with a combination of stone and wooden walls, Colonial-style hardware made at the Center, and industrial-looking steel window sash.

In June 1939 Mrs. Roosevelt endeared herself to the local citizenry by coming "at the wheel of her own car" to lay the cornerstone of the Wood-working Shop, the Center's first building, and then engaging easily with officials and the boy trainees "as if in the intimacy of her own family circle." The fifty NYA boys (girls later were employed in the Textile or Wool Shop) had already quarried stone and laid the foundation for the shop, and those who had carved the cornerstone ("N Y A 1939") and made the ceremonial trowel were given special recognition at the ceremony. Other boys were chosen to show the president's wife where future buildings would rise, as well as explain blueprints for the buildings, which incorporated ideas from the boys. Mrs. Roosevelt wrote about the event in her widely read column, "My Day": "I can imagine no more wonderful

*XXI-18. NYA
Wood-Working Shop*

place for these boys to be, for all around them are people who are experts in some art or craft who, at the same time, have made a study of a way of life which should be helpful to these young people." Anita Smith, who attended the cornerstone ceremony, later credited the boys with building fine stone walls for their workrooms under the supervision of sculptor Tom Penning, while the woodworking instructor directed the boys in carpentry for completion of the buildings.

The following August, Mrs. Roosevelt returned with Elinor Morgenthau, wife of Treasury Secretary Henry Morgenthau, to attend the flag-raising ceremony at the Training Center. The *Kingston Daily Freeman* reported that "the base of the flag pole was designed and carved by N.Y.A. youth of the stone cutting unit under the direction of Tomas Penning of High Woods." The octagonal base is fitted with eight bluestone panels with sculptured reliefs pertinent to the activities of the Center, including stone, wood, and metalworking. (An elephant sculpted in bluestone by the NYA about 1940 and given to their physician, Dr. Henry L. Bibby, has been on exhibit at the Senate House Museum in Kingston.)

It is unclear who designed the Center's buildings. In December 1940 *The Overlook* credited Tomas Penning with designing "the new metal building," and three months later it announced that Albert Graeser "has joined the State N.Y.A.

staff as architect for the center's proposed building program," implying that Graeser had not designed the earlier buildings. However, Evers credits him with designing the Wood-Working Shop as well. As America prepared for war, stone craft was dropped in favor of metalworking, but by May 1942 most of the Center was scheduled for closing. After the war the Art Students League ran a summer school in the former NYA buildings from 1947 until 1979. Since 1981 the Woodstock School of Art, founded by Robert Angeloch, has maintained its school in this landmark of the New Deal.

XXI–19* New Theatre (unexecuted proposal)
1931. Frank Lloyd Wright.

In 1931 America's greatest twentieth-century architect, Frank Lloyd Wright, made sketches for a project called the New Theatre that was to be built in Woodstock, then bustling with theatrical activity. Wright's drawings show the low, blocky shapes of the theater would relate to the mountain profile he sketched rising in the distance. The *Woodstock Press* (September 11, 1931) reported that the theater, designed by Wright "in a thoroughly modern manner," was planned for a site near the country club (on Mill Hill Road), and that Joseph Patrick McEvoy (1895–1958), an author and playwright,

XXI-19. New Theatre (drawings by Wright, 1931 [© 2011 Frank Lloyd Wright Foundation/ Artists Rights Society], reproduced in Pfeiffer, **Frank Lloyd Wright Drawings***)*

was the leading promoter. McEvoy, according to Alf Evers, found Hervey White's Maverick Festivals "old-fashioned" and wanted to bring to Woodstock the culture of "smart people" from Broadway and Hollywood.

About the same time, McEvoy was also involved with a plan for an experimental summer theater designed by Frederick J. Kiesler. The structure was to be of metal tubing, steel grating, and fireproofed canvas. Alf Evers wrote that the exterior of this "Universal Theater" would have "something of the look of a space vehicle come to earth from a far more advanced world than ours." Neither Wright's nor Kiesler's proposal came to fruition.

At his own estate on the Woodstock-Bearsville road, McEvoy apparently used local architect Myron Teller to remake a decaying old Dutch barn into what Teller called "a game house" with, as McEvoy wrote, "a hardwood floor for dancing, a fireplace big enough to roast an ox, a billiard table and a system for amplifying records."

XXI–20* Woodstock Playhouse
Mill Hill Rd. 1938 (destroyed by fire 1988). Albert Edward Milliken.

The 1938 playhouse was the successor to the Woodstock Playhouse, which opened in 1929 in a converted barn but burned in 1931. The new,

high-roofed, wooden playhouse had barnlike qualities and followed the Byrdcliffe-Maverick ideal that a building should fit easily into the landscape. At the Maverick colony Hervey White had designed and built a dirt-floored theatre (1924) of such rusticity that it was impractical; tree-trunk posts hindered the view of the stage.

Robert Elwyn managed and directed the Maverick Theatre for four seasons, and then decided to erect his own theatre, taking the name and building near the site of the earlier Woodstock Playhouse. Its design was a collaboration between Elwyn and Kingston architect Albert (Ned) Milliken, who had been an assistant to Norman Bel Geddes, the well-known New York stage set and industrial designer. The interior was simple and open—wood benches, roof supported by arched trusses, no posts. Milliken described his work as "functional architecture," and the arched volume has something in common with contemporary aircraft hangars whose design Bel Geddes had praised.

Construction took just six weeks. The local press declared the result "a building of such architectural beauty and mechanical perfection Mr. Elwyn must feel obligated to present the best the stage has to offer." The inaugural play, *Yes, My Darling Daughter*, had been produced in 1937 by Woodstock's Alfred de Liagre, Jr. Milliken himself wrote *Sun Metal*, a romantic drama about archeologists in the Andes Mountains, that Elwyn put into production. The architect-playwright later recalled that "the setting was in an Inca temple from which one saw the sweeping grandeur of the mountain vastness. So all we had to do was build the Andes Mountains—not a painted drop, but worked out in relief, so that the background responded to the lights played upon it. ..."

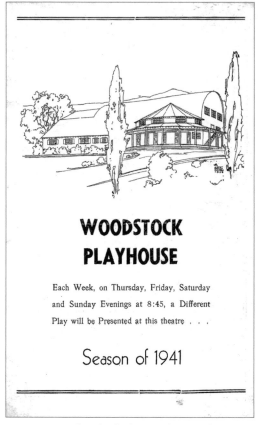

XXI-20. Woodstock Playhouse (drawing by Milliken, 1941 program)

Notes

Abbreviations

AML: Adriance Memorial Library, Poughkeepsie

FDRL: Franklin D. Roosevelt Library, Hyde Park

FHK: Friends of Historic Kingston

HABS: Historic American Buildings Survey

HHHC: Haviland-Heidgerd Historical Collection, Elting Memorial Library, New Paltz

HHS: Historic Huguenot Street, New Paltz

HVVAN: *Hudson Valley Vernacular Architecture Newsletter*

KDF: *Kingston Daily Freeman*

NPI: *New Paltz Independent*

NPN: *New Paltz News*

NPT: *New Paltz Times*

NYSL: New York State Library, Albany

NYT: *The New York Times*

SRL: Stone Ridge Library

ST: *Saugerties Telegraph*

UCHS: Ulster County Historical Society, Marbletown

VCL: Vassar College Libraries

WAA: Woodstock Artists Association

Introduction

Collections of the Ulster Historical Society, I (Kingston, 1860), xxii; Sylvester, II, 200; Hastings, 94–95; Reynolds, *Dutch Houses in the Hudson Valley before 1776*; Teller, *The Early Stone Houses of Ulster County*; Benepe, *Early Architecture in Ulster County*; on Alton B. Parker's Rosemount, see Elizabeth Burroughs Kelley, "West Park and Esopus," 141–143; on Chagall's house, see Jackie Wullschlager, *Chagall* (New York: Knopf, 2008), 433, and *Marbletown Album*, 99; on Sojourner Truth's birthplace, see *Kingston Journal and Weekly Freeman*, Feb. 4, 1886, and Carleton Mabee, *Sojourner Truth* (New York: New York University Press, 1993), 1–2; Wick, *Esopus*, 90; *Narrative of Sojourner Truth* (Battle Creek, 1878, reprinted 1994 by Oxford University Press), 14; John H. Coe, "Lloyd," in Clearwater, *History of Ulster County*, 273; Hilary Stout, "Time For a Place In the Country?" *NYT*, Oct. 3, 2010; *Town of Esopus Story*, 38; *KDF*, Oct. 5, 2010; *HVVAN*, (Oct.–Dec. 2010): 20.

Chapter I. Town of Denning

Sylvester, II, 332.

I-1.   De Lisser, "Townships of Denning and Harden-bergh," *Picturesque Ulster*, 148; Rhoads, "The Artist's House," 89–90; Lewis I. Sharp, *John Quincy Adams Ward* (Newark, Del.: University of Delaware Press, 1985), 23–24, 66; Paul R. Baker, *Richard Morris Hunt* (Cambridge: MIT Press, 1980), 159, 271; *NYT*, Sept. 6, 1896; "Chat of Collectorship," *The Collector*, 7 (Sept. 15, 1896), 291.

I-2.   De Lisser, "Denning and Hardenbergh," 146–48; Kenneth E. Hasbrouck, compiler, "History of the Town of Denning," *History of Ulster County* (1983), 29; Evers, *The Catskills*, 594–95; *Who's Who in America*, 1906; Phillips, *Charmed Places*, fig. 91; *KDF*, Aug. 11, 1893; *NYT*, July 4, 1894; De Lisser, "Olive," *Picturesque Ulster*, 134; *NYT*, Mar. 17, 1915.

I-3.   Sylvester, II, 331.

I-4.   Galusha, *Build Strong*; Meike Cryan, "The Forstmann Hunting Lodge," undergraduate paper for Art of the Hudson Valley, SUNY New Paltz, 1977; Julius Forstmann's obituary, *NYT*, Oct. 28, 1939; *NYT*, Mar. 24, 1912, Mar. 28, 1926; Barrus, II, 255; *NYT*, Dec. 9, 1924, Apr. 23, 1918, Mar. 10, 1918, Aug. 14, 1929, Jan. 9, 1942; White and Willensky, 407; *KDF*, Aug. 1, 2007.

I-5.   Lancaster, *Japanese Influence*, 144–49, 195, 198; Ted B. Hilton phone conversation, Nov. 11, 2008, and email, Dec. 2008; Mark Kessenich, undergraduate paper on Grey Lodge for Art of the Hudson Valley, 1987; *NYT*, July 10, 1952, Feb. 13, 1904, Jan. 7, 1905, June 9, 1919, July 17, 1938, Dec. 8, 1932, Sept. 16, 1930; Aug. 28, 1900; *Who's Who in New York*, 1907; Henry F. du Pont to Sarah Lounsbery, Oct. 1, 1937, HF 350, Winterthur Library; *American Architect & Building News*, Dec. 7, 1907.

Chapter II. Town of Esopus

Mary E. Polhemus, "Town of Esopus," *History of Ulster County* (1983), 39; Wallace Bruce, *The Hudson by Daylight Map* (Brooklyn: Bryant Union, c. 1907).

II–1. Kelley, "West Park and Esopus," 121, 132; Harold S. Brigham, *The First Century of Ulster County Savings Institution* (1951), 21, 26, 33, 35; Sylvester, I, 261; *NYT*, Apr. 21, 1871, June 23, 1912; Richard Foy on Archibald Russell: http://academic2.marist.edu/foy/esopus/esop03.html#ArchibaldRussell.

II–2. Kelley, "West Park and Esopus," 126; *KDF*, Apr. 27, 1936; *NYT*, July 8 and Oct. 5, 1933.

II–3. Kelley, "West Park and Esopus," 128; Hilda Worthington Smith, *Opening Vistas in Workers' Education: An Autobiography of Hilda Worthington Smith* (Washington, 1978); *NYT*, May 7, 1901; *The Workers Look at the Stars* (Vineyard Shore, 1927); press release of Bryn Mawr Summer School, Mar. 29, 1939, at www.smlr.rutgers.edu/library; Blanche Wiesen Cook, *Eleanor Roosevelt* (New York: Viking, 1999), II, 356.

II–4. Kelley, "West Park and Esopus," 121, 129–30.

II–5. Kelley, "West Park and Esopus," 129; Barrus, I, 355; Koyl, 1962, 721.

II–6. Barrus, I, 134, 154, 165–171, 178, 232, 248, II, 81; John Burroughs Journal, Mar. 28, 1888 and Oct. 4, 1889, John Burroughs Papers, Archives & Special Collections Library, VCL; John Burroughs, "Mellow England," *Scribner's Monthly*, 8 (Sept. 1874): 567; Charles E. Benton, *Troutbeck* (Dutchess County Historical Society, 1916): 26; Rhoads, *Kingston*, 50, 165; Burroughs, "House-Building," 331–41; Burroughs, "Roof-Tree," 273–89; John Burroughs, untitled fragment of an essay on art, c. 1863–1872, Box 14, Folder 14, John Burroughs Papers, VCL; William B. Rhoads, "Donald G. Mitchell and the Colonial Revival," *Nineteenth Century*, 4 (Autumn 1978): 76–83; E. C. Gardner, *Homes and How to Make Them* (Boston: James R. Osgood, 1874), 64; Renehan, 115; Jeff Walker, "The Roughest of Shells ... ," *American Transcendental Quarterly*, 21 (Sept. 2007); Stickley, 577–78; Kelley, *John Burroughs Naturalist*, 68, 258; Julian Burroughs, "Boyhood Days with John Burroughs," *Craftsman*, 22 (July 1912): 360; John Burroughs, *My Boyhood with a conclusion by ... Julian Burroughs* (Garden City: Doubleday, Page, 1922), 157; Julian Burroughs, typed memoirs, p. 10, Box 5, Folder 1, Julian Burroughs Papers, NYSL.

II–7. Julian Burroughs, *Memories,* 43, 83; Julian Burroughs, "Country House," 415–16; Kelley, *Naturalist,* 170, 171, 247; Barrus, II, 28, 71, 207; John Burroughs, "Roof-Tree," 269; John Burroughs Journal, Feb. 18, 1902 to Aug. 9, 1902; Julian Burroughs, "Boyhood Days with John Burroughs," *Craftsman*, 22 (July 1912): 360; photos in Julian Burroughs Papers, NYSL, boxes, 8, 9, 19; Julian Burroughs to John Burroughs, Feb. 16, 1903, and May 10, 1903, Box 19, John Burroughs Papers, VCL; Julian Burroughs, "Using Slabs and Bark as a House Covering," *Craftsman*, (Mar. 1911): 619–21; Benepe, 200.

II–8. Wilson Brothers, *Catalogue*; Kelley, "West Park," 116.

II–9. H. A. Haring, ed., *The Slabsides Book of John Burroughs* (Boston: Houghton, Mifflin, 1931), 10, 15, 17, 48; John Burroughs, "Wild Life about My Cabin," *Far and Near* (Boston: Houghton, Mifflin, 1904), 131–56; John Burroughs Journal, Mar. 22, 1888, July 23, 1891, Aug. 12 and 24, 1895, Dec. 14 to 18, 1910; Elizabeth Kelley notes to Burroughs Journal, 1895, p. 643, and Aug. 24, 1895; Kelley, *Slabsides,* 3, 17–23, 41, 70, 78; John Burroughs, "House-Building," 269; Barrus, I, 169, 250, 254, 297, 348–49, 356, 359, 365, 394, II, 86, 97, 110; Clara Barrus, *The Retreat of a Poet Naturalist* (Boston: Poet Lore, 1905), 4, 18–20; Renehan, 60, 190, 257; James Perrin Warren, "John Burroughs' Writing Retreats," *Hudson River Valley Review*, 25 (Autumn 2008): 28; Stickley, 580; John Burroughs, "Picturesque Aspects of Farm Life in New York," *Scribner's Monthly*, 17 (Nov. 1878): 43; John Burroughs, "Roof-Tree," 263; Edward Kanze, *World of John Burroughs* (New York: Abrams, 1993), 63–64, 96–97; Green, 128, 225; Kelley, "West Park," 141; Ingersoll, 139; *John Burroughs and Ludella Peck* (New York: Harold Vinal, 1925), 10, 16, 24; *NYT*, July 25, Aug. 15, and Dec. 18, 1910.

II–10. Kelley, "West Park," 125.

II–11. *Holy Cross Magazine*, Nov. 1902, via holycrossmonastery.com; *KDF*, May 20, 1904; Kelley, "West Park," 127; *NYT*, Apr. 20, 1904, Aug. 7, 1964; Shand-Tucci, 176–77; Kenneth

Rexroth, *Autobiographical Novel* (Garden City: Doubleday, 1966), 310, 333–34.

II–12. *Kingston Sunday Freeman*, July 4, 1976; Dennis Steadman Francis, *Architects in Practice, New York City, 1840–1900* (New York: Committee for the Preservation of Architectural Records, 1980), 44; Ingersoll, 139; Kelley, "West Park," 122–23, 135, 139; *NYT*, July 14, 1913, May 13, 1926, Sept. 6, 1934, Sept. 6, 1936; *NPI*, Oct. 10, 1878; Paul E. Parker, "Historical Sketch," in Town of Lloyd Historian's Office.

II–13. Julian Burroughs, *Memories*, 89–90, 97; *NYT*, Nov. 16, 1911, Oct. 24, 1913, Oct. 1, 1934; *KDF*, Sept. 23, 1909, Oct. 1, 1934; Foy; Kelley, "West Park," 134, 137–38; Hewitt, *Carrere & Hastings*, II, 109, 279; *NPT*, Sept. 24, 2009; Kelley, *West Parker*, 53, 62; Julian to John Burroughs, Oct. 8, 1913, VCL; Emma Larson to Julian Burroughs, Apr. 8 and Nov. 17, 1914, Jan. 14 and 16, 1915, Box 2, Julian Burroughs Papers, NYSL; Julian to John and Ursula Burroughs, "Sun. eve" [1914], Box 1, Julian Burroughs Papers, NYSL; Julian to same, Sept. 10, 1915, VCL; Herbert Peck, *Book of Rookwood Pottery* (New York: Crown, 1968), 95.

II–14. *Chronological Biography of the Hon. Zadock Pratt* (New York: Shoe and Leather Reporter Press, 1868); Sylvester, I, 156–57; Ulster Historical Society, 254–60.

II–15. Alfred Hopkins, *Modern Farm Buildings* (New York: McBride, Nast, 1913); Julian Burroughs, *Memories*, 89, 96; Julian to John Burroughs, Aug. 3, 1914, July 29, 1916, Jan. 23, 1918, "Wed." [Feb. 1918], VCL; Foy; Kelley's note on photo of plaque, Box 9, Julian Burroughs Papers, NYSL.

II–16. Emma Larson to Julian Burroughs, Jan. 3, 1915, Box 2, Julian Burroughs Papers, NYSL; Julian to John Burroughs, Aug. 8, 1915, VCL.

II–17. Hewitt, *Carrere & Hastings*, II, 279; *KDF*, June 28, 1917.

II–18. *KDF*, May 17, 1904; Child, 82–84; Sylvester, II, 120; Ulster Historical Society, xxxiii.

II–19. John V. McGuire, *The Esopus Story: A History of the Redemptorist House of Studies, Mount Saint Alphonsus* (Esopus, 1957), 42, 49–50, 59, 68, 73, 84, 132; Withey (on Untersee), 609; *KDF*,

May 17, 1904; Sara Delano Roosevelt to Franklin D. Roosevelt, Feb. 7, 1915, Roosevelt Family Papers, FDRL; Kelley, "West Park," 146; *A Century of Blessings. Centennial Jubilee. Mount Saint Alphonsus, Esopus, 1907–2007*, 36–37, 53.

II–20. Mary Polhemus and Janice Torrens, "Early Homes and Historic Sites," *Town of Esopus Story*, 44; *Kingston Sunday Freeman*, June 29, 1975.

II–21. www.esopuslighthouse.org.

II–22. *KDF*, Oct. 1, 1930; *Railroad Magazine*, 24 (Sept. 1938): 107; William B. Rhoads, "The Machine in the Garden: The Trolley Cottage as Romantic Artifact," *Perspectives in Vernacular Architecture*, 8 (2000): 17–32.

II–23. Sylvester, I, 105, II, 117–18; consistory minutes and other early records preserved by the church.

II–24. *KDF*, Feb. 24, 1879, Mar. 26, 1946, Nov. 26, 1946; Ulster Historical Society, xiv, xxv, xxxiv, 163; Sylvester, I, 103–05, 140; Wick, *Esopus*, 54; DeWitt, 131; Withey (on Lienau), 371; library.marist.edu/archives/MHP/bechfamily.

II–25. www.nycoveredbridges.org (text by Raymond W. Smith); Allen, 86–87; *Kingston Weekly Freeman*, Feb. 4, 1886; Hubertis Cummings, "Theodore Burr and His Bridges across the Susquehanna," *Pennsylvania History*, 23 (Oct. 1956): 476–86; Miller, 18–22.

II–26. Child, 82; Sylvester, II, 121; *Maple Lanes*, 98–99; New Paltz newspaper copying the Kingston *Leader*, Apr. 12, 1895; *NPI*, July 19, 1895, Aug. 5, 1954; a New Paltz newspaper, May 15, 1914.

Chapter III. Town of Gardiner

Mabee, *Gardiner*, 4, 7; Mabee, "Gardiner's Tuthilltown Grist Mill," *Ulster County Gazette*, 36 (June 2003): 1; Child, 86; Beers, 117–18.

III–1. Neil Larson, "Interpretations of Locust Lawn and the Evolving New Paltz Cultural Landscape," 2002, www.huguenotstreet.org; Roth, *For the Village*, 34; "Colonel Josiah Hasbrouck House," 2-page typescript, Huguenot Historical Society, c. 1955; Leslie LeFevre-Stratton, "Locust Lawn: An Unfolding History," *On Huguenot Street*, 4 (Winter 2005): 1, 4–5; Benepe, 128–29.

III–2. Hasbrouck, *Gardiner*, 23–24; Neil Larson & Associates, "Jenkins-DuBois Farm & Mill Site,

Historic Conditions Report," Jan. 2001 (at HHHC).

III–3. Hasbrouck, *Historic New Paltz*, 58; Sadie Penzato, *Growing Up Sicilian and Female* (New York: Bedford Graphics, 1991), 25, 27; author's conversation with Anthony Aiello, May 13, 2009.

III–4. "Report from ... Trustees of Gardiner School District No. 1," Jan. 1, 1857, in HHHC; Hasbrouck, *Gardiner*, 22; Mabee, *Gardiner*, 72; www.hrvh.org/exhibits/show/leah/Earlylife/the-kettleborough-school.

III–5. Mabee, *Whistle*, 70–71.

III–6. Hasbrouck, *Gardiner*, 57; Mabee, *Gardiner*, 51–52; *NYT*, Apr. 18 and Sept. 26, 1897; William B. Rhoads, "The Colonial Revival and the Americanization of Immigrants," in *The Colonial Revival in America* (New York: W. W. Norton, 1985), 341–61.

III–7. *Report of the Board of Water Supply of the City of New York*, 1916, 76–79; *Catskill Aqueduct*, 53, 131.

III–8. Hasbrouck, *Gardiner*, 38; Mabee, *Gardiner*, 35.

III–9. Hasbrouck, *Gardiner*, 43; Mabee, *Whistle*, 28–31, 135.

III–10. Mabee, *Gardiner*, 30, 37; unidentified newspaper clipping, Oct. 3, 1929, HHHC.

III–11. Mabee, *Gardiner*, 72; Margaret C. Conrads, *Winslow Homer* (Princeton: Princeton University Press, 2001), 46.

III–12. "The Ancestry of William Edmund Bruyn ... compiled by Joseph Brown Turner," 1926, Bruyn Collection, HHS; "Estate of William E. Bruyn," *Architectural Record*, 68 (Nov. 1930): 396–99; Harriet Sisson Gillespie, "Early Dutch Architecture in Hudson Valley," *Arts & Decoration*, 34 (June 1931): 28–29, 72; Marc B. Fried, "A Tale of Two Houses: The Bruyn and Smedes Homesteads," *de Halve Maen* (Fall 2006): 43–50; Larson, *Masonry Architecture*, 51; author's conversation with Harry Halverson, Nov. 14, 1984; *Teller & Halverson Architects*; NPI, May 3, 1928; *NYT*, Sept. 4, 1927; *Proceedings of the Ulster County Historical Society*, 1938–39, 46A.

III–13. "Minnewaska Golf and Country Club," brochure in author's collection; information from David, Susanna, and Richard Lent, by phone, Mar. 11, 2008; Mabee, *Gardiner*, 58; *NYT*, Dec. 4, 1925 and Jan. 21, 1927.

Chapter IV. Town of Hardenburgh

Howard Hendricks, "Town of Hardenbergh," in Clearwater, 258; Sylvester, II, 329.

IV–1. *NYT*, Sept. 15, 1886, Aug. 16, 1891, Mar. 12 and July 31, 1892, Oct. 2, 1894, Aug. 28, 1898, June 24, 1900; Ingersoll, 172; *Picturesque Wallkill Valley 1900* (Walden: Wallkill Valley Farmers' Association), 45; Rhoads, *Kingston*, 172.

IV–3. Miller, 45–46.

IV–4. *NYT*, Aug. 29 and 31, 1888, Nov. 11, 1893, May 27, 1894, Apr. 21, 1910, June 28, 1914, Mar. 25, 1924; George Gould in *Who's Who*, 1899; Evers, *Catskills*, 546; Private Papers of the Kingdon Gould Family: Samuel G. Dimmick to George Gould, Jan. 27, 1890, correspondence between Andrew F. Mason and George Gould, Jan. 7, 1890 to Aug. 24, 1891, Samuel Dimmick to Mrs. Gould, Mar. 11, 1890, George Gould to H. Neill Wilson, Oct. 21, 1891, Francis L. V. Hoppin to "Lady Bountiful," July 14, 1913; *New York World*, July 19, 1891; Ingersoll, 173; DeLisser, 175; conversation with Kingdon Gould, Oct. 3, 2010; Kingdon Gould email to author, Apr. 21, 2009; Rollin Hillyer Cooke, *Historic Homes and Institutions ... of Berkshire County* (New York: Lewis, 1906), 316–17; Richard S. Jackson, Jr., and Cornelia Brooke Gilder, *Houses of the Berkshires* (New York: Acanthus, 2006), 152.

Chapter V. Town of Hurley

Sylvester, II, 149; Olive Clearwater, "Hurley," in *History of Ulster County*, 104; Spafford, 247; Eberlein, *Manors*, 256.

V–1. Schoonmaker, 320 (engraving of "House at Hurley where Council of Safety met"); Reynolds, 231; Blackburn, 145; Eberlein, *Manors*, 256–66; George W. Nash, "How We Went Shopping for a Country House," *Country Life in America* 12 (June 1907): 208–09; Nash, "The Transformation of Our Country House," *Country Life in America*, 16 (July 1909): 322–24; Nash, "Turning a Doorway into a Fireplace," *Country Life in America*, 20 (Sept. 1, 1911): 55; Nash, "Some Early American Hardware," *Architectural Record*, 34 (Oct. 1913): 329–33; Richard Le Gallienne, "Old Kingston,"

Harper's Monthly, 123 (Nov. 1911): 926; *KDF*, Oct. 9, 1937.

V-2. Rhoads, "Keefe," 4–5; *KDF*, July 5, 1950; "In the Dutch Tradition," *House & Garden*, 87 (May 1945): 86–87; Keefe drawings, FHK.

V-3. Sylvester, II, 154; conversation with Don Kent, George Kent's son, Jan. 15, 1985; historical notes provided by Don Kent; HABS No. 4–302; Keefe drawings, FHK and author's collection.

V-4. De Lisser, 113; Deana F. Decker, *Images of America: Hurley* (Charleston: Arcadia, 2007), 39; Reynolds, 223–24; Waldron Phoenix Belknap, Jr., *American Colonial Painting* (Cambidge: Harvard University Press, 1959), 257, pl. 69.

V-5. Rhoads, "Hervey White and the Architecture of the Maverick," in Bloodgood, 46–48.

V-6. Rhoads, "Hervey White," in Bloodgood, 42–45.

V-7. Conversation with T. Jay Rifenbary, son of Jay W. Rifenbary, Nov. 7, 1984; construction photos formerly in T. J. Rifenbary collection; Alice Schoonmaker, "Historical Notes on the Town of Rochester," in *History of Ulster County*, 311; phone conversation with Lachlan Pitcairn, Oct. 16, 2008; notes on Glen Tonche compiled by Helen Chase for 1995 annual meeting of the Catskill Center for Conservation & Development; Raymond Pitcairn in *Who's Who*, 1942; *NYT*, July 13, 1966; www.philadelphiabuildings.org; *KDF*, Oct. 3, 2005; www.allairestudios.com/views; Augustus R. Schrowang to author, April 24, 2009; 66 architectural drawings in Mellor, Meigs & Howe Collection, Architectural Archives, University of Pennsylvania.

V-8. Sylvester, II, 152; Allen M. Rowe, *Old West Hurley Revisited* (Saugerties: Hope Farm Press, 1999), 45.

Chapter VI. City of Kingston

VI-1. Ford, *Images*, 15; *KDF*, Dec. 28, 1904, June 22, 2001; Kenneth Hewes Barricklo, Historic Structure Report: The Matthewis Persen House, for the Ulster County Department of Buildings and Grounds, 2000; Lowell Thing, phone interview with Paul Huey, June 16, 2003.

VI-2. Roderic H. Blackburn, "The Fred J. Johnston Museum," *Magazine Antiques*, 152 (August 1997): 168–77.

VI-3. Jacob Landy, *The Architecture of Minard Lafever* (New York: Columbia University Press, 1970), 44; Krattinger.

VI-4. Sylvester, I, 216–17; C. M. Ryon in De Lisser, 66; Ford, *Images*, 48; Rhoads, *Kingston*, 33, 123–24.

VI-5. *KDF*, Mar. 31, 1904, Oct. 16, 1905, Oct. 5, 1909; plans by Teller, FHK.

VI-6. William De Witt, 42; www.rupco.org/kirklandhistory; National Register registration form provided by Guy Kempe.

VI-7. William De Witt, 65; *KDF*, Apr. 14, 1903, Apr. 15, 1905.

VI-8. Ford, *Images*, 20; Schoonmaker, 295, 456; information compiled by Jane Kellar.

VI-9. De Lisser, 35; *Commemorative Biographical*, 377–78; National Register registration form provided by Jane Kellar.

VI-10. *KDF*, Mar. 30, 2001; www.rupco.org.

VI-11. *American Builder* (Dec. 1876); *NYT*, Jan. 10, 1881; Sylvester, I, 153.

VI-12. James Sullivan, ed., *History of New York State* (New York: Lewis Publishing, 1927), 364–65; author's conversations with Augustus Schrowang, Jr., July 20 and Aug. 1, 2007; notes provided by Augustus Schrowang, Jr., Jan. 26, 2009.

VI-13. Hewitt, *Architect*, 278; *NYT*, Sept. 19, 1915; *International Studio*, 37 (June 1909): xcii; *Architectural Record*, 28 (Oct. 1910): 261–67; *American Architect*, 99 (Apr. 12, 1911); Lewis Colt Albro and Harrie T. Lindeberg, *Domestic Architecture* (New York, 1912); Phil M. Riley, "A Country House That 'Fits,'" *Country Life in America*, 18 (Oct. 1910): 638–40; William De Witt, 138; *KDF*, Oct. 24, 1908; National Register registration form, Galli-Curci Estate, prepared by Kathleen LaFrank, 2010, with research by Maureen Nagy.

VI-14. *KDF*, Oct. 2, 1907, July 21, 1911, June 10, 1912; *Craftsman*, 19 (Nov. 1910): 202; *Carle's Directory, City of Kingston*, 1899.

VI-15. Plans by Teller, 1915–16, FHK; Chester H. Liebs, *Main Street to Miracle Mile* (Boston: Little, Brown, 1985), 83; *KDF*, Mar. 2, 1927; *NYT*, Apr. 3, 1945.

VI-16. De Lisser, 36; Withey, 45; *NYT*, July 20, 1889, Dec. 3, 1894, July 11, 1904, Feb. 9, 1940; "The

High Altar and Triptych in the Church of the Holy Cross," 1925 pamphlet provided by the Rev. David L. Bronson; Shand-Tucci, 115; C. M. Hall in Clearwater, 470; William De Witt, 26.

VI–17. Beers, 71; Sylvester, I, 263; William De Witt, 419; *NYT*, Mar. 27, 1898; George E. Woodward, *Woodward's Country Homes* (New York, 1865), 9, 18; Woodward's drawings for the Bray house, Catalogue 54, Bookpress Ltd., Williamsburg, Va., Winter 1990.

VI–18. Beers, 31; De Lisser, 40; William De Witt, 76; Lowell Thing email to author, Jan. 27, 2009.

VI–19. Correspondence at Winterthur Library: Fred Johnston to Henry Francis du Pont, May 26, 1945 and Sept. 4, 1945; du Pont to Johnston, Sept. 29, 1945; Sweeney, 152–53.

VI–20. Child, 241; *KDF*, May 7, 2007; Geoffrey Miller email to author, Dec. 8, 2010.

VI–21. Benson Lossing, *Pictorial Field-Book of the Revolution*, 2 vols. (New York: Harper, 1851–52), I, 388; Ford, *Street Whys*, 67; National Register registration form prepared by Kevin McEvoy, 2008; Sylvester, I, 276.

Chapter VII. Town of Kingston

Sylvester, I, 14, II, 334; Kathleen Burton Maxwell in *History of Ulster County*, 146; Ernest Jarrold, *Mickey Finn Idylls* (New York: Doubleday & McClure, 1899), 114, 205.

VII–1. Maxwell in *History of Ulster County*, 148.

Chapter VIII. Town of Lloyd

Sylvester, II, 125, 128; *KDF*, Nov. 16, 1937; Child, 104; Mabee, *Promised Land*, 73–79.

VIII–1. Mabee, *Bridging*, 7, 8, 36, 41–49, 55; Thomas C. Clarke, "Hudson River Bridge at Poughkeepsie," *Scientific American Supplement*, 25 (May 19, 1888): 10311–13; Plowden, 140, 165–66; *KDF*, Oct. 2, 2009; ny.existingstations.com.

VIII–2. *NYT*, July 4, 1937, June 28, 1940; Norman Bel Geddes, *Horizons* (Boston: Little, Brown, 1932), 222–23; Plowden, 243; *KDF*, Oct. 10, 1925, Aug. 26, 1930; William B. Rhoads, "Artistic Patronage of Franklin D. Roosevelt," *Prologue* 15 (Spring 1983): 15–16.

VIII–3. Christopher Gray in *NYT*, Nov. 21, 2004; Gutman, 232, 262; Engle, 121.

VIII–4. Adams; unidentified New Paltz newspaper, Apr. 13, 1871.

VIII–5. *Highland Post*, July 20, 1923; Rhoads, *Kingston*, 45; Jackman, 49, 51, 71.

VIII–6. *NPT*, Apr. 22, 1896; Jackman, 56.

VIII–7. *Commemorative Biographical*, 517–18; Clarence J. Elting to Helen W. Reynolds, Aug. 9 and Aug. 31, 1925, AML; *ST*, Nov. 30, 1934; Wadlin, 144–45; Jackman, 66.

VIII–8. Unidentified newspaper, May 8, 1896, HHHC; *Commemorative Biographical*, 296; Wadlin, 253; Chris DiMattei email to author, Jan. 11, 2011; George F. Barber, *The Cottage Souvenir No. 2* (Knoxville, 1890; reprinted as *Victorian Cottage Architecture* [Mineola: Dover, 2004]), Design No. 53, 113.

VIII–9. Rhoads, *Kingston*, 146; *Commemorative Biographical*, 673; "Map of Ulster County ... from original surveys by Oliver J. Tillson and P. Henry Brink," HHHC; Child, 195; Jackman, 67.

VIII–10. Sylvester, II, 129, 133; Beatrice Wadlin in *History of Ulster County*, 169; *NPI*, Sept. 6, 1869; Jackman, 68, 98; Child, 200; Charles Cullen to author, Aug. 22, 2007.

VIII–11. J. H. French, "Map of Ulster County," 1858; information from Cynthia Lee; *NPI*, Sept. 26, 1902; Child, 195; *Highland Post*, Apr. 27, 1891.

VIII–12. Upjohn; information in Town of Lloyd Historian's Office; *NPI*, Dec. 15, 1870, Aug. 21, 1873, July 8, 1875; *Kingston Daily Leader*, July 12, 1901; Jackman, 44.

VIII–13. Sylvester, II, 129; *Vail's Poughkeepsie City Directory*, 1873–74.

VIII–14. Raymond Riordon, "Interlaken, An Outdoor School," *Craftsman*, 22 (May 1912): 185; David Cathers, *Gustav Stickley* (New York: Phaidon, 2003), 189–90; Charles Hamilton, *Roycroft Collectibles* (San Diego: Barnes, 1980), 107; Raymond Riordon, "An Outdoor School," *Craftsman*, 26 (April 1914): 92, 94; Jackman, 74; Elbert Hubbard II, "The Boy and Opportunity," *Raymond Riordon School*, undated pamphlet in Lloyd Historian's Office, and other pamphlets and photos in this office and the collections of Vivian Wadlin and the author; unidentified newspaper, Dec. 31, 1915, HHHC; *Poughkeepsie Sunday Courier*, May 5 and Dec. 19? 1940; "The Wilderness Camp at Horseshoe," *Touchstone*, 8 (Oct. 1920): 60–5; *Who's Who*, 1922; *KDF*, April 22 and Dec. 23, 1940; *NYT*, April 23, 1940; plaques in private collection, Lloyd.

Chapter IX. Town of Marbletown

Child, 105; Beverly Russell, "1765 Mill Grinds into Action," *House & Garden*, (1977? [clipping in Ulster County Community College Library]): 36–40; (Harry Hansen), "Rest Plaus Rural Historic District," *Ulster County Gazette*, 37 (June 2004): 1–7; Sylvester, II, 188.

IX–1. Reynolds, 236; Gary Tinterow, "What I Learned about the Wynkoop House," lecture at Marbletown Community Center, Apr. 5, 2003; Tinterow, Marbletown Landmark Designation Application, April 10, 2008; Long, 58–63; William Walton, "Hudson Valley Heritage: Restoring a House where Washington Laid His Head," *Architectural Digest* (June 1995): 144–53; Sylvester, II, 200; correspondence at FDRL: H. F. du Pont to F. D. Roosevelt, Aug. 21, 1933, Roosevelt to du Pont, Aug. 25, 1933, Roosevelt to Postmaster General, Aug. 25, 1933; correspondence at Winterthur Library: du Pont to Sarah Lounsbery, May 23, 1935, du Pont to Lounsbery, Feb. 27, 1953, du Pont to Fred Johnston, Jan. 25, 1954; author's phone conversation with Sarah Lounsbery, Aug. 11, 1978; Sara Jatcko, of Winterthur Museum, conversation with author, Nov. 13, 2007; *HVVAN*, (July 1999 and Aug. 2001).

IX–2. Benepe, 58; Reynolds, 219; Report by Harry Hansen, Minutes of Marbletown Historic Preservation Commission, Oct. 9, 2010 (www.marbletown.net/government/historic_preservation.cfm); Elsie Lathrop, *Early American Inn and Taverns* (1926; reprint New York: Blom, 1968), 259–60; printed ephemera from Sarah Lounsbery's Sally Tock's Inn, UCHS; unidentified newspaper, 1914, SRL; guest register preserved at UCHS; William B. Rhoads, "Roadside Colonial: Early American Design for the Automobile Age," *Winterthur Portfolio*, 21 (Autumn 1986): 133–52; Judith A. Barter et al., *American Arts at the Art Institute of Chicago* (Chicago, 1998), 31; *NYT*, Mar. 4, 1961 and Dec. 20, 1994; plans by Teller, FHK; Teller's photos of the inn before alterations,

SRL; Gertrude Stein, *The Autobiography of Alice B. Toklas* (New York: Harcourt, Brace, 1933), 195, 209; Leggett, 279; H. F. du Pont to E. C. Chadbourne, Oct. 1, 1937, Chadbourne to du Pont, Oct. 15, 1937, Winterthur Library; Kevin D. Murphy, "'Secure from All Intrusion': Heterotopia, Queer Space, and the Turn-of-the-Century American Resort," *Winterthur Portfolio*, 43 (Summer/Autumn 2009): 185–228.

IX–3. Benepe, 56; www.stoneridgelibrary.org/library_history; Zimm, 125; Report by Hansen cited in note IX–2.

IX–4. Gary Tinterow, Marbletown Landmark Designation Application, Dec. 1, 2008.

IX–5. Sylvester, II, 194; Deweese DeWitt, 15.

IX–6. www.marbletown.net/about/buildinghistory; Leggett, 82–3, 247; Laura Shane Cunningham, "A Place in the Country," *New Yorker* (Aug. 2, 1999): 47, 49; www.ridgely.org/greatsummer; *NYT*, May 26, 1894, Dec. 16, 1899, Aug. 16, 1901, Aug. 16, 1924, Oct. 24, 1951; "Ridgely Park in the Shawangunk Mountains," c. 1894 brochure, and Ken Davenport, "Ridgely Manor, Stone Ridge," Nov. 11, 1976, both in SRL; White and Willensky, 384; W. Barksdale Maynard, *Buildings of Delaware* (Charlottesville: University of Virginia Press, 2009), 253.

IX–7. Gravestones of Sanger and Harriet Carleton, Fairview Cemetery, Stone Ridge; *NYT*, Aug. 31, 1941; author's conversations with the Rev. David L. Bronson.

IX–8. Ryan, "Old World Traditions," 109; Fitchen, 6, 9; *Marbletown Album*, 30–1; Greg Huber, "The Case of the Vanishing Barn," *Ulster* (Winter 1995): 72, 75; Huber in *HVVAN* (Feb.–Mar. 2007): 2–6, and (Apr.–June 2010): 15.

IX–9. Benepe, 158; *Marbletown Album*, 29; author's conversations with Julian and Shannon Schreibman.

IX–10. Sylvester, II, 196; Harry Hansen, report on Main Street Historic District, 1988, SRL; *KDF*, July 31, 1920, Jan. 24, 1940, and undated (1930s) clipping, SRL; Katharine Hasbrouck, "The Fun of Fixing Up a Farmhouse," *Garden & Home Builder* (May 1928); A. J. Canaday, "The Shop in the Garden," *Gift and Art Shop* (Feb. 1934); Zimm, 198; Shop in the Garden postcards, postmarked Jan. 12, 1933 and Aug. 17, 1935, author's collection; Ryan, "Old World Traditions," 56; Teller's plans for Dr. John Roswell Hasbrouck, FHK; Brian L. Taylor emails to author, Feb. 15 and Apr. 27, 2010; Lucy Van Sickle, *Images of America: Marbletown* (Charleston: Arcadia, 2008), 21; *Marbletown Album*, 16.

IX–11. *NYT*, Dec. 26, 1929, Apr. 11 and Oct. 3, 1937, Jan. 16, 1938; Sarah Allaback, *The First American Women Architects* (Urbana: University of Illinois Press, 2008), 214–16; *American Architect*, 146 (Jan. 1935): 41–2; *Architectural Record*, 78 (Aug. 1935): 28.

IX–12. Report on Bevier House by Myron Teller to Louis Bevier, Apr. 1953, UCHS; Kenneth Hewes Barricklo, "Historic Structure Report, The Bevier House at Marbletown," 2002, UCHS; Neil Larson, "Building a Stone House in Ulster County, New York, in 1751," *HVVAN* (Apr.–June 2011): 5–11; *KDF*, Aug. 16, 1938 and May 20, 1953; Teller, 2; *NYT*, Oct. 3, 1981.

IX–13. Benepe, 154; Child, 200.

IX–14. Benepe, 70; *KDF*, Oct. 3, 2007; William Heidgerd dated the origin of the house to 1730 and identified the builder as Daniel Schoonmaker, while a stone above a doorway is inscribed 1785, according to Heidgerd's notes on his photos of the house in HHHC.

IX–15. Clearwater, 279; Alison Lurie, review of *Small Wonder* in *New York Review of Books*, Dec. 4, 2008.

IX–16. *Marbletown Album*, 66; *KDF*, May 21, 2010.

IX–17. "What's Dutch," 21; "Early American Homes: Van Idah," *The Jeffersonian*, 1933, provided by Janet M. Leas; *NYT*, July 20, 1951; Teller's photos and notes, including "Observation Records ... Ulster Old Houses," SRL; *KDF*, July 31, 1920.

IX–18. Reynolds, 226, pl. 92; Marijn Manuels, "Hudson Valley Wall Paneling," www.metmuseum.org/Works_of_Art.

IX–19. Sylvester, II, 188; Ryan, "Old World Traditions," 58; Benepe, 74–5; www.depuycanalhouse.net.

IX–20. Charles W. Cullen, "Notes on St. John's Memorial Church, High Falls," Jan. 2000, D & H Canal Museum; Robert M. Vogel, *Roebling's Delaware & Hudson Canal Aqueducts* (Washington: Smithsonian, 1971); Wakefield, 169–75; Rochelle Riservato, "The Saga of High Falls' Elsie Crawford," *Blue Stone Press*, Mar. 17, 2006.

IX–21. Burgess; Josephson, *Mohonk*; brochures and correspondence in the Mohonk Mountain House Archives: "Exercises Had at the Dedication of the New Parlor," 1899; "Lake Mohonk Mountain-House, 1876"; Joan LaChance, "The Evolution of Mohonk Mountain House from 1869 to 1902"; Alfred Smiley to Albert Smiley, Sept. 24 and 27, 1872, Sept. 20 and Oct. 7, 1874; James E. Ware to Albert K. Smiley, Nov. 29, 1898; Michel LeBrun to Mr. Smiley, Oct. 17, 1892; Michel LeBrun to Albert K. Smiley, July 9 and Nov. 8, 1887. A New Paltz newspaper, July 2, 1869, Sept. 28, 1900; *NYT*, Aug. 14, 1882; "The Same Only Better," *Hudson Valley* (Oct. 2005): 51–55; www.akspl.org/history; Partington, 113.

IX–22. Sylvester, II, 199; Deweese DeWitt, 55; conversations with Robert A. Larsen and Robi Josephson, Oct. 2006.

IX–23. Larson, "Village of New Paltz," IV–15; Josephson, 13; Ryan, "Old World Traditions," 34, 50; Benepe, 78; Burgess, 120.

Chapter X. Town of Marlborough

Sylvester, II, 83–84; Barber and Howe, 558; Mary Lou Mahan, "The Adopted Son," *Southern Ulster Times*, Feb. 8, 2006; *KDF*, Oct. 20, 1885; Lizzie W. Champney, "Summer Haunts of American Artists," *Century Magazine*, 30 (Oct. 1885): 846; Sue Rainey, "Mary Hallock Foote," *Winterthur Portfolio*, 42 (Summer/Autumn 2007) 123.

X–1. Blackburn, 149–53; Holly Snyder, "The Gomez Family and Their Hudson Valley Connections," lecture at SUNY New Paltz, Sept. 27, 1997; Natalie Curtis, "An Historic House on the Hudson," *Craftsman* 17 (Oct. 1909): 3–11; www.stormking.org/history; Dard Hunter, *My Life with Paper* (New York: Knopf, 1958), 58–71; Cathleen A. Baker, *By His Own Labor: The Biography of Dard Hunter* (New Castle: Oak Knoll, 2000), 68–85; "Gomez Mill House" brochure, 2007; *NYT*, Jan. 27, 1939; unidentified newspaper (re demolition of Deepdene), Aug. 23, 1978; www.gomez.org.

X–2. Upjohn, 180, 212; Sylvester, II, 91; Charles M. Hall in Clearwater, 467; Margaret Armstrong, *Five Generations* (New York: Harper, 1930),

401; *Biographical Cyclopaedia of American Women* (New York: Halvord, 1924), 50; David Maitland Armstrong, *Day before Yesterday* (New York: Scribner's, 1920), 24.

X–3.   *NYT*, Mar. 27, 1938.

X–4.   *ST*, June 26, 1868; *NPN*, Feb. 14, 1979; Adams; Sylvester, II, 85.

X–5.   *KDF*, Aug. 7, 1936 and Dec. 11, 1937; Park & Markowitz, 122.

X–6.   Wilson Brothers, 13.

X–7.   Reynolds, 201–02; Eberlein, *Manors*, 271–74; Le Fevre, 341; conversation with George Rusk, Jr., June 25, 2010.

X–8.   Clearwater, 254; unidentified newspaper, Apr. 1924, in Marlboro Free Library for Woosley's obituary.

X–9.   Sylvester, II, 94.

X–10. Richard Upjohn, *Upjohn's Rural Architecture* (New York: Putnam, 1852).

X–11. National Register of Historic Places, registration form, "Milton Railroad Station," 2007; Wilson Brothers, 13.

X–12. *KDF*, Sept. 12, 1912, June 29, 1926; Kirsten Scott to author, Dec. 5, 1978; "The Ashbee Journals," June 1915, typescript in Marlboro Free Library; W. Scott Braznell, "The Early Career of Ronald Hayes Pearson," *Winterthur Portfolio*, 34 (Winter 1999): 185–213; *Picture Book*, 27; Hanna Astrup Larsen, "The Craft Work on the 'Hill of Fairies,'" *Craftsman*, 30 (Sept. 1916): 634–37; Elverhoj brochures and photos, Bruce Weiss collection; conversation with Bruce Weiss, June 27, 2009; Mabee, *Promised Land*, 68–72; Marylou Mahan, *The First Hundred Years* (Lincoln, Neb.: Universe, 2002), 141; *NYT*, Aug. 9, 1938.

Chapter XI. Town of New Paltz

Roth, "'where ye walloens dwell,'" 347–54; Roth, *For the Village*; Barber & Howe, 559; *Souvenir of the Wallkill Valley* (Walden: Wallkill Valley Farmers' Assoc., 1898), 55; Eberlein, *Manors*, 267.

XI–1. John G. Waite Associates, Architects, *DuBois Fort, Historic Structure Report* (Albany: Mt. Ida Press, 2001); John H. Braunlein, "Huguenot Street," *Ulster County Gazette*, 37 (Nov. 2004): 3; conversation with William Heidgerd, Nov. 18,

1986; Gladys Gottlieb, *Recipes and Memories: The Old Fort Restaurant* (Kearney, Neb.: Morris, 2007), 5; *NYT*, May 31, 1954; HABS, "The Dubois Fort," p. 8; *NPI*, Dec. 15 and 22, 1938, Sept. 26, 1940; *NPN*, Aug. 2, 1956.

XI–2. *NPI*, Dec. 2, 1869, Dec. 28, 1894, Jan. 3, 1919; Neil Larson in *Newsletter of the Huguenot Historical Society*, 5 (Fall 2004): 4–5; Crawford & Stearns and Neil Larson & Associates, "Historic Structure Report for the Jean Hasbrouck House," Fall 2002, 2.28; Blackburn, 123; Roth, *For the Village*, 11; [New Paltz] *Normal Review* 1 (June 1894): 11; *NYT*, July 26, 1970.

XI–3. *NPI*, Sept. 5, 1972; Kenneth E. Hasbrouck, "Our French Church," typescript, 1973; Rhoads, *Architectural History*, 1–3; Roth, "'where ye walloens dwell,'" 346; *NPT*, May 16, 1862.

XI–4. *NPT*, May 4, 1887 and May 2, 1894; *NYT*, June 8, 1952; John G. Waite Associates, "Deyo House, Historic Structure Report," 1997; Jacquetta Haley, "Deyo House, Furnishing Plan," 2001; *NPI*, March 1887.

XI–5. Roth, *For the Village*, 18; *NPI*, Dec. 28, 1894; Reynolds, 183; lecture by Leslie LeFevre-Stratton at Elting Memorial Library, July 21, 2005; Joseph E. Diamond, "Archaeological Field School," *Newsletter of Historic Huguenot Street*, 8 (Fall 2009): 2.

XI–6. Reynolds, 204; *Hudson Valley Sunday Courier*, Oct. 14, 1942; *NPI*, July 1, 1948; William B. Rhoads, "Ivar Elis Evers: New Paltz Watercolors, 1930–1950," typescript for Dorsky Art Museum, SUNY New Paltz, 1998; Roth, *For the Village*, 36; *NYT*, Apr. 24, 1955 and May 31, 1957; Blackburn, 130.

XI–7. Consistory minutes and other records, archives of the New Paltz Reformed Church; Rhoads, *Architectural History*; Clearwater, "Old Dutch Church at Shawangunk," 1; *NPN*, Sept. 28, 1983; Gary A. Trudgen, "John Bailey," *Colonial Newsletter*, 30 (July 1990): 1154–85.

XI–8. Le Fevre, 160–62; *NPI*, Jan. 9, Oct. 9, Dec. 18, 1873, Dec. 17, 1874, Mar. 18, 1875, Aug. 12, 1881.

XI–9. Beers, 134; *NPI*, Oct. 22 and Nov. 19, 1874, Feb. 18 and 25, 1875, Nov. 27, 1914; Child, 189; Beers, 134; Johnson and Ryan, 37.

XI–10. *NPT*, Aug. 17 and 31, Nov. 23, 1892, July 19,

1893; *NPI*, July 3, 1891, Nov. 4, 1892; conversation with Mildred Radley Hague, 1975; Lang, 45; [New Paltz] *Normal Review,* 1 (Feb. 1895): 5.

XI–11. *NPI*, Nov. 6, 1891, Mar. 5, 1936; Rhoads, *Kingston*, 172.

XI–12. Larson, "Village of New Paltz," IV, 28; *KDF*, July 31, 1920; *NPI*, Aug. 5, 1920, June 28, 1928, Mar. 4, 1937, Apr. 1, 1954, Mar. 8, 1962; Leon H. Smith to Nettie, May 23, 1920, HHHC; William Heidgerd, "The New Paltz Library," unidentified New Paltz newspaper, June 27, 1962; Johnson & Ryan, 61; Carol A. Johnson, *Elting@100: A History of the Elting Memorial Library* (Elting Memorial Library, 2009); Teller & Halverson records, FHK.

XI–13. *NPI*, Mar. 20, 1924; Sept. 15, 1933; Apr. 18, 1935, Sept. 19, 1935, Dec. 3, 1936; conversation with Harold Wood, Mar. 20, 1978.

XI–14. Johnson & Ryan, 80; *NPT*, May 18, 1871; note by Cyrus (Freer), Jan. 14, 1908, HHHC.

XI–15. Johnson & Ryan, 44; *NPT*, Apr. 12, 1893; Wheeler's plans and specifications for the Luther Hasbrouck house remain at the house.

XI–16. Sylvester 19; White & Willensky, 41; *NPI*, Sept. 15, 1870; unidentified New Paltz newspaper, Jan. 14, 1887; William B. Rhoads, "8 Church Street," typescript for Village of New Paltz Historic Preservation Commission, 2004.

XI–17. *NPI*, May 28, 1925, Feb. 3 and Mar. 17, 1927, June 28 and Nov. 22, 1928, May 30, 1930; *KDF*, Nov. 21, 1928; Teller & Halverson's drawings for the proposed and completed church, FHK; Rhoads, *Teller & Halverson*, 13–15.

XI–18. Standard Homes Co., *Better Homes at Lower Cost* (Washington, 1923); *NPI*, June 20, 1929 and June 12, 1952.

XI–19. *NYT*, Oct. 3, 1894; New York Couch Bed Co. catalogue, HHHC; *NPI*, Jan. 18 and Feb. 22, 1907, Mar. 27, 1924; Reiff, 186; Pamela H. Simpson, *Cheap, Quick, & Easy: Imitative Architectural Materials* (Knoxville: University of Tennessee Press, 1999), 11; conversation with Peter Harp, July 21, 1975; Johnson & Ryan, 112; Larson, "Village of New Paltz," IV, 131–35.

XI–20. Conversations with O. Lincoln Igou, May 28, 1976 and Jan. 10, 2009; Koyl, 1962, 483; *NYT*, Aug. 23, 1947 and Aug. 28, 2001; *NPI*,

Apr. 12 and Nov. 1, 1951, Apr. 9, 1958; Miller's drawings for the Igou house, HHHC.

XI–21. *NPI*, Jan. 26, 1937; Reiff, 238–39; Katherine Cole Stevenson and H. Ward Jandl, *Houses by Mail* (Washington: Preservation Press, 1986), 158.

XI–22. *NPI*, May 11, 1871, July 31, 1873, June 28, 1907; Ruth Mack Havens bookplate, Special Collections, Sojourner Truth Library; "An Era Topples," Office of Information, State University College, New Paltz, copy in HHHC.

XI–23. Lang, 11, 22–27, 42, 68–70; *Manufacturer & Builder*, 16 (June 1884): 128; "New Paltz, Education, Normal School, 1919," I, bound newspaper clippings, HHHC; Cornelia Brooke Gilder, "George L. Heins," in *Architects in Albany* (Albany: Mt. Ida Press, 2009), 50; *NYT*, June 29, 1935; architectural records at SUNY New Paltz.

XI–24. Lang, 96–100; *NPI*, Mar. 17, 1927, Oct. 31, 1930, June 1, 1934; *NYT,* Feb. 12, 1928, Oct. 9 and 25, 1930; Bruyn Hasbrouck to Franklin D. Roosevelt, Apr. 30, 1931, FDRL; unidentified newspaper, June 10, 1932; architectural plans at SUNY New Paltz.

XI–25. Lang, 136–39; *NPI*, Dec. 12, 1946; *New Paltz*
and 26 *Alumni News*, May 9, 1955, 1; *Progressive Architecture*, 47 (Jan. 1966): 142–47 and 49 (Sept. 1968): 132–39; architectural plans at SUNY New Paltz.

XI–27. *NPT*, May 31 and July 5, 1861, Apr. 22, 1864, Oct. 20, 1870; www.portjervisny.org/rivercit; *NPI*, Sept. 28, 1894, May 10 and June 7, 1895, Aug. 5, 1920; Luther B. Hill, *A History of the State of Oklahoma* (Chicago: Lewis, 1908), 95–96; *KDF*, Apr. 14, 1915; Fackler, 18–22.

XI–28. Larson, "Village of New Paltz," IV, 30.

XI–29. J. H. French, *Gazetteer of the State of New York* (Syracuse: R. P. Smith, 1860), 661; *NPT*, July 20, 1860 and Mar. 2, 1887; *NPI*, July 10, 1873, Apr. 9 and Nov. 12, 1886, May 27, 1904, Aug. 11, 1905; www.co.ulster.ny.us/poorhouse; syracusethenandnow.org; Rhoads, *Kingston*, 180; *Proceedings of the Board of Supervisors of Ulster County* (Kingston, 1889), 157; *KDF*, July 31, 1920 and Oct. 3, 2004; *NPN*, Oct. 12, 1977; Johnson & Ryan, 92.

XI–30. Johnson & Ryan, 28–29; Mabee, *Gardiner*, 15.

XI–31. Burgess, 53; Mohonk Mountain House Archives:

James E. Ware & Sons to A. K. and D. Smiley, Jan. 11, 1908, *The Golden Day 1857–1907*, 38, *Dedicatory Exercises of the Smiley Testimonial Gateway*, Oct. 14, 1908, architectural records and drawings; unidentified New Paltz newspaper, Oct. 10, 1908; *Who's Who*, 1906.

XI–32. Mohonk Mountain House Archives: "Dedicatory Exercises—A. K. Smiley—Tower, Aug. 30, 1923," *The Golden Day*, 1857–1907, 12, "To All Mohonk Guests," c. 1920, Charles F. Miller address at cornerstone laying, Aug. 30, 1921, Alfred to Albert Smiley, Mar. 16 and June 15, 1872, Ben Matteson, "The Story of Skytop," *Mohonk Winter Bulletin*, 84 (1996–97): 1, "To All Mohonk Guests," May 2, 1921, Francis R. Allen to Charles F. Miller, Sept. 13, 1920, Albert K. Smiley to W. H. P. Fraunce, Nov. 3, 1920, Fraunce to Miller, Sept. 13, 1920, Daniel Smiley address at cornerstone laying, Aug. 30, 1921, Allen to Fraunce, Dec. 7, 1921, architectural plans; Partington, 54, 70–71.

XI–33. Johnson & Ryan, 17; *NPI*, June 14, 1893 and July 24, 1941.

XI–34. *Who's Who*, 1942; Fackler, 18–22; unidentified New Paltz newspaper, Nov. 4, 1898 and Apr. 28, 1921; *NPI*, Dec. 8, 1899, Nov. 15, 1901, July 9, 1942; photos and other views and documents preserved at the Culinarians' Home; *KDF*, Dec. 29, 1941; Zimm, 213; Karl Schriftgiesser, *Oscar of the Waldorf* (New York: Dutton, 1943), 78–79, 97, 183.

XI–35. Betty Lent interviewed by Irene Martin, Feb. 21, 1986, HHHC; *NPI*, Apr. 15 and July 1, 1932, Dec. 23, 1943; Village of New Paltz Historic Preservation Commission, Landmark Designation Form for 30 Center St.

XI–36. Johnson & Ryan, 27; postcard, HHHC; *NPI*, Aug. 12, 1920 and June 6, 1946; Larson, "Village of New Paltz," IV, 182–83.

XI–37. *NPI*, Oct. 12, 1894; Rhoads, *Architectural History*, 11.

Chapter XII. Town of Olive

Sylvester, II, 294, 297, 302; Ford, *Street Whys*, 309; Child, 119–20; Rhoads, *Kingston*, 61, 118; Lowell Thing email to author, Sept. 3, 2010, correctly dates the Samson house c. 1858.

XII–1. Architectural League of New York, *Year Book*, 1925; *NYT*, Nov. 12, 1908, July 9, 1911, Oct. 14, 1917, May 6, 1944; David Stradling, *Making Mountains: New York City and the Catskills* (Seattle: University of Washington Press, 2007), 167; Allen M. Rowe, *Old West Hurley Revisited* (Saugerties: Hope Farm Press, 1999), preface; *Catskill Aqueduct Celebration*, 20, 87 and *passim*; Steuding, 107; Bone, 123–28; *KDF*, June 26, 1936 and Aug. 26, 2010; Diane Galusha, *Liquid Assets: A History of New York City's Water System* (Fleischmanns: Purple Mountain Press, 1999); Arthur Gray Adams, *Guide to the Catskills* (Albuquerque: Sun Books, 1977), 41; Vera M Sickler in *History of Ulster County*, 254.

XII–2. Postcard in author's collection.

XII–3. Rhoads, *Teller & Halverson*, 6–8; *NYT*, Dec. 29, 1934; Board of Water Supply, *Annual Report*, 1912, 113; David E. Tarn, "A Study in Local Adaptation," *Architectural Record*, 34 (October 1913): 319–28; C. Matlack Price, "A Reversion to Type," *Arts & Decoration*, 3 (Oct. 1913): 397–400.

XII–4. *NYT*, Mar. 14, 1955; *Woodstock Press*, Feb. 27, 1931.

XII–5. Postcards in author's collection; Rhoads, *Teller & Halverson*, 21; *KDF*, May 18, 1916; "The Transformation of a Wayside Inn," *New Country Life*, 32 (Dec. 1917): 70–71; Christopher Gray in *NYT*, June 19, 2011.

XII–6. John Burroughs Journal, Aug. 24, 1909; Barrus, II, 257, 270; Thomas Morris Longstreth, *The Catskills* (New York: Century, 1918), 239–45.

XII–7. Deweese DeWitt, 16.

XII–8. *NYT*, Apr. 21, 1914; postcards in author's collection; *KDF*, July 30, 1947; www.conciergesuggests.com/Brunel; www.ebrunelgallery.com.

XII–9. ny.existingstations.com; Ham and Bucenec, 9, 92.

XII–10. skellyloy.com; "Adam's Journey's photostream," flickr.com/photos; unidentified New Paltz newspaper, June 24, 1891.

XII–11. *NYT*, Dec. 6, 1955, Feb. 4, 1971, Oct. 25, 1996; blueprint and other documents preserved at the Lodge by Robert McBroom; *Time*, June 6, 1932.

XII–12. Galusha, *Another Day*, 39, 47–66; *KDF*, June 22 and July 25, 1933, Dec. 21, 1935; http://digilab.browardlibrary.org.

XII–13. "He Couldn't Buy It ... So He Made It," *American Architect*, 137 (Feb. 1930), 48–51; *KDF*, Mar. 23, 1915.

Chapter XIII. Town of Plattekill

Child, 121; Sylvester, II, 180; Werlau, 8; Spafford, 417.

XIII–1. P. N. Mitchell, *The History of the Village of Clintondale* (Poughkeepsie? 1894); Shirley V. Anson and Betty Walker in *History of Ulster County*, 287.

XIII–2. Harrison Meeske, *The Hudson Valley Dutch and Their Houses* (Fleischmanns: Purple Mountain Press, 1998), 115; Ken Walton in *HVVAN* (Aug.–Sept. 2009): 9.

XIII–3. Sylvester, II, 179.

XIII–4. Mabee, *Gardiner*, 55–56; Neil Larson and Harry Hansen, "Cole-Hasbrouck Farm Historic District," National Register of Historic Places Registration Form, 1994; Anson and Walker in *History of Ulster County*, 271; Werlau, 70.

XIII–5. Sylvester, II, 177; *Christian Intelligencer*, May 24, 1905.

XIII–6. Sylvester, II, 177; "A Guide to Huguenot Street and Preservation Efforts of the Huguenot Historical Society," 1974, 38–40; David Decker, "A Historical Luncheon," *NPT*, Aug. 25, 2005; Jerome and Elizabeth Hurd, *The Village of Clintondale from Its Beginning to 1959* (Clintondale, 1959), 19; Anson and Walker in *History of Ulster County*, 287.

Chapter XIV. Town of Rochester

Harry Hansen, "Town of Rochester, Historic Resources Report, Reconnaissance Survey," 1995 and 2008 (www.accord-kerhonkson.com/HistoricReconnaissance-1995.pdf); Sylvester, II, 207–08, 224; Deweese DeWitt, 19.

XIV–1. Marie Blank, "George Stokes Cabins," *Accordian*, 18 (Dec. 2008).

XIV–2. Reynolds, 234; Friends of Historic Rochester, "Second Annual Tour of Stone Houses," Oct. 11, 1997, 11.

XIV–3. Harry Hansen, "Krom House," Building-Structure Inventory Form, #51, July 1994; Sinclair and Sahler, 40.

XIV–4. Harry Hansen, "Benjamin Schoonmaker House," Building-Structure Inventory Form, #35, July 1994; Alice Cross, "Appledoorn Farm," *Accordian*, 20 (June 2010): 1–3; *KDF*, Jan. 17, 1903, Nov. 7, 1931, July 29, 1937; *Who's Who*, 1942; *NYT*, Feb. 22, 1966; Myron S. Teller to Harriet S. Gillespie, Feb. 2, 1939, SRL; conversation with Harry Halverson, Nov. 14, 1984; Dirck Teller to author, July 25, 2002.

XIV–5. "The O&W Railway in the Town of Rochester," *Accordian*, 17 (Sept. 2007): 2–3; vintage photos of Anderson house, Friends of Historic Rochester.

XIV–6. Reynolds, 228; Harry Hansen, "DeWitt Residence," Building-Structure Inventory Form, #10, July 1994.

XIV–7. John Cross in *Accordian*, 17 (Sept. 2007): 4–5; 1927 schedule provided by Eastern Correctional Facility, 2007.

XIV–8. John S. and Alice Cross emails to author, Jan. 19, 21, and 25, Feb. 20, 2008; Harry Hansen, "Lawrence-Cross House," Building-Structure Inventory Form, #24, July 1994.

XIV–9. Sylvester, II, 227–28; Harry Hansen, "Jacobus Van Wagenen House," Building-Structure Inventory Form, #14, July 1994.

XIV–10. Sylvester, II, 228; Harry Hansen, "Westbrook House," Building-Structure Inventory Form, #871, July 1994; Alice Cross, "Dreamland Farm," *Accordian*, 10 (July 1996): 1–4.

XIV–11. Beers, 134; "Old School Houses," notebook in Friends of Historic Rochester Museum and Library; conversation with Alice Cross, Feb. 20, 2008.

XIV–12. Benepe, 162–63; Harry Hansen, "Catherine Harnden House," Building-Structure Inventory Form, #20, July 1994; Child, 232; Beers, 74; Sylvester, II, 198; Deweese DeWitt, 53–54.

XIV–13. Burgess, 23; William E. Doughty, *Lake Minnewaska* (New York: Herbert Spencer, 1960), 30; J. M. Wilson in Minnewaska Guest Ledger, Aug. 4–Aug. 16, 1879, HHHC; Alfred to Albert Smiley, Sept. 21, 1875, Mohonk Mountain House Archives; Fried, *Shawangunk*, 17, 30; *NPI*, May 17, 1877 and Oct. 17, 1878; Jervis McEntee Diary, Aug. 28, 1878 and July 29, 1879 (www.aaa.si.edu/guides/site-jervis); "Lake Minnewaska House," 1886, 1889, 1901, 1922, 1925, 1926 brochures; unidentified New Paltz newspaper, Apr. 21, 1893, Mabee, *Gardiner*, 89, 94, 96.

Chapter XV. Town of Rosendale

Fried, *Shawangunk*, 71; Child, 125–26; Sylvester, II, 233, 239–41; Beers, 93; Century House Historical Society, *Natural News*, 11 (Spring 2009): 10.

XV–1. Sylvester, II, 243–44; *Natural News*, 10 (Fall 2008): 8–9.

XV–2. Zimm, 56; W. & J. Sloane to A. J. Snyder, Jan. 29, 1941, Snyder Papers, HHS; *Natural News*, 7 (Summer 2005): 6–7.

XV–3. "Harry Halverson, A.I.A., List of Commissions: 1924–1972," #650 and #728, drawings at FHK.

XV–4. Sylvester, II, 230; *NYT*, Mar. 19, 1872; *Guide Book to Lake Mohonk* (Providence: Rhode Island Printing, 1875); www.centuryhouse.org/news-letr/summ2000/kingbrdg.html.

XV–5. Postcard, Vivian Wadlin collection.

XV–6. Sylvester, II, 237–38; Withey, 150; *NYT*, Jan. 7, 1882; *American Builder*, Dec. 1876 and Aug. 1877; *NPI*, Dec. 9, 1869.

XV–7. Shirley V. Anson and Laura M. Jenkins, *Quaker History and Genealogy of the Marlborough Monthly Meeting* (Baltimore: Gateway, 1980), 31.

XV–8. Benepe, 182; Gregory D. Huber in *HVVAN*, 12 (Aug.–Sept. 2009): 13–19.

XV–9. Postcards, author's collection; *KDF*, Aug. 1, 1932; William B. Rhoads, "The Colonial Revival and the Americanization of Immigrants," in *The Colonial Revival in America* (New York: Norton, 1985), 341–61.

Chapter XVI. Town of Saugerties

Child, 129; Sylvester, II, 29, 34, 40, 42, 60, 74.

XVI–1. Reynolds, 199–200; Reynolds field notes, AML; Sylvester, II, 73; Stevens, 280–81; Benepe, 32; *KDF*, Dec. 21, 2003.

XVI–2. *School Buildings and Grounds*, vol. 3 of 11th Annual Report of the State Department of Education, 1917, 182; *NYT*, Jan. 1, 1937; Park and Markowitz, 147; *Antiques & the Arts Weekly*, May 14, 1993, May 19, 1995.

XVI–3. *ST*, Sept. 17, 1915; Rhoads, *Kingston*, 104; Joseph L. Wheeler and Alfred Morton Githens, *The American Public Library Building* (Chicago: American Library Association, 1941), 134; Abigail A. Van Slyck, *Free to All: Carnegie Libraries and American Culture* (Chicago: University of Chicago Press, 1995), 157, 186–87,

190; Cleota Reed, *Henry Chapman Mercer and the Moravian Pottery and Tile Works* (Philadelphia: University of Pennsylvania Press, 1987), 141, 147–50; Christopher Gray, *NYT*, Dec. 23, 1990; Withey, 345.

XVI–4. Selma Rattner, "James Renwick," *Dictionary of Art* (New York: Grove, 1996); Pugin, 44–45; Sylvester, II, 46; *ST*, July 10, 1868, Nov. 5 and 12, 1875, Nov. 6, 1879.

XVI–5. Darius Bryjka, "Sibling Rivalry Good for Illinois Architecture: The Meskers' Sheet-Metal Business," *Historic Illinois*, 28 (April 2006): 3–10; www.gotmesker.com.

XVI–6. *Saugerties Daily Post*, Oct. 10, 1942.

XVI–7. Hassinger, 67.

XVI–8. Adams; engraving of Seamon Bro's Building, "Dealers in Fine Grades of Furniture," Senate House Museum; *KDF*, Sept. 30, 1882; *ST*, Mar. 22, 1883; Rhoads, *Kingston*, 168.

XVI–9. Rhoads, "Franklin D. Roosevelt"; *KDF*, Sept. 29, 1934, Mar. 31, 1936; correspondence in box 6064, Washington National Records Center: Louis Simon to Frederick Darrow, Apr. 19, 1934; Darrow to Procurement Division, Apr. 21, 1934; Darrow to Margaret LeHand, Nov. 18, 1934; Royal Copeland to Henry Morgenthau, Nov. 30, 1934; W. E. Reynolds to Copeland, Nov. 19, 1934; Peoples to Morgenthau, Nov. 30, 1934; Neal Melick to Simon, Dec. 3, 1934; correspondence in FDRL: Darrow to LeHand, Dec. 3, 1934; Roosevelt to Admiral Peoples, Nov. 22, 1934.

XVI–10. One-page, framed history of the church, at the church; Sylvester, II, 51; *NYT*, Apr. 9, 1855; Central Committee, General Congregational Convention, *A Book of Plans for Churches and Parsonages* (New York: Daniel Burgess, 1853); Rhoads, "Poughkeepsie's Architectural Styles," 21.

XVI–11. Beers, 36, 136; Hassinger, 33; Poll & Elia, 41.

XVI–12. *ST*, Mar. 15, 1883.

XVI–13. Richard Burtsell in Clearwater, *History of Ulster County*, 421; Sylvester, II, 48; Mgr. Thomas J. Shelley, "Proud Legacy," *Catholic New York*, Dec. 23, 1999; Louis Dow Scisco, *Political Nativism in New York State* (1901, reprint New York: AMS, 1968), 168; Alastair Duncan, *Tiffany Windows* (New York: Simon & Schuster, 1980), 207.

XVI–14. www.saugertieslighthouse.com.

XVI–15. A. Charles Sewter, *The Stained Glass of William Morris and His Circle* (New Haven: Yale University Press, 1975), 225–26; "The William Morris Window," *Scribner's Monthly*, 6 (June 1873): 245–46; Emma Simmons Sidman, "A History of Trinity Church," in *Trinity Church Centennial* (Brooklyn, 1931), 5–9; *The Pearl*, 1 (Dec. 1875): 96; www.trinitychurchsaugerties.org/history; Sylvester, II, 40, 47, 59; Beers, 41; *KDF*, Sept. 17, 1874; Pugin, 55–56; Sarah Bradford Landau, *Edward T. and William A. Potter* (New York: Garland, 1979), 462.

XVI–16. *Practical Book* in author's collection; *NYT*, Nov. 13, 1925, Aug. 13, 1949; Henry Corse, "A Small English Manor in America," *Arts & Decoration*, 28 (Feb. 1928): 42–43.

XVI–17. Sylvester, II, 60; Karlyn Knaust Elia, "The House That Sheffield Built," *Saugerties Times*, May 15, 2003; *NYT*, July 1 and 7, 1888; White and Willensky, 221.

XVI–18. Hassinger, 4; *NYT*, Aug. 22, 1909; *KDF*, Aug. 17, 2006; Mary Beckert and Lloyd Loop in *History of Ulster County*, 358; Marjorie F. Block, *Saugerties* (Charleston: Arcadia, 2010), 51, 54.

XVI–19. http://ny.existingstations.com/counties/Ulster.html.

XVI–20. Poll and Elia, 50; Brink, 76–78, 252; "Initial Stones in Katsbaan Church Wall," *Olde Ulster* (Nov. 1911): 339–41; Sylvester, II, 45; Deweese DeWitt, 25; www.katsbaanchurch.org.

XVI–21. Beers, 32; Child, 253; The Rev. William R. Phinney, "West Camp-Asbury Methodist Church," www.rootsweb.ancestry.com/~nygreen2/asbury_circuit.htm.

XVI–22. *HVVAN*, 5 (Feb. 2003): 1–7; menu in author's collection; *KDF*, Jan. 20, 2003, Jan. 28, 2008.

XVI–23. *NYT*, Aug. 3, 1968; "Harvey Fite's Opus 40," brochure, before 1976; *Overlook*, June 8, 1934; Tad Richards emails to author, Oct. 22 and 23, 2008; Liam Nelson in Wolf, *Woodstock's Art Heritage*, 89; www.opus40.org.

XVI–24. Town of Saugerties, "Historic Resources Survey," 2005; Sylvester, II, 46; Deweese DeWitt, 49; *KDF*, July 6, 1937; *NYT*, July 6, 1937; Cynthia Koch, "Franklin Roosevelt's 'Dutch-ness,'" in *Dutch New York* (Yonkers: Hudson River Museum, 2009), 364.

XVI–25. Sylvester, II, 46; Peter S. Beekman, *History of the Reformed Church of Flatbush, N.Y., 1807–1907* (Kingston: W. R. Anderson, 1907).

XVI–26. Evers, *Catskills*, 527–28, 658, 764; Wick, *Kingston and Ulster*, 70; *KDF*, Nov. 9, 1978; *Ulster Arts* (Winter 1978–79); *Schmidt* (Burlington, Vt.: Fleming Museum, 1975).

Chapter XVII. Town of Shandaken

Child, 132; Sylvester, II, 306, 308, 313; *ST*, Aug. 14, 1868; Best, 181.

XVII–1. *NYT*, June 28, 1921, June 25, 1933, May 1, 1938, Apr. 28, 1947, Dec. 10, 1990; Rhoads, *Kingston*, 145; William DeWitt, 223; information at Zen Mountain Monastery including Jean Jian Fitzpatrick, "Birth of the Dragon," 11, 17; *MIT Technology Review* (April 1923): 314; White and Willensky, 289; "Zen Mountain Monastery. State and National Historic Site," brochure.

XVII–2. Ham and Bucenec, 9, 29; John M. Ham and Robert K. Bucenec, *The Old 'Up and Down,' Catskill Mountain Branch of the New York Central* (Hunter: Stony Clove & Catskill Mountain Press, 2003), 177, 195, 235.

XVII–3. Adams; *KDF*, Apr. 25, 1883.

XVII–4. *KDF*, June 20, 1879, Aug. 4, 1879; *NYT*, June 30, 1889, Mar. 19, 1895; Annon Adams, "The Grand Hotel," lecture, Town of Middletown Historical Society, July 25, 2010; Evers, *Catskills*, 484–85, 674; Best, 64; K. E. Hasbrouck in *History of Ulster County*, 375.

XVII–5. De Lisser, 195; Fr. Phil Tran email to author, Nov. 21, 2008; Richard Burtsell in Clearwater, *History of Ulster County*, 444; *75th Anniversary of St. Francis de Sales Parish, 1902–1977*.

XVII–6. Information at Shandaken Historical Museum; Engle, 197.

XVII–7. SIRIS Art Inventories Catalog; *NYT*, Aug. 17, 1986; information on plaque at site.

XVII–8. Galusha, *Another Day*, 51–2; Galusha email to author, Oct. 13, 2008.

XVII–9. Gale, 22; *NYT*, Sept. 2, 1924; Barrus, II, 109.

XVII–10. Dakin Morehouse in http://woodlandvalleyview.blogspot.com/2008/02; Gale, 22; Elizabeth Kelley notes to John Burroughs Journal,

June 19, no year, VCL; Barrus, II, 109; *KDF*, Sept. 12, 1914; *NYT*, Apr. 27, 1924.

XVII–11. *NYT*, June 2, 1906, June 13, 1911, Sept. 25, 1913; information at Shandaken Historical Museum.

XVII–12. Herbert L. Shultz, *A Winnisook Chronicle, 1886–1986*; *NYT*, Aug. 6, 1893, Aug. 25, 1896, Aug. 15, 1904, Sept. 6, 1923; Barrus, I, 341; John Burroughs Journal, July 15–17, 1905, VCL.

XVII–13. Gale, 76; Nancy T. Smith, *Pine Hill* (1976), 26; Evers, *Catskills*, 507; *NYT*, July 1 and Sept. 2, 1894, June 3, 1899, Dec. 15, 1901; *Jersey City Journal*, Feb. 19, 1902; *Pine Hill Sentinel*, Feb. 13 and Apr. 23, 1904; architectural plans dated Dec. 1, 1902, Shandaken Historical Museum; information provided by Maureen Nagy.

XVII–14. Evers, *Catskills*, 504–12; Best, 36, 39, 66; Annon Adams, "The Grand Hotel," lecture, Town of Middletown Historical Society, July 25, 2010; Ingersoll, 171.

XVII–15. *NYT*, July 14, 1895; Clearwater, *History of Ulster County*, 578.

XVII–16. Best, 66; *Manufacturer & Builder*, 16 (Jan. 1884); *Catskill Mountain Resorts Reached by the Ulster & Delaware R.R.* (1909), 167.

XVII–17. *NYT*, July 24, 1904; Margherita Arlina Hamm, *Eminent Actors in Their Homes* (New York: James Pott, 1902), 167–77.

Chapter XVIII.
Town of Shawangunk

Fried, *Shawangunk*, 3; Sylvester, II, 157.

XVIII–1. Mauritz, 89–98; McCausland, 202; *Windy Summits*, 36; Clearwater, "Old Dutch Church," 2; Hasbrouck, *Shawangunk*, 45.

XVIII–2. John Bonafide, National Register of Historic Places nomination, 2000.

XVIII–3. Reynolds, 189–90; Mary Anne Hunting, "The Johannes Decker Farm in Ulster County, New York," *Magazine Antiques,* 153 (April 1998): 572–81; *NYT*, Feb. 18, 1948; Edward B. Edwards to Helen Reynolds, Dec. 7, 1925, AML; Benepe, 112–13; *HVVAN*, June 2003; Blackburn, 134–42.

XVIII–4. Reynolds, 190; note by Helen Reynolds, AML; undated *Middletown Record* article by Eileen

Lubhart on the inn; *Times Herald–Record*, Mar. 25, 2008.

XVIII–5. Reynolds, 209; Historical Society of Shawangunk & Gardiner, *Newsletter*, Summer 2003; *HVVAN*, April 2003.

XVIII–6. *1776–1976 Town of Shawangunk* (Wallkill: Bicentennial Committee, 1976), 23; Child, 272; Historical Society of Shawangunk & Gardiner, *Newsletter*, Fall 2003; Clearwater, *History of Ulster County*, 378.

XVIII–7. John G. Waite Associates, Architects, "Historic Structure Report. Andries DuBois House, Wallkill, New York," 2005.

XVIII–8. *Rondout Courier* reprinted in a New Paltz newspaper, March 3, 1881; *NPI*, Feb. 3 and June 2, 1881; www.arch.columbia.edu/Studio/Spring 2003/up/Brewster; Mentz, 108; Mott Iron Works to John G. Borden, Feb. 4, 1886, HHS; *NYT*, Dec. 22, 1881; Rinaldi and Yasinsac, 183.

XVIII–9. *NPI*, Jan. 20, Feb. 17, June 2, 1881; Hasbrouck, *Shawangunk*, 16; John G. Borden to Ladies Temperance Union, Wallkill (Oct. 1884?), HHS; *NYT*, Apr. 22, 1888; brochures from "Borden Day," Wallkill, 2004, 2005.

XVIII–10. Mentz, 21–22.

XVIII–11. *NPI*, Oct. 27, 1870; Sylvester, II, 167; www. geocities.com/wallkillreformed/churchhistory.

XVIII–12. Mauritz, 44–45; Walden *Citizen Herald*, Oct. 14, 1935; Hanford's blueprints, Mar. 7 and May 6, 1935, at the library.

XVIII–13. Ollie Burgess, *Hometown Memories: Main Street, Wallkill, N.Y.*

XVIII–14. Kenneth E. Hasbrouck in *History of Ulster County*, 392–93; Sylvester, II, facing 157; *HVVAN* (Apr.–June 2011): 2; *NPI*, June 2, 1881, Oct. 8, 1886, Aug. 7, 1891; *Appleton's Cyclopaedia of American Biography*, 8: 129; *NYT*, Apr. 22, 1888; Eric Strangfeld, "Chasing a Dream: The Borden Family in Wallkill," *New Paltz Historical Review* (Spring 1998): 40; brochures from "Borden Day," 2004, 2006; *Historic Wallkill and Hudson River Valleys* (Walden: Wallkill Valley Publishing, 1905), 30; *Sunday Record*, July 24, 1988; *Ulster County Press*, Jan. 31, 2007.

XVIII–15. Alfred Hopkins, *Prisons and Prison Building* (New York: Architectural Book Publishing,

1930), pl. II, 138–39; information and photos from David L. Miller, May 2009; Norman Johnston, *The Human Cage: A Brief History of Prison Architecture* (New York: Walker, 1973), 44; *Eighth Annual Report of the State Commission of Correction for the Year 1934*, 69; *Wallkill Valley World*, Feb. 20, 1932; *NYT*, Feb. 17 and Aug. 17, 1931, Aug. 28, 1934, Aug. 17, 1939; www.correctionhistory.org; *NPI*, Nov. 9, 1944; www.prisontalk.com/forums/archive/index.php/t-86088.html.

Chapter XIX. Town of Ulster

Hutton, 84, 205.

XIX–1. Reynolds, 213–14; Sylvester, II, after 336.

XIX–2. Robert Sweeney email to author, Jan. 29, 2007; National Register of Historic Places, 2005-12-07, nomination form; HABS NY, 56-KING, V, 6, NY-6131; Reynolds, 223; Fay Campbell Kaynor, "Thomas Tileston Waterman: Student of American Colonial Architecture," *Winterthur Portfolio*, 20 (Summer 1985): 117; correspondence between H. F. du Pont and Fred Johnston, Aug. 18 to Sept. 27, 1937, Oct. 21 to Nov. 11, 1938, Feb 24 and Apr. 21, 1939, Winterthur Library; *HVVAN*, Sept. 2004.

XIX–3. E. C. Holtzoper, "The Planning of a House," *Country Life*, 8 (Oct. 1905): 621; Charles Edward Hooper, *The Country House* (New York: Doubleday, Page, 1906), 38, 67; *KDF*, Sept. 20, 1919; Le Fevre, 366; Rhoads, *Kingston*, 81; deed research on the Saugerties Road property by Sally M. Rhoads; Betsy Fahlman, "Wilson Eyre in Detroit," *Winterthur Portfolio*, 15 (Autumn 1980): 269; Clearwater, *History of Ulster County*, 607.

XIX–4. *KDF*, Mar. 15, May 26–27, 1949.

Chapter XX. Town of Wawarsing

Fried, *Shawangunk*, 12; Sylvester, II, 252, 258, 272; Child, 139–44.

XX–1. Sweeney, 36–39; Reynolds, 202–03; Katharine T. Terwilliger, "Before Today's Headlines: The Johannis G. Hardenbergh House," undated *Ellenville Journal*; Frederick S. Dellenbaugh, *The Hardenberghs* (Ellenville: Ellenville Journal, 1935); *Proceedings of the Ulster County Historical Society*, 1930–31, 13, 1931–32, 10–11, 1933–34, 20–21; *KDF*, Sept. 29, 1934; HABS NY 4125, Works Progress Administration Project 265–6907; at Winterthur Archives: M. Elinor Betts to John A. H. Sweeney, Mar. 15, 1955; correspondence between Fred Johnston and H. F. du Pont, June 10, 1938 to April 24, 1940; photos of workmen removing woodwork; *Winterthur Newsletter*, Dec. 12, 1957.

XX–2. *NYT*, Apr. 19, 1922, Mar. 18, 1950; Clearwater, *History of Ulster County*, 603; Myrtle Clark to Mr. Gray, Feb. 4, 1915, author's collection; Kuhlmann, 42; Katharine Terwilliger in *History of Ulster County*, 432; www.soyuzivka.com.

XX–3. *NYT*, Dec. 8, 1933, Mar. 30, 1950, Feb. 17, 1964; "Who's Who in Architecture," *American Art Annual*, 21 (1924–25): 441; Architectural League of New York, *Year Book*, 1922.

XX–4. Neil Larson, National Register nomination form, 1983.

XX–5. Terwilliger, *Napanoch*, 49–67, 85; Rhoads, "Poughkeepsie's Architectural Styles," 18; Deweese DeWitt, 43–44.

XX–6. Terwilliger, *Napanoch*, 43, 48, 206.

XX–7. Terwilliger, *Napanoch*, 147–48; Wakefield, 159; Withey, 595; *NYT*, Aug. 29, 1901; *Eastern New York Correctional Facility 1900–2000* (New York State Department of Correctional Services), 2–4; www.correctionhistory.org/easternny100.

XX–8. *NYT*, Apr. 28, 1948; information on the station (including architectural plans of Feb. 1902) and Eastern Correctional Facility provided 1998 by David L. Miller, Superintendent, and staff member Jeff Rubin, of Eastern.

XX–9. Harris; *KDF*, Sept. 30, 1907; Carlyle Ellis, "Yama-no-uchi and Its Trout," *American Homes and Gardens*, 7 (July 1910): 271–74; Kuhlman, 71; notes by Elizabeth Burroughs Kelley to John Burroughs Journal, Sept. 1908, VCL; Josephson, "In the 'Silent Sweet Woods'"; Wendy Harris email to author, May 31, 2007, citing "Hall Clock" brochure, Sept. 15, 1914, re Stickley's visit; Lancaster, 152,198; *Yama Farms Inn: Where It Is, Why and What It Is* (New York: Frank Seaman, Inc., 1914?); *NYT*, May 11, 1914, Nov. 13, 1920. For updated information, see Wendy E. Harris, "Yama Farms Inn:

A Home in the Mountains," http://www.yama-farmsinn.net.

XX–10. Gutman, 262; Engle, 209.

XX–11. Terwilliger, *Wawarsing*, 227.

XX–12. Newspaper clippings in Ellenville Public Library & Museum; Marion M. Dumond in *Wawarsing.NetMagazine*, March 2004; Koyl, 1956, 625; *NYT*, Oct. 29, 1899; Laura Linke email to author, Feb. 23, 2011; Helen Binkerd Young obituary by Mrs. Robert V. Morse, 1959, Cornell University Library.

XX–13. Adams.

XX–14. Terwilliger, *Napanoch*, 151; *Timeline, Terwilliger House Museum* (Spring 2006); *Portrait and Biographical Record of Orange County* (New York: Chapman, 1895), 174.

XX–15. www.huntmemorial.com/history.

XX–16. Rhoads, "Franklin D. Roosevelt"; *KDF*, May 12 and Oct. 25, 1938, Aug. 21, 1940; *Ellenville Journal*, Dec. 30, 1937, May 25 and Nov. 30, 1939, Oct. 31, 1940; Withey, 566; Child, 143; Sylvester, II, 257–58, Katharine Terwilliger in *History of Ulster County*, 429; correspondence, May–June 1939, OF 400 NY, FDRL; correspondence, May–Sept. 1939, Box 5702, Washington National Records Center; correspondence, Jan. 1940–June 1942, RG 121, National Archives; Katharine Terwilliger to Nicolai Cikovsky, Jr., June 13, 1972, and to author, May 2, 1979.

XX–17. Carolyn Blouin email to author, June 22, 2006; Sylvester, II, 265; McCausland, 42.

XX–18. Adams; Sylvester, II, 265; Beers, 106.

XX–19. Dorothy Hurlbut Sanderson, *St. John's Memorial Episcopal Church*, 1973; *Middletown Record*, May 26, 2000.

XX–20. *KDF*, Apr. 28, 1909; *Who's Who*, 1914; *NYT*, Nov. 24, 1958.

XX–21. Peter D. Barton to Thomas Woltman, June 18, 1980; Woltman to Dale Stein, 1980; Manville B. Wakefield, *To the Mountains by Rail* (Grahamsville: Wakefair Press, 1976), 218.

XX–22. Kuhlman, 81.

XX–23. Mary Ann Van Benschoten, "The Schultz Legacy," *Terwilliger House Museum, Timeline* (Fall 2002); Aaron Imbt email to author, Mar. 12, 2007; *Who Was Who in American Art*; *NYT*,

Sept. 12, 1902, Apr. 17, 1958.

XX–24. *HVVAN*, 8 (Feb. 2006): 6; Reynolds, 184–85, 191; Reynolds notes, AML; *KDF*, Oct. 15, 1938; Fred Johnston to H. F. du Pont, Aug. 24, 1936, Winterthur; G. Wurts DuBois to Reynolds, Aug. 15, 1925, AML.

XX–25. Katharine Terwilliger in *History of Ulster County*, 437; Helen Reynolds notes, AML; Calvert Vaux, *Villas and Cottages* (New York: Harper, 1869), 217–22; Marion M. Dumond, *Wawarsing.Net Magazine*, Dec. 2002.

XX–26. McCausland, 38; Buff, 1056; Rhoads, "Artist's House," 90–91; E. L. Henry to E. V. Valentine, Feb. 7, 1880, in Amy Kurtz Lansing, *Historical Fictions: Edward Lamson Henry's Paintings of Past and Present* (New Haven: Yale University Art Gallery, 2005), 25.

XX–27. *KDF*, July 13, 1908; Hakam and Houghtaling, 17; *NYT*, Nov. 10, 1942.

XX–28. *Who's Who*, 1928; Velma Warner and Harriet Woodruff, *A Brief History of the Cragsmoor Free Library* (1975); "Cragsmoor, The History and the Artists," and other information provided by Hattie Grifo, Director, May 15, 2007.

XX–29. Buff, 1061; Harry Hansen, "Orchard Cottage," Building Structure Inventory Form, #92, Apr. 1995; "Cragsmoor Day Historic House Tour, 2006."

XX–30. Buff, 1067; *NYT*, Apr. 10, 1913, Mar. 1, 1943.

XX–31. Harry Hansen, "Building Structure Inventory Form, #55, Apr. 1995; information provided by Sally Matz, May 12, 2007; *NYT*, Feb. 3, 1896, Sept. 19, 1913, Nov. 16, 1930; *Vespers* illustrated in *E. L. Henry's Country Life* (Cragsmoor Free Library, 1981), 12; Harry Hansen, "Hillcrest," Building Structure Inventory Form, #53, Apr. 1995.

XX–32. Harry Hansen, "Endridge," Building Structure Inventory Form, #67, Apr. 1995; Frederick S. Dellenbaugh, *The North-Americans of Yesterday* (New York: Putnam's, 1906), 195; Dellenbaugh on the "log house" in Russell Sturgis, *A Dictionary of Architecture and Building* (New York: Macmillan, 1902), II, 786; Barrus, II, 86.

XX–33. Buff, 1059; Hansen, "The Barnacle," Building Structure Inventory Form, #69, Apr. 1995.

XX–34. Harry Hansen, "Cragsmoor Historic District,"

National Register of Historic Places, section 7, 12; "Cragsmoor Day Historic House Tour, 2006"; Emily C. Liang to Sandra S. Phillips, July 25 and Nov. 17, 1985.

XX–35. *Cragsmoor Journal*, July 10, 1910; Jalenak, 55–56; Jane Ward Faquin and Maia Jalenak, *Helen M. Turner: The Woman's Point of View* (Memphis: Dixon Gallery and Gardens, 2010), 12, 17, fig. 5.

XX–36. Harry Hansen, "Windy Hearth" Site, Building Structure Inventory Form, #88, Apr. 1995; Jalenak, 67.

XX–37. *NYT*, Apr. 8 and June 21, 1903, June 10, 1906, Sept. 22, 1929, Nov. 28, 1963; *Windy Summits*, 5, 12–13, 26; Harry Hansen, "Chetolah," Building Structure Inventory Form, #139; Hakam and Houghtaling, 22.

XX–38. Marion M. Dumond, "Huckleberry Memories," *Wawarsing.Net Magazine* (Aug. 2004): 20–21; www.nature.org/wherewework/northamerica/states/newyork/science/art22249.html.

Chapter XXI. Town of Woodstock

Evers, *Catskills* and *Woodstock*; Child, 148.

XXI–1. *Life*, 5 (Aug. 22, 1938): 24; Evers, *Woodstock*, 647; Fallon-Mower, 23; *Hue & Cry*, June 20, 1925.

XXI–2. Carl Eric Lindin, "The Woodstock Art Gallery," *Plowshare*, 9 (July 1920); Tom Wolf, *The Founders of the Woodstock Artists Association* (WAA, 2000), 1; summary of minutes of Artists' Realty Co., 1919–20, WAA Archives; information from Emily Jones and Tom Wolf, Apr. 2009; *Overlook*, May 14, 1937; William A. Boring to Charles S. Keefe, Mar. 5, 1925, author's collection.

XXI–3. Evers, *Woodstock*, 612; *Overlook*, May 3 and July 26, 1935, June 12, July 3, Nov. 6, 1936, Jan. 8, Feb. 2 and 19, Mar. 5, Apr. 9, May 14, June 25, July 30, Aug. 27, Sept. 17 and 24, Oct. 1 and 8, Nov. 19, 1937, Feb. 24, Mar. 31, Nov. 3, 1939; Koyl, 1962, 258; *KDF*, Dec. 28, 1950 and Jan. 3, 1953.

XXI–4. Alf Evers, "A Brief History of the John F. Carlson Painting at the Woodstock Town Offices," www.woodstockhistory.org/CarlsonStory.html; *NYT*, June 24, 1929; Frank E. Wallis, *How to*

Know Architecture (New York: Harper, 1910), 277, 290.

XXI–5. Evers, *Woodstock*, 493, 499–500; *KDF*, June 5, 1928, Aug. 6, 1929; www.colonycafe.com/history; Rhoads, *Kingston*, 147–48.

XXI–6. Evers, *Woodstock*, 548; Fallon-Mower, 18, 20; *KDF*, May 28, 1928; *Hue and Cry*, July 7, 1928; *Overlook*, Nov. 19, 1937.

XXI–7. *Who's Who*, 1942; Smith, 89, 136, 194–95; *Overlook*, June 18, 1937; Andy Mele, "The Artists' Cemetery," *Woodstock Review*, Mar. 9, 1972; Allen Staley, "Byrdcliffe and the Maverick," M.A. thesis, Yale University, 1960, 32; *Overlook*, June 18, 1937; www.meredithmusic.com.

XXI–8. Smith, 80, 136; *Life*, 5 (Aug. 22, 1938): 26–27; Elsie Speicher, "Studio Home in the Foothills of the Catskills," *Arts & Decoration*, 50 (May 1939): 10–13; *Arts & Decoration Book of Successful Houses* (New York: McBride, 1940), 15–18; Wolf, 55, 132–33; *Eugene Speicher* (New York: American Artists Group, 1945); Michael Quick, *Paintings of George Bellows* (New York: Abrams, 1992), 82.

XXI–9. Ralph Radcliffe Whitehead, "A Plea for Manual Work," *Handicraft*, 2 (June 1903): 60; Green, editor, 68, 124, 225 and *passim*.

XXI–10. *Overlook*, Apr. 14, 1939; *Herald Tribune*, Sept. 1, 1940; Smith, 203.

XXI–11. Evers, *Woodstock*, 582–83; Fallon-Mower, 51; Gale, 70.

XXI–12. Evers, *Woodstock,* 499; Rinaldi and Yasinsac, 111–17.

XXI–13. Martin Podskoch, *Fire Towers of the Catskills* (Fleischmanns: Purple Mountain Press, 2000), 72, 105; *KDF*, July 23, 2008; www.catskillcenter.org/towers/overlook; www.michiganfiretowers.com; www.nysfiretowers.com/overlook.

XXI–14. Wolf, 104–05; Josephine Bloodgood, *At Woodstock, Kuniyoshi* (Woodstock Artists Association, 2003), 15; *Life*, 5 (Aug. 22, 1938): 27.

XXI–15. *House and Garden* (June 1941): 16; Park and Markowitz, 43, 135, 138.

XXI–16. Evers, *Woodstock*, 547–48; postcard of "De Liagre House, Zena Road, M. S. Teller Restoration," sent by Alfred De Liagre to Myron S. Teller, Apr. 12, 1929, SRL; *Overlook*, July 30,

1937, July 29, 1938; *Architectural Record*, 83 (Apr. 1938): 146; Herbert Williams, "The Pelican Surveys Modern Architecture," *Arts & Decoration*, 50 (May 1939): 22–25; *NYT*, Apr. 21, 1931, Jan. 18, 1933, Feb. 3, 1990; Koyl, 1955, 398; Alfred De Liagre to William Muschenheim, Aug. 1, 1938, additional correspondence, drawings, and documents, Avery Library; *KDF*, Mar. 20, 2009.

XXI–17. Wolf, 94; Katherine Morrow Ford and Thomas H. Creighton, *Quality Budget Houses* (New York: Rheinhold, 1954), 36–37; *NYT*, May 25, 1946, June 22, 1949.

XXI–18. Blanche Wiesen Cook, *Eleanor Roosevelt* (New York: Viking, 1992), II, 270; Richard S. Wallach, Director, NYA for New York State, text for brochure, July 2, 1940, Historical Society of Woodstock; www.nps.gov/museum/exhibits/elro/valkill.html; Evers, *Woodstock*, 598; Rhoads, "Franklin D. Roosevelt," 438; *Overlook*, June 30, 1939, Dec. 20, 1940, Mar. 21, 1941; *Woodstock Press*, May 15, 1942; Eleanor Roosevelt, "My Day," June 28, 1939, FDRL; Smith 173; *KDF*, Aug. 20, 1940, May 29, 1981.

XXI–19. *Woodstock Press*, Sept. 11, 1931; Evers, *Woodstock*, 525, 546; Bruce Brooks Pfeiffer, *Frank Lloyd Wright Drawings* (New York: Abrams, 1990), 122, 141; Evers in *50 Years of Theater* (Woodstock Playhouse, 1975), 4; Myron Teller's notes on photos of barn, SRL; J. P. McEvoy, *Charlie Would Have Loved This* (New York: Duell, Sloan and Pearce, 1956), 149–50.

XXI–20. Evers, *Woodstock*, 505, 585, 587; Norman Bel Geddes, *Horizons* (Boston: Little, Brown, 1932), 283; "History," in Woodstock Playhouse program, 1941; Rhoads in Bloodgood, 49–50; *Overlook*, July 1, 1938; Fallon–Mower, 13; Alf Evers and Albert E. Milliken in *50 Years of Theater* (Woodstock Playhouse, 1975).

Selected Bibliography

Archival Sources

John Burroughs Papers, Archives and Special Collections Library, Vassar College Libraries, Poughkeepsie; Julian Burroughs Papers, New York State Library/Manuscripts & Special Collections, Albany; Henry Francis du Pont Papers, Winterthur Library: Winterthur Archives, Winterthur, Del.; Fred Johnston Papers, Friends of Historic Kingston; Charles S. Keefe Architectural Drawings and Papers, Friends of Historic Kingston; Teller & Halverson Architectural Drawings, Friends of Historic Kingston; William Muschenheim Collection (Project: Alfred de Liagre), Avery Library, Columbia University; Helen Wilkinson Reynolds Collection (Ulster County files for her *Dutch Houses in the Hudson Valley*), Adriance Memorial Library, Poughkeepsie; Upjohn Collection (Christ Church, Marlborough), Avery Library, Columbia University.

Newspapers and Directories

The New York Times (*NYT*), which can be searched through Proquest, was an extremely valuable resource, as were the *Kingston Daily Freeman* and New Paltz newspapers—the latter in well-organized clipping files at the Haviland-Heidgerd Historical Collection. The *Freeman* for 1895 and 1903–12 can be searched via Hudson River Valley Heritage's Historical Newspapers Web site, while other years are on microfilm at the Kingston Library. Woodstock newspapers were read at the Woodstock Library and Woodstock Historical Society. Kingston city directories were consulted at the Kingston Library.

Books, Articles, and Unpublished Papers

Adams, Annon. "J. A. Wood's Ulster County Buildings." Typescript, February 15, 2007.

Allen, Richard Sanders. *Covered Bridges of the Northeast*. Brattleboro: S. Greene, 1974.

Anderson, Stott. *Ulster County's Old Timbered Crossings*. n.p., n.d. [1965?]

Barber, John W., and Henry Howe. *Historical Collections of the State of New York*. New York: S. Tuttle, 1841.

Barrus, Clara. *The Life and Letters of John Burroughs*. 2 vols. Boston: Houghton Mifflin, 1925.

Beers, F. W. *County Atlas of Ulster, New York*. New York: Walker & Jewett, 1875. Reprinted by Ulster County Genealogical Society, 1975.

Benepe, Barry. *Early Architecture in Ulster County*. Kingston: Junior League of Kingston, 1974.

Best, Gerald M. *The Ulster and Delaware. Railroad through the Catskills*. San Marino, Calif.: Golden West, 1972.

Blackburn, Roderic, et al. *Dutch Colonial Homes in America*. New York: Rizzoli, 2002.

Bloodgood, Josephine, Tom Wolf, and William B. Rhoads, *The Maverick: Hervey White's Colony of the Arts*. Woodstock Artists Association and Museum, 2006.

Bone, Kevin, editor. *Water-Works: The Architecture and Engineering of the New York City Water Supply*. New York: Monacelli, 2006.

Breiner, Charles M., and William E. Scott. *A Guide to the New York, Ontario & Western Railway's Monticello, Port Jervis & Kingston Division*. Middletown: Ontario & Western Railway Historical Society, n.d.

Brink, Benjamin Myer. *The Early History of Saugerties*. Kingston: R. W. Anderson & Son, 1902.

Buff, Barbara. "Cragsmoor, an Early American Art Colony." *Magazine Antiques* 114 (November 1978): 1056–1067.

Burgess, Larry E. *Mohonk: Its People and Spirit*. New Paltz: Mohonk Mountain House, 1980.

Burroughs, John. "House-Building." *Scribner's Monthly*, 11 (January 1876): 333–341.

———. "Roof-Tree." *Signs and Seasons*. Boston: Houghton, Mifflin, 1886.

Burroughs, Julian. "How I Built My Own Country House." *Country Life in America*, 9 (February 1906): 415–417.

———. *Hudson River Memories*. West Park:

Riverby Books, 1987.

Catskill Aqueduct Celebration. Souvenir Edition. Municipal Engineers Journal. October 12–14, 1917.

Chase, Helen K. "Glen Tonche," compiled for the 1995 annual meeting of the Catskill Center for Conservation and Development.

Child, Hamilton. *Gazeteer and Business Directory of Ulster County, New York.* Syracuse: Hamilton Child, 1871.

Clearwater, Alphonso T. *The History of Ulster County, New York.* Kingston: W. J. Van Deusen, 1907.

———. "The Old Dutch Church at Shawangunk." *Year Book of the Holland Society of New York, 1928 and 1929* (copyright 1931).

Commemorative Biographical Record of Ulster County, New York. Chicago: J. H. Beers, 1896.

"Cragsmoor Day Historic House Tour." Cragsmoor, 2006.

De Lisser, Richard Lionel. *Picturesque Ulster.* (published in parts) Kingston: Styles & Bruyn, 1896–1905.

DeWitt, Deweese W. *Ulster County's Reformed Church Legacy.* Kingston: Old Dutch Men's Club, 1977.

DeWitt, William C. *People's History of Kingston.* New Haven, 1943.

"Early American Homes: Van Idah, Major Van Lear Woodward's Residence." *The Jeffersonian* (September 1933): 14–15, 28–29.

Eberlein, Harold Donaldson. *The Manors and Historic Homes of the Hudson Valley.* Philadelphia: J. B. Lippincott, 1924.

Eberlein, Harold Donaldson, and Cortlandt Van Dyke Hubbard. *Historic Houses of the Hudson Valley.* New York: Bonanza, reprint of Architectural Book Publishing, 1942.

Elia, Karlyn Knaust. "The House That Sheffield Built." *Saugerties Times,* May 15, 2003.

Ellis, Carlyle. "Yama-no-uchi and Its Trout." *American Homes and Gardens* (July 1910): 271–274.

Engle, Michael, and Mario Monti. *Diners of New York.* Mechanicsburg, Penn.: Stackpole Books, 2008.

Evers, Alf. *The Catskills: From Wilderness to*

Woodstock. Garden City: Doubleday, 1972.

———. *Woodstock: History of an American Town.* Woodstock: Overlook Press, 1987.

Fackler, Jon. "Oscar's Farm." *Ulster Magazine* (Winter 1995): 18–22.

Fallon-Mower, Janine. *Woodstock (Images of America).* Charleston: Arcadia, 2002.

Fitchen, John. *The New World Dutch Barn.* Syracuse: Syracuse University Press, 1968.

Ford, Edwin Millard. *Images of America: Kingston.* Charleston: Arcadia, 2004.

———. *Street Whys: Anecdotes and Lore about the Streets of Kingston, New York.* Round Top: Ford Printing, 2010.

Foy, Richard. (detailed history of the Oliver Hazard Payne estate in Esopus: http://academic2.marist.edu/foy/esopus).

Fried, Marc. *The Huckleberry Pickers: A Raucous History of the Shawangunk Mountains.* Hensonville: Black Dome Press, 1996.

———. *Shawangunk Place-Names.* Gardiner: the Author, 2005.

Gale, Lonnie, and Ruth Gale. *Shandaken, New York: A Pictorial History.* Fleischmanns: Purple Mountain Press, 1999.

Galusha, Diane. *Another Day, Another Dollar: The Civilian Conservation Corps in the Catskills.* Hensonville: Black Dome Press, 2008.

———. *Build Strong: The History of Camp Wawayanda/Frost Valley YMCA.* Claryville: Frost Valley YMCA Press, 2001.

Gomez Mill House. Marlboro: Gomez Foundation for Mill House, n.d.

Green, Nancy E., editor. *Byrdcliffe: An American Arts and Crafts Colony.* Ithaca: Herbert F. Johnson Museum of Art, Cornell University, 2004.

Gutman, Richard J. S., *American Diner.* New York: Harper/Collins, 1993.

Hakam, Margaret, and Susan Houghtaling. *Cragsmoor: An Historical Sketch.* Cragsmoor Free Library, 1983.

Ham, John M., and Robert K. Bucenec. *The Grand Old Stations and Steam Locomotives of the Ulster & Delaware.* Hunter: Stony Clove & Catskill Mountain Press, 2005.

Hansen, Harry. Historic Resources Reconnaissance

Survey. Town of Rochester, 1995.

Hansen, Harry, et al. Cragsmoor Building Structure Inventory Forms for Cragsmoor Free Library, 1991 and 1995.

Harris, Harold, Wendy E. Harris, and Dianne Wiebe. *Yama Farms: A Most Unusual Catskills Resort*. Cragsmoor: Cragsmoor Historical Society, 2006.

Hasbrouck, Kenneth E. *Historic New Paltz*. New Paltz, 1959.

———. *History of the Township of Gardiner*. Gardiner: Town Board of Gardiner, 1953.

———. *History of the Township of Shawangunk*. Shawangunk: Kenneth E. Hasbrouck, 1955.

Hassinger, Ernest, compiler. *Old Home Week. Official Program*. Saugerties, 1911.

Hastings, Helen M. "The Old Stone Houses of Esopus." *Architectural Record*, 49 (January 1921): 91–95.

Hewitt, Mark A. *The Architect & the American Country House*. New Haven: Yale University Press, 1990.

Hewitt, Mark Alan, et al. *Carrere & Hastings Architects*. 2 vols. New York: Acanthus, 2006.

History of Ulster County, with emphasis upon the last 100 years, 1883–1983. Kingston: Ulster County Historians, 1984.

Hutton, George V. *The Great Hudson River Brick Industry*. Fleischmanns: Purple Mountain Press, 2003.

Ingersoll, Ernest. *Rand, McNally & Co.'s Handy Guide to the Hudson River and Catskill Mountains*. Chicago: Rand, McNally, 1897.

Jackman, Ethan P. *Images of America: Highland and the Town of Lloyd*. Charleston: Arcadia, 2009.

Jalenak, Maia. "Helen M. Turner, American Impressionist." M.A. thesis, Louisiana State University, 2000.

Johnson, Carol A. *Images of America: New Paltz Revisited*. Charleston: Arcadia, 2010.

Johnson, Carol A., and Marion W. Ryan. *Images of America: New Paltz*. Charleston: Arcadia, 2001.

Josephson, Roberta. "In the 'Silent Sweet Woods': John Burroughs in and around the Shawangunks." M.A. thesis, SUNY New Paltz, 1990.

Josephson, Robi. *Images of America: Mohonk Mountain House and Preserve*. Charleston: Arcadia, 2002.

Kelley, Elizabeth Burroughs. *John Burroughs' Slabsides*. Rhinebeck: Moran, 1974.

———. *John Burroughs Naturalist*. New York: Exposition, 1959.

———. "West Park and Esopus." *Town of Esopus Story*. Town of Esopus, 1979.

———. *A West Parker Remembers When*. West Park: Riverby Books, 1987.

Koyl, George S., editor. *American Architects Directory*. New York: R. R. Bowker, 1955; second edition, 1962.

Krattinger, William. "First Reformed Protestant Dutch Church, Kingston" National Historic Landmark Nomination, 2006.

Kuhlmann, Pamela. *Wawarsing*. Charleston: Arcadia, 2009.

Lancaster, Clay. *The Japanese Influence in America*. New York: Walton H. Rawls, 1963.

Landau, Sarah Bradford. *Edward T. and William A. Potter: American Victorian Architects*. New York: Garland, 1979.

Lang, Elizabeth, and Robert Lang. *In a Valley Fair: A History of the State University College of Education at New Paltz, N.Y.* New Paltz: State University College, 1960.

Larson, Neil. *The Masonry Architecture of Ulster County, New York: An Evolution, 1665–1935*. Vernacular Architecture Forum, 1986.

Larson, Neil, & Associates. "Jenkins-DuBois Farm & Mill Site, Historic Conditions Report." 2001.

———. "Village of New Paltz, Reconnaissance-Level Historic Resource Survey." Woodstock, 2004.

Le Fevre, Ralph. *History of New Paltz, New York, and Its Old Families*. Second edition. Albany: Fort Orange Press, 1909.

Le Gallienne, Richard. "Old Kingston." *Harper's Monthly Magazine,* 123 (November 1911): 917–926.

Leggett, Frances. *Late and Soon: The Transatlantic Story of a Marriage*. Boston: Houghton, Mifflin, 1968.

Long, Gregory. *Historic Houses of the Hudson River Valley*. New York: Rizzoli, 2004.

Mabee, Carleton. *Bridging the Hudson: The Poughkeepsie Railroad Bridge and Its Connecting Rail Lines*. Fleischmanns: Purple Mountain Press, 2001.

———. *Images of America. Gardiner and Lake Minnewaska*. Charleston: Arcadia Publishing, 2003.

———. *Listen to the Whistle: An Anecdotal History of the Wallkill Valley Railroad in Ulster and Orange Counties*. Fleischmanns: Purple Mountain Press, 1995.

———. *Promised Land: Father Divine's Interracial Communities in Ulster County, New York*. Fleischmanns: Purple Mountain Press, 2008.

McCausland, Elizabeth. *The Life and Work of Edward Lamson Henry*. Albany: New York State Museum, 1945.

Maple Lanes: The History of Woodcrest and The Rifton Valley. Rifton: Woodcrest School, Hutterian Brethren, 1989.

A Marbletown Album 1669–1977. Stone Ridge Library, 1977.

Mauritz, Jacqueline, editor. *The History of the Town of Shawangunk*. Town of Shawangunk, 1988.

Mentz, Frank. *Shawangunk Hearths: Recollections of an Old Timer as Told to Vera Seely*. Wallkill Public Library, 1974.

Miller, Patricia Bartels. *Timbers of Time: The Existing Covered Bridges of Ulster County*. Arkville: Erpf Catskill Cultural Center, 1977.

Morgan, William Davis. "The Architecture of Henry Vaughan," Ph.D. dissertation, University of Delaware, 1971.

Park, Marlene, and Gerald E. Markowitz. *New Deal for Art*. Hamilton: Gallery Association of New York State, 1977.

Partington, Frederick E. *The Story of Mohonk*. New Paltz: Smiley Brothers, 1970 (originally published 1911).

Phillips, Sandra S., and Linda Weintraub, editors. *Charmed Places*. New York: Abrams, 1988.

Picture Book: As We Were ... As We Are, Marlboro-Milton, N.Y. Marlborough: Town of Marlborough, c. 1977.

Plowden, David. *Bridges: The Spans of North America*. New York: Viking, 1974.

Poll, Edward, and Karlyn Knaust Elia. *Saugerties*.

Dover, N.H.: Arcadia, 1997.

Pugin, A. W. N. *True Principles of Pointed or Christian Architecture*. 1841, reprint New York: St. Martin's, 1973.

Reiff, Daniel D. *Houses from Books*. University Park: Pennsylvania State University Press, 2000.

Renehan, Edward J., Jr. *John Burroughs, An American Naturalist*. Post Mills, Vt.: Chelsea Green, 1992.

Reynolds, Helen Wilkinson. *Dutch Houses in the Hudson Valley before 1776*. New York: Payson and Clark, 1929. Reprinted by Dover Publications, 1965.

Rhoads, William B. *An Architectural History of the Reformed Church, New Paltz, New York*. New Paltz: Reformed Church, 1983.

———. "The Artist's House and Studio in the Nineteenth-Century Hudson Valley and Catskills." *Charmed Places*. New York: Abrams, 1988.

———. "Charles S. Keefe: Colonial Revivalist." *Preservation League of New York Newsletter*, 11 (Sept. 1985): 4–5.

———. "Franklin D. Roosevelt and Dutch Colonial Architecture." *New York History*, 59 (Oct. 1978): 430–64.

———. *Kingston, New York: The Architectural Guide*. Hensonville: Black Dome Press, 2003.

———. "Poughkeepsie's Architectural Styles, 1835–1940." *Dutchess County Historical Society, Year Book*, 72 (1987): 18–55.

———. *Teller & Halverson: Masters of the Colonial Revival in Ulster County*. Kingston: Friends of Historic Kingston, 2005.

Rinaldi, Thomas E., and Robert J. Yasinsac. *Hudson Valley Ruins*. Hanover, N.H.: University Press of New England, 2006. (See also their web site: hudsonvalleyruins.org.)

Roth, Eric J. *For the Village: The Story of Huguenot Street*. New Paltz: Historic Huguenot Street, 2009.

———. "'where ye walloens dwell': Rethinking the Ethnic Identity of the Huguenots of New Paltz and Ulster County." *New York History*, 89 (Fall 2008): 347–54.

Ryan, Thomas R. "Cultural Accommodations in the Late-Eighteenth-Century Architecture of

Marbletown, New York." *Shaping Communities. Perspectives in Vernacular Architecture*. VI. Knoxville: University of Tennessee Press, 1997, 137–149.

———. "Old World Traditions and Modern Sensibilities: Late-Eighteenth-Century Domestic Architecture in Marbletown, New York." M. A. thesis, University of Delaware, 1994.

Schoonmaker, Marius. *The History of Kingston, New York*. New York: Burr Printing, 1888.

Seaman, Frank. Unpublished memoir, 1930s. Courtesy of Ken Chase and Wendy Harris.

Shand-Tucci, Douglass. *Ralph Adams Cram: An Architect's Four Quests*. Amherst: University of Massachusetts Press, 2005.

Sinclair, Peter, and Susanne Sahler. *Report on Historic Barns and Timber Framing*. Town of Rochester Historic Preservation Commission, 1997.

Smith, Anita M. *Woodstock: History and Hearsay*. Second edition with additions by Weston Blelock and Julia Blelock. Woodstock: Woodstock Arts, 2006.

Spafford, Horatio Gates. *Gazetteer of the State of New York*. Reprint of 1824 edition. Interlaken: Heart of the Lakes, 1981.

Steuding, Bob. *The Last of the Handmade Dams: The Story of the Ashokan Reservoir*. Fleischmanns: Purple Mountain Press, 1985.

Stevens, John R. *Dutch Vernacular Architecture in North America, 1640–1830*. West Hurley: Society for the Preservation of Hudson Valley Vernacular Architecture, 2005.

Stickley, Gustav. "A Day with John Burroughs at Riverby and Slabsides." *Craftsman*, 8 (August 1905): 564–583.

Sweeney, John A. H. *The Treasure House of Early American Rooms*. New York: Viking, 1963.

Sylvester, Nathaniel Bartlett. *History of Ulster County, New York*. Philadelphia: Everts & Peck, 1880.

Teller, Myron S. *The Early Stone Houses of Ulster County*. Ulster County Historical Society, 1959.

Teller & Halverson Architects: A Portfolio of Recent Work. New York: Architectural Catalog Co., 1933.

Terwilliger, Katharine T. *Napanoch*. Ellenville: Ellenville Public Library & Museum, 1982.

———. *Wawarsing*. Ellenville: Rondout Valley Publishing, 1977.

Town of Esopus Story. Town of Esopus Bicentennial Committee, 1979.

Ulster Historical Society. *Collections*. Kingston: Hommel & Lounsbery, 1860.

Upjohn, Everard M. *Richard Upjohn, Architect and Churchman*. New York: Columbia University Press, 1939.

Van Benschoten, Mary Ann. "The Schultz Legacy." *The Timeline*. Terwilliger House Museum, Ellenville, Fall 2002.

Wadlin, Beatrice Hasbrouck. *Times and Tales of Town of Lloyd*. 1974.

Wakefield, Manville B. *Coal Boats to Tidewater: The Story of the Delaware & Hudson Canal*. South Fallsburg, 1965.

Werlau, Elizabeth. *Images of America: Plattekill*. Charleston: Arcadia, 2008.

"What's Dutch: Country Seats Tour." Hudson River Heritage and Hudson Valley Vernacular Architecture, 2009.

White, Norval, and Elliot Willensky. *AIA Guide to New York City*. New York: Three Rivers, 2000.

Wick, Karl R., and Susan B. Wick. *Images of America: Esopus*. Charleston: Arcadia, 2003.

Wick, Susan B., and Karl R. Wick. *Images of America: Kingston and Ulster Townships*. Charleston: Arcadia, 2009.

Wilson Brothers & Co. *Catalogue of Work Executed*. Philadelphia: J. B. Lippincott, 1885. [google books]

Windy Summits, Fertile Valleys: An Artistic Journey through the Shawangunk Mountains. Cragsmoor Free Library, 1982.

Withey, Henry F., and Elsie Rathburn Withey. *Biographical Dictionary of American Architects*. Los Angeles: Hennessey and Ingalls, 1970.

Wolf, Tom. *Woodstock's Art Heritage*. Woodstock: Overlook Press, 1987.

Zimm, Louise Hasbrouck. "Ulster County." *Southeastern New York*. New York: Lewis Historical Publishing, 1946.

Illustration Sources

Photographs were taken by the author or are illustrations from the author's collection, unless otherwise credited.

Marie Blank: XIV–1

Century House Historical Society (Rosendale, NY): XV–2A

The Culinarian's Home: XI–34, 34A

Erma DeWitt Photos, Haviland-Heidgerd Historical Collection, Elting Memorial Library: II–23, V–1, IX–3, 14, 18, 19, XI–5, 9, 12, XIX–2

Ellenville Public Library & Museum: XX–7, 12, 15, 25, 25A

Esopus Meadows Lighthouse & Robert Arnouts: II–21

First Reformed Protestant Dutch Church, Kingston: VI–3

Edwin M. Ford, City of Kingston Historian: VI–19

Friends of Historic Kingston: VI–2, XVI–26

Haviland-Heidgerd Historical Collection, Elting Memorial Library: XI–11, 16A, 20, 23

Historical Society of Woodstock: XXI–11

Carol LeFevre: III–6

Mohonk Mountain House (Smiley Brothers, Inc.): XI–32, front and back covers

National Archives & Records Administration: XX–16A

Sean and Patty Roche: XV–6

Saugerties Historical Society: XVI–21

Scoresby Hose Hook & Ladder Company: XX–12A

Herbert L. Shultz: XVII–12

Sojourner Truth Library, SUNY New Paltz: XXI–16

Stone Ridge Library: IX–8, 17

Town of Lloyd Historian: II–6A

Ulster County Historical Society/Bevier House Museum: IV–4, V–4, VI–4, IX–12, XVI–1, XVII–15

Bruce Weiss: X–12, 12B

Vivian Yess Wadlin Collection: II–2, 15, 17, VIII–3, 7, 14, 14A, X–6, 12A, XV–5

Winterthur Museum: XX–1

Tom Wolf: XXI–14

Frank Lloyd Wright Foundation, Scottsdale, AZ/ Artists Rights Society, NY: XXI–19

Acknowledgments

I was introduced to Ulster County's historic architecture by my parents, Paul and Mary Rhoads, on a family vacation trip from our home in Harrisburg, Pennsylvania, to the Hudson Valley in 1948 when I was a boy of four. Along with my older brothers John and Henry, I was influenced by my parents' (and especially my mother's) keen interest in studying history by visiting old buildings, historic landscapes, and artifacts. The stone houses of our Pennsylvania German roots were similar enough to Hurley's stone houses to merit a trip across the Hudson from Hyde Park on that trip.

My study of American and European architectural history at Princeton under Professors Donald Drew Egbert and David R. Coffin gave me a solid basis for exploring a variety of architectural topics, culminating now in this study of Ulster County. Arriving at SUNY New Paltz in 1970 to teach art and architectural history, I benefited from the knowledge of and enthusiasm for regional history passed on to me by Professors Dale Stein and Alfred H. Marks. Colleagues outside the college who have provided essential advice and support for this book include Jane Kellar and Patricia Murphy of the Friends of Historic Kingston and Carol Johnson of Elting Memorial Library's Haviland-Heidgerd Historical Collection. Annon Adams, an independent historian, has generously shared the results of her comprehensive research into the career of architect J. A. Wood, and Vivian Wadlin has kindly provided illustrations from her extensive collection. John Winthrop Aldrich was a careful reader of the text and corrected several errors. He and Christopher Pryslopski were kind enough to offer their reviews of the book for the benefit of potential readers. Since 1966 my most important and dedicated advisor has been my wife, Sally M. Rhoads, who has been a helpful companion and map reader on countless auto adventures around Ulster County.

In researching the architecture of the county, I have also benefited from the assistance of: the late Anthony Aiello, Amico Anderson (Scoresby Hose Company), Shirley Anson, Barry Benepe, Anne Carpenter Bienstock, Marie Blank, Carolyn Blouin, Bob Boucher (Woodcrest), the Rev. David L. Bronson, Mary Lou Carolan (Wallkill Public Library), Anne Cotton, Alice and John Cross (Friends of Historic Rochester), Charles Cullen, Tildy and Bill Davenport, Diane De Chillo, the late William and Gladys DuBois, Marion M. Dumond, Edwin M. Ford, Richard Foy, Diane Galusha, Larry Gobrecht, the late William T. Golden, Asha Golliher and staff of the Ellenville Public Library & Museum, Kingdon Gould and his assistant Mrs. Ambrose, Linda Greenow, Hattie Grifo (Cragsmoor Free Library), Steve Grim (Riverby), Wendy E. Harris, Richard R. Hasbrouck, Mary Herrmann (Shandaken Historical Museum), Ted B. Hilton, Terry Howell, Tim Hunt, Paul Huth (Daniel Smiley Research Center of the Mohonk Preserve), Sandra H. Hutton, the late O. Lincoln Igou, Aaron Imbt, the late John Jacobson, Sara Jatcko (Winterthur Museum), Emily Jones (Woodstock Artists Association & Museum Archives), Paul Kellar, Guy Kempe, Mark Kessenich, Joan LaChance (Archives, Mohonk Mountain House), Neil Larson, Barbara Lavino, Edwin Lavino, Janis M. Leas, Leslie LeFevre-Stratton (Historic Huguenot Street), the late Elizabeth Lent, Donna Light, Suzanne Lown, Carleton Mabee, Robert McBroom (Onteora Mountain House), Marian McCorkle-Beckerman, Jo Margaret Mano, Konrad Ryushin Marchaj and Danica Ankele (Zen Mountain Monastery), Lord Margesson and his wife Helena, staff of the Marlboro Free Library, Irene Martin, Sally Matz, David L. Miller (Retired Superintendent, Eastern New York Correctional Facility), Geoffrey Miller, Maureen Nagy (Pine Hill and Shandaken), Paula Nelson (Woodstock School of Art), Hanne Nielsen (Pewabic Pottery), Betty O'Connell, Thomas G. Olsen (Village of New Paltz Historic Preservation Commission), Ontario & Western Railway Historical Society, the late William Peters, Sandra Phillips, Lachlan Pitcairn, Mary Prevo, Lee Pritchard, Christopher Pryslopski (Marist College), Maureen Radl, Bill Reinhart, Richard Rider (Friends of Historic Rochester), the late

T. Jay Rifenbary, Frank Rivera (Wallkill Correctional Facility), Sean and Patty Roche, Libby Ross, Eric Roth (Historic Huguenot Street), Jeff Rubin (Eastern New York Correctional Facility), George Rusk, Jr., William L. Schnitzer, Julian and Shannon Schreibman, Augustus R. Schrowang, Terry Scott (former Town of Lloyd Historian), Stephen Q. Shafer, Peter Sinclair, Lisa Smith (Mount St. Alphonsus), Michael S. Smith, Susan Stessin-Cohn, Rob Sweeney, Brian L. Taylor, Lowell Thing, Gary Tinterow, Fr. Phil Tran, Martin and Jeannine Tully, Rick Umble (Ulster County Information Services), Gary Van Aken, the late Beatrice Wadlin, Robin Walsh (Ulster County Community College), Bruce Weiss, the late Dietrich Werner, Tom Wolf (Bard College), Raymond and Kathleen Wood.

Black Dome Press has been a faithful partner during the long gestation of this book. Deborah Allen early expressed confidence in the project and ably assisted with its development until its final stages. Steve Hoare has been a wise editor throughout, and in the final phases of producing the book has expertly handled countless tasks with calm assurance. Ron Toelke created the book's handsome and fitting design, while Ruth Elwell has contributed the indispensable index. Rick Remsnyder, Director of Ulster County Tourism, was very supportive in granting permission to use the map, as was the Mohonk Mountain House and the Elting Memorial Library in allowing us to use their photographs for the front cover. Natalie Mortensen served with distinction as proofreader.

It is an honor to have Joan K. Davidson's foreword, which so movingly expresses the belief that in chaotic times our historic structures "can provide a longed-for sense of steadiness, and contentment."

W.B.R.
October 2011

About the Author

William B. Rhoads is a professor emeritus of art history at SUNY New Paltz, where he taught from 1970 to 2005. His publications include studies of Colonial Revival architecture and Franklin Roosevelt's sponsorship of architecture and art. Rhoads's Kingston, New York: The Architectural History & Guide *was published by Black Dome Press in 2003.*

Index

M

Y

Z